SECOND EDITION

The Bilingual Special Education Interface

Leonard M. Baca
Director, BUENO Center for Multicultural Education
University of Colorado

Hermes T. Cervantes
School Psychologist, Denver Public Schools
Denver, Colorado

Merrill Publishing Company
A Bell & Howell Information Company
Columbus Toronto London Melbourne

Cover Photo: Ulrike Welsch

Published by Merrill Publishing Company
A Bell & Howell Information Company
Columbus, Ohio 43216

This book was set in Garamond Book

Administrative Editor: Vicki Knight
Production Coordinator: Julie Higgins
Art Coordinator: Lorraine Woost
Cover Designer: Brian Deep

Library of Congress Catalog Card Number: 88-62585
International Standard Book Number: 0-675-20833-5
Printed in the United States of America
1 2 3 4 5 6 7 8 9—92 91 90 89

This book is affectionately dedicated to our own bilingual exceptional families, including our parents Marcus and Victoria and Jesus and Esther; our spouses Eleanor and Cecilia; and our children Elena, Carmela, Julianna, Michelle, Rosalinda, Rafael, and Ziomara..

Con cariño y amor,
Leonard and Hermes

CONTRIBUTORS

JAMES BRANSFORD
Director, Bilingual Education Center
College of Education
University of New Mexico
Albuquerque, New Mexico

CATHERINE COLLIER
Assistant Professor
Bilingual Special Education Program
University of Colorado
Boulder, Colorado

KATHLEEN C. HARRIS
Associate Professor
Division of Special Education
California State University, Los Angeles
Los Angeles, California

TIMOTHY E. HERON
Professor
Department Human Services Education
Ohio State University
Columbus, Ohio

JOHN J. HOOVER
Assistant Professor, Special Education
University of Texas, Tyler
Tyler, Texas

MICHAEL KALK
Professor, Special Education
University of Colorado
Boulder, Colorado

ALBA A. ORTIZ
Associate Professor
Director, Bilingual Special Education
University of Texas, Austin
Austin, Texas

ROSE M. PAYAN
Professional Associate
Educational Testing Service
Research and Advisory Services
Berkeley, California

SISTER PHYLLIS SUPANCHECK
Assistant Professor
Department of Education
Loyola Marymount University
Los Angeles, California

JAMES R. YATES
Assistant Dean
College of Education
University of Texas, Austin
Austin, Texas

PREFACE

This book is about children who are learners and who are bilingual as well as exceptional. We see a tremendous need for a meaningful interface between Bilingual Education and special education. During the 1950s and 1960s and until just recently, special education classes were overpromoted and misused in many parts of the United States. The process of declaring a student "mentally retarded" or otherwise in need of special education and placing the child in a special class became an accepted method of educating ethnically, linguistically, and socioeconomically different children. In some cases these children were authentically handicapped, but in other cases their linguistic or cultural background was the primary factor for their low test scores and subsequent special education placement.

On the other hand, because of the tremendous increase in the numbers of Asian, Hispanic, and Native American students, school districts have been unable to ignore the need for adjusting instructional programs to better serve these groups and other linguistically and culturally different individuals. One result has been the great expansion of Bilingual Education to provide for the educational needs of students with limited proficiency in English. But what of the bilingual student who is also handicapped? It is on this group of learners that we focus our attention in this text. By interfacing the programs and methodologies of Bilingual Education and special education, we believe that this group can achieve success and maximize their potential.

Dewey's famous dictum that what the best and wisest of fathers wants for his child, the state should want for all its children has a special significance today. For us the word *all* has special significance. By all, we mean Anglo, Asian, Hispanic, Native American, Black, the poor, the rich, and all other linguistic, ethnic, cultural, and socioeconomic groups in the United States.

Objective of the Book

This book has been written as a resource for teacher trainers and others engaged in the preparation of ancillary school personnel; for example, school counselors, psychologists, and speech and language specialists. It is designed to familiarize educators with the major needs of the exceptional child with limited skills in English. It also provides information on models, curriculum, and strategies for better educating this unique population of students.

Organization and Flexibility of the Book

The book is organized to emphasize the interface between bilingual and special education. The chapters have been carefully sequenced to familiarize the reader with key issues from each of the two areas. Particular attention has been given to the creative convergence that can result when these two educational approaches are meaningfully integrated with each other. The major issues within the emerging field of Bilingual Special Education have all been included in the text. A strong effort has been made to strike a balance between the theoretical and the practical dimensions of the material.

The book is written to promote great flexibility as well as breadth of coverage. While it is designed as a text for courses in special education, Bilingual Education, and Bilingual Special Education, certain chapters can also be used as supplementary material for many other education courses. By using the reference lists and appendix, greater depth and breadth of treatment can be achieved.

Features of the Second Edition

In response to comments from users of the first edition and from our reviewers, we have made some important changes and additions to the second edition of this text. First, we have updated the existing material. Furthermore, we have added new material and current references to all the chapters. We have totally revised the chapter on language acquisition to reflect the current research in this area. We have deleted the chapter on model programs, since such programs vary so much from school to school depending on the unique needs and resources of individual communities. A new chapter on consultation greatly strengthens the text. A more detailed chapter on methods and materials increase the practical value of the book.

Acknowledgments

We are greatly indebted to the many colleagues and individuals, as well as exceptional children, who have motivated and assisted us in numerous ways. One person who was very instrumental is Rose Payan of the Educational Training Service, and we are most thankful for her contribution in conceptualizing, designing, and writing two of the major chapters. We would also like to acknowledge the fine assistance and excellent work of our contributing authors: Michael Kalk, James Yates, Alba Ortiz, Catherine Collier, John J. Hoover, Sister Phyllis Supancheck, Kathy Harris, Tim Heron, and Jim Bransford. In addition we wish to thank those who reviewed the text at various stages of its development: Jozi DeLeon, University of New Mexico; Phyllis Maslow, California State University, Long Beach; Anne Y. Gallegos, University of Texas at El Paso; Al G. Prieto, Arizona State University; and Linda McCormick, University of Hawaii. Their input made a positive contribution to the text. Our gratitude is extended to Vicki Knight, our administrative editor at Merrill Publishing Company, for her support and assistance. Many friends and colleagues assisted with typing, proofreading, and technical editing—we extend a special word of thanks to Gerry Schafer, Margarita Miller, and Michele Roscoe.

Finally we wish to extend our sincere appreciation to our wives, Eleanor Baca and Cecilia Cervantes, as well as to our children, who provided constant and immeasurable encouragement and support while this text was in preparation.

Leonard M. Baca
Hermes T. Cervantes

CONTENTS

CHAPTER EIGHT
Assessment Procedures for the Exceptional Child 153

CHAPTER NINE
Staffing and the Development of Individualized Educational Programs for the Bilingual Exceptional Student 183
Alba A. Ortiz, James R. Yates

CHAPTER TEN
Bilingual Special Education Curriculum Development 205
Catherine Collier, Michael Kalk

CHAPTER ONE

Background and Rationale for Bilingual Special Education

- Equal Educational Opportunity
- Right to an Appropriate Education
- Cultural Pluralism and Education
- Bilingual Education as a Worldwide Phenomenon
- Language Policy in the United States
- Incidence Figures on Bilingual Students
- Overrepresentation of Bilingual Students in Special Education
- Call for Bilingual Special Education
- Definition of Bilingual Special Education
- Summary

Objectives

- To introduce the concept of equal educational opportunity
- To present information on the right to an appropriate education
- To discuss cultural pluralism as it related to Bilingual Education
- To review language policy in the United States
- To present incidence figures on bilingual students
- To propose a rationale for Bilingual Special Education

Bilingual students, including those with handicaps, have finally established their right to be educated in their stronger or more proficient language. These students have been referred to as the "triple threat students" because they have three strikes against them before they even start school (Rueda & Chan, 1979). The first is their handicap. The second is their limited English proficiency. The third is their lower socioeconomic status. When our schools teach them in their native language, they build on their cultural and linguistic strengths. This is compatible with sound educational practice (Krashen & Biber, 1988).

During the past half century special education has developed into a strong and effective part of our overall public school system. The expansion of special education reached its peak with the passage in 1974 of P.L. 94–142, which is known as the Education for All Handicapped Children Act (Haring & McCormick, 1986). A review of recent national legislation and appropriations provides evidence that the education of the handicapped continues to be a strong national priority today.

Bilingual Education is not a new phenomenon; it is as old as education itself (Noboa, 1987). But the past 20 years have seen a renewed interest in Bilingual Education in the United States. Congress passed the Bilingual Education Act (P.L. 90–247) in 1968. This law made it possible for local school districts to receive federal funding through a competitive grant process for the implementation of bilingual programs designed to meet the needs of students with limited English proficiency (LEP).

More recent developments in litigation and educational research dealing with exceptional children of limited English proficiency suggest that educators must seriously address the issues related to designing and implementing Bilingual Special Education programs. This book addresses the complex issues and challenges related to merging the delivery systems of Bilingual Education and special education. The remainder of this chapter discusses the major issues related to the establishment of Bilingual Special Education.

Equal Educational Opportunity

The development of Bilingual Special Education can be viewed as an extension of the equal educational opportunity movement. Equal educational opportunity has a long and rich history that can be traced back to the founding of our nation. For example, the Declaration of Independence asserts that "all men are created equal." In addition the Fourteenth Amendment to the Constitution ensures equal protection under the law. At one time Thomas Jefferson proposed a plan to promote equal educational opportunity. McClellan et al. (1980) state:

> Equalitarian rhetoric first came to be attached to formal education in the Revolutionary era when Thomas Jefferson, among others, proposed a national system of schooling that would provide scholarships for talented youngsters of modest means who might otherwise have little chance to achieve social prominence. Such a system, thought Jefferson, would bring a measure of equality of opportunity to a society where social

station and access to education had so often depended solely on the accidents of birth.

The concept of equal educational opportunity has continued to evolve to the present day. Two factors have substantially influenced educational policy regarding equal educational opportunity. They are the *Brown v. Board of Education of Topeka* (1954) decision and the *Coleman Report.*

In the *Brown v. Board of Education* decision, the U.S. Supreme Court ruled:

> . . . in these days it is doubtful that any child may reasonably be expected to succeed in life if he is denied the opportunity of an education. Such an opportunity, where the state has undertaken to provide it is a right which must be made available to all on equal terms. (Brown v. Board of Education, 347 U.S. 483, 74 S.Ct. 686, 91 L.Ed. 873)

The Court set a precedent by ruling that the segregation of Black and White children in state public schools on the basis of race denied Black children equal protection guaranteed by the Fourteenth Amendment (Jarolimek, 1981). In effect, the Court held that the doctrine of separate but equal education was inherently unequal. According to Jarolimek (1981), for a period of 25 years this landmark decision was followed by one judicial decision after another extending the concept of equal educational opportunity.

The *Coleman Report,* entitled "Equality of Educational Opportunity," was commissioned by the U.S. Office of Education, as mandated by the 1964 Civil Rights Act. In defining equal educational opportunity, Coleman (1968) identifies these components:

1. Providing a free education up to a given level that constituted the principal entry point to the labor force
2. Providing a common curriculum for all children, regardless of background
3. Providing that children from diverse backgrounds attend the same school
4. Providing equality within a given locality, since local taxes provided the source of support for schools

This approach to equal educational opportunity stresses that all students be treated the same and places the responsibility for achieving equality upon the students. Another approach to equality emphasizes the school as the agent in providing what is fitting and appropriate for the student (Komisar & Coombs, 1974). According to Jarolimek (1981), the concept of individualized instruction, which has been an accepted part of educational thought, if not practice, for at least 50 years, is the embodiment of the "equality as fitting or appropriate" principle. Deciding what is fitting or appropriate for a given student or group of students is the responsibility of school personnel. However, what school officials think is the appropriate program for a child may not really be what the child needs at all.

Another approach, called the "equality of outcomes," (Padilla & Sue, 1986) protects students from placement in programs not suited for their needs. Jencks (1972) refers to this approach not as equal opportunity but as equal results. Equality becomes the responsibility of the school rather than the student. This allows the school to use a variety of teaching methods and approaches as long as the student learns the required material.

The establishment of Bilingual Special Education programs to meet the needs of exceptional children of limited English proficiency is an extension of this equal educational opportunity and equal educational benefits movement.

Right to an Appropriate Education

Only within the last several years has the right of handicapped children to an education appropriate to their needs been recognized and accepted by our society (Heward & Orlansky, 1986). Former U.S. Commissioner of Education

Sidney Marland (1971) addressed this issue at the international convention of the Council for Exceptional Children:

> The right of a handicapped child to the special education he needs is as basic to him as the right of any other young citizen to an appropriate education in the public schools. It is unjust for our society to provide handicapped children with anything less than a full and equal educational opportunity they need to reach their maximum potential and attain rewarding, satisfying lives.

Providing this appropriate education in a language that is intelligible to the student would appear to be a basic prerequisite, an integral part of what could be considered "appropriate education." Fifteen years ago it would have been impossible to find a school district that provided a Bilingual Special Education program. Today, however, this type of program can be found in most major school districts across the country.

The right to an appropriate education should be viewed as an extension of a more basic concept and fundamental right referred to by the courts as the "right to education." The development of the right to education policy has its roots in the Fourteenth Amendment to the U.S. Constitution, which provides that no state may deny to any person within its jurisdiction the equal protection of the law. According to Hockenberry (1979), case law has advanced a series of interpretations of the Fourteenth Amendment preventing government from denying governmental benefits to persons because of their unalterable characteristics, that is, because of age, sex, race, or handicap. The *Brown v. Board of Education* case of 1954 established an important precedent for subsequent right to education cases for all children, including the handicapped.

If a state agrees to provide a free public education for all school-aged children, it cannot exclude the handicapped. When such exclusion has been found, court rulings have declared that equal protection of the law was denied to the handicapped on the basis of their unalterable trait—their handicap (Turnbull & Turnbull, 1978).

The most significant cases dealing with a right to an education are the *Pennsylvania Association for Retarded Children (PARC) v. Pennsylvania* (1971) and *Mills v. Board of Education of D.C.* (1972). Both cases involved equal protection arguments. The plaintiff class in the *PARC* case consisted of all school-age, mentally retarded children excluded from the public schools. The plaintiff class in the *Mills* case consisted of all school-age children with any form of disability who were excluded from public education. In both cases the court ruled in favor of the plaintiffs and mandated that a free public program of education appropriate to the child's capacity be provided. It is interesting to note the court's use of the word *appropriate.* According to Hockenberry (1979), subsequent cases involving the right to education for handicapped children have closely followed the arguments made in the *PARC* and *Mills* cases, with similar decisions and relief granted by the courts. In addition to court cases, right to education policy has been further strengthened by the Rehabilitation Act of 1973. Section 504 of this act is of particular importance.

- The child must be furnished an individualized education program (IEP) (Sec. 121a.342).
- The child is entitled to a due process hearing if educational appropriateness is in doubt (Sec. 121a.506).
- The student is entitled to appropriately and adequately trained teachers (Sec. 121a.12).
- The child has the right of access to school records (Sec 121a.562).
- The student's representatives (parents or others) are entitled to participate in and be

given notice of school actions affecting special education programs and the student's own education (Sec. 121a.345).

- The child is entitled to a due process hearing if educational appropriateness is in doubt (Sec. 121a.506).

Using this detailed procedural definition of "appropriate education," one could argue that a special bilingual program of instruction could easily be called for under certain circumstances. A series of cases in New York have raised this very issue. The most significant of these was *Dyrcia S. et al. v. Board of Education of New York* (1979). This case was filed on October 2, 1979, on behalf of LEP handicapped Puerto Rican and other Hispanic LEP children residing in New York City who require Bilingual Special Education programs. On December 14, 1979, a judgment was issued calling for the provision of appropriate bilingual programs for all handicapped children with both high and low incidence disabilities.

The issue of the right to an appropriate education is clearly at the heart of any discussion of Bilingual Special Education.

Cultural Pluralism and Education

Bilingual Special Education, as has been pointed out thus far, is closely related to equal educational opportunity and the right to an appropriate education. It is also closely related to cultural pluralism.

The National Coalition for Cultural Pluralism (1973) has defined pluralism as:

> A state of equal co-existence in a mutually supportive relationship within the boundaries or framework of one nation of people of diverse cultures with significantly different patterns of belief, behavior, color and in many cases with different languages.

Contemporary American society is made up of people from many different cultural backgrounds. Any effective educational program in today's schools should reflect this cultural pluralism (Garcia, 1982). As Hunter (1974) has stated:

> It is therefore apparent, if education in the United States is to meet the needs of its peoples, then it must have a life blood of multicultural content in order to be sociologically relevant, philosophically germane, and pedagogically apropos.

Cultural pluralism is not a concept that enjoyed strong support in the early years of the United States. On the contrary, cultural assimilation—the melting pot theory—was expected. According to the melting pot theory, individuals of all nations should be melted down into one common new "race" of Americans. In other words, all immigrants to this country were expected to relinquish their native language and culture and adopt the new American way of life. This attempt to Americanize all immigrants was strongly reinforced by World War I. At that time, there was concern that some immigrants would support their native countries against the United States. According to Kopan (1974), World War I led to a crash program of Americanization in schools, factories, and churches. The purpose of the Americanization program was to assert Nordic superiority by encouraging immigrants to abandon their native cultures and become American. During this time other languages were excluded from the curriculum. This forced Americanization created an atmosphere of suspicion and mistrust that has never been completely eliminated.

Israel Zangwill (1909) first used the term *melting pot* as the title of a play that became an instant success on Broadway in 1908. The following excerpt from the play illustrates the thinking upon which the melting pot theory is based.

> America is God's Crucible. The great Melting Pot where all the races of Europe are melting and

> reforming! Here you stand, good folk, think I, when I see them at Ellis Island, here you stand in your fifty groups with your fifty language histories, and your fifty hatreds and rivalries, but you won't be long like that, brothers, for these are the fires of God. A fig for your feuds and vendettas! Germans and Frenchmen, Irishmen and Englishmen, Jews and Russians—into the Crucible with you all! God is making the American.... The real American has not yet arrived. He is only in the Crucible, I tell you—he will be the fusion of all races, the coming superman.

Actually the "real American," the "coming superman," has never arrived. To a large extent the melting pot theory has failed to work. The existence of a myriad of distinct racial and ethnic subgroups within the United States is a confirmation of this failure. Despite the fact that the melting pot approach has failed in many ways, it has nonetheless had a strong influence on American educators. Kobrick (1972) sums it up as follows:

> America's intolerance of diversity is reflected in an ethnocentric educational system to "Americanize foreigners or those who are seen as culturally different." America is the great melting pot, and, as one writer recently stated it, "If you don't want to melt, you had better get out of the pot." The ill-disguised contempt for a child's language is part of a broader distaste for the child himself and the culture he represents. Children who are culturally different are said to be culturally "deprived." Their language and culture are seen as "disadvantages." The children must be "remodeled" if they are to succeed in school.*

This monocultural and ethnocentric approach to education has been gradually changing toward a pluralistic multicultural model. This change of emphasis is documented by Carpenter (1974):

> In 1909 an educator wrote that a major task of education in American cities was to "break up these immigrant groups or settlements, to assimilate and amalgamate these people as part of our American race, and to implant in their children, so far as can be done, the Anglo Saxon conception of righteousness, law and order, and popular government. . . ."
>
> Sixty years later the Congress of the United States passed the Ethnic Heritage Studies Act giving official "recognition to the heterogeneous composition of the nation and the fact that in a multiethnic society, a greater understanding of the contributions of one's own heritage and those of one's fellow citizens can contribute to a more harmonious, patriotic, and committed populace . . ."

This change in thinking in favor of cultural pluralism is long overdue. Finally ethnic and cultural diversity are being viewed as positive aspects of American society. According to Trueba, Guthrie, and Hu-Pei-Au (1981), cultural pluralism is gaining momentum among educators and social scientists. Cortez (1986) has suggested that the melting pot metaphor be replaced by the metaphor of a mosaic. He refers to cultural pluralism as a "constantly-shifting mosaic in which the multi-hued pieces do not always fit together perfectly, as if an on-going historical earthquake has been challenging the society to attempt to resolve the unresolvable." When translated into the schools, cultural pluralism becomes muticultural education. Multicultural education teaches children to recognize and appreciate the contributions of all cultural groups to the development of this nation. In their attempt to promote multicultural education, Stone and De Nevi (1971) stressed these points:

1. We possess in America diverse and linguistic heritages, a tremendous untapped natural resource which is worth preserving and extending. Diversity of culture and language enriches all of us.

---

*From Kobrick, J.W. The compelling case for bilingual education. *Saturday Review,* April 19, 1972, pp. 54–58. © 1972 Saturday Review Magazine Co. Reprinted by permission.

2. We ought to consciously encourage bilingualism in our schools. Teachers must become adept at interweaving non-Anglo contributions and material into the curriculum, using such material to enrich all students.

3. Non-White literature, music, art, dance, sports, and games should become part of the curriculum.

4. Non-White teachers must be sought, recruited, trained, retrained, and supported in opportunities to work with non-Anglo pupils.

5. School information (and school meetings) intended for parents of minority group children should be made available in all appropriate languages.

Support for cultural pluralism and multicultural education continues to grow. Not only minority group members advocate a multicultural approach to education. Many supporters of this concept are members of the dominant society. Even national educational associations have adopted strong statements in support of multicultural education. One difficulty in the implementation of multicultural education has been the lack of appropriate training for teachers. It is interesting to note the National Council for the Accreditation of Teacher Educators (NCATE) established a special standard in 1980 requiring accredited teacher training institutions to include training in multicultural education for all prospective teachers.

One of the most eloquent statements in support of multicultural education was issued by the American Association of Colleges for Teacher Education (AACTE) in 1973. This statement, entitled *No One Model American,* serves as a guide for addressing the issue of multicultural education. In part, it reads:

> Multicultural education is education which values cultural pluralism. Multicultural education rejects the view that schools should seek to melt away cultural differences or the view that schools should merely tolerate cultural pluralism. Instead, multicultural education affirms that schools should be oriented toward the cultural enrichment of all children and youth through programs rooted to the preservation and extension of cultural diversity as a fact of life in American society, and it affirms that this cultural diversity is a valuable resource that should be preserved and extended. It affirms that major education institutions should strive to preserve and enhance cultural pluralism.

Other observations, explicit in the AACTE statement and crucial to an understanding of multicultural education, are summarized here:

> Cultural pluralism does not acknowledge the concept of a model American. Rather, it is a movement and an idea which endorses the health of the entire society based on the strengths of its unique parts.
>
> Cultural pluralism rejects assimilation and separation. No single group lives in isolation. Education, if it is to be meaningful to the ideals of the multicultural movement, must include: (1) the teaching of diverse cultural values, (2) the incorporation of ethnic cultures into the mainstream of economic and political life, and (3) the exploration of alternative life-styles.
>
> A commitment to multiculturalism must be established at all levels of education in order for the concept to become a social reality. This is especially true for teacher education.
>
> Above all, multicultural education acknowledges the right of different cultures to exist.

As can be seen from the preceding remarks, multicultural education is not the addition of an instructional unit or a course on multiculturalism. Rather it is a philosophical orientation or attitude that permeates the entire curriculum. Multicultural education is not limited to elementary or regular education but applies to all educational programs. Thus multicultural education should be a part of special education. The Council for Exceptional Children (CEC) has promoted this position through several topical conferences; the most recent addressed the concerns of the culturally diverse exceptional children. These meetings were held in October 1988 in Denver. Special educators are also beginning to see the need for incorporating multiculturalism into programs. The establishment of Bilingual Special Education programs may be viewed as part of a larger movement attempting to infuse multiculturalism into the schools.

Bilingual Education as a Worldwide Phenomenon

The concept of Bilingual Education requires a detailed explanation, which will be provided in the following chapter; however, a broad and generally accepted definition was developed by Parker (1978):

> Bilingual education refers to some configuration of instruction through the medium of two languages.
>
> In the U.S., this means teaching skills in English as well as another language and teaching content through the medium of both languages. Attempts to put this definition into practice have resulted in a wide variety of programs.

Almost all countries in the world have bilingual populations. Many of these countries have Bilingual Education programs (Noboa, 1987). Approaches to Bilingual Education throughout the world show much diversity. Some countries have mandatory bilingual policies while others do not. Because Bilingual Education may be found in most countries, it is considered a universal phenomenon.

Some countries are multilingual. For example, Singapore and Switzerland each have four official languages. Many other countries are legally designated as bilingual. Among these are Afghanistan, Belgium, Canada, Finland, India, Ireland, and South Africa. Most countries that have only one official language still have bilingual schooling. Such is the case in France, Denmark, Norway, West Germany, Greece, Jordan, Mainland China, the Philippines, Egypt, Mexico, and Guatemala (Fishman, 1976). Therefore the establishment of Bilingual Special Education is in keeping with a worldwide tradition of Bilingual Education.

Language Policy in the United States

Because the issue of language policy is usually raised in any discussion involving bilingualism, it seems appropriate to discuss briefly the history and status of language policy in the United States.

This nation is made up of more than 230 million people who have come from or have ancestral ties to hundreds of different countries where a vast number of different languages were spoken. Uniting a large number of immigrants through the use of a common language was a critical concern for America in 1776. Interestingly enough, however, the nation chose not to initiate language planning. According to Heath (1977), many language policies were proposed in those early days but none was accepted. Instead of a mandatory national language policy being established, a permissive language policy evolved.

At the outset, Bilingual Education programs were implemented at the local level in several different regions of the country. According to Andersson and Boyer (1970):

> Before 1800 German schools flourished throughout the country. Also this period saw the beginning of many French schools in New England and many Scandinavian and some Dutch schools in the Midwest. Many of these schools were not actually bilingual in their curricula; they were non-English schools where English was taught as a subject.

According to Zirkel (1978), an estimated 1 million students were in bilingual public school programs during the 19th century. This does not include the thousands of students who were in private schools. For example, there were many French-English parochial school programs in Louisiana and Spanish-English parochial school programs in New Mexico.

No official language policy existed at the federal level during the early history of the country. At the state level, most of the early school laws and administrative policies were silently permissive as to the languages of instruction. According to Zirkel (1978):

> Some states specifically authorized using a language other than English as a medium of instruction. For example, a Pennsylvania statute passed in 1837 and an Ohio statute passed in 1839 specifically permitted German-English public schools. Similarly, the California and New Mexico constitutions were drafted in the context of linguistic equality between Spanish and English.
>
> By not adopting an official language policy, the United States chose a permissive language policy (Dozier, 1956). According to Heath (1977), during this early period language was viewed as a social matter, not a political one. It was felt that legislation of social and cultural habits would restrict the guaranteed basic freedoms.

World War I ushered in a new era of language policy in the United States. During this period bilingual instruction was prohibited in most states, the result of a national paranoia that set in with the outbreak of the war. During this time everything foreign became suspect. Immigrant groups who were in any way associated historically with the enemy were under scrutiny regarding their loyalty. This national fear continued into World War II and ultimately led to the internment of thousands of Japanese-Americans in concentration camps. The "English-only era" continued until the mid-1960s. The passage of Title VII of the Elementary and Secondary Education Act of 1968, known as the Bilingual Education Act, finally ended this era and initiated a new period of a permissive bilingual policy, which exists today. This policy has been supported by a number of recent court decisions, which are discussed in Chapter 4.

Language policy formulation has been brought into the forefront recently with the English-only initiative. A national organization known as U.S. English has been diligently lobbying for an amendment to the U.S. Constitution to make English the official language of the United States. In addition to this national effort there are 37 states that have either passed or will be voting on similar measures in the near future (McLean, 1988). Historical analysis reveals that every large wave of immigration into this country evokes a reaction that, like the English-only movement, tries to limit language freedom in this country.

Because of the permissive language policy, our predominantly monolingual and monocultural country has allowed a strong and consistent bilingual tradition to develop and continue to this day. Kloss (1977) has documented this in her book, *The American Bilingual Tradition*. The development of Bilingual Special Education programs is certainly compatible with existing language policy.

Incidence Figures on Bilingual Students

Available data sources show that the population of LEP students continues to grow at a brisk pace. The 1980 census (U.S. Bureau of the Census, 1984) indicated that 19.3 million people (8.8% of the population) in the United States are native speakers of a language other than English. These figures represent an increase from 17 million people (8.5% of the population) reported in 1976 (U.S. Bureau of the Census, 1976). Based on the 1980 Census and Immigration and Naturalization Services record on legal immigration, it is estimated that there are 7.9 million school-age language minority children in the United States.

An examination of the older 1976 data in Table 1–1 shows that this bilingual population is

Table 1–1
Numbers and Percentages of Non-English Background Children (1976)

Data from Brown, G., et al. (1980). *The condition of education for Hispanic Americans,* Washington, DC: U.S. Government Printing Office.

	Total School-Age Children	Total Non-English-Background Children	Percentage of Non-English-Background Children
All states	50,326,000	5,032,000	10
Alabama	886,000	15,000	1
Alaska	98,000	15,000	15
Arizona	555,000	161,000	29
Arkansas	503,000	15,000	1
California	4,786,000	1,105,000	23
Colorado	616,000	82,000	13
Connecticut	716,000	77,000	11
Delaware	140,000	15,000	4
Florida	1,820,000	194,000	11
Georgia	1,200,000	27,000	2
Hawaii	206,000	53,000	26
Idaho	208,000	15,000	6
Illinois	2,655,000	233,000	8
Indiana	1,283,000	47,000	4
Iowa	690,000	16,000	2
Kansas	520,000	22,000	4
Kentucky	829,000	15,000	0.5
Lousiana	1,000,000	140,000	14
Maine	259,000	22,000	8
Maryland	989,000	48,000	5
Massachusetts	1,346,000	109,000	8
Michigan	2,318,000	91,000	4
Minnesota	988,000	26,000	3

distributed throughout the United States with heavier concentrations in the southwest and northeastern regions. The highest concentration of language minority students is in the large urban areas (Rueda, 1985). Perhaps the best example of this is in California where, as Figure 1–1 indicates, the number of LEP students has increased dramatically in the past few years.

The United States Department of Education provides much lower estimates of LEP students by using much more stringent criteria than the Census Bureau, such as only counting students who score below the 19th percentile in overall achievement (Crawford, 1987). Waggoner (1987) believes that the Department of Education figures are a significant underestimate of the actual LEP population.

Considering the overall LEP population in the United States, a critical question for bilingual special educators is: How many of these students are also handicapped? If the U.S. Office of Special Education figure of 12% is used, this would indicate that 948,000 children are both linguistically different and handicapped. This constitutes a substantial population who could benefit from Bilingual Special Education services.

Table 1–1 Continued

	Total School-Age Children	Total Non-English-Background Children	Percentage of Non-English-Background Children
Mississippi	615,000	15,000	1
Missouri	1,096,000	24,000	2
Montana	191,000	15,000	4
Nebraska	367,000	16,000	4
Nevada	146,000	15,000	9
New Hampshire	200,000	17,000	8
New Jersey	1,697,000	182,000	11
New Mexico	316,000	154,000	49
New York	4,073,000	785,000	19
North Carolina	1,219,000	22,000	2
North Dakota	162,000	15,000	4
Ohio	2,524,000	184,000	4
Oklahoma	624,000	36,000	6
Oregon	524,000	25,000	5
Pennsylvania	2,656,000	140,000	5
Rhode Island	206,000	21,000	10
South Carolina	723,000	15,000	1
South Dakota	166,000	15,000	3
Tennessee	971,000	15,000	1
Texas	2,952,000	846,000	29
Utah	322,000	19,000	6
Vermont	114,000	15,000	6
Virginia	1,168,000	38,000	3
Washington	826,000	37,000	5
Wisconsin	1,149,000	27,000	2
West Virginia	407,000	15,000	0.5
Wyoming	92,000	15,000	6

When discussing the incidence figures of the non-English-speaking population, the projections made for the future growth of this group should be considered. A study conducted by Inter-America Research Associates (Oxford et al., 1980) reports a growth in this population from 28 million in 1976 to 34.7 million by 1990 and nearly 40 million by 2000. Figure 1–2 illustrates these projections by language groups.

The states of California, New York, and Texas are projected to have the largest number of non-English-speaking populations in the future. Table 1–2 illustrates the projections for these areas of the country.

Although children in the public schools of our country represent a large number of diverse language backgrounds, the single largest group is Hispanic. At present this population comprises 75% of the children of limited English proficiency. The data in Table 1–3 illustrate the diversity and geographic location of this group of students, and Figure 1–3 lists the states with Hispanic populations of at least 5%.

Another sizable group of children with a

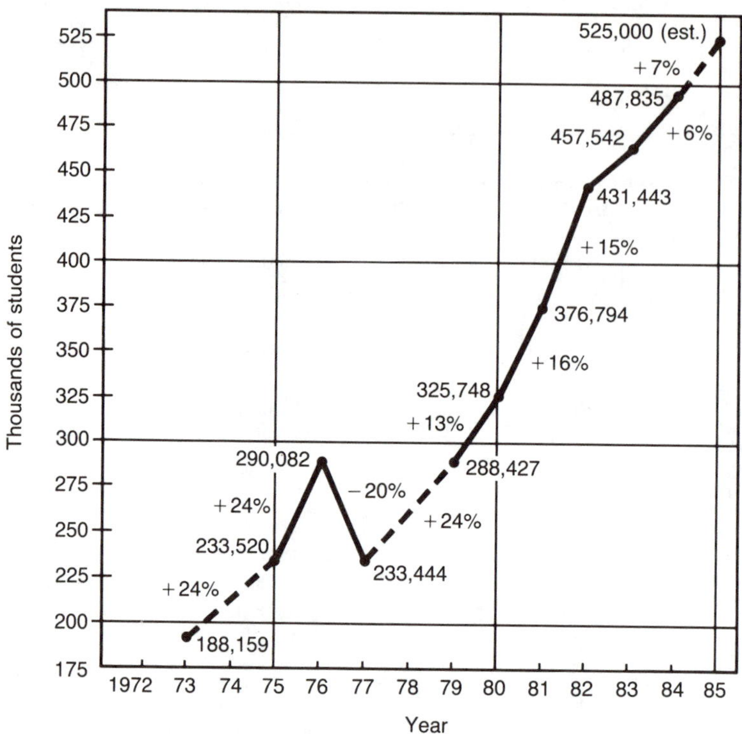

Figure 1–1
Numbers of Limited English Proficient Students in California Public Schools, 1973 to 1984
Data from California Department of Education.

non-English background consists of refugees. In 1981 there were 103,550 refugee children in the 12 states reporting the largest enrollments of such students. Table 1–4 summarizes the distribution by state and grade level (elementary or secondary).

Overrepresentation of Bilingual Students in Special Education

A cursory review of the literature of the past 25 years indicates that bilingual children have not had a positive experience with special education. It has been well established that bilingual children and minority children in general have historically been misplaced and thus overrepresented in self-contained special classes—particularly those for the mentally retarded and learning disabled (Mercer, 1973; Ortiz & Yates, 1983). Mercer (1973) reported that Mexican-American children were placed into classes for the mentally retarded at a rate that was much higher than would have been expected. According to her study, Mexican-Americans were 10 times as likely to be placed in special education as were their White counterparts.

Although overrepresentation continues to be an issue in some school districts, a new problem of underrepresentation has also emerged in some areas (Ovando and Collier, 1985). This new difficulty seems to have come

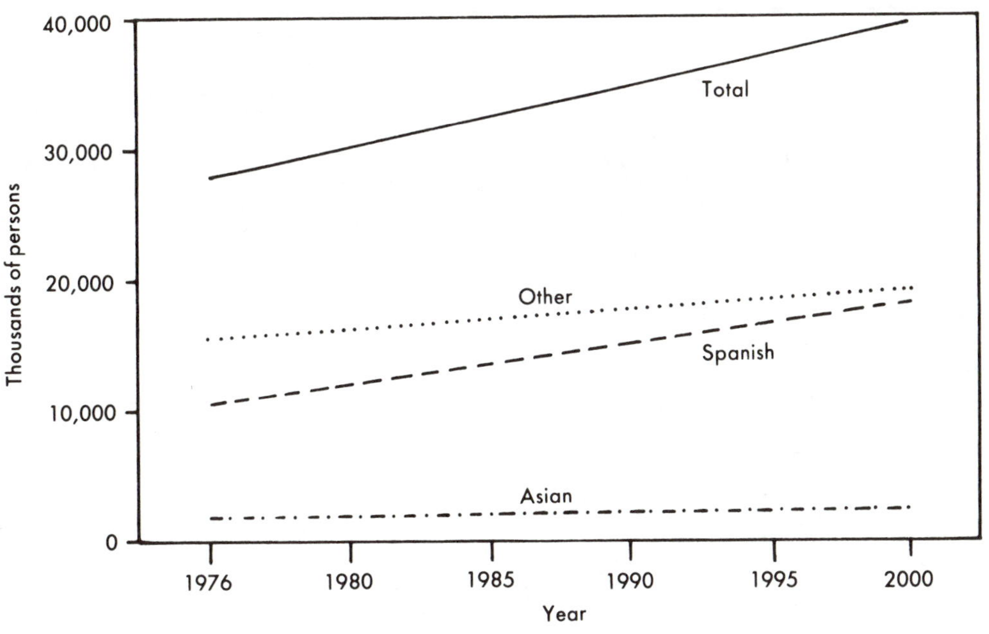

Figure 1–2
Non-English Language Background Projections by Language Group—1976 to 2000 (All Ages)

From Projections of non-English language background and limited English proficient persons. in the United States to the year 2000, Rosslyn, Va., 1980. National Clearinghouse for Bilingual Education.

Table 1–2
Non-English Language Background Projections by Major States—1976 to 2000 (All Ages)

Data from Projections on non-English language background and limited English proficient persons in the United States to the year 2000, Rosslyn, Va., 1980, National Clearinghouse for Bilingual Education.

	State (numbers in thousands)				
Year	**California**	**New York**	**Texas**	**Remainder**	**Total**
1976	5,220.5	4,432.8	3,040.8	15,291.3	27,985.1
1980	5,744.1	4,534.3	3,414.6	16,262.0	29,954.0
1985	6,350.9	4,653.2	3,917.6	17,630.0	32,280.7
1990	6,996.3	4,792.1	4,466.7	18,487.6	34,741.7
1995	7,648.1	4,927.4	5,041.1	19,542.7	37,158.3
2000	8,300.7	5,051.8	5,637.4	20,505.6	39,493.5

State†	Number of Hispanics (000s)	Percent of Population—Hispanic	Percent Distribution — Hispanic Subgroup: Mexican American	Puerto Rican	Cuban	Central or South American	Other Hispanic
United States	11,193	5.6	61	14	6	7	11
Arizona	350	15	91	*	*	*	7
California	3,348	16	82	3	1	7	8
Colorado	278	11	76	*	*	*	21
Connecticut	81	3	*	71	*	*	*
Florida	669	8	5	6	62	9	19
Georgia	23	1	*	*	*	*	*
Hawaii	27	3	*	*	*	*	*
Idaho	28	3	73	*	*	*	*
Illinois	412	4	54	32	*	6	*
Indiana	84	2	68	*	*	*	*
Iowa	22	1	*	*	*	*	*
Kansas	43	2	77	*	*	*	*
Lousiana	85	2	*	*	*	24	52
Maryland	31	1	*	*	*	*	*
Massachusetts	89	1	*	49	*	24	*
Michigan	96	1	70	*	*	*	*
Minnesota	20	1	*	*	*	*	*
Missouri	25	1	*	*	*	*	*
Nebraska	25	2	88	*	*	*	*
Nevada	36	6	62	*	*	*	*
New Jersey	385	5	*	47	24	15	12
New Mexico	420	36	51	*	*	*	48
New York	1,439	8	*	59	5	20	14
Ohio	85	1	52	26	*	*	*
Oklahoma	38	1	66	*	*	*	*
Oregon	40	2	71	*	*	*	*
Pennsylvania	125	1	*	80	*	*	*
Texas	2,557	21	97	*	*	*	2
Utah	41	3	70	*	*	*	*
Virginia	56	1	*	*	*	*	36
Washington	74	2	74	*	*	*	*
Wisconsin	34	1	*	*	*	*	*

Table 1–3

Geographical Distribution of Hispanics among Selected States, by Subgroup, 1976

Data from U.S. Department of Health, Education and Welfare, National Center for Education Statistics, Survey of Income and Education, Spring 1976, special tabulations.

*Percentage not shown when estimate is less than 20,000 persons.

†Only those states with an estimated Hispanic population of at least 20,000 are listed.

NOTE: Details may not add to totals because of rounding.

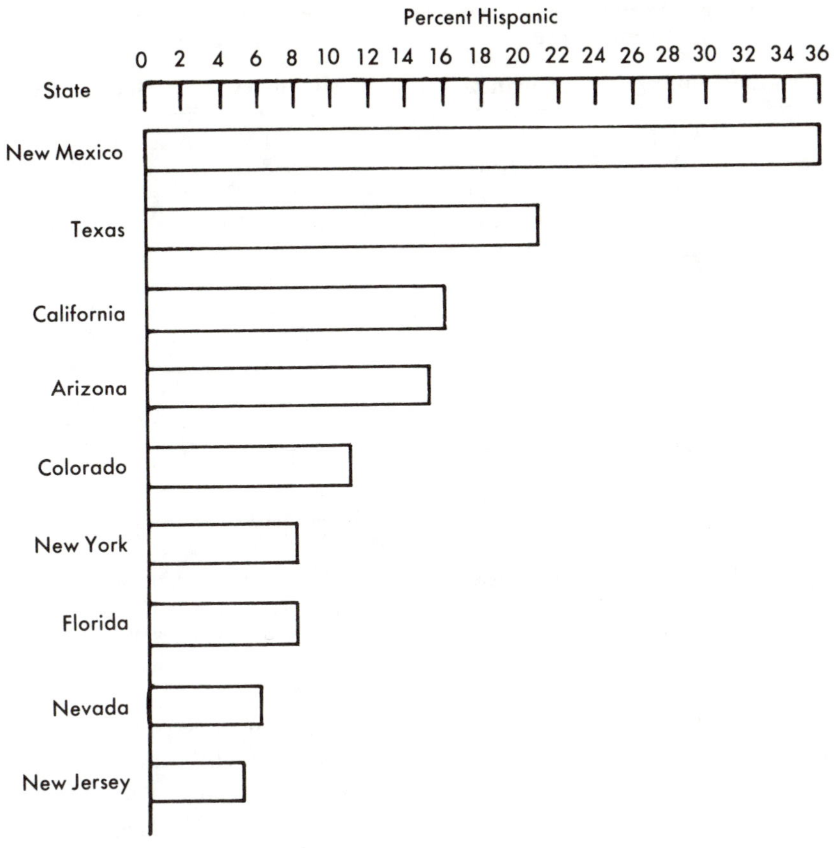

Figure 1–3
States with Hispanic Population of at Least 5%

From U.S. Department of Health, Education and Welfare, National Center for Education Statistics, Survey of Income and Education, Spring, 1976, Special Tabulations.

about because many LEP handicapped students are being placed in Bilingual Education as an alternative to special education.

The principal reason for the overrepresentation of bilingual children in special education classes, however, is biased assessment practices. Jones (1976) maintains that bias is involved at three different levels:

(1) at the content level where the decisions are first made about what items to include in a test,
(2) at the level of standardization where decisions are made about the population for whom the test is appropriate, and
(3) at the point of validation where efforts are undertaken to determine whether or not tests accomplish what they have been designed to accomplish.

The courts have been involved in the issue of biased assessment for many years. For example, the decision handed down in the *Larry P. v. Wilson Riles* (1979) case banned the use of the

State	Indochinese		Other		Total
	Elementary	Secondary	Elementary	Secondary	
California	20,073	15,871	1 ,981	1,488	39,413
New York	2,706	1,141	5,938	1,357	11,142
Florida	1,711	1,112	2,941	1,980	7,744
Texas	4,135	3,167	—	—	7,302
Pennsylvania	2,383	1,928	2,094	590	6,995
Washington	3,384	3,015	40	11	6,450
Illinois	2,384	1,946	1,086	751	6,167
Minnesota	2,628	2,285	60	41	5,014
Oregon	2,394	1,696	13	4	4,107
Virginia	1,887	1,699	127	107	3,820
Louisiana	2,038	889	14	7	2,948
Wisconsin	1,524	771	132	21	2,448
TOTALS	47,247	35,520	14,426	6,357	103,550

Table 1–4
List of 12 States with Largest Enrollment of Refugee Children
Data from Projections of non-English language background and limited English proficient persons in the United States to the year 2000, Rosslyn, Va., 1980, National Clearinghouse for Bilingual Education.

IQ test with Black children in the California public schools. In his decision of 1979, which was reiterated in 1986, Federal Judge R. F. Peckham stated:

> We must recognize at the outset that the history of the IQ test, and of special education classes built on IQ testing is not the history of neutral scientific discoveries translated into educational reform. It is, at least in the early years, a history of racial prejudice, of social Darwinism, and of the use of the scientific "mystique" to legitmate such prejudices.

As a result of the decision the California State Department of Education issued regulations and guidelines banning or limiting the use of IQ tests for the placement of minority children in special education classes. Perhaps other states will follow California's lead.

In addition to litigation, legislation is also being used in an attempt to minimize biased assessment practices. The Education for All Handicapped Children Act (P.L. 94–142) includes a section on nondiscriminatory testing. This law stipulates that children must be tested in their native or home language whenever possible.

Another important factor causing overrepresentation is examiner bias. A critical area of difficulty in using standardized tests is not a factor of the tests themselves but of those who administer them (Fishman, 1971). A study by Flanigan and Schwartz (1971) investigated the concept of examiner bias in the administration of individual intelligence tests. Three qualified psychological examiners evaluated 21 children using the Wechsler Intelligence Scale and the Stanford-Binet test. Striking differences were attributed to the examiners rather than to the instruments used.

The preparation and training of psychometrists, psychologists, counselors, and other test administrators varies from university to university and from state to state. Examiners are not always adequately prepared. Linden and Linden (1968) stated:

> Each year testing does a great deal of harm to thousands of children in the U.S. Many counselors have not been trained adequately and most are not prepared even to use tests as aids . . . if testing is to remain an important function then those who administer tests must become well versed in their use.

The ethnic background of the examiner is another important variable. Although research on this topic is limited, it appears that matching the ethnic and language background of the examiner and the student does make a significant difference. Palomares and Johnson (1966) conducted an interesting study in this regard. Each of them tested a number of Mexican-American children who had been recommended for classes for the educable mentally retarded (EMR). After testing the children with standard instruments, Johnson, who speaks no Spanish, found 73% of his 33 students eligible for classes for the educable mentally retarded. On the other hand, Palomares, a Spanish-speaking psychologist, recommended that 26% of his 35 pupils be placed in classes for the educable mentally retarded.

In the *Journal of Mexican American Studies,* Chandler and Plakos (1971) found that Mexican-American students are placed in classes for the educable mentally retarded at rates two to three times higher than their Anglo peers. Yet when properly evaluated by a psychologist conversant in Spanish who uses standard instruments translated into Spanish, the IQs of these so-called mentally retarded students increase some 13 points.

Professionals within the field of special education began to question the educational practices involving minority children as far back as the early 1960s. The most striking and effective condemnation of these practices was issued by Dunn in 1968:

> A better education than special class placement is needed for socioculturally deprived children with mild learning problems who have been labeled educable mentally retarded . . . The number of special day classes for the retarded has been increasing by leaps and bounds. The most recent 1967–1968 statistics compiled by the U.S. Office of Education now indicate that there are approximately 32,000 teachers of the retarded employed by local school systems—over one-third of all special educators in the nation. In my best judgment about 60–80 percent of the pupils taught by these teachers are from low status background—including Afro-Americans, American Indians, Mexicans and Puerto Rican Americans; those from nonstandard English speaking, broken, disorganized and inadequate homes; and children from other non-middle class environments. This expensive proliferation of self contained special schools and classes raises serious educational and civil rights issues which must be squarely faced. It is my thesis that we must stop labeling these deprived children as mentally retarded. Furthermore we must stop segregating them into our allegedly special programs.

Even though these serious problems were identified, the question still remains as to how best to educate bilingual children who are indeed truly handicapped.

Call for Bilingual Special Education

Large numbers of bilingual children are authentically handicapped and do require special education services. For some of them special placement in a class for the educable mentally retarded or the learning disabled would be the most appropriate placement and would provide them the opportunity for maximum development. What about the curriculum for these children? Should it be the same as that provided for monolingual children? Bernal (1974) was one of the first to endorse a bilingual approach:

> It is critically important that the exceptional child encounter as few traumatic emotional discontinuities in the educational process as possible. Accommodating the special education curriculum to the motivational, relational, expectational

> styles of Chicano children would ease their adaptation to formal educational settings. For this reason, I believe special education for Chicano children should be bilingual.

In response to this statement, one could raise this objection: It is difficult enough to teach a handicapped child the most basic skills; isn't it asking too much of special educators to include additional material on culture and on a second language? In reality the opposite is true. In other words, the imparting of basic skills may be facilitated considerably if one understands that the child's culture and language are the foundations upon which an appropriate education may be built.

The basic educational paradigm is to move the child from the known to the unknown through a linguistic or communicative medium that is already mastered. Consequently, the question is not one of additional material on culture but of the basic materials for education. In short, building on children's acquired repertories is fundamental to sound educational practice. The English language and Anglo cultural skills are actually the additional materials.

Definition of Bilingual Special Education

What is meant by Bilingual Special Education? Ideally, Bilingual Special Education may be defined as the use of the home language and the home culture along with English in an individually designed program of special instruction for the student. Bilingual Special Education considers the child's language and culture as foundations upon which an appropriate education may be built. The primary purpose of a Bilingual Special Education program is to help each individual student achieve a maximum potential for learning. Above all the program is concerned with the child's cognitive and affective development. It would be misleading to assume such a program is primarily concerned with teaching or maintaining a second language or culture. Here, language and culture are used as appropriate means rather than as ends in themselves.

In some cases a bilingual exceptional child could be placed in a self-contained Bilingual Special Education Program or could participate in a bilingual resource room for a short period each day. The handicapped bilingual child could also be served by an itinerant Bilingual Special Education teacher. The major determinants of the Bilingual Special Education program design would be the unique educational needs of the students.

Summary

This chapter introduced the emerging concept of Bilingual Special Education. Throughout the United States there are a sizable number of handicapped children of limited English proficiency whose educational needs are not being met adequately. The development of Bilingual Special Education programs was proposed as an innovative means of addressing this need.

Several significant issues related to Bilingual Special Education were discussed. It was stated that the establishment of Bilingual Special Education was an extension of the equal educational opportunity movement. Bilingual Special Education was shown to be closely related to the issue of the right to an appropriate education. Cultural pluralism and multicultural education were presented as part of the philosophical framework supporting Bilingual Special Education. Bilingualism was discussed as a worldwide phenomenon. The history and status of language policy in the United States was reviewed and the compatibility of Bilingual Special Education with this policy was shown. A review of the incidence figures on bilingual students revealed that approximately 7.9 million students in this country come from non-English language backgrounds. It was estimated that 948,000 of this group were both bilingual and handicapped. Finally, the development of Bilingual Special Education was proposed as the most effective way of meeting the special needs of these young learners.

Discussion Questions

1. Based on legislative mandates and court rulings, discuss the meaning and implications of equal educational opportunity. What is the underlying rationale for equal education?

2. What factors contribute to the right for an appropriate education?

3. Upon what concepts is the notion of cultural pluralism based?

4. Numerous factors contributed to a tradition of Bilingual Education in the United States. Identify the historical trends and discuss their implications in terms of the statistics in Tables 1–1 through 1–4 and in Figures 1–1 through 1–3.

5. The educational needs of LEP and LEP handicapped children have increased with the population. Discuss the projections and their implications for the classroom teacher and school districts.

6. The emphasis on Bilingual Education during the latter part of the 20th century has been an outgrowth of legislation during the past 50 years. Discuss the development, intent, and application of legislation over this period.

7. The purpose of multicultural education is implicit in the AACTE statement on p. 7. Discuss the rationale for the position taken.

References

American Association of Colleges for Teacher Education (1973). No one model American. *Journal of Teacher Education*. 24:264.

Andersson, T., & Boyer, M. (1970). *Bilingual schooling in the United States*. Austin, TX: Southwest Educational Development Laboratory.

Bernal, E. (1974, May). A dialogue on cultural implications for learning. *Exceptional Children*. 40:552.

Brown v. Board of Education of Topeka (1954). 347 U.S. 483, 74 S.Ct. 686, 91 L.Ed. 873.

Brown, G., et al. (1980). *The condition of education for Hispanic Americans*. Washington, DC: U.S. Government Printing Office.

Carpenter, J. (1974). Educating for a new pluralism. In J. Herman (Ed.), *The scholar and group identity*. New York: Institute on Pluralism and Group Identity.

Chandler, J. T., & Plakos, J. (1971). An investigation of Spanish speaking pupils placed in classes for the educable mentally retarded. *Journal of Mexican American Studies*. 1:58.

Coleman, J. S. (1968, Winter). The concept of equality of educational opportunity. *Harvard Educational Review*. 38:1.

Cortez, C. (1986). The education of language minority students: A contextual interaction model. In *Beyond language*. Los Angeles: Evaluation, Dissemination and Assessment Center, California State University.

Crawford, J. (1987, April 1). Bilingual education: Language, learning and politics. *Education Week*. 6(27): 19–49.

Dozier, E. (1956). Two examples of linguistic acculturation: The Yaqui of Sonora and the Tewa of New Mexico. *Language*. 32(1):146.

Dunn, L. M. (1968, September). Special education for the mildly retarded: Is much of it justifiable? *Exceptional Children*. 34:5.

Dyrcia S. et al. v. Board of Education of New York (1979). 79 C. 2562 (E.D.N.Y.).

Fishman, J. A. (1971). Testing special groups: The culturally disadvantaged. In L. C. Delighton (Ed.) , *The encyclopedia of education,* vol 9. New York: Macmillan.

Fishman, J. A. (1976). *Bilingual education: An international sociological perspective*. Rowley, MA: Newbury House.

Flanigan, P.J., & Schwarz, R. H. (1971, September). Evaluation of examiner bias in intelligence testing. *American Journal of Mental Deficiency.* 56:252.

Garcia, R. (1982). *Teaching in a pluralistic society: Concepts, models, strategies.* New York: Harper & Row.

Haring, N. G., & McCormick, L. (1986). *Exceptional children and youth: An introduction to special education.* Columbus, OH: Merrill Publishing Co.

Heath, S. (1977). Viewpoint: social history. In *Bilingual education: Current perspectives,* vol. 2. Arlington, VA: Center for Applied Linguistics.

Heward, W. L., & Orlansky, M. D. (1986). *Exceptional children: An introductory survey of special education.* Columbus, OH: Merrill Publishing Co.

Hockenberry, C. (1979). *Policy issues and implications on the education of adjudicated handicapped youth.* Reston, VA: Council for Exceptional Children.

Hunter, W. A. (1974). *Multicultural education: Through competency based teacher education.* Washington, DC: American Association of Colleges for Teacher Education.

Jarolimek, J. (1981). *The schools in contemporary society.* New York: Macmillan.

Jencks, C. (1972). *Inequality: A reassessment of the effect of family and schooling in America.* New York: Basic Books.

Jones, R. L. (1976). *Mainstreaming and the minority child.* Minneapolis: Council for Exceptional Children.

Kloss, H. (1977). *The American bilingual tradition.* Rowley, MA: Newbury House.

Kobrick, J. W. (1972, April 19). The compelling case for bilingual education. *Saturday Review* (pp. 54, 58).

Komisar, P., & Coombs, J. (1974). The concept of equality in education: Studies in philosophy and education. In C. Tesconi and E. Hurwitz (Eds.), *Education for whom?* New York: Dodd, Mead & Co.

Kopan, A. (1974). Melting pot—myth or reality? In E. Eppr (Ed.), *Cultural pluralism.* Berkeley, CA: McCutchan.

Krashen, S., & Biber, D. (1988). *On course: Bilingual education's success in California.* Sacramento, CA: California Association for Bilingual Education.

Larry P. v. Wilson Riles (1979). C-71-2270 FRP. Dis. Ct.

Linden, F. W., & Linden, K. W. (1968). *Tests on trial.* Boston: Houghton Mifflin.

Marland, S. (1971). Papers presented at the International Convention of the Council for Exceptional Children, Miami.

McClellan, B. E., et al. (1980). *Education and American culture.* New York: Macmillan.

McLean, G. (1988, Winter). American myths, official English and the need for action. *Cross Cultural Special Education Network.*

Mercer, J. R. (1972). *Labeling the mentally retarded.* Berkeley, CA: University of California Press.

Mills v. D.C. Board of Education (1972). 348 F. Supp. 866 (D.D.C.)

National Coalition for Cultural Pluralism (1973). In M. Stent, W. Hazard, and N. Rivlin (Eds). *Cultural pluralism in education: A mandate for change.* New York: Appleton-Century-Crofts.

Noboa, A. (1987). Bilingualism: An important imperative. *Family Resource Coalition Report,* 6(2), Chicago.

Ortiz, A. A., & Yates, J. R. (1983). Incidence of exceptionality among Hispanics: Implications for manpower planning. *NABE Journal.* 7:41–54.

Ovando, C., & Collier, V. (1985). *Bilingual and ESL classrooms: Teaching in multicultural contexts.* New York: McGraw-Hill.

Oxford, R., et al. (1980). *Projections of non-English language background and limited English proficient persons in the United States to the year 2000.* Rosslyn, VA: National Clearinghouse for Bilingual Education.

Padilla, A., & Sue, S. (1986). Ethnic minority issues in the U.S.: Challenges for the educational system. In *Beyond language.* Los Angeles: Evaluation, Dissemination and Assessment Center, California State University.

Palomares, U. H., & Johnson, L. L. (1966, April). Evaluation of Mexican American pupils for educable mentally retarded classes. *California Education.* 3:27.

Parker, L. (1978). *Bilingual education: Current perspectives, synthesis.* Arlington, VA: Center for Applied Linguistics.

Pennsylvania Association for Retarded Citizens (PARC) v. Pennsylvania (1971). 334 F. Supp. 1257 (E.D. Pa.)

Rueda, R., & Chan, K. (1979). Poverty and culture in special education: Separate but equal. *Exceptional Children.* 45 (7): 422–431.

Stone, S. C., & De Nevi, D. P. (Eds.). (1971). *Teaching multicultural populations: Five heritages.* New York: Van Nostrand Reinhold.

Trueba, H., Guthrie, G., & Hu-Pei-Au, K. (1981). *Culture and the bilingual classroom: Studies in classroom ethnography.* Rowley, MA: Newbury House.

Turnbull, H., & Turnbull, A. (1978). *Face appropriate public education—law and implementation.* Denver: Love Publishing Co.

U.S. Bureau of the Census (1976, July). Language usage in the United States, July 1975. *Current Population Studies.*

U.S. Bureau of the Census (1984). 1980 Census of Population, Chapter D, Detailed Population Characteristics, Part I, U.S. Summary (p680–1–d1). Washington, DC: U.S. Government Printing Office.

Waggoner, D. (1987, April 1). In J. Crawford, Bilingual education: Language, learning and politics. *Education Week* 6(27).

Zangwill, I. (1909). *The melting pot.* New York: Macmillan.

Zirkel, P. (1978). The legal vicissitudes of bilingual education. In H. Fontaine, B. Persky, and L. Golubchick (Eds.), *Bilingual education.* Wayne, NJ: Avery Publishing Group.

CHAPTER TWO

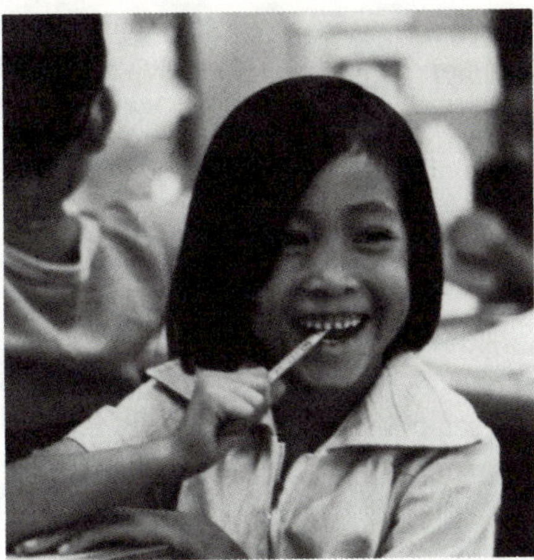

Bilingualism and Bilingual Education

- Clarification of Terms
- Goals of Bilingual Education
- Rationale for Bilingual Education
- Impact on Cognitive Development
- Impact on Language Arts Skills
- Impact on Attitude and Self-Concept
- Bilingual Program Designs
- Bilingual Methodology
- Program Staffing
- Effectiveness of Bilingual Education
- Summary

Objectives

- To present an overview of the field of Bilingual Education
- To clarify issues related to the goals of Bilingual Education
- To discuss the rationale for Bilingual Education
- To provide information on the impact of Bilingual Education on cognitive development, language arts skills, and self-concept
- To discuss program design and methodology
- To present information on the effectiveness of Bilingual Education

A better understanding of the types of services needed by culturally/linguistically different exceptional students requires familiarity with the services provided by Bilingual Education and special education. The next two chapters provide a comprehensive overview of these two important programs.

The main purpose of this chapter is to acquaint the reader with the principal issues and practices in the field of Bilingual Education. This includes a review of the basic concepts and terms related to bilingual instruction and with the various goals of bilingual programs. Aspects of curricular design, methodology, and staffing are explored and discussed as well. Finally, research data that describe the effectiveness of Bilingual Education in different contexts are presented.

Clarification of Terms

The terms *bilingualism* and *Bilingual Education* appear frequently in the literature. However, there is a great deal of variation with regard to the meaning of these terms (Hakuta, 1986). To be considered bilingual generally means an individual has the ability to use two different languages. Confusion arises when the degree of proficiency in each language is discussed. Some authorities claim that a bilingual person must have nativelike fluency in both languages (Bloomfield, 1933). Other experts maintain that minimal competency in two languages is sufficient to be called bilingual (Haugen, 1956; Diebold, 1961). This problem is best resolved by following the advice of Hornby (1977), who maintained that bilingualism is not an all-or-none property. Rather, it is an individual characteristic that may exist to varying degrees from minimum ability to complete fluency in more than one language. The term *balanced bilingual* is used frequently in the literature, referring to someone who is fully competent in both languages (Lambert, Hovelka, & Gardner, 1957). The designation, however, is not too useful, because most people tend to be more proficient in one language.

The issue of Black English is raised occasionally in the context of bilingualism (Castellanos, 1985). Is a Black child who speaks a combination of standard English and Black English bilingual? Most authorities would say no (Lyons, 1968). However, Taylor (1976) defines a bilingual person as one who speaks two or more "languages, dialects, or styles of speech that involve differences in sound, vocabulary, and syntax." According to this definition, the Black child could be considered bilingual. Because the issue of Black English is most complex and requires extensive discussion, it will not be included within the scope of this text.

Bilingual Education is another term requiring clarification because of its variation of meaning in different circles. According to Cohen (1975), Bilingual Education may fall into that category of terms much talked about but little understood. A commonly accepted definition of Bilingual Education is Cohen's definition (1975), which is as follows:

> "Bilingual Education" is the use of two languages as media of instruction for a child or a group of children in part or all of the school curriculum.

Because it is impossible to totally separate language from culture (Ovando & Collier, 1985), the term *Bilingual Education* includes the concept of bicultural education.

The U.S. Congress in P.L. 95–561, which is known as the Bilingual Act, defines the term *program of Bilingual Education* as follows:

> A program of instruction, designed for children of limited English proficiency in elementary or secondary schools, in which, with respect to the years of study to which the program is applicable . . . there is instruction given in, and study of, English and, to the extent necessary to allow a child to achieve competence in the English language, the native language of the children of limited English proficiency, and such instruction is given with appreciation for the cultural heritage of such children, and of other children in American society, and with respect to elementary and secondary school instruction, such instruction shall, to the extent necessary, be in all courses or subjects of study which will allow a child to progress effectively through the educational system.

The basic definition of Bilingual Education, generally agreed upon by both scholars and laypersons, is the "use of two languages as media of instruction." In other words, there is agreement regarding what the process of Bilingual Education is, but confusion arises when the philosophy and goals of Bilingual Education are discussed.

Goals of Bilingual Education

The goals of Bilingual Education may be organized into four categories: cognitive development, affective development, linguistic growth, and cultural enrichment.

According to Blanco (1977), the consensus of experts in the field of Bilingual Education is that its primary goals are in the areas of cognitive and affective development rather than in the linguistic and cultural realms. In other words, the primary goal of Bilingual Education is not to teach English or a second language per se but to teach children concepts, knowledge, and skills through the language they know best and to reinforce this information through the second language. The definition proposed by Andersson and Boyer (1970) stresses this approach. Accordingly, Bilingual Education is:

> A new way of conceiving the entire range of education especially for the non-English child just entering school. Bilingual learning necessitates rethinking the entire curriculum in terms of a child's best instruments for learning, of his readiness for learning various subjects, and his own identity and potential for growth and development.

When educators, legislators, or parents lose sight of cognitive and affective development as the primary goals of Bilingual Education, confusion, controversy, and disagreement are likely to be the outcome. What occurs most often is that the linguistic and cultural goals are taken out of context and made the primary purpose of the program. For example, legislators might say: "The main purpose of this program is to teach them English as soon as possible and get them into the mainstream of education." On the other hand, parents might say: "The main purpose of this program should be to maintain their native language and culture while they learn English." The issue of transition versus maintenance is certainly an important one, but it should not become the central issue when the primary goals of the program are discussed.

The linguistic and cultural goals of Bilingual Education can be viewed from four different philosophical perspectives: transition, maintenance, restoration, and enrichment.

A bilingual program with a *transitional* linguistic and cultural goal is one that uses the native language and culture of the student only to the extent necessary for the child to acquire English and thus function in the regular school curriculum. This program does not teach the student to read or write in the native language.

A bilingual program with linguistic and cultural *maintenance* as a goal also promotes English language acquisition. In addition, it endorses the value of linguistic and cultural diversity. Therefore linguistic and cultural maintenance encourages children to become literate in their native language and to develop bilingual skills throughout their schooling even into their adult lives. All state and federal legislation supports the transitional approach to Bilingual Education. These laws, however, do not prohibit local districts from going beyond the law into a maintenance program using local resources. Although legislation favors the transitional approach, local districts are free to implement a maintenance approach if they so desire.

A bilingual program with linguistic and cultural *restoration* as a goal would restore the language and culture of the student's ancestors, which may have been lost through the process of assimilation. For example, if a group of Lakota Indian children had lost the ability to speak the Lakota language, an appropriate bilingual program could help them revitalize their ancestral language and culture.

A bilingual program with linguistic and cultural *enrichment* as a goal concerns itself with adding a new language and culture to a group of monolingual children. A good example would be a program for monolingual English-speaking children designed to teach them the Spanish language and culture simply as an enrichment of their education.

Another program sometimes confused with Bilingual Education is English as a Second Language (ESL). The learning of English is an essential part of every bilingual program in this country (Troike, 1986). The teaching of English as a Second Language, however, does not in and of itself constitute a bilingual program. A good bilingual program, however, will include an English as a Second Language component (Ovando & Collier, 1985).

Bilingual and ESL education share a common objective: Both strive to promote English proficiency on the part of limited English proficient (LEP) students (Krashen, 1985). The major difference between the two programs is the approach. Bilingual Education accepts and develops the native language and culture in the instructional process. ESL instruction relies exclusively on English as the medium of teaching and learning. Bilingual Education is more comprehensive in orientation. It teaches not only English, as does ESL, but also cognitive skill development and subject matter concepts throughout the regular school curriculum in the general areas of math, science, language arts, and social studies. Bilingual Education and ESL are compatible. However, when either approach is used to the exclusion of the other, it is the LEP students who are slighted.

Rationale for Bilingual Education

The concept of Bilingual Education is supported by the idea that schools may use the culture and language of the home to maximize learning for LEP children. At the same time, Bilingual Education enriches learning for children of the dominant culture. It is an instructional strategy to help the LEP child to achieve maximum cognitive development. It is also an approach for providing a fuller educational experience for the non-LEP child of the majority culture.

At the center of the Bilingual Education movement is the conviction that the country is best served by preserving the varied contributing cultures that make up this nation instead of seeking to reduce cultures to a monochromatic, homogeneous amalgam. Bilingual Education may be justified as (1) the best way to attain the maximum cognitive development of linguistically different students, (2) a means of achieving equal educational opportunity and/or results, (3) a means of easing the transition into the dominant language and culture, (4) an approach to eventual total educational reform, (5) a means of promoting positive interethnic relations, and (6) a wise economic investment to help linguistic minority children to become maximally productive in adult life for the benefit of themselves and society.

According to Andersson and Boyer (1970), the rationale for Bilingual Education in the United States rests on the following propositions:

> 1. American schooling has not met the needs of children coming from homes where non-English languages are spoken; a radical improvement is therefore urgently needed.
>
> 2. Such improvement must first of all maintain and strengthen the sense of identity of children entering the school from such homes.
>
> 3. The self-image and sense of dignity of families that speak other languages must also be preserved and strengthened.
>
> 4. The child's mother tongue is not only an essential part of his sense of identity; it is also his best instrument for learning, especially in the early stages.
>
> 5. Preliminary evidence indicates that initial learning through a child's non-English home language does not hinder his learning English or other school subjects.
>
> 6. Differences among first, second, and foreign languages need to be understood if learning through them is to be sequenced effectively.
>
> 7. The best order of learning basic skills in a language—whether first or second—needs to be understood and respected if best results are to be obtained; for children this order normally is listening comprehension, speaking, reading, and writing.
>
> 8. Young children have an impressive learning capacity especially in the case of language learning; the young child learns the sound system, the basic structure, and the vocabulary of a language more easily and better than adolescents or adults.
>
> 9. Closely related to bilingualism is biculturalism, which should be an integral part of bilingual instruction.
>
> 10. Bilingual education holds the promise of helping to harmonize various ethnic elements in a community into a mutually respectful and creative pluralistic society.*

Additional insights on the rationale for Bilingual Education may be gained from a review of information presented by Garrader (1975). Accordingly, an appropriate Bilingual Education will:

1. Avoid retardation when the child's English is not adequate
2. Establish mutually supporting relationship between home and school
3. Defend and strengthen the child's self-concept
4. Exploit career potential of the non-English language
5. Conserve cultural (including linguistic) heritage of our people
6. Uphold the basic right of every people to rear and educate their children in their own image
7. Establish the superiority of foreign medium instruction over foreign language instruction
8. View bilingualism and Bilingual Education as instruments of politics

The rationale for Bilingual Education is clearly multifarious and comprehensive. Many different variables enter into the rationale, and

---

*From *Bilingual schooling in the United States* (pp. 43–44) by T. Andersson and M. Boyer, 1970, Austin, TX: Southwest Educational Development Laboratory. Copyright © 1970. Reprinted by permission.

the reasons for Bilingual Education are not only pedagogical but also social, psychological, and economic.

Impact on Cognitive Development

The basic and primary goal of Bilingual Education is the promotion of the maximum cognitive development of the student. Proponents of Bilingual Education advance a logical and pragmatic argument supporting this contention. Basically, they claim an LEP child is able to learn more effectively in a language the child understands (Cummins, 1981; Garcia, 1982). Moreover, children are able to learn new concepts and skills at a normal rate while at the same time learning English. If the same children were in an English-only program, they would fall behind in concept and skill acquisition until English was learned. For many children this would mean falling behind their peers in cognitive skill development and achievement by at least one or two years. This initial disadvantage generally becomes more pronounced as the children progress through school.

Before discussing the research related to the impact of Bilingual Education on cognitive development, it is important to understand the notion of cognitive development as a complex one with a long academic history. Many definitions and theories have sought to describe cognition and cognitive development. Flavell (1979) describes three general approaches: traditional, information processing, and developmental.

The *traditional* position views cognition as a state involving the higher mental processes. This would include thinking, problem solving, imagination, and conceptualization. The *information processing* position considers cognition analogous to a highly sophisticated computer that stores, retrieves, transforms, and processes information. Finally, the *developmental* position, influenced by Piaget, stresses the gradual development of cognitive abilities through a constant interaction, assimilation, and accommodation with the environment.

The early studies conducted during the 1920s and 1930s used a more traditional approach to cognition when examining the effects of bilingualism on cognitive development. This movement was characterized by emphasis on intelligence test scores as dependent measures. Ramirez (1977) noted that the period was dominated by attempts to relate bilingualism to performance on IQ tests. Ben-Zeev (1979) maintained that the majority of the early studies demonstrated that bilingualism had a negative impact on intelligence. MacNamara (1966) emphasized the important distinction between intelligence and IQ, arguing that many studies measured IQ rather than intelligence. However, there were serious methodological problems with the early studies, as Lambert (1977) has noted. For example, control for social and economic influences was lacking. Most of the early studies concluded that bilingualism decreases intelligence. A few of the early studies found no relationship between bilingualism and intelligence. Two of these studies concluded that bilingualism increased intelligence. Summarizing the findings of these early studies, Lambert stated:

> The largest proportion of these investigators concluded that bilingualism has a detrimental effect on intellectual functioning; a smaller number found little or no relation between bilingualism and intelligence; and only two suggested that bilingualism might have favorable effects on cognition.

Beginning in the 1960s, the more recent studies have shown a much more positive impact of bilingualism on cognitive development (Lambert, 1977). These studies were influenced by the developmental approach to cognition. In a development-oriented study with over 200 subjects, Duncan and De Avila (1979) found:

> Proficient bilingual children significantly outperformed all other monolingual and bilingual children on cognitive perspectivism tasks as well as on two cognitive perceptual components of field dependent/independent cognitive style. This finding is clearly supportive of the (1962) Peal and Lambert study, as well as the subsequent empirical and theoretical work of Ianco-Worrall, De Avila and Duncan, Cummins, and others regarding the potential cognitive advantages of bilingualism. The extent of the advantages revealed in this study is significant across a series of tasks. The nature of these differences or advantages can be described in terms of superior development of perspectivism or ability to intellectually restructure or reorganize a three-dimensional display; in relative use of separating out part of an organized field from the field as a whole, and in level of development of articulation of body concept. . . .

The results of this study also revealed a positive, monotonic relationship between degree of relative linguistic proficiency (RLP) and cognitive functioning. In other words, the more proficient the children were in each of their languages, the better they performed on the dependent measures. However, contrary to commonly held views, the "deficiencies" of limited bilingual children appear to be linguistic rather than intellectual.*

According to Parker and Heath (1978), a review of the research on bilingualism and cognitive development shows that Bilingual Education has a positive effect on cognitive development.

Barik and Swain (1974) suggests that immersion programs may contribute to the bilingual student's cognitive development. Lambert (1977) maintains there is a definite academic advantage enjoyed by bilingual children in the domain of cognitive flexibility. Supporting a similar position, De Avila and Duncan (1979) argue that bilingual children are potentially advanced with respect to metalinguistic awareness and conclude that their research supports the hypothesis of a cognitive advantage for the bilingual child. Krashen (1985) concludes that continued first language development has practical benefits, helps develop a healthy sense of biculturalism, and can result in superior cognitive development. Even though the literature is not conclusive at this point, Bilingual Education does not cause cognitive retardation as does an English-only program for bilingual children.

Impact on Language Arts Skills

It is well documented that linguistically different students generally do poorly in school when compared to their White peers. This is especially true in the area of reading achievement. The Education Commission of the States found, for example, that Hispanic reading achievement was consistently below that of White students (National Assessment of Educational Progress, 1977). Many of these children do poorly in reading English because they were taught to read before they had mastered the language. In bilingual programs reading is taught in the child's native language to ensure initial reading success. Rather than assuming cultural and linguistic experiences the child does not have in reading instruction, Bilingual Education capitalizes on the familiar experiences and knowledge of the child's own language. Thus children are not being taught reading skills and a new language at the same time (U.S. Commission on Civil Rights, 1975).

Once children have learned to read in their native language they can also learn to read English much more easily, because basic reading skills are transferable from one language to another (Reyes, 1987). Several studies conducted with widely disparate populations (Indians in

---

*From "Bilingualism and cognition: Some recent findings" by S. E. Duncan and E. A. De Avila, Fall 1979, *NABE Journal, 4(1),* p. 43. Copyright © 1979. Reprinted by permission.

Mexico, Blacks and Puerto Ricans in New York, Irish students in Ireland) reveal positive indications that bilingual instruction does not hinder reading ability in the second language. Actually, children in bilingual programs appear to be able to read the second language at grade level or above when compared with control groups (Parker & Heath, 1978; Reyes, 1987).

Cohen's findings (1975) on this topic are negative. According to his Redwood City study, Spanish-speaking children in a bilingual program scored lower in English reading than the control group. In this particular program children were taught to read English and Spanish simultaneously. This practice no longer enjoys strong support by bilingual educators. Although the research findings on second language reading are somewhat mixed, it appears that ample evidence supports the teaching of reading in the native language before the introduction of English reading. Thonis (1981) concurred when she wrote:

> The case for native language reading instruction for language minority students is strong. The rationale can be defended on logical grounds and empirical evidence. The perceptual, sensory-motor, and cognitive processes learned and practiced in any language have tremendous potential for transfer when developmental and learning principles are not violated. Once language minority students have learned to read well and have understood strategies for obtaining meaning from print, these abilities provide a solid foundation for literacy skills in the second language. The essential characteristic of first language skills available for supporting the additions of the second language is strength. Only strong learning transfers. Lastly, premature introduction to the second writing system may result in two weak sets of skills, neither of which serves well enough to be the carrier of content in school subjects.

A more recent ethnographic study by Moll and Diaz (1985) confirms the positive value of teaching reading in the native language to LEP students. They indicate that the students acquired advanced reading skills as a result of their participation in the Spanish language classroom. They argue that their research provides strong support for native language reading instruction.

The latest Government Accounting Office (GAO) report in 1987 also supports the claim that the extant research evidence in the field of Bilingual Education upholds the positive impact of native language instruction on the development of enhanced language arts skills.

Impact on Attitude and Self-Concept

To maximize learning potential, the child must have a positive attitude and a positive self-concept. Educational research has demonstrated a positive correlation between self-concept and academic achievement (Gay, 1966; Lumpkin, 1959). One goal of Bilingual Education is to improve the self-concept of the students in the program. Advocates of Bilingual Education argue that a program that accepts and respects the language and culture of its students will do more to enhance their self-concept than a program that does not accept and respect their language and culture. Even though this seems reasonable, and although many parents and program directors claim self-concepts are improved through Bilingual Education, the position is not yet supported by sufficient research data. Some studies have reported improved self-concept as a result of participation in bilingual programs (Markowitz & Haley, 1973; Rivera, 1973). Because of the many difficulties involved in the measurement of self-concept, these findings are tentative. However, one thing is certain: Bilingual Education does not harm the self-concept of students. This is more than can be said of English-only programs.

Bilingual Program Designs

Although Bilingual Education is defined as the use of two languages as media of instruction, programs may be designed and implemented in many different ways. The critical factors determining the design of the programs include (1) student needs, (2) linguistic ability of staff, and (3) program philosophy. School administrators must carefully assess these areas before establishing a program model.

Fishman and Lovas (1970) classify bilingual programs into four categories:

Type I Transitional Bilingualism
: The native language is used only until the children adjust to school and are able to participate in academic subjects in the second language.

Type II Monoliterate Bilingualism
: Programs of this nature have as a goal the development of oral language in the native language and the second language, but reading is taught only in the second language. Programs of this type represent an intermediate step between language shift and language maintenance.

Type III Partial Bilingualism
: These programs have as an objective fluency and literacy in both languages, but literacy in the national language is limited to some content areas, preferably those that have direct relation to the culture of the linguistic group.

Type IV Full Bilingualism
: In programs in which full bilingualism is the main goal, students are taught all skills in both languages in all domains.

These four models are based primarily on the program philosophy on which the school's curriculum committee has agreed. Gonzales (1975) describes five similar models:

Type A ESL/Bilingual (Transitional)
: Strictly remedial/compensatory orientation.

Type B Bilingual Maintenance
: Student's fluency in another language is seen as an asset to be maintained and developed.

Type C Bilingual/Bicultural (Maintenance)
: Similar to Type B, but it also integrates history and culture of the target group as an integral part of curricular content and methodology.

Type D Bilingual/Bicultural (Restorationist)
: A strong attempt is made to restore to children the option of learning the language and culture of their ancestors that may have been lost in the process of assimilation.

Type E Culturally Pluralistic
: Students are not limited to a particular target group. Rather, all students are involved in linguistically and culturally pluralistic schooling.

These models are also determined primarily by the philosophy and goals of Bilingual Education adopted by the school district. When a school district has adopted a particular philosophical position toward Bilingual Education, it can then choose one of these language scheduling models:

Alternate day plan. One language is used one day and the other is used the next day as deemed appropriate by the instructional staff.

Half day plan. The home language is used for instruction during one part of the day and English for the other part of the day (similar to the alternate day plan).

Mixed. Some subjects are taught in one language while other subjects are taught in the second language. In some programs the same lessons are repeated in both languages.

Bilingual support. This model is used in situations in which there are too few limited English-speaking (LES) and non-English-speaking (NES) students in one language background for the school to provide a full bilingual program; in such programs, resource materials and people (teachers, aides, and tutors) who speak the language are identified and placed on call to assist the student in or out of the classroom through tutoring in subject areas and to help teach the student skills (such as reading, writing, and computation) in the home language; meanwhile the student participates in regular English medium instruction with monolingual children.

No Bilingual Education program should be designed without a comprehensive needs assessment of the students who will be involved in the program. This needs assessment should focus on first and second language proficiency, on academic needs, and on affective needs. This information should be provided for both the linguistically different as well as the nonlinguistically different students who wish to participate in the program. Once the school district knows the needs of its students it can then begin to review and select an appropriate dual language instruction schedule from the models shown in Figure 2–1.

The linguistic ability of the staff is one factor to consider before selecting a program design. Answers should be given to such critical questions as these: Are sufficient numbers of bilingual aides available? Are they sufficiently skilled in assisting teachers in reinforcing instruction? Are they fluent enough to teach in the native language?

In summary, the program design is selected when compatibility exists between the needs of the students, the linguistic ability of the staff, and the philosophy of school district.

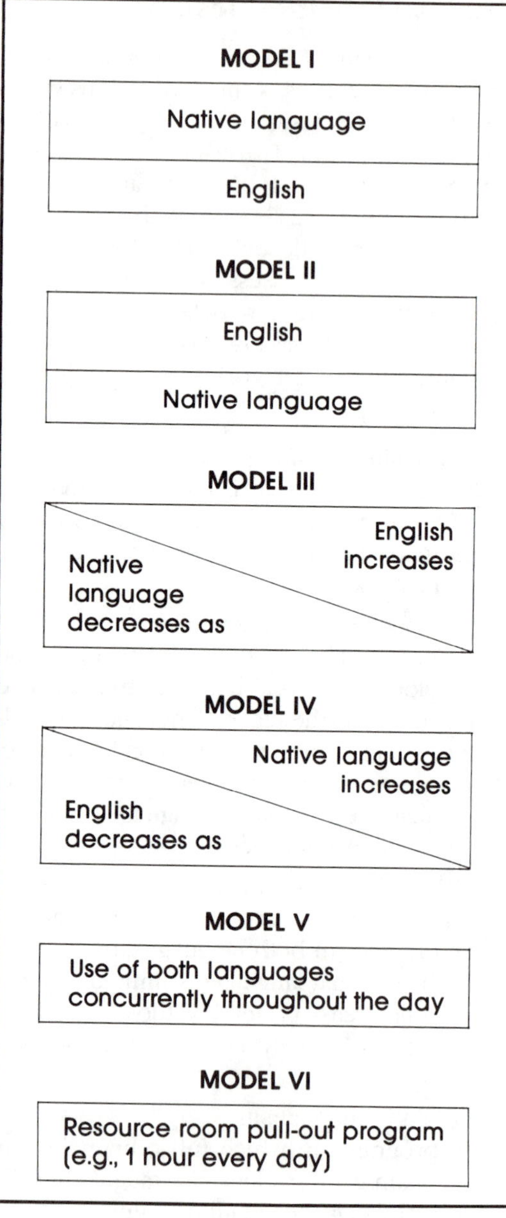

Figure 2–1
Bilingual Instruction Models

From *Models for bilingual programs* by C. Savédra, 1979, Colorado State Department of Education: Bilingual Institute. Copyright © 1979. Reprinted by permission.

Bilingual Methodology

Bilingual methodology varies from program to program. It is usually based on the program philosophy. An important factor to consider is whether the program is the maintenance type or the transitional type. The most common dual language instruction methods are:

1. **Translation method**
With the translation method the aide literally translates what the teacher says. Found in transitional programs, it is not too popular because it is time consuming and awkward.

2. **Preview-review method**
With the preview-review method, the lesson is begun in the home language, then presented in English, and summarized in the home language.

3. **Alternate day method**
This is mainly a matter of scheduling. In this approach the two languages could be alternated; English could be used on Monday, Wednesday, and Friday, and the home language on Tuesday and Thursday, for example. Variations of this method could be the alternate week or month approach.

4. **Concurrent method**
The concurrent method consists of a natural shifting from one language to the other as the teacher sees fit. It is a natural and relaxed form of code switching facilitated by the teacher.

5. **ESL method (English as a Second Language)**
The ESL method is used by the teacher when working with small groups of children who are not dominant in English. It is not a bilingual method per se, but it is used in most bilingual programs.

6. **SSL method (Spanish as a Second Language)**
This is exactly the same as the ESL method except Spanish is offered to those students who are not Spanish dominant.

7. **Eclectic method**
The eclectic method is the combination of two or more of the previously discussed approaches by the teacher for whatever reasons deemed appropriate.

8. **Total immersion**
Total immersion is a more intense approach where the total curriculum is taught in the chosen language, either English or the home language, for an extended period of time.

In selecting any of these methods it is important to consider the needs of the students as well as the abilities of the teachers and the philosophy of the program.

Program Staffing

As with most other programs, there are several ways of staffing a bilingual program. The most acceptable model is the self-contained class with a fully qualified bilingual teacher and a bilingual aide. Team teaching with a bilingual and a monolingual teacher working together is an acceptable model. Several variations of team teaching can be implemented. Removing children from their regular classes and placing them in resource rooms for brief periods during the day is not considered a quality approach and is not acceptable in some school districts.

Effectiveness of Bilingual Education

The following review of the literature on Bilingual Education discusses the findings of studies conducted in a variety of bilingual program settings. It presents information about bilingual projects that exist or have existed in the United States, as well as those from other countries.

Modiano's study (1968) of the comparison of Spanish direct teaching and the Indian language approach in Chiapas, Mexico, indicates that after three years, students who had been initially taught in their native language and then in Spanish had higher reading comprehension, as measured by a Spanish reading test, than those children who had been taught only in Spanish. Modiano's findings supporting the use of the child's native language in initial reading tasks are substantiated by other studies such as those of Barrera-Vasquez (1953) with Tarascan Indians, Burns's study (1968) of Quechua Indians, and Osterberg's findings (1961) from his study on dialect-speaking Swedish children.

Gudschinsky (1971) studied the native language approach used in the mountains of Peru. The children in this project were exposed to Quechua, their native language, as the medium of instruction for the first two years and then were moved into Spanish. Gudschinsky found that more children remained in schools under this system, and the work done was superior to that done by comparable students who were not in the bilingual program.

Worral (1970) studied Afrikaans-English bilingual students, ages 4 to 6 and 7 to 9, in Pretoria, South Africa. She matched each bilingual child with two monolingual children—one Afrikaans-speaking and the other English-speaking—on intelligence, age, sex, school grade, and social class. On a phonetic preference test, the preschool bilingual children showed greater ability to separate the sound of a word from its meaning than did either of the monolingual groups.

She concluded that bilingual children are aware that different words can mean the same thing earlier than monolinguals because they are used to giving the same object two names, one for each of their languages. Blank (1973) claims that a major characteristic of low-functioning preschool children is that they have not developed what she calls the "abstract attitude" acquired by the more successful preschool children. Blank concludes that the primary goal of teaching children who function poorly should be to develop the precursors of abstract thinking so that they will have an internalized, readily available symbolic system. She believes that if "learning sets" have any value in preschool education, they should be "metaset" or the learning set par excellence. The metaset is a step beyond specific learning sets. It is a more abstract or sophisticated skill that enables the child to adapt and transfer other learning sets as needed. Worral's findings (1970) appear to be one instance in which this hypothesis is substantiated.

Malherbe (1969) reported that children involved in the bilingual schools in South Africa performed significantly better in language attainment (in both languages), geography, and arithmetic when compared with comparable monolingual children. Malherbe's study is one of the few that controlled for student's intelligence, and as a result of his investigation he stated:

> There is a theory that while the clever child may survive the use of the second language as a medium the duller child suffers badly. We, therefore, made the comparison at different intelligence levels and found that not only the bright children, but also the children with below normal intelligence do better school work all around in the bilingual school than in the unilingual school. What is most significant is that the greatest gain for the bilingual school was registered in the second language by the lower intelligence groups.

Richardson's findings (1973) about the Coral Way Elementary School in Florida support Matherbe's findings regarding the benefit of bilingual education. The Coral Way program was similar to that used in the South Africa study, because the subject matter was taught in both languages and the student population was mixed. After a three-year study, his findings indicated:

> . . . that while the students, English-speaking and Spanish-speaking, were not yet as proficient in their second language as in their native language, they had made impressive gains in learning their second language. The study also indicated that the bilingual curriculum was as effective as the traditional curriculum in helping the students progress in paragraph meaning, word meaning, spelling, arithmetic, reasoning, and computation.

The alternate days approach in the Philippines' bilingual program was similar in structure to the South African bilingual schools. At the end of the first year, the bilingual class performed equally as well as the Filipino class on tests, conducted in Filipino, of reading, science, and nonverbal social studies as did the English class. Both control and experimental groups performed equally well on oral English (Tucker, et al., 1972).

The San Antonio, Texas, bilingual study was designed to test the effectiveness of intensive oral language instruction in English and Spanish. Taylor's assessment (1976) of oral language skills at the fourth and fifth grades showed that the intensive Spanish group scored the highest on the English oral test. Arnold (1969) also found these children had better reading retention. This finding is similar to those reported by Lambert & Tucker (1972), indicating transfer and learning in the other language without direct teaching. A five-year longitudinal study of the Santa Fe, New Mexico, bilingual program (Leyba, 1978) found children in the bilingual program performed better consistently on academic achievement tests than the nonbilingual control group. The cumulative effect after the five-year period was statistically significant. Cohen (1975), in his study of the Redwood City, California, bilingual program, reported:

> 1. That Mexican-American children who are taught in the academic curriculum in Spanish and English for several years are as proficient in English language skills as comparable Mexican-American children taught only in English;
>
> 2. Bilingually schooled children are, to a limited extent, more proficient in Spanish language skills than comparable children taught only in English;
>
> 3. A bilingual program promotes a greater use of Spanish among its Mexican-American participants than found among comparable non-project participants;
>
> 4. Mexican-American children, following a bilingual program, perform at least as well—and at one group level significantly better—in relation to the comparison group on tests of a nonlanguage matter such as mathematics;
>
> 5. Students in the bilingual program perform better than the comparison students at one level and the same at the other two levels on measures of academic aptitude;
>
> 6. Mexican-American students in the bilingual program gained more positive appreciation of Mexican culture than the comparison group. This positive gain in cultural appreciation was not achieved at the expense of their esteem for the Anglo culture;
>
> 7. The school attendance of the Mexican-American students in the bilingual program was much better than that of Mexican-American students in the comparison group;
>
> 8. Those students who had been in the bilingual program the longest had more positive attitudes toward school than did comparison students who had been schooled conventionally for the same period of time;
>
> 9. The bilingual group parents were more positive than the comparison parents about the virtues of the Spanish language, not only as a means of preserving their heritage but also for practical reasons such as enhancing their children's education and helping them to get a job.

In 1976 the U.S. Government Accounting Office (GAO) issued a report on Bilingual Education entitled *Bilingual Education: An Unmet Need*. The report indicated that the gains made by the English-dominant students on the average were better than those of the non-English-dominant students. For example, the data showed that 45% of the English-dominant students made normal or better reading progress. But only 33% of the non-English-dominant students made normal or better progress in reading. The report goes on to state that two possible causes for these results are not enough native language instruction and too many monolingual English speakers in the program. While these reasons may be valid, it should be pointed out that testing the students in English only is not consistent with the principles of Bilingual Education. Students in these programs should be evaluated in both languages.

A more current GAO report (1987), however, claims that federal bilingual programs have been found effective for educating LEP students. It appears that Bilingual Education programs are improving with age.

A study by Troike (1978) cited several programs that have documented success. Included among the programs are:

1. **Philadelphia, PA (Spanish)**
In a third-year program, English- and Spanish-speaking kindergarten students in the bilingual program exceed the citywide mean and a control group on the Philadelphia Readiness test (a criterion-referenced test), and attendance records were better than in the control group.

2. **San Francisco, CA (Chinese)**
Chinese-dominant students in the Title VII bilingual program in 1975–76 were at or above district and national norms in English and math in three of six grades, and only .1 (one month) below in two others, as measured by the Comprehensive Test of Basic Skills (CTBS). In addition, English-speaking students in the program performed at or above national and district norms in all grades, demonstrating that the time spent learning Cantonese did not detract from the English language development.

3. **San Francisco, CA (Spanish)**
The Spanish Title VII bilingual program students in the seventh grade showed two months greater gain than regular district students on the CTBS during 1975–76, and were only .1 below other district students in the same schools. Additionally, the absenteeism among bilingual program students was less than one-third that of the regular program students (3.6 percent compared to 12.1 percent).

4. **Lafayette Parish, LA (French)**
Students in grades K–3 in the French-English bilingual program performed as well or significantly better than a control group of students in the regular program in all areas tested, including reading and reading readiness, linguistic structures, writing, math concepts, and social science. Instruments used included the Primary Abilities Test, the Metropolitan Achievement Test, and a criterion-referenced test for French.

5. **Artesia, NM (Spanish)**
On the Comprehensive Test of Basic Skills, Spanish-dominant children in the bilingual program scored significantly higher than the control group in grades three and four in English and reading, while even English-dominant children in the program scored higher than their control group. In general, the control group children continued to lose positive self-image while the bilingual program children maintained or increased it.*

Troike in a more recent article (1986) points out that bilingual programs have demonstrated that they can raise achievement scores to or above the national norms and that the effect of the program is cumulative, with the greatest gains made after five and six years of participation in the program.

The most thoroughly conceived, carefully conducted, and academically respected longitu-

---

*From *Research evidence for the effectiveness of bilingual education* (pp. 5–6) by R. Troike, 1978, Rosslyn, VA: National Clearinghouse for Bilingual Education. Copyright © 1978. Reprinted by permission.

dinal study in the literature on Bilingual Education was the one conducted by Lambert and Tucker (1972) in Canada. This study differed radically from other studies in these respects:

> 1. It was not a comparison of two models but rather a demonstration of the value of the Direct Approach.
>
> 2. The children in this study were speakers of the dominant language (English) and were learning the non-dominant language (French) in Montreal. In all other studies, the subjects have been minority groups who were to learn the language of the majority.
>
> 3. The parental input differed. The parents were middle class and active in the education of their children. Parents conceived this project and supported it through 6 years.

This well-designed and tightly controlled study indicates:

1. Children in the pilot group were identical to the English control group on achievement and intelligence. Their achievement is apparently unhampered by learning in a weaker language for four years.

2. Retesting in the sixth grade showed that the children in the program were equivalent to English speakers on English exams.

3. The children in general had a high self-concept, and they identified fairly completely with the English-Canadian set of values. However, in a questionnaire given to fourth and fifth graders, the children rated themselves as both English and French Canadian. Thus, they may be gaining some qualities of biculturalism.

4. The experimental program resulted in no native language or subject matter deficit or retardation of any kind.

5. The experimental students appear to be able to read, write, speak, understand, and use English as competently as students in the English control group.

6. During the same period of time and with no apparent personal or academic costs, the experimental children developed a competence in reading, writing, speaking, and understanding French that could never be matched by English students following a standard French as a Second Language program (Lambert and Tucker, 1972).

Peal and Lambert (1962), in reference to the St. Lambert experimental program, stated:

> The picture that emerges of the French/English bilingual in Montreal is that of a youngster whose wider experiences in two cultures have given him advantages, which a monolingual does not enjoy. Intellectually, his experience with two language systems seems to have left him with a mental flexibility, superiority in concept formation, and a more diversified set of mental abilities, in the sense that the patterns of abilities developed by bilinguals were more heterogeneous . . . In contrast, the monolingual appears to have a more unitary structure of intelligence which he must use for all types of intellectual tasks.

The research discussed and other bilingual studies demonstrate the success of Bilingual Education. Children involved in learning environments employing two languages are performing at a level equal to or higher than their monolingual counterparts. Dulay, Burt, and Zappert (1976) in their summary of research findings state:

> Contrary to widespread belief, the research contracted to date is not contradictory with regards to the effects of bilingualism and bilingual education on student performance. If one applies objective criteria for applicability and soundness of research design, most of the studies show a significant positive effect, or a nonsignificant effect, on student performance. Of the 66 studies reviewed only 1% was negative; 58% were positive and 41% were neutral.

Troike (1986) in the *Compendium of Papers on the Topic of Bilingual Education* prepared for the Committee on Education and Labor of the 99th Congress states that the increased use of the native language in the classroom results in higher academic achievement as measured in English and in better language skills.

Hakuta and Snow (1986) conclude that Bilingual Education is indeed superior to submersion, that poorly conducted evaluation research has observed this fact, and that evaluation research conducted with greater rigor would bear out the superiority of Bilingual Education as an instructional method in many educational contexts.

Willig (1985) in her meta-analysis study of Bilingual Education concluded that the bilingual programs she examined were more effective than nonbilingual programs.

Krashen (1985) and Krashen and Biber (1988), experts in English as a Second Language, also concluded that well-organized bilingual programs are very effective in teaching English as a Second Language, often more effective, in fact, than all-day English programs that "submerse" the child in English.

From this brief review of literature, Bilingual Education is established as an effective educational methodology. It not only works well with the average child, but it has also been shown to work with children of limited intellectual ability (Malherbe, 1969). Thus it appears that Bilingual Special Education may also be an effective method of providing an appropriate education for the bilingual handicapped child.

Summary

This chapter attempted to familiarize the reader with the basic concepts related to Bilingual Education. Various terms were defined and classified. The philosophy and goals of Bilingual Education were discussed at some length. It was pointed out that the basic and primary goal of Bilingual Education is the cognitive and affective development of the student. Various designs and teaching methodologies were described. Finally, research evidence on the effectiveness of Bilingual Education was presented.

Although there is a great need for additional research, enough studies have been conducted that show the positive effects of bilingual instruction. It is anticipated that these same positive results will also be encountered in Bilingual Special Education programs. Bilingual Special Education is based on many of the same theoretical principles as Bilingual Education. The crossover between Bilingual Education and Bilingual Special Education will be discussed in Chapter 5.

Discussion Questions

1. Compare and contrast the definitions of Bilingual Education. Which seems the most comprehensive? The most appropriate? Why?

2. The primary or central goal of Bilingual Education is frequently misunderstood. Given the various goals, determine how this misunderstanding occurs.

3. Describe and compare the four types of bilingual programs, as categorized by Fishman and Lovas (1970), then choose the most appropriate and provide a rationale for the choice.

4. Which of the language instruction methods would best serve the primary goal of Bilingual Education? Why?

5. What are the critical factors that influence the design of a bilingual program?

6. Discuss the differences between the various Bilingual Education methodologies.

7. What evidence supports the cognitive and affective effectiveness of Bilingual Education?

References

Andersson, T., & Boyer, M. (1970). *Bilingual schooling in the United States.* Austin, TX: Southwest Educational Development Laboratory (pp. 43–44, 63).

Arnold, R. (1969, January). Reliability of test scores for the young bilingual disadvantaged. *Reading Teacher* (pp. 341–346).

Barik, H., & Swain, M. (1974). English-French bilingual education in the early grades: The Elgin Study. *Modern Language Journal.* 54:392.

Barrera-Vasquez, E. (1953). The Tarascan project in Mexico. In *Use of vernacular languages in education.* Paris: UNESCO.

Ben-Zeev, S. (1979). Mechanisms by which childhood bilingualism affects understanding of language and cognitive structures. In P. Hornby (Ed.), *Bilingualism: Psychological, social and educational implications.* New York: Academic Press.

Blanco, G. (1977). *Bilingual education: Current perspectives.* Arlington, VA: Center for Applied Linguistics (p. 60).

Blank, M. (1973). A tutorial language program to develop abstract thinking in socially disadvantaged preschool children. *Child Development.* 39:379.

Bloomfield, L. (1933). *Language.* New York: Holt, Rinehart & Winston.

Burns, D. (1968). Bilingual education in the Andes of Peru. In J. Fishman (Ed.), *Language problems of developing nations.* New York: John Wiley & Sons.

Castellanos, D. (1985). *The best of two worlds: Bilingual-bicultural education in the U.S.* Trenton, NJ: New Jersey State Department of Education.

Cohen, A. (1975). *A sociolinguistic approach to bilingual education.* Rowley, MA: Newbury House (pp. 18, 261).

Cummins, J. (1981). The role of primary language development in promoting educational success for language minority students. In *Schooling and language minority students: A theoretical framework* (pp. 3–49). Sacramento, CA: Office of Bilingual Bicultural Education, California State Department of Education.

De Avila, E. & Duncan, S. (1979). Bilingualism and the metaset. *Journal of the National Association for Bilingual Education.* 3(2):1.

Diebold, R. (1961). *Bilingualism and biculturalism in a Hauve community.* Doctoral dissertation, Yale University, New Haven, CN.

Dulay, H., Burt, M., & Zappert, L. (1976). *Why bilingual education? A summary of research findings.* Berkeley, CA: BABEL/LAU Center.

Duncan, S., & De Avila, E. (1979, Fall). Bilingualism and cognition: some recent findings. *NABE Journal.* 4(1):43.

Fishman, J., & Lovas, J. (1970). Bilingual education in sociolinguistic perspective. *TESOL Quarterly.* 4(31):251.

Flavell, J. (1979). The cognitive and affective development of children. In H. Trueba and C. Barnett-Mizrahi (Eds.), *Bilingual multicultural education and the professional: From theory to practice.* Rowley, MA: Newbury House.

Garcia, R. (1982). *Teaching in a pluralistic society: Concepts, models, strategies.* New York: Harper & Row.

Garrader, B. (1975). The rationale behind bilingual-bicultural education. In F. Von Moltitz (Ed.), *Living and learning in two languages* (pp. 66–67). New York: McGraw-Hill.

Gay, C. (1966). *Academic achievement and intelligence among Negro eighth grade students as a function of the self-concept.* Unpublished doctoral dissertation, North Texas State University, Denton TX.

Gonzales, J. (1975, February). Coming of age in bilingual bicultural education: An historical perspective. *Inequality of Education.* 19(5):5.

Gudschinsky, S. (1971, November 22–24). *Literacy in the mother tongue and second language learning.* Paper presented at the Conference of Child Language, Chicago.

Hakuta, K. (1986). *Mirror of language: The debate on bilingualism.* New York: Basic Books.

Hakuta, K. & Snow, C. (1986). The role of research in policy decisions about bilingual education. In *Compendium of Papers on the Topic of Bilingual Education of the 99th Congress.* Washington, DC: U.S. Government Printing Office.

Haugen, E. (1956). *Bilingualism in the Americas; a bibliography and research guide.* Montgomery, AL: University of Alabama Press.

Hornby, P. (1977). *Bilingualism: Psychological, social, and educational implications.* New York: Academic Press.

Krashen, S. D. (1985). *Inquiries and insights: Second language teaching, immersion and bilingual education literacy.* Hayward, CA: Alemany Press.

Krashen, S., & Biber, D. (1988). *On course: Bilingual education success in California.* Sacramento, CA: California Association for Bilingual Education.

Lambert, W. (1977). The effects of bilingualism on the individual: Cognitive and sociocultural consequences. In P. Hornby (Ed.), *Bilingualism: Psychological, social, and educational implications* (p. 5). New York: Academic Press.

Lambert, W., Hovelka, J. & Gardner, R. (1957). Linguistic manifestation of bilingualism. *American Journal of Psychology.* 72:77.

Lambert, W., & Tucker, R. (1972). *Bilingual education of children: The St. Lambert experiment* (pp. 144–152). Rowley, MA: Newbury House.

Leyba, C. (1978). *Longitudinal study, Title VII bilingual programs, Santa Fe Public Schools.* Los Angeles: National Dissemination and Assessment Center.

Lumpkin, D. (1959). *The relationship of self-concept to achievement in reading.* Unpublished doctoral dissertation, University of Southern California, Los Angeles.

Lyons, J. (1968). *Introduction to theoretical linguistics.* Cambridge, England: Cambridge University Press.

MacNamara, J. (1966). *Bilingualism and primary education: A study of Irish experience.* Edinburgh: Edinburgh University Press.

Malherbe, E. (1969). Commentary to N.M. Jones, How and when do persons become bilingual. In L. Kelley (Ed.), *Description and measurement of bilingualism* (p. 78). Toronto: University of Toronto Press.

Markowitz, A., & Haley, F. (1973). *A bilingual Navajo curriculum project: Profiles of promise.* ERIC No. ED 095073. Washington, DC: National Institute of Education.

Modiano, N. (1968). Bilingual education for children of linguistic minorities. *America Indigina.* 28:405.

Moll, L., & Diaz, S. (1985). Ethnographic pedagogy: Promoting effective bilingual instruction. In E. Garcia and R. Padilla (Eds.), *Advances in bilingual education research.* Tucson, AZ: University of Arizona Press.

National Assessment of Educational Progress (1977, May). *Hispanic student achievement in five learning areas: 1971–1975.* Report No. BR-2.

Osterberg, T. (1961). *Bilingualism and the first school language.* Umea, Sweden: Vasberbottens Tryekeri.

Ovando, C. J. & Collier, V. P. (1985). *Bilingual and ESL classrooms: Teaching in multicultural contexts.* New York: McGraw-Hill.

Parker, L., & Heath, S. (1978). *Center for Applied Linguistics: Bilingual education current perspective-synthesis.* Arlington, VA: Center for Applied Linguistics.

Peal, E., & Lambert, W. (1962). *The relation of bilingualism to intelligence.* Psychological Monographs—General and Applied 75(27).

Ramirez, J. L. (1977). Chicano psychology. New York: Academic Press.

Reyes, M. de la L. (1987). Comprehension of content area passages: A study of Spanish/English readers in third and fourth grade. In S. R. Goldman and H. T. Trueba (Eds.), *Becoming literate in English as a second language.* Norwood, NJ: Ablex Publishing Corp.

Richardson, J. (1973). Two patterns of bilingual education in Dade County, Florida. In I. Bird (Ed.), *Foreign language learning: Research and development.* Meneska, WI: George Banta Co.

Rivera, E. (1973). *Academic to achievement; bicultural attitudes and self-concepts of pupils in bilingual and non-bilingual programs.* Unpublished doctoral dissertation, Fordham University, Bronx, NY.

Savedra, C. (1979). *Models for bilingual programs.* Unpublished papers, Colorado State Department of Education, Bilingual Institute.

Taylor, I. (1976). *Introduction to psycholinguistics* (p. 238). New York: Holt, Rinehart & Winston.

Tonis, E. (1981). Reading instruction for language minority students. In *Schooling and language minority students: A theoretical framework* (p. 178). Los Angeles: Office of Bilingual and Bicultural Education, California State Department of Education.

Troike, R. C. (1986). Improving conditions for success in bilingual education programs. In *Compendium of papers on the topic of bilingual education of the 99th Congress.* Washington DC: U.S. Government Printing Office.

Troike, R. (1978). *Research evidence for the effectiveness of bilingual education* (pp. 5–6). Rosslyn, VA: National Clearinghouse for Bilingual Education.

Tucker, G., et al. (1972). An alternate days approach to bilingual education. In J. Alatis (Ed.), *Report of the 21st annual round table meeting on linguistics and language studies.* Washington, DC: Georgetown University Press.

U.S. Commission on Civil Rights (1975). *A better chance to learn: Bilingual bicultural education.* U.S. Commission on Civil Rights Clearinghouse Publication No. 51., Washington, DC: U.S. Government Printing Office.

U.S. Government Accounting Office (1987). *Bilingual education: A new look at the research evidence.* Washington, DC: U.S. Government Printing Office.

U.S. Government Accounting Office (1976). *Bilingual education: An unmet need.* Washington, DC: U.S. Government Printing Office.

Willig, A. C. (1985). A meta-analysis of selected studies on the effectiveness of bilingual education. *Review of Educational Research.* 55(3):269–317.

Worrall, A. (1970). *Bilingualism and cognitive development.* Doctoral dissertation, Cornell University, Ithaca, NY.

CHAPTER THREE

The Education of Children with Exceptional Needs

- Classification of Children
- Exceptional Children Defined
- Incidence and Prevalence of Exceptional Children
- The Bilingual Exceptional Child
- Special Education Services
- Efficacy of Special Classes
- Summary

Objectives

- To understand how children are classified within the school setting and labeled as exceptional
- To explore the differences between incidence and prevalence with respect to students identified as exceptional
- To review the historical development of special education programs and the individuals who contributed to their success
- To understand how valid special education classes are for children

In a general educational sense, all children have exceptional needs. However, in this chapter we are concerned with children whose needs are significantly different from those of other children in some important dimension of their general functioning. For these children a physical, emotional, cognitive, or social factor makes it difficult for them to realize their full potential. They need skilled intervention and care to succeed both academically and socially.

Such exceptional children include the hearing and vision impaired, the physically handicapped, the mentally retarded, the learning disabled, and the emotionally disturbed, among others. Even gifted and talented children with high intelligence and creative talents must be recognized as special, because they also need skilled intervention to succeed in school.

Classification of Children

Over the years many terms have been used to refer to children with exceptional needs, such as *dysfunctional, disabled, handicapped,* and *gifted.* The educational literature and the special education literature in particular have emphasized considerably the process of defining exceptionalities. However, the emphasis has shifted from developing new definitions to focusing on the consequences of applying definitions to exceptional children. Heightened public awareness and social concern can be partly attributed to this shift in emphasis.

Unlike the case of children in "regular" education, definitions have become central to the educational placement of exceptional children and, in turn, to the design of instructional activities. Definitions are considered important because:

1. They are a means to distinguish students whose abilities dictate specific instructional approaches.
2. They are a necessary form of communication for personnel at local, district, state, and federal levels who provide services for exceptional children.

Meyen (1982) believes these explanations make sense. One must be able to identify children whose emotional, cognitive, or social characteristics require special instruction. Teachers, administrators, and other educational consultants must understand the terminology used to describe these children. Unfortunately, he points out, what has occurred in the history of special education has been a compromise in the treatment of definitions.

As school systems gradually included special education services, they found it necessary to use definitions and guidelines to determine whether children were eligible or ineligible for a particular special education program. At another level, state departments of education used definitions as a basis for approving children for placement into special programs.

It is understandable why definitions of exceptional children have developed as they have. However, definitions included as part of state regulations, guidelines, or laws have had significant influence at the local or district level. For example, if teachers and parents read in their state regulations that a student with an intelligence score of 75 is classified as "mentally retarded," they believe the statement to be true because it is in the state regulations.

These definitions became even more influential as they developed into conditions for allocating district, state, and federal financial assistance for services to exceptional children. The impact on public school systems has been significant. As if overnight, the number of exceptional children defined increased tenfold and the financial aid increased accordingly. However, as many school districts are seeing, the snowball effect can be particularly devastating during periods of economic recession, inflation, and declining student enrollments.

Additional disadvantages to the use of definitions can be noted at the school level. Definitions provided a basis from which the classroom teacher could refer an exceptional child out of the classroom. For many teachers, referring children for specialized services became a practice that aimed at removing children from the regular class, thus reducing the teacher's work load. In many cases such practices resulted in school dropouts.

Most definitions tended to emphasize limitations and weaknesses rather than strengths. Criteria included in most definitions focused on physical limitations, inability to see or hear, low intelligence, unusual or bizarre behavior, or inappropriate classroom behavior. Children were classified on the basis of what they could not do rather than on what they could do. In the process of being identified as an exceptional child, the child acquired a label that provided eligibility for a special education program but included a stigma that frequently followed the child far beyond the school setting.

Another negative effect was the assumption that if a child was classified as exceptional, that child would remain exceptional and would always need special education programs. An example has been the treatment of the educable mentally retarded. Historically, once these children were identified as educable mentally retarded, they were placed in special education classes. After placement, consideration was rarely given to returning the child to the regular classroom. Placement became permanent and stigmatizing (Meyen, 1982).

The use of definitions has had some positive benefits however. The development of specific special education programs based on definitions of student needs contributed to mandated education for all exceptional children. Without definitions, most exceptional children would not be receiving specialized assistance and would be required to succeed in a classroom without the necessary skills and competencies.

Exceptional Children Defined

The term *exceptional* has for the most part been interpreted by the public to refer to the gifted. However, parents of an educable mentally retarded child, for example, might associate the term *exceptional* with *handicapped.* Scriven (1976) suggests the term is misleading. He related:

> I cannot condone the euphemistic use of the term "exceptional children" to refer to handicapped children. There are exceptional pupils whose problems we are not discussing; they happen to be the ones from whom the term "exceptional children" was stolen because of its honorific connotations. We will not help children by misrepresenting them . . . and it is a terrible foundation for such an effort to begin by misrepresenting the entire group of such children.

Although teachers, administrators, psychologists, and other professionals apply the term *exceptional* without explanation, it does not communicate the same meaning to everyone. An examination of several texts in the field reveals trends with respect to the definition of exceptionality.

Kirk and Gallagher (1983) state that the exceptional child is defined:

> As the child who deviates from the average or normal child (1) in mental characteristics, (2) in sensory abilities, (3) in neuromuscular or physical characteristics, (4) in social or emotional behavior, (5) in communication abilities, or (6) in multiple handicaps to such an extent that he requires a modification of school practices, or special education services, in order to develop to his maximum capacity.

Others have responded to the definition out of concern for mislabeling and overreferral. Dunn's (1973) is one such definition:

> An exceptional child is so labeled only for that segment of his school career (1) when his deviating physical or behavioral characteristics are of such a nature as to manifest a significant learning asset or disability for special education purposes; and therefore, (2) when, through trial provisions, it has been determined that he can make greater all-round adjustment and scholastic progress with direct or indirect special education services than he could with only a typical regular school program.

Hallahan and Kauffman (1986) and Gearheart and Weishahn (1984) look at the definition from the perspective of special services needed. According to Hallahan and Kauffman (1986):

> Exceptional children are those who require special education and related services if they are to realize their full human potential.

Similarly, Gearheart and Weishahn (1984) state that:

> For purposes of this text, the exceptional child shall be considered to be one whose educational requirements are so different from the average or normal child, that he cannot be effectively educated without the provisions of special educational programs, services, facilities or materials.

An examination of the literature, including state rules and regulations, indicates little substantive variance in how the specific categories of exceptional children have been defined. The language used to describe the different categories varies but, in general, overall definitions have been similar.

The *Federal Register* (1982) includes definitions that are accepted by the U.S. government as well as by most school districts, particularly if they wish to continue to receive financial assistance. Because these definitions are included in the Handicapped Children's Act (P.L. 94–142), they are pertinent. Section 300.4 of the proposed rules for P.L. 94–142 includes the following definitions:

> A. As used in this part, the term "handicapped child" means a mentally retarded, hard of hearing, deaf, speech impaired, visually handicapped, seriously emotionally disturbed, orthopedically impaired, other health impaired, deaf-blind, or multi-handicapped child, or a child with a specific learning disability whose impairment adversely affects the child's ability to benefit from a regular education program, and who by reason thereof requires special education and related services after an evaluation in accordance with 300.142.
>
> B. The terms used in this definition are defined as follows:
>
> 1. "Deaf" means having a hearing impairment which is so severe that the child is impaired in processing linguistic information through hearing, with or without amplification.
>
> 2. "Deaf-blind" means having concomitant hearing and visual impairments, the combination of which causes such severe communication and other developmental and educational problems that the child cannot be accommodated in special education programs solely for deaf or blind children.
>
> 3. "Hard of hearing" means having a hearing impairment, whether permanent or fluc-

tuating, which is not included under the definition of "deaf" in this section.

4. "Mentally retarded" means having significant sub-average general intellectual functioning existing concurrently with deficits in adaptive behavior and manifested during the developmental period.

5. "Multihandicapped" means having concomitant impairments (such as mentally retarded-blind, mentally retarded-orthopedically impaired, etc.), the combination of which causes such severe educational problems that the child cannot be accommodated in special education programs solely for one of the impairments. The term does not include a deaf-blind child.

6. "Orthopedically impaired" means having a severe orthopedic impairment. The term includes an impairment caused by a congenital anomaly (e.g., clubfoot, absence of some member, etc.), an impairment caused by disease (e.g., poliomyelitis, bone tuberculosis, etc.), and an impairment from any other cause (e.g., cerebral palsy, amputations, and fractures or burns which cause contractures).

7. "Other health impaired" means having an (a) autistic condition which is manifested by severe communication and other developmental and educational problems, or (b) limited strength, vitality or alertness due to chronic or acute health problems such as a heart condition, tuberculosis, rheumatic fever, nephritis, asthma, sickle cell anemia, hemophilia, epilepsy, lead poisoning, leukemia, or diabetes.

8. "Serious emotionally disturbed" means having a condition exhibiting one or more of the following characteristics over a long period of time and to a marked degree:

a. An inability to learn which cannot be explained by intellectual, sensory, or health factors:

b. An inability to build or maintain satisfactory interpersonal relationships with peers and teachers;

c. Inappropriate types of behavior or feelings under normal circumstances;

d. A general pervasive mood of unhappiness or depression; or

e. A tendency to develop physical symptoms or fears associated with personal or school problems;

f. Being schizophrenic.

9. "Specific learning disability" means a disorder in one or more of the basic psychological processes involved in understanding or in using language, spoken or written, which may manifest itself in an imperfect ability to listen, think, speak, read, write, spell, or to do mathematical calculations. The term includes such conditions as a perceptual handicap, brain injury, minimal brain dysfunction, dyslexia, and developmental aphasia. The term does not include a learning problem which is primarily the result of a visual, hearing or motor handicap, of mental retardation, or of environmental, cultural, or economic disadvantage.

10. "Speech impaired" means having a communication disorder, such as stuttering, impaired articulation, a language impairment, or a voice impairment.

11. "Visually handicapped" means having a visual impairment with or without correction. The term includes both partially seeing and blind children. (*Federal Register,* 1982, p. 33845.)

Incidence and Prevalence of Exceptional Children

The question of student numbers has been a concern throughout the history of special education. State and district policies of most states contain numerous sections that discuss in some detail caseloads, identification surveys, pupil-teacher ratios, and funding formulas based on the number served versus the number thought to exist.

The concern of educators on pupil-teacher ratios within the special education classroom has been influential in setting limits on the number of exceptional children who can be assigned to a special education classroom. These children need intensive pupil-teacher attention almost impossible in larger classroom settings. Smaller classroom settings are further encouraged by the power of financial aid, which is tied to approval requirements pertaining to class size.

Although most states have had legislation mandating educational programs for exceptional children, and school districts have developed systematic evaluative procedures, accurate estimates on the number of exceptional children are not available. Eligibility criteria for program placement change frequently. As more children qualify for a program, financial aid increases proportionately. For example, if a district adjusts test score requirements upward for program placement, the number of children who can be identified also increases. This variability in eligibility criteria for program placement can be found across school districts and states. Data bases of exceptional children are clouded and districts find it difficult to make accurate predictions on the number of exceptional children within their district.

Needs assessment studies conducted in certain geographical areas were, until recently, the primary data sources on the numbers of exceptional children. These studies are useful for their particular geographical area, but the results cannot always be generalized to other areas for reasons related to the circumstances that cause handicaps. For example, most children who have been identified as mentally handicapped live in geographical areas generally characterized by social and economic problems. Similarly, an outbreak of meningitis possibly would increase the numbers of children with learning disabilities as compared to a similar geographical area that did not experience such an outbreak.

The terms *incidence* and *prevalence* are often used interchangeably in speaking of the number of exceptional children. However, their meanings are different. *Incidence* refers to the number of children who at some point in their life span might be considered exceptional. *Prevalence* refers to the number of exceptional children currently existing.

MacMillan (1977) described the difference:

> To illustrate how the two distinct statistics can be derived, suppose you wanted to know how widespread chicken pox was in your neighborhood. You could go from door to door asking three questions: (1) How many children live here? (2) How many of them have had chicken pox within the past six months? (3) How many have ever had chicken pox? With these figures totaled for the whole neighborhood, you could derive two different statistics, one for incidence and one for prevalence.
>
> To determine the prevalence of chicken pox in the neighborhood you would divide the total number of b's (those who had chicken pox within the past six months) by the total number of a's (all children living at home) and multiply the answer by 100 to express it as a percentage.
>
> Prevalence, incidentally, does not always refer to a six-month period. For instance, you could have asked instead how many children had chicken pox within a year. The important thing to remember is that prevalence refers to a specific time frame.
>
> To determine incidence you would divide the total c's (all children who have ever had chicken pox) by the total a's (all children living at home) and multiply the answer by 100 to find the percentage of children in the neighborhood who have ever had chicken pox. Obviously, this would be a higher figure than the one you got for prevalence.*

---

*From *Mental Retardation in School and Society* by D. L. MacMillan, 1977, Boston: Little, Brown. Copyright © 1977 by Little, Brown. Reprinted by permission.

Table 3–1 presents the prevalence estimates of various handicaps according to the U.S. Office of Education. The word *estimates* must be emphasized because the data were determined from a composite of federal- and state-level reports as well as from other sources. It is quite likely that the actual figures are much higher, but how much higher is unknown. However, Table 3–1 does give a general idea of the magnitude of the problem for various handicaps.

P.L. 94–142 requires that each handicapped child be identified and that districts report data on handicapped children served. Section 300.51 of the Proposed Rules for P.L. 94–142 states:

> In its report, the State education agency shall include a table which shows: (1) The number of handicapped children receiving special education and related services on December 1 of that school year; (2) The number of those handicapped children within each disability category, as defined in the definition of "handicapped child" in Section 300.4(b)(4); and (3) The number of those handicapped children within each of the following age groups: (a) three through five; (b) six through seventeen; and (c) eighteen through twenty-one (*Federal Register,* 1982, p. 33849).

Table 3–2 reveals that for the 1982–83 school year, 4,298,327 children in preschool through grade 12 received special education services. By far the largest category receiving special education services was identified as learning disabled. Indeed, within the last 10 years it is the one category that has increased significantly while others have remained the same or decreased. In part this is due to the acceptability of being labeled learning disabled rather than mentally retarded.

After the learning disabled group, the next largest categories of children were classified as speech impaired and mentally retarded.

The figures for both Table 3–1 and Table 3–2 show a substantial difference between the total estimate of the prevalence of handicaps and the

Table 3–1
Prevalence Estimates of Various Handicaps

Data from the U.S. Department of Education, 1984. Based on 1983 population estimates.

Disability Group	Ages 3–5	Ages 6–17	Ages 18–21	Total
Mentally retarded	19,052	557,909	76,121	653,082
Hard of hearing	3,634	29,622	3,464	36,720
Deaf	1,740	8,682	1,517	11,939
Speech impaired	168,176	941,847	4,666	1,114,689
Visually handicapped	1,736	17,021	2,489	21,246
Emotionally disturbed/ behaviorally disordered	5,860	299,536	15,203	320,599
Orthopedically impaired	7,031	34,941	3,227	45,199
Other health impaired	4,015	41,767	3,833	49,615
Learning disabled	19,204	1,699,070	70,592	1,788,866
Deaf-blind	139	1,150	158	1,447
Multihandicapped	12,500	33,083	5,123	50,706
Totals	243,087	3,664,628	186,393	4,094,108

Table 3–2
Children Receiving Special Education Services
Data (preschool through grade 12) from the U.S. Department of Education, 1984. Based on 1983 population estimates.

Exceptionality	Percent Enrolled in Special Classroom	Number Enrolled in Special Education
Learning disabled	4.40	1,745,871
Speech impaired	2.86	1,134,197
Mentally retarded	1.92	780,831
Emotionally disturbed/ behaviorally disordered	0.89	353,431
Other health impaired	0.13	52,026
Multihandicapped	0.16	65,479
Hard of hearing and deaf	0.18	75,337
Orthopedically impaired	0.14	57,506
Visually handicapped	0.07	31,096
Deaf-blind	0.01	2,553
Total	10.76	4,298,327

actual number of children receiving specialized services. Such figures have been matters of controversy for decades. It is, however, clear that some categories are overrepresented in the school population while others are underrepresented. The difficulties are related to confusing categories, assessment problems, and political concerns, as well as financial issues.

The Bilingual Exceptional Child

We are able to identify school-age children in the United States who were diagnosed as handicapped. Unfortunately, we are currently unable to determine accurately the number of limited English-proficient (LEP) children who have been identified as handicapped. But it is possible to estimate the number of bilingual exceptional children.

The National Center for Educational Statistics estimates that in the spring of 1980 there were approximately 30 million people in the United States whose primary language was not English. Of these, about 9.2 million were of school age (3 to 21 years old). If one assumes that anywhere from 10.7% to 15% of this population may be handicapped, then anywhere from 984,400 to 1,380,000 students were linguistically different, as well as handicapped, during the spring of 1980. It is important to remember that these figures are only estimates and that the actual figures for LEP exceptional children have not been recorded as far as we were able to determine.

Public education has been severely criticized as being inadequate in meeting the needs of language minority children. Gearheart and Weishahn (1984) noted that special classes were "dumping grounds," modes of segregation, and "in certain geographical areas a convenient way to do something about culturally different, bilingual children without actually initiating a bilingual program."

The view of special education programs by Jones and Wilderson (1976) was much more critical:

> From the perspective of minority group members, self-contained special classes were to be indicted on several counts, including but not limited to beliefs (a) that minority group children were overrepresented in special classes, particularly for the mentally retarded; (b) that assessment practices are biased; (c) that special education labels are stigmatizing; and (d) that teachers hold negative attitudes toward the potential of minority group children. These views, reinforced by professional special educators in some instances, have served to highlight for many minority parents and professionals the view that institutionalized racism is part and parcel of educational practice.

Historically and to some extent even today, the dominant policy for dealing with children who presented behavioral or instructional difficulties for the classroom teacher was to refer the child out of the classroom to the special services staff. The end result was typically a special education program placement. For the language-minority child, the situation was significantly compounded by the classroom teacher's lack of understanding of the child's background. The background was interpreted as inadequate linguistic skills, unresponsiveness to learning, and low achievement.

Therefore it was not surprising that language-minority children were significantly more frequently presumed to need specialized services. Linguistically and culturally different children also acquired an additional label that increased the problems they were already encountering in school, in the community, and in society in general.

Some language-minority children have been appropriately placed in special education classes, but the evidence is clear that generally they have been disproportionately represented in special classes, especially those for the mentally retarded (Dunn, 1973; Gearheart & Weishahn, 1984; Hallahan & Kauffman, 1986; Jones & Wilderson, 1976; Mercer, 1973).

The identification of language-minority children as being significantly more likely to be labeled mentally retarded is related to the major contributions of Mercer (1973) and Silberberg & Silberberg (1974). Mercer (1973) reported that the rate of placement of Hispanic children in special classes was four times higher than would be expected, based on the proportion of Hispanics in the population. Silberberg and Silberberg (1974) noted that value judgments played an important role in program placement based on a child's ethnicity:

> If a black and a white child are not learning well, chances are that the black will be called mentally retarded and the white will be called learning disabled. The latter term has a much more positive image, suggesting that the learning disabled white child is average but needs extra remedial help to fulfill his potential. The black child is seen as inferior and needing much less of a challenge, including much less of the monies set aside for special programs.

Though discriminatory practices toward language minorities continued to be criticized through the late 1960s, the early and middle 1970s saw considerable progress. In the early 1980s, progress has been substantial. The degree to which needs of exceptional children from language minority groups are met in the middle and late 1980s and beyond greatly depends on the efforts of special educators in:

1. Reducing the impact of labels
2. Improving assessment instruments and procedures
3. Preparing teachers to be responsive to the unique needs of exceptional children from language minority groups and more sensitive to their cultural heritage
4. Maintaining due process procedures that protect the welfare of children

Special Education Services

Along with the changes in the history of special education, there have been changes in the methods used in public schools to provide services to exceptional children. Placement in a special classroom rather than an institution was a major change of the delivery of special education services to exceptional children.

Today the treatment model required by exceptional children is special instruction aimed at improving academic, vocational, or social competencies. Of course, some children may require other assistance, such as physical treatment, medical treatment, or psychotherapy.

Special education may be viewed as having three important components:

1. Establishment of the most accurate diagnostic base for identification of exceptionality
2. Determination of the most appropriate instructional program according to individual need
3. Selection of the most efficient and effective administrative staff for the delivery of service

To have an effective special education program, all three components must be included. Accurate diagnosis and effective administrative structures are inadequate unless instructional resources and materials have been incorporated into the program. It is not unusual to visit a school district that has well-defined organizational structures, which contribute to precise diagnosis and appropriate placement, and not enough emphasis on curriculum and individualized learning materials.

The literature reveals that the trend toward the least restrictive environments clearly has influenced the design of service delivery models as well as the language to describe them (Gearheart & Weishahn, 1984; Hallahan & Kauffman, 1986; Jones & Wilderson, 1976). However, many models could be criticized because of their complicated designs as well as their frequent use of unique terms. In addition, there is a tendency to overemphasize the procedures for the delivery of services and not the actual services.

The following section describes program options for special education services, according to Meyen (1982). Though one finds a variety of terms used in describing special education services across different school districts, an effort will be made to use the most commonly used terms.

1. *Regular class placement.* Placement in a regular class becomes a service option when it can meet the exceptional student's specific needs. It is assumed that in such a placement, the regular classroom teacher has specialized training in adapting instructional materials for the specific needs of the exceptional child. It is also assumed that the teacher has the necessary curriculum and resource materials.

2. *Self-contained special class placement.* The self-contained special class becomes an option for a student when full-time specialized assistance is required. However, for most exceptional children, the self-contained special class is becoming less and less of a primary option.

   Generally, in the self-contained special classroom, a group of children with similar handicaps would be assigned to a teacher responsible for their educational program. In addition to the teacher, one might find a classroom aide, parent, or other paraprofessional. The option of a self-contained special classroom generally is considered for students with moderate to severe handicapping conditions.

3. *Part-time special class placement.* One option used more frequently is the part-time placement in a special class. In this option the child is assigned to the special class for at least half the school day. Generally what occurs is that the students receive special educational instruction in basic skill areas and then are mainstreamed into regular classes for other subjects.

4. *Resource room placement.* Resource room placement is becoming a favorable mode of service delivery of special education for the learning disabled. Generally, students are referred to a

special education teacher on the basis of assessed academic deficiencies. In addition, instruction is typically provided on an individualized basis dependent on the student's particular skills. The primary concern of the special education teacher is the delivery of remedial and supplemental instruction based on objectives and prescribed activities for individual students.

Placement in the resource room is on a short-term basis; that is, it is expected that the student will be returned to the regular classroom when sufficient academic progress is realized. For a majority of exceptional children, the combination of the resource room and the regular class placement remains as a more appropriate, less restrictive alternative.

5. *Resource center.* The resource center option is becoming a popular service delivery model for handicapped children. One finds resource centers organized into one or two classrooms and staffed by at least two special education teachers. Teachers are assigned to the resource center as a team to work with handicapped students having a variety of disabilities. Resource centers are more frequently found in junior and senior high schools. Students are assigned to the resource center between one and three periods a day and seldom for more than three periods or three hours a day. Again, instruction is provided by the team teachers based on specific objectives and activities for individual student academic needs.

6. *The itinerant teacher.* In the itinerant teacher option, the direct services to handicapped children are provided by a special education teacher who is not responsible for a classroom. Such teachers provide tutorial assistance as a supplement to instruction provided by the student's regular classroom teacher. It is important to note here that itinerant teachers provide instructional assistance to handicapped students while the student remains in the regular classroom. A requirement for implementation of the itinerant teacher option is the cooperation and coordination of instruction between the regular classroom teacher and the itinerant teacher. This option has been used quite extensively with visually handicapped students.

7. *The consulting teacher.* In this option the consulting teacher provides consultation to teachers and other school staff members involved in the exceptional child's program. Consulting teachers do not provide direct services to handicapped children. Their purpose basically is to assist the regular classroom teachers to understand the exceptional children in their room and to aid them in adjusting their instruction accordingly.

With the growing emphasis on the least restrictive environment, the regular classroom teacher is being called upon more and more to assume responsibility for the educational needs of exceptional children. This service model will very likely soon become the major option as more and more exceptional children are educated in the regular classroom.

8. *Homebound instruction.* When a student's education is interrupted by a short- or long-term illness, homebound instruction is routinely employed. Special education teachers visit the student at home on a regular basis, generally every day. These teachers provide individualized instruction and also coordinate the instruction from the student's regular classroom teacher. This option is designed to function on a short-term basis and is rarely a student's primary source of instruction. Homebound instruction is used most frequently for health reasons such as illnesses or accidents, as well as for some behavioral disorders.

9. *Hospital instruction.* Hospital instruction is an option for students who are confined to a hospital. Instruction here is similar to homebound instruction. An important condition, as in homebound instruction, is that educational activities be adjusted according to the child's physical and emotional state. In some large school districts, there is a cooperative effort between the district and children's hospitals such that special education teachers are part of the hospital staff.

In keeping with the provisions of the Education for All Handicapped Children's Act (P.L. 94–142), it is the responsibility of the public schools to place each special child in as normal a classroom as possible, given the child's disability. Such placement in the least restrictive environment is generally considered to be the regular classroom within the public school setting. One way of looking at how students should be placed, given the least restrictive environment, was developed by Reynolds (1962, 1976). Figure 3–1 presents Reynolds's Special Education Placement Cascade.

This cascade is a series of optional placements in the schools. Any of these placements may be the least restrictive environment for a special child at some time, depending on the child's needs. The least restrictive environment in this model is the regular classroom. Each subsequent step upward becomes increasingly more restrictive.

Basic to Reynolds's placement cascade is the notion that the child should be moved only as far as necessary from the regular classroom to obtain the specialized assistance necessary and then returned to the regular classroom or to a less restricted environment as soon as feasible.

Efficacy of Special Classes

The question of just how valid special classes actually are is one that is not discussed extensively in special education texts (Cummins, 1984; Taylor, 1984; Gearheart & Weishahn, 1984; Hallahan & Kauffman, 1986; Jones & Wilderson, 1976; Haring & McCormick, 1986). However, much of the current impetus for questioning the validity of special classes came from an article by Dunn (1968) entitled "Special Education for the Mildly Retarded—Is Much of it Justifiable?" Dunn concluded in this article that there was no evidence to justify the existence of special classes for this population.

Others, however, argue that Dunn's comments were inaccurate primarily because subjects were not randomly assigned to special classes versus regular classes (Keogh & Levitt, 1976; MacMillan & Becker, 1977; Robinson & Robinson, 1976). Thus those selected to go into special classes could very likely have been much more difficult to teach to begin with than those who were left in the regular classroom.

Goldstein, Moss, and Jordan (1965) in their study randomly assigned children with IQs below 85 to a special class or a regular class. Their findings revealed that for mildly retarded children with relatively high IQs (between 75 and 85), placement in regular classes significantly benefited their academic achievement. On the other hand, the opposite was true for children with lower IQs (below 75).

Carlberg (1979) and Carlberg and Kavale (1980) in a comprehensive effort have investigated the effect of special class placement versus regular class placement. Using a meta-analysis (a statistical technique that puts the comparisons of many studies into the same scale of measurement) of 50 research studies on special versus regular class placement, they found that with respect to achievement, learning disabled, emotionally disturbed, and behaviorally disordered children performed better in the special class than in the regular one. On the other hand, for students with low IQs (below 90), roughly 57% were better off in regular classrooms than their average counterpart in special classes. They concluded (1980):

> When integrated statistically, the results of 50 efficacy studies failed generally to disclose any dramatic relationship among size of treatment effect, type of treatment, and variables descriptive of the subjects. Only one prominent feature emerged, and that was related to the category of exceptionality. The findings suggest no justification for placement of low I.Q. children (SL and EMR) in special classes. Some justification in the form of positive gain in academic and social variables was found in special class placement of LD and BD/ED children.

Though it is certainly not conclusive, there appears to be some evidence that special education classes are beneficial for children with learning disabilities and emotional disturbances. There is also evidence to indicate that the regular classroom may be a better setting

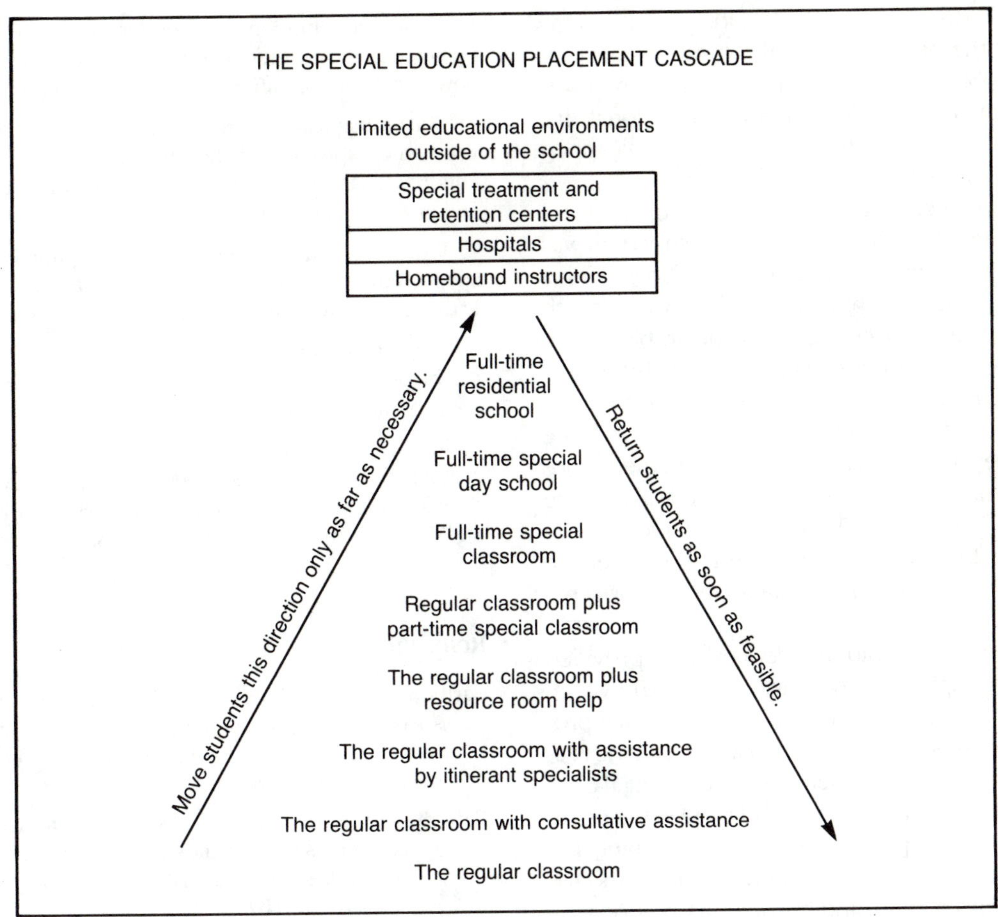

Figure 3–1
The Special Education Placement Cascade

From "A Framework for Considering Some Issues in Special Education" by M. C. Reynolds, 1962, *Exceptional Children* 28:367–370.

than the special classroom for both the academic and the social growth of children with low IQs (between 75 and 85).

Summary

All children are exceptional. Some, however, differ from other children in a significant way, such as giftedness, deafness, blindness, mental retardation, or some other handicap. Defining *exceptional* is a difficult and complex task that has been made more difficult by state regulations, guidelines, and federal and state statutes. Definitions have their advantages and disadvantages, including (1) facilitating legislation, (2) enhancing referrals, (3) labeling, and (4) affecting the student's self-concept.

In this chapter several definitions for the exceptional child were provided. Definitions included discussions of deviation from some norm, the need for special education services, the problem of excessive mislabeling, and over-referral. The last definition of exceptional discussed was the one included in the Handicapped Children's Act (P.L. 94–142).

Incidence and prevalence of exceptional children were discussed. The distinction was made between incidence and prevalence, with a point made that prevalence data were much more useful, accurate, and desirable when speaking of numbers of exceptional children.

With respect to language-minority exceptional children, the evidence appears to indicate that they have been significantly identified more frequently than other children for classes for the mentally retarded. This occurred more often before 1970; the present trend is to exercise considerable caution with language-minority exceptional children.

Special education services are provided with an emphasis on the least restrictive environment. Options in which such services are provided in most public school districts include regular class placement, self-contained special class placement, part-time special class placement, resource room placement, resource center, the itinerant teacher, the consulting teacher, homebound instruction, and hospital instruction.

Just how effective special classes are is a question that is not extensively discussed in most standard special education texts. The literature does appear to indicate that special education classes are beneficial for children with learning disabilities as well as emotional disturbances. There is also evidence to indicate that the regular classroom may be a better place than the special classroom for children with IQs between 75 and 85.

Discussion Questions

1. Applying definitions to exceptional children has positive and negative points. Discuss some of these.

2. Present a definition of exceptionality from those included in the chapter or prepare your own. Explain how this definition differs from the others presented.

3. The terms *incidence* and *prevalence* are frequently used when speaking of the number of exceptional children. Discuss the difference between these terms and give an example for each.

4. From the point of view of minority individuals, special education classes have been criticized on at least four major points. Explain these four points.

5. Program options for special education services can be provided in several ways. Explain seven different program options.

6. Just how effective special classes are compared to regular classes has been hotly debated for over a decade. Discuss the findings of the Carlberg (1979) and Carlberg and Kavale (1980) studies.

References

Carlberg, C. (1979). Meta-analysis of the effects of special classes, resource rooms and other treatments on exceptional children. *Dissertation Abstracts.* 40:1998–1999.

Carlberg, C., & Kavale, K. (1980). The efficacy of special versus regular class placement for exceptional children: A meta-analysis. *Journal of Special Education.* 14:295–309.

Cummins, J. (1984). *Bilingualism and special education: Issues in assessment and pedagogy.* San Diego: College-Hill Press.

Dunn, L. M. (1968). Special education for the mildly retarded—Is much of it justifiable? *Exceptional Children.* 35:5–22.

Dunn, L. M. (Ed.) (1973). *Exceptional children in the schools.* (2nd ed.). New York: Holt, Rinehart & Winston.

Federal Register (1982, August). Part II. No. 150 (p. 33845). Washington, D.C., Department of Health, Education and Welfare.

Gearheart, B. R., & Weishahn, M. W. (1984). *The handicapped student in the regular classroom,* (2nd ed.). St Louis: Mosby.

Goldstein, H., Moss, J., & Jordan, L. J. (1965). *The efficacy of special class training on the development of mentally retarded children.* Urbana, University of Illinois Press.

Hallahan, D. P. & Kauffman, J. M. (1986). *Exceptional children.* Englewood Cliffs, NJ: Prentice-Hall.

Haring, M. G., & McCormick, L. (Eds.) (1986). *Exceptional children and youth: An introduction to special education.* Columbus, OH: Merrill Publishing Co.

Jones, R. L., & Wilderson, F. B. (1976). Mainstreaming and the minority child: An over of issues and a perspective. In R. L. Jones (Ed.), *Mainstreaming and the minority child.* Reston, VA: Council for Exceptional Children.

Keogh, B. K., & Levitt, M. L. (1976). Special education in the mainstream: A confrontation of limitations? *Focus on Exceptional Children.* 8:1–11.

Kirk, S. A., & Gallagher, J. J. (1983). *Educating exceptional children.* Boston: Houghton Mifflin.

MacMillan, D. L. (1977). *Mental retardation in school and society.* Boston, Little, Brown.

MacMillan, D. L. & Becker, L. D. (1977). Mainstreaming the mildly handicapped learner. In R. D. Kneedler & S. G. Tarver (Eds.), *Changing perspectives in special education,* Columbus, OH: Merrill Publishing Co.

Mercer, J. R. (1973). *Labeling the mentally retarded.* Berkeley, CA: University of California Press.

Meyen, E. L. (Ed.) (1982). *Exceptional children and youth: An introduction,* Denver: Love Publishing Co.

Reynolds, M. C. (1962). A framework for considering some issues in special education. *Exceptional Children.* 28:367–370.

Reynolds, M. C. (1976, November 23). *New alternatives through a new cascade.* Paper presented at the Sixth Annual Invitational Conference on Leadership in Special Education Programs. New York, NY.

Robinson, N. M. & Robinson, H. B. (1976). *The mentally retarded child.* New York: McGraw-Hill.

Scriven, M. (1976). Some issues in the logic and ethics of mainstreaming. *Minnesota Education.* 2:61–67.

Silberberg, N. E. & Silberberg, M. C. (1974). *Who speaks for the child?* Springfield, IL: Charles C. Thomas Publishing.

Taylor, R. L. (1984). *Assessment of exceptional students: Educational and psychological procedures.* Englewood Cliffs, NJ: Prentice-Hall.

CHAPTER FOUR

Bilingual Special Education: A Juridical Perspective

- Federal Legislative History of Special Education
- State Education Laws for the Handicapped
- Special Education and the Courts
- Federal Legislative History of Bilingual Education
- State Bilingual Education Laws
- Bilingual Education and the Courts
- Bilingual Special Education: The Law and the Courts
- Summary

Objectives

- To review federal legislation for special education
- To analyze state education laws for the handicapped
- To review landmark special education court cases
- To present the federal legislative history of Bilingual Education
- To discuss state legislation related to Bilingual Education
- To review landmark Bilingual Education court cases
- To present a Bilingual Special Education interface from a juridical perspective

This chapter discusses the legal background and history of Bilingual Special Education. It also describes the impact of the major court decisions related to Bilingual Special Education. Finally, it presents the current status of Bilingual Special Education from a legislative and judicial point of view.

At present there are no laws that have been formulated to deal specifically with Bilingual Special Education. What does exist is a legal history dealing with Bilingual Education and a legal history dealing with special education. To discuss the legal perspective of Bilingual Special Education it will be necessary to treat each of these two areas separately and point out where some interface exists.

Federal Legislative History of Special Education

Legislation specifically designed to protect the rights of the handicapped is a fairly recent phenomenon in the United States; such legislation did not exist until the second half of this century. In the United States, attitudes toward and treatment of the handicapped have evolved through five distinct stages.

1. Neglect of the handicapped. From 1776 to 1817 the handicapped were rejected and removed as far as possible from society.

2. Asylum. A sense of pity characterized the period 1817 to 1869. The handicapped were "stored away" and isolated from society in large institutions; the establishment of these large asylums was a practice imported from Europe.

3. Day school classes. States began to provide special day schools for the handicapped from 1869 to 1913.

4. Public school programs. From 1913 to 1950 public school programs for the handicapped were established throughout the United States.

5. Equity for the handicapped. The years since 1950 have been characterized by an emerging recognition that the handicapped deserve the same rights and opportunities enjoyed by all other citizens. During this period there has been a great deal of legislation, at both the state and the national levels, designed to implement a variety of special education programs. More has been done to promote the rights of the handicapped in the past 15 years than ever before in the history of this country.

Federal legislation dealing with the education of the handicapped was passed in 1864. This law established Gallaudet College, a national college for the deaf. In 1879 additional legislation created the American Printing House for the Blind. These were the only federal laws that benefited the handicapped until the middle of the 20th century. In 1958 the Congress passed P.L. 85–905, the Captioned Films for the Deaf Act. This law provided educational as well as recreational films for the deaf on a loan basis. This same year Congress also passed P.L. 85–926, which provided for the training of teacher trainers for the mentally retarded. Three years later, in 1961, the Congress passed P.L. 87–276, the Act to Train Teachers for the Deaf. This legislation was amended in 1963 to include the training of educational personnel for all disability groups. This law, P.L. 88–164, was called the Mental Retardation Facilities and Community Mental Health Centers Construction Act. It was signed by President Kennedy, a staunch supporter of special education for the handicapped. This same law also provided for research and demonstration grants to explore problems related to the education of exceptional children.

The federal government's most extensive involvement in education came with the passage of P.L. 89–10, known as the Elementary and Secondary Education Act of 1965 (ESEA). This measure provided large sums of money for the educationally disadvantaged and the handicapped. Several other laws were passed in 1965 that provided educational opportunities for the handicapped. One of the most significant of these was P.L. 89–313, the Aid for Education of Handicapped Children in State Operated Institutions Act. This measure provided monies for the education of handicapped children who were in state-operated institutions for the handicapped.

In 1966 the U.S. House of Representatives formed a subcommittee to assist the educational needs of handicapped children and the extent to which the federal government was involved in meeting these needs. The major findings of the subcommittee were incorporated into the 1976 amendments to the ESEA. These amendments established ESEA Title VI, a program of grants-in-aid to the states for special education. Under the program's provisions each state could submit to the Office of Education a plan established by a state advisory committee detailing the special education needs of the state and priorities for meeting those needs. In addition, Congress mandated the Office of Education to establish the Bureau of Education for the Handicapped to administer all federal programs for handicapped children (Weintraub, 1971).

The 90th Congress took another bold step toward providing better educational services for handicapped children when it passed P.L. 90–538, the Handicapped Children's Early Education Assistance Act, in September 1968. With minor exceptions, this law represents the first time that Congress passed specific legislation for special education. In the past, federal legislation for special education was tied to the coattails of general education or health legislation. The 1968 law provides for the establishment of experimental demonstration centers for the education of preschool handicapped children and reflects a clear concern on the part of the federal government about meeting the unique needs of all handicapped children.

In addition, the 90th Congress amended three major general education laws to assure special education's access to their provisions. Title III of the ESEA, which provides for the establishment of innovative regional centers, was amended by the earmarking of 15% of the funds for special education purposes. In addition, Congress required that state and national Title III advisory councils have special education representation. A similar approach was followed in the 1968 amendments to the Vocational Education Act of 1963 by the requirement that 10% of state grant funds be used for special education purposes and that special education be represented on state and national advisory councils. The 1968 amendments to the Higher Education Facilities Act of 1963 reflected Congress's concern that many academically capable handicapped students were not being given access to higher education because of varying secondary effects of their disabilities.

In 1969 the Congress, through P.L. 91–61, established a National Center on Educational Media and Materials for the Handicapped to facilitate the use of new educational technology in programs for handicapped persons. The 1970 ESEA amendments, P.L. 91–230, extended the major aid programs for the handicapped under

ESEA and in addition created a program of special grants for research, training, and establishment of model centers for the education of children with specific learning disabilities. In the past such children have not been included in existing programs for the handicapped, and with this legislation, for the first time they are receiving the more appropriate educational assistance that their problems demand (Carey, 1971).

In 1974 the Congress passed P.L. 93–380, the Educational Amendments of 1974. This law required that the states, to remain eligible for federal funds for the education of handicapped children, adopt amendments to existing state plans for fiscal year 1975. These amendments included provisions such as a full services goal, priority to unserved children, and evaluation-placement safeguards. Evaluation safeguards included a provision for nondiscriminatory testing, which applied directly to bilingual children. This was the first time the special education legislation included initial provisions for limited English proficiency (LEP) children.

In 1975 the Congress passed P.L. 94–142, the Education for All Handicapped Children Act, which is without doubt the most significant legislation on behalf of handicapped children to date. For the bilingual exceptional child, this legislation not only included a provision for nondiscriminatory testing but also called for an appropriate education for each child, which is to be accomplished through an individualized educational plan (IEP) for each child. With the passage of this law, the legal foundation for Bilingual Special Education was initiated.

In 1978 President Carter signed the Educational Amendments of 1978 (P.L. 95–561), which reorganized and extended for five years the current ESEA programs, including services to the handicapped. In summary, there is now special education legislation that mandates a free and appropriate education for all handicapped children. For the bilingual exceptional child this means that testing must be done in a nondiscriminatory manner and that an individualized educational program must be set up, which could require that the instruction be carried out in a bilingual manner.

State Education Laws for the Handicapped

Because education is primarily the responsibility of the states, every state in our country has formulated a comprehensive code of school law. For nonhandicapped children, this regular school law is sufficient and provides the basis for an equal educational opportunity in the theoretical domain. However, this has not been the case for the exceptional children of the United States. Advocates for the handicapped have fought for and acquired additional legal provisions on behalf of the handicapped students in our schools. To protect children who have various physical, mental, emotional, and learning impairments, legal provisions have been established that facilitate the provision of specialized aids and services designed to ameliorate the barriers these students face in school. Every state has enacted some form of special education legislation. This state-sponsored legislation is the basis on which handicapped children are able to gain access to free public education, which is the responsibility of each state to provide (Abeson, 1973).

State laws relating to the education of the handicapped vary from state to state; it is beyond the scope of this chapter to provide a comprehensive analysis of these many laws. An attempt will be made, however, to deal with general patterns and trends in state legislation. According to Abeson (1973), there are four patterns that are used by the states to determine which children are eligible for special education programs. The essential difference in the laws is the degree of specificity in the descriptions of the various categories of handicapped children.

The most specific laws create and define specific disability categories. A case in point is a statute from South Carolina. This law defines emotionally handicapped children very specifically as children with demonstrable adequate intellectual potential who, because of emotional, motivational, or social disturbance, are unable to benefit from the normal classrooms of the public schools but who can benefit from special services suited to their needs.

The second common pattern in state eligibility laws lists the actual categories of children. For example, the Kansas statute names nine different handicapping categories, including children who (1) are crippled, (2) are visually defective, (3) are hard of hearing, (4) are speech impaired, (5) have heart disease, (6) have tuberculosis, (7) have cerebral palsy, (8) are emotionally or socially maladjusted or intellectually inferior or superior, or (9) are physically or mentally defective.

The third type of law is more flexible. An example is the New York law, which defines the handicapped child as "one who, because of mental, physical or emotional reasons, cannot be educated in regular classes but can benefit by special services. . . ." (Sec. 4401 N.Y. Stats.).

The fourth type of law establishes authority for special education and designates a state agency to develop definitions of children who are eligible for services. The following excerpt from the Maryland law is an example: "It shall be the duty of the State Board of Education to set up standards, rules and regulations for the examination, classification and education of such children in the counties of the state who can be benefited under the provisions of this subtitle." (Sec. 77–241 ACM).

The issue of mandatory or permissive legislation has high priority in the struggle to provide an appropriate education for the handicapped; it is sometimes referred to as the "shall" or "may" controversy. There are various forms of mandatory and permissive legislation. Mandatory legislation does not by any means guarantee an adequate or even better education for the handicapped. In fact, it has been argued that some states with permissive legislation provide better services. All things being equal, however, mandatory legislation of some type is more effective, since such mandates for services are more readily available for direct judicial review. Mandatory legislation is certainly the trend in many states.

This review of state and federal legislation shows a strong legal basis for the education of the handicapped. Both the federal and the state governments have passed numerous laws ensuring that the handicapped have an equal educational opportunity. None of these laws refers directly to bilingual exceptional children. P.L. 94–142 does, however, require nondiscriminatory assessment as well as the establishment of an individualized educational program for each handicapped child, including LEP children. This individualized program will require Bilingual Education in some instances.

Special Education and the Courts

Legislation on behalf of the handicapped has had a strong positive impact on the improvement of educational opportunity. Added to this is another very important advocacy force: litigation through the courts. The American educational system has not always been responsive to the needs of the handicapped. Much of the progress that has been made in the past 20 years has resulted from litigation. Cases brought by parent groups and comprehensive class action suits have been vehicles for reform. These suits can generally be grouped into three categories. The first group has dealt with the right of handicapped children to acquire an appropriate tax-supported education. The emphasis here has been on both "appropriate" and "tax-supported." The plaintiffs have argued that for a handicapped child to have access to just any educational program is not enough. The education the handicapped learner receives must be appropriate to the child's unique needs. Parents have maintained that they should not have to pay high tuition for an appropriate and quality education for their handicapped children, but rather that the proper program should be provided through the public schools at taxpayers' expense.

The second group of suits deals with the right to adequate treatment. These lawsuits have demanded that the handicapped who are institutionalized receive proper services, including education.

The third category of cases has concerned the improper classification and placement practices that have restricted opportunities for the appropriate education of the handicapped.

According to Abeson (1977), these suits have occurred because the appropriate remedies did not come through legislative and administrative channels. Although litigation is very costly and time consuming, it has been a highly effective way of obtaining positive public policy changes for the handicapped. It is interesting to note that the plaintiffs and the defendants in many of these cases have often agreed regarding the needed remedies but had to use the courts to bring about the desired changes. For example, Abeson (1977) states that "in some cases the defendants have spent days preparing defenses for the suit, and nights assisting the plaintiffs to prepare their arguments."

The concept of a right to an appropriate education was introduced in Chapter 1. From the standpoint of legal history, the establishment of this basic concept that no child can be denied or excluded from a publicly supported education because of handicap comes from two cases: *Pennsylvania Association for Retarded Children (PARC) v. Pennsylvania* (1971), and *Mills v. D.C. Board of Education* (1972). Although *PARC* ended in a consent agreement and was not fully litigated, *Mills* did go to trial and the opinion by Judge Waddy does represent the leading case in the area. *Mills* was a class action suit that established the constitutional right of handicapped children to a public education commensurate with their ability to learn. The problem behind this suit was the fact that the city was not providing the necessary funds for children who needed special education. Many of the children were being forced to remain at home without any formal education. In August 1972 Federal Judge Joseph Waddy ruled in favor of the plaintiffs and ordered the District of Columbia to provide an appropriate education for all the handicapped children within 30 days.

A good example of a "right to adequate treatment" case is the precedent case of *Wyatt v. Aderholt* (1974). This case involved institutionalized handicapped adults and children. It was found that two state hospitals for the mentally ill and a home for the mentally retarded were understaffed and that the services provided were extremely inadequate. As a result of this suit a set of treatment standards was adopted and the state was ordered to hire 300 new employees. Included in the treatment standards were educational standards dealing with teacher-student ratios and length of school days. Another aspect of this case established the right of the mentally retarded to receive services in the least restrictive setting. Abeson (1977) described the precedent-setting value of this case; this was the first time a court had ruled that the institutionalized mentally retarded have a constitutional right to adequate treatment. It also represented the first time measurable and judicially enforceable standards for adequate treatment have been established. The minimum standards established in the case included the implementation of individual treatment plans, length of school days, and teacher-student ratios. Also included were detailed physical standards, minimum nutritional requirements, and the requirement that the mentally retarded person be provided the least restrictive setting for habitation.

There has been a great deal of discussion in the literature of litigation related to the improper classification and placement of LEP children into special education programs and classes. Three of the more significant cases originated in California from 1968 through 1970. In chronological order they were *Arreola v. Santa Anna Board of Education* (1968), *Diana v. California State Board of Education* (1970), and *Covarrubias v. San Diego Unified School District* (1971). All three cases challenged the validity of using IQ tests to measure the mental ability of linguistically and culturally different children. *Arreola* established the due process rights of parents and children to have a hearing before placement into classes for the educable mentally retarded (EMR). In the *Diana* agreement the school districts agreed to several procedures to ensure improved placement practices. These included testing in the children's primary language, the use of nonverbal tests, and the collection and use of extensive supporting data.

A unique issue raised in the *Covarrubias* case was the requirement of informed parental consent before EMR placement. The plaintiffs in this class action suit were predominantly Spanish-speaking Chicano parents and students. There were also a few Chinese and Black parents and children included in the lawsuit.

According to Casso (1973), each of the three lawsuits resulted in retesting of the plaintiff children; they were found not retarded and should never had been placed into EMR classes. Each of the three lawsuits also demonstrated the damage that was caused the children as a result of misplacement. During the late 1960s and 1970s the educational community became painfully aware of these testing and placement problems and abuses through the court actions discussed and others throughout the country involving Hispanics.

Once the problem was exposed and acknowledged, educators as well as legislators and policymakers began to take steps to improve the testing and classification procedures of children in general and minority and LEP children in particular. In the early and middle 1970s several states, including Arizona, California, and Texas, began making legislative, regulatory, and educational changes that promoted more accurate assessment and placement procedures for these children. Likewise, the federal government began to make provisions for ensuring that minority and LEP children be evaluated in a nondiscriminatory manner and instructed in a more appropriate way. A good example of this can be seen in the following excerpt from the U.S. Office of Education (1980) guidelines of 1974. It reads as follows:

> A procedure also should be included in terms of a move toward the development of diagnostic prescriptive techniques to be utilized when for reasons of language differences or deficiencies, non-adaptive behavior, or extreme cultural differences, a child cannot be evaluated by the instrumentation of tests. Such procedures should ensure that no assessment will be attempted when a child is unable to respond to the tasks or behavior required by a test because of linguistic or cultural differences unless culturally and linguistically appropriate measures are administered by qualified persons. In those cases in which appropriate measures and/or qualified persons are not available, diagnostic-prescriptive educational programs should be used until the child has acquired sufficient familiarity with the language and culture of the school for more formal assessment.

The problem of misplacement and overrepresentation of minority as well as LEP children has been ameliorated but not yet resolved to the complete satisfaction of many parents and educators. As this problem of overinclusion has been addressed and partly resolved, a new problem of underinclusion has begun to develop in some areas of the country. Some students who are handicapped as well as limited in their use of

English are not being referred and placed into the special education programs they need. To a certain extent this seems to be the result of an overreaction to the misplacement issue. This phenomenon, along with related litigation, is addressed later in this chapter.

Federal Legislative History of Bilingual Education

It was pointed out in Chapter 2 that Bilingual Education is not a new educational innovation. Bilingual Education has a longstanding, rich historical tradition worldwide. Federal support for Bilingual Education in the United States is, however, a relatively new phenomenon. The federal government's involvement in Bilingual Education came about through the passage on January 2, 1968, of the Bilingual Education Act (P.L. 90–247), known as Title VII of the Elementary and Secondary Education Act. The act in part states:

> The Congress declares it to be the policy of the United States, in order to establish equal educational opportunity for all children (A) to encourage the establishment and operation, where appropriate, of educational programs using bilingual educational practices, techniques, and methods, and (B) for that purpose, to provide financial assistance to local education agencies, and to State education agencies for certain purposes, in order to enable such local educational agencies to develop and carry out such programs in elementary and secondary schools, including activities at the preschool level, which are designed to meet the educational needs of such children; and to demonstrate effective ways of providing, for children of limited English speaking ability, instruction designed to enable them, while using their native language, to achieve competence in the English language.

When this initial law was passed it carried with it an appropriation of $7.5 million to fund 76 local school district programs. To qualify for the programs children had to be identified as having limited English speaking ability (LESA) and as coming from low-income families who lived in environments where the dominant language was other than English. The primary purpose of the law was to assist students in developing greater competence in English. It also promoted native language improvement, the study of the history and culture associated with the student's native tongue, and the enhancement of the child's self-esteem. The passage of this law marked the first time that a lack of English proficiency was acknowledged at the federal legislative level as a barrier to equal access to educational opportunities.

The 1968 Bilingual Education Act, once implemented, was found to be limited in certain areas. Therefore Congress amended it with the passage of P.L. 93–380 in 1974. The requirement that a LESA child be from a low-income family was removed, thus increasing the population of students qualified to receive services. Additional language groups became eligible for services. Some of these language groups included the French, Portuguese, Italian, and Greek. Another weakness in the 1968 legislation was its failure to provide a means of assessing the success of the bilingual program. This was remedied in the 1974 amendments; the Secretary of the Interior was given the responsibility of reviewing and evaluating Bilingual Education programs. The 1974 legislation did not take a definitive position on the transitional approach versus the maintenance approach to Bilingual Education. This can be seen from the language used in the project application manual (U.S. Office of Education, 1980) published after the passage of the 1974 legislation. According to this manual, both the maintenance and the transitional approaches to Bilingual Education are acceptable:

> It is intended that children participating in this program will develop greater competence in English, become more proficient in their dominant language, and profit from increased educational opportunity. Though the Title VII, ESEA program affirms the primary importance of English, it also recognizes that the use of the chil-

dren's mother tongue in school can have a beneficial effect upon their education. Instructional use of the mother tongue can help to prevent retardation in school performance until sufficient command of English is attained. Moreover, the development of literacy in the mother tongue as well as in English should result in more broadly educated adults.

In 1978 the Bilingual Education Act was further amended by P.L. 95–561. Through these amendments the definition of the target population changed from LESA (limited English speaking ability) to LEP (limited English proficient), again expanding the population of eligible participants. Limited English proficiency was defined to include children with limited English reading, writing, speaking, and understanding. The 1978 statute formally included the American Indian and Alaskan native language groups. To promote a multicultural environment and to protect the LEP student from segregation, the law set up a 60:40 ratio requirement. This meant the monolingual English speaker could participate in the program but only up to a maximum of 40% of the total number of children.

The uses of the native language and culture in Bilingual Education were maintained in the 1978 legislation, but as Leibowitz (1980) points out, they were subordinated to a stronger English language emphasis. Another strong emphasis included in the 1978 legislation was the support included for research. The act itself states:

> The Commissioner [of Education] is charged to carry out a research program through competitive contracts with institutions of higher education, private and nonprofit organizations, state educational agencies, and individuals.

The research activities to be funded are set forth in the statute and are wide-ranging. Almost all arose in 1978 as a result of Senate initiative:

1. Studies to determine and evaluate effective models for bilingual/bicultural programs
2. Studies to determine
   a. language acquisition characteristics
   b. the most effective method of teaching English within the context of a bilingual/bicultural program
3. A five-year longitudinal study to measure the effect of bilingual education on students who have non-English language proficiencies
4. Studies to identify the most effective and reliable method of identifying students entitled to bilingual education services
5. Studies to determine the most effective methods for teaching reading to children and adults who have language proficiencies other than English
6. Studies to determine the effectiveness of teacher training preservice and inservice programs funded under this title
7. Studies to determine the critical cultural characteristics of selected groups of individuals to teach about culture in the program
8. The operation of a clearinghouse of information for bilingual education.

In 1984 the Bilingual Education Act was again amended and signed by the President as P.L. 98–511. In addition to this legislation, other related statutes also support Bilingual Education. These include the bilingual vocational training provisions of Carl Perkins Vocational Education Act of 1984, the refugee education provisions of the Refugee Act of 1980, and provisions of the Emergency Immigrant Education Act of the Education Amendments of 1984.

The 1984 Bilingual Education Act reauthorized Bilingual Education for four years through September 30, 1988. According to Stein (1984), the following are the key funding provisions of the act:

1. At least 60% of the funds for the act as a whole are to be set aside for financial assistance for Bilingual Education programs (Part A).
2. At least 75% of the Part A amount is to be reserved for transitional Bilingual Education programs.

3. From 4 to 10% of the overall funds are to be set aside for special alternatives instructional programs (these are English-only programs).

4. At least 25% of the funds are to be reserved for training and technical assistance (Part C).

5. The national Advisory and Coordinating Council for Bilingual Education is to receive up to 1% of the funds not reserved for Parts A and C.

6. State education agencies are eligible for grants of at least $50,000, not to exceed 5% of the funds received under Part A the previous fiscal year.

The 1984 amendments introduced several new program options. Included among these are the six following types of programs.

1. Transitional Bilingual Education programs. These programs combine structured English language instruction with a native language component. These programs also incorporate the students' cultural heritage into the curriculum.

2. Developmental Bilingual Education programs. These are programs of English and second language instruction designed to help children achieve competence in English and a second language.

3. Special alternative instructional programs. These are specially designed programs in which native language instruction need not be used.

4. Academic excellence programs. These are programs of transitional Bilingual Education, developmental Bilingual Education, or special alternative instruction that have an established record of providing effective, academically excellent instruction for limited English proficient (LEP) students. These programs must be designed to serve as models of exemplary Bilingual Education programs and to disseminate information on effective Bilingual Education practices.

5. Family English literacy programs. These are programs designed to help adults and out-of-school youth achieve English language competency. Preference will be given to the immediate families of LEP students in programs funded under this act. The program curriculum includes instruction on how parents and family members can assist LEP children with educational achievement.

6. Preschool, special education, and gifted programs. Under the act, one- to three- year grants may be awarded to conduct preschool, special education, and gifted and talented programs. The programs, however, are to be "preparatory or supplementary to programs such as those assisted under this Act."

As can be seen, the Bilingual Education Act of 1968 has gone through a number of significant changes over the past 20 years. The changes have gradually expanded the population of eligible students, opened up new program options, and put much more emphasis on the acquisition of English language proficiency. The passage of P.L. 100–297 on April 28, 1988 increased the cap on special alternative programs from 10% to 25%.

In terms of financial support the federal bilingual effort has gone from an initial appropriation in 1968 of $7.5 million, serving 76 school districts and 25,521 students, to a high of $167 million, serving 565 school districts and 350,000 students in 1981. The ensuing dropoff in the number of children served is attributable to the effects of inflation and to smaller local programs for low-incidence language groups, such as various American Indian tribes. The 1981–84 congressionally authorized ceiling of $139 million marks the beginning of a gradual decline and leveling off of federal funding for all of education, including Bilingual Education (see Table 4–1).

Table 4–2 highlights the salient features of the Bilingual Education Act as it has been amended through the legislative process over the past 20 years.

Table 4–1
Federal Title VII Bilingual Education Appropriations
Data from the National Clearinghouse for Bilingual Education.

Year	Appropriation (in millions of dollars)	Number of Basic Programs	Number of Students
1969–70	$ 7.5	76	25,521
1970–71	21.25	131	51,918
1971–72	25	164	83,748
1972–73	35	217	108,816
1973–74	35	209	129.380
1974–75	68	383	339,595
1975–76	85	319	162,124
1976–77	98	400	191,718
1977–78	115	425	259,364
1978–79	135	565	302,000
1979–80	158	565	350,000
1980–81	167	565	350,000
1981–82	158	554	223,000
1982–83	138	494	176,000
1983–84	138	566	216,000
1984–85	139	581	221,000
1985–86	139	641	205,494
1986–87	143	605	266,486
1987–88	146	609	268,322
1988–89*	149	612	270,482

*estimate

State Bilingual Education Laws

Because education is a state responsibility, it is not surprising that most states have addressed the broader issue of the use or prohibition of non-English languages in the school. As mentioned in Chapter 1, Bilingual Education flourished in many states during the 1880s. During the post–World War I era, however, the trend throughout the country was for states to pass laws that prohibited the use of non-English languages for purposes of instruction, with the

Table 4–2
Provisions of the Bilingual Education Act (1968–88)

	Eligibility	Student Mix	Number of Programs	Children Served
1968	limited English speaking and low income	NA	76	25,521
1974	limited English speaking	NA	383	339,595
1978	limited English proficient and American Indian and Alaskan Native	60% LEP 40% non-LEP	565	302,000
1984	Same as 1978	Same as 1978	581	221,000
1988	Same as 1978	Same as 1978	609	268,322

Table 4–3
State Bilingual Education Legislation and Funding Summary

From Center for Applied Linguistics: *Papers in Applied Linguistics, Bilingual Education Series: 9. The current status of bilingual education legislation: An update.* Washington, DC: Author, 1981. Reprinted by permission.

	Type of Statute			
State	**Bilingual Education Forbidden**	**Permits Funding**	**Mandates Funding**	**No Provision Stated**
Alabama				●
Alaska			●	
Arizona		●		
Arkansas				●
California			●	
Colorado			●	
Connecticut		●		
Delaware	●			
Florida		●		
Georgia				●
Hawaii		●		
Idaho				●
Illinois			●	
Indiana		●		
Iowa		●		
Kansas		●		
Kentucky				●
Louisiana			●	
Maine		●		
Maryland		●		
Massachusetts			●	
Michigan			●	
Minnesota			●	
Mississippi				●

exception of foreign language education at the secondary level. This anti–second language legislative trend began to reverse itself with the advent of the civil rights movement in the 1960s.

In 1971, 20 states did not permit bilingual instruction in the public schools (Cordasco, 1976). These states were Alabama, Arkansas, Connecticut, Delaware, Idaho, Indiana, Iowa, Kansas, Louisiana, Michigan, Minnesota, Montana, Nebraska, North Carolina, North Dakota, Oklahoma, Oregon, South Dakota, West Virginia, and Wisconsin. Five years later, in 1976, seven of these states—Connecticut, Indiana, Kansas, Michigan, North Dakota, Oregon, and South Dakota—repealed their English-only legislation. By 1984 only two states still prohibited Bilingual Education: Delaware and West Virginia.

The types of Bilingual Education statutes passed by the various states were similar to the special education laws in terms of their permis-

Table 4–3 *continued*

State	Type of Statute			
	Bilingual Education Forbidden	**Permits Funding**	**Mandates Funding**	**No Provision Stated**
Missouri				•
Montana				•
Nebraska				•
Nevada				•
New Hampshire		•		
New Jersey			•	
New Mexico			•	
New York			•	
North Carolina		•		
North Dakota				•
Ohio				•
Oklahoma		•		
Oregon			•	
Pennsylvania			•	
Rhode Island			•	
South Carolina				•
South Dakota				•
Tennessee				•
Texas			•	
Utah			•	
Vermont				•
Virginia				•
Washington			•	
West Virginia	•			
Wisconsin			•	
Wyoming				•

sive and mandatory provisions. According to the Center for Applied Linguistics (1981), 30 states had Bilingual Education legislation that was either mandatory (18 states) or permissive (12 states). Table 4–3 summarizes this legislation. It is interesting to note that states such as Texas, California, New Mexico, Illinois, and New York, which have large numbers of LEP students, all have mandatory statutes. Florida, however, which also has a high concentration of LEP students, has permissive legislation.

Bilingual Education and the Courts

The legislative and, to an extent, the executive branches of our government have had a significant role in advancing the cause of equal educational opportunity for all citizens, including the handicapped and the limited English proficient. The role of the judicial branch of government, however, is perhaps the most critical in guaranteeing that the rights of these individuals are not only protected but facilitated. The decisions of the courts at both the state and federal levels in Bilingual Education are therefore of utmost importance to the field of Bilingual Special Education. These decisions are even more significant to the parents and children who are directly affected by them.

Any contemporary discussion of Bilingual Education litigation should be centered around the unanimous U.S. Supreme Court decision in *Lau v. Nichols* (1974). This is without question the landmark case par excellence in this field of study. *Lau* was a class action suit brought on behalf of 1,800 Chinese students in California. The Court did not involve itself directly in the specifics of school curriculum by mandating Bilingual Education. It did, however, state in its opinion "that there was no equality of treatment merely by providing students with the same facilities, textbooks, teachers, and curriculum, for students who do not understand English are effectively foreclosed from any meaningful education." The Court went on to further stipulate that special language programs were necessary if schools were going to provide equal educational opportunity. According to Teitelbaum and Hiller (1977), the *Lau* decision is significant because even though it did not expressly endorse Bilingual Education per se, it "did legitimize and give impetus to the movement for equal educational opportunity for non-English speakers as only a unanimous Supreme Court ruling can."

Before examining the implications of the *Lau* decision and discussing the other related cases subsequent to *Lau,* it seems appropriate to discuss briefly the rationale upon which *Lau* was based as well as the trend of cases before *Lau.* A careful analysis of the decision itself shows that the Court relied exclusively on Title VI of the Civil Rights Act of 1964. The decision states:

> We do not reach the Equal Protection Clause argument which has been advanced but rely solely on section 601 of the Civil Rights Act of 1964, 42 U.S.C. 200d to reverse the Court of Appeals. That section bans discrimination based "on the ground of race, color or national origin," in "any program or activity receiving Federal financial assistance."

Another factor that highly influenced the Supreme Court in its decision was the so-called May 25th Memorandum of 1970. This was a regulatory document published by the U.S. Department of Health, Education and Welfare in an attempt to assist school districts to comply with the Civil Rights Act of 1964. This directive told school districts that they must correct English language deficiencies by taking affirmative steps that go beyond the provision of the same books and teachers to all students.

Only a few cases before *Lau* dealt with the use of non-English languages. Teitelbaum and Hiller (1977) discuss two significant cases in this regard: *Meyer v. Nebraska* (1923), and *Yu Cong v. Trinidad* (1925). In the *Meyer* case a teacher had been convicted for giving German instruction in a private school; the court ruled in favor of the teacher and overturned the conviction. The *Yu Cong* decision upheld the use of foreign languages in commerce by striking down a Philippine criminal statute called the Chinese Bookkeeping Act, which permitted only the use of English and Spanish (the Philippines were under U.S. rule at the time).

It can be seen from this discussion that before the *Lau* decision, issues related to Bilingual Education had never been directly considered by the courts. In these early cases the rights of individuals to use non-English languages in private schools, in commerce, and, to an extent, in the exercise of one's civic responsibilities were upheld. It is also important to note that although *Lau* is closely related to the *Brown v. Board of Education of Topeka* (1954) in terms of equal educational opportunity, it was not decided directly on the equal protection principle of the Fourteenth Amendment of the Constitution as was the *Brown* case. The *Brown* case, decided by the Supreme Court some 34 years ago, is a landmark decision in the area of school desegregation and civil rights generally. It in effect outlawed socially segregated systems of public education as inherently unfair and unconstitutional (Baca & Chinn, 1982). The *Brown* case is also important to the handicapped and to the limited English proficient because it played such a major role in the development of our current social and educational policy, helping to create the climate that made possible the passage of the Civil Rights Act of 1964 and the Education for All Handicapped Children Act of 1975.

The impact of *Lau* on the public schools, on subsequent legislation, and on the courts has been significant as well as controversial. Teitelbaum and Hiller (1979) point out that *Lau* raised the nation's consciousness of the need for Bilingual Education and in so doing encouraged both federal and state legislation, motivated federal enforcement efforts through the U.S. Office of Civil Rights, and set the stage for a number of additional lawsuits.

According to Applewhite (1979) the aftermath of *Lau* can be more easily interpreted by examining the cases that spell out what he calls the "legal dialect" of Bilingual Education. The critical cases are as follows: *Keyes v. Denver School District No. 1* (1976); *Serna v. Portales Municipal Schools* (1974), New Mexico; *Aspira of New York, Inc. v. Board of Education of the City of New York* (1973); *Otero v. Mesa County Valley School District No. 51* (1975), Colorado; and *Rios v. Reed* (1977), New York.

In the *Serna* case segregation was not an issue. According to Applewhite (1979), the court voted that although an equal education in terms of teachers, classrooms, and textbooks was provided to the Spanish-speaking student, the district did not address the English language deficiencies of the students. The court mandated the adoption of a bilingual program. Both *Serna* and *Keyes* relied heavily on the Fourteenth Amendment principle of equal protection under the law in arriving at their final decision (Teitelbaum & Hiller, 1979). The 10th Circuit Court of Appeals upheld the *Serna* decision and held that the students had a right to a Bilingual Education.

The *Aspira* case is another very significant case dealing with Bilingual Education. Puerto Rican as well as Hispanic students sued the New York City Board of Education for not living up to its publicly stated commitment to provide Bilingual Education. Tens of thousands of students were getting no instruction related to their language and cultural needs, and many were receiving instruction in English as a Second Language (ESL) only. At the same time that the *Aspira* case was being argued, the *Lau* decision was handed down. Seven months later in August 1974 the parties consented to a decree, which required the district to design and implement an approved method for assessing the English and Spanish language skills of students to determine who is eligible for Bilingual Education. The decree also addresses teacher qualification and recruitment and explicitly forbids the use of a pull-out program that would remove children from their regular classroom. Teitelbaum and Hiller (1979) point out that *Aspira* is perhaps the most far-reaching court-ordered bilingual program ruling since *Lau*. They also point out, however, that *Aspira,* unlike *Lau,* is limited to Spanish-speaking students only and to Spanish speakers who are more proficient in Spanish than in English.

The *Otero* case is important because it is the only case that was decided in favor of the defendants and did not require the district to provide Bilingual Education. The court found that the low level of achievement of Chicano students was caused by socioeconomic factors rather than by the type of educational program. According to Applewhite (1979), the low number of affected students was an important factor in this decision. The right to Bilingual Education was not upheld.

The *Rios v. Reed* case is also significant because it introduced for the first time the issue of effectiveness or quality of a district's bilingual program. In this case a school district in Long Island, New York, was told that the critical question is not simply the provision of a bilingual program but rather whether the program is effective. The court stated, "An inadequate program is as harmful to a child who does not speak English as no program at all."

Finally, *Casteneda v. Pickard,* (1981) set up court standards for reviewing remediation plans and said that although a school policy for programs may have once been appropriate, nevertheless it is subject to review in the future if in practice it has failed to remediate. Table 4–4 summarizes the outcomes of these cases.

Bilingual Special Education: The Law and the Courts

To this point we have reviewed the major legislation and litigation relative both to special education and to Bilingual Education. No laws have been passed to date that specifically mandate Bilingual Special Education for bilingual exceptional students. Existing laws, however, in both Bilingual Education and special education do apply to bilingual exceptional children because both Title VI of the Civil Rights Act of 1964 and section 504 of the Rehabilitation Act prohibit discrimination based on race, national origin, and handicaps under any program receiving federal financial assistance. What this means in practice is that a bilingual exceptional child qualifies for services under both special education and Bilingual Education. Just because a bilingual exceptional child qualifies for services under special education does not automatically disqualify the child for services under Bilingual Education or vice versa. For some bilingual exceptional students the ideal situation would be to receive Bilingual Special Education services through one teacher who has the training and expertise to provide the special education services within a bilingual instructional environment.

Bilingual Special Education services for bilingual exceptional children are not only guaranteed through Title VI of the Civil Rights Act and Section 504 of the Rehabilitation Act. The Education for All Handicapped Children Act (P.L. 94–142) as well as the *Lau* remedies also support the provision of Bilingual Special Education services when a student's needs call for it. Bergin (1980) also supports this position. She puts it this way:

> The law guarantees minority language handicapped students equal access to education. Special education and bilingual education must come together within the administrative structure of a school system to provide, in practice, what the law requires.

In terms of litigation it is important to note that issues related to Bilingual Special Education have been addressed in several New York court cases. In *Lora v. Board of Education of the City of New York* (1984) a program for Hispanic and Black students in a day school for the emotionally disturbed was found to be inadequate. *Jose P. v. Ambach* (1983) filed in 1979, charged that handicapped children were being denied a free and appropriate education because of a lack of timely evaluation and placement in an appropriate program. The case of *United Cerebral Palsy (UCP) of New York v. Board of Education of the City of New York* (1979) charged that children who have disabilities resulting from brain injury or other impairments to the central nervous system were not receiving appropriate special education services.

The most significant of these cases was *Dyrcia S. et al. v. Board of Education of the City of New York* (1979). The plaintiffs were Puerto Rican and other Hispanic children living in New York City who were both LEP and handicapped

Table 4–4
Dates and Unique Outcomes of Court Cases on Bilingual Education

Case	Date	Unique Outcome
Lau	1974	Affirmative steps must be taken to rectify language deficiency
Aspira	1973	Required use of proficiency tests to determine student eligibility for a bilingual program
Serna	1974	Mandated bilingual programs
Keyes	1976	Established bilingual education as compatible with desegregation
Otero	1975	Low achievement of Chicanos caused by socioeconomic factors: low number of students with real language difficulty does not warrant a bilingual program
Rios	1977	Bilingual program must emphasize quality and be effective in meeting students' needs
Casteneda	1981	Set court standards for reviewing remediation plans

and who required bilingual/bicultural special education programs for which they were not being promptly evaluated and placed. Because these cases were all so closely related to one another in terms of location, content, and timing, a consolidated judgment was issued in the *UCP* and *Dyrcia S.* cases, which incorporated the provisions of the *Jose P.* case. In summary, the relief that was ordered affects all the special education programs and procedures in the city of New York. What follows is a brief summary of the court order particularly as it relates to the bilingual provisions. The relief included these provisions:

1. Identification of children needing special education services with the inclusion of an outreach office with adequate bilingual resources.
2. Appropriate evaluation through the establishment of school-based support teams to evaluate children in their own environment with a bilingual, nondiscriminatory evaluation process.
3. Appropriate programs in the least restrictive environment, including a comprehensive continuum of services with the provision of appropriate bilingual programs at each level of the continuum for children with limited English proficiency.
4. Due process and parental student rights, including a Spanish version of a parent's rights booklet, which explains all the due process rights of children and parents. Also included is the hiring of neighborhood workers to facilitate parental involvement in the evaluation and development of the individualized educational program.

Summary

This chapter has discussed the legislative history of special education at both state and federal levels, which has involved five stages. The early period from 1776 to 1817 was known as the period of neglect of the handicapped. The age of the asylum, from 1817 to 1869, was followed by the period of day schools for the handicapped from 1869 to 1913. From 1913 to 1950 was the age of public school programs for the handicapped. The final period from 1950 to the present is called the age of equity for the handicapped; most of the major legislation authorizing education services for the handicapped has been formulated during this age of equity. The two most significant pieces of legislation were P.L. 99–10, which is known as the Elementary and

Secondary Education Act of 1965, and P.L. 94–142, the Education for All Handicapped Children Act of 1975. Through this landmark legislation LEP handicapped students are entitled to nondiscriminatory assessment and an individualized educational program that could include bilingual instruction.

The bilingual legislation at the federal level was instituted in 1968 with the passage of P.L. 90–247, which is known as the Bilingual Education Act. The law, amended in 1974, 1978, and 1984, provided financial support to school districts for the provision of bilingual instruction to children of limited English proficiency. Nothing in the law precludes the participation of bilingual exceptional children in these programs.

State legislation in Bilingual Education has followed the general pattern that occurred in state special education legislation. Many of the states historically had statutes that excluded handicapped children from the schools. Similarly, many states had statutes that forbade the use of non-English languages for instruction. The next trend in state legislation was to initiate permissive legislation, which allowed school districts to provide programs for both handicapped students and LEP students. The final trend was the passage of mandatory legislation, which compelled districts to provide both special education services and Bilingual Education Services.

In terms of litigation, suits related to special education can be grouped into three categories: (1) right to an education, (2) right to adequate treatment, and (3) improper classification and placement. The decisions have established the rights of the plaintiffs to more appropriate services. In the area of Bilingual Education the rights of the LEP student to special services, including Bilingual Education, have been firmly established. In some instances bilingual programs have been mandated and their quality has been considered. The litigation dealing specifically with Bilingual Special Education has also established the rights of bilingual exceptional children and their parents to receive bilingual instruction and supportive services.

Discussion Questions

1. Discuss the salient cases that have upheld the rights of plaintiffs in the area of Bilingual Education.

2. Discuss the salient cases that have upheld equity for the handicapped.

3. Discuss the impact of current laws and mandates in the areas of bilingual and special education in your local school district.

4. What impact has *Lau v. Nichols* (1974) had on your local school district?

5. Discuss your familiarity with any two of the eight concepts listed on p.00.

6. Select any two cases mentioned in this chapter and show their relation to the concepts of equal and adequate treatment of children.

References

Abeson, A. (1973). *Legal chance for the handicapped through litigation.* Reston, VA: Council for Exceptional Children.

Abeson, A. (1977). Litigation. In F. J. Weintraub et al. (Eds.), *Public policy and the education of exceptional children.* Reston, VA: Council for Exceptional Children.

Applewhite, S. R. (1979). The legal dialect of bilingual education. In R. V. Padilla (Ed.), *Bilingual education and public policy in the United States.* Ypsilanti, MI: Eastern Michigan University.

Arreola v. Santa Anna Board of Education (1968). No. 160–577, Orange County, Calif.

Aspira of New York, Inc. v. Board of Education of the City of New York (1973). 58 F.R.D. 62.

Baca, L., & Chinn, P. (1982, February). Coming to grips with cultural diversity. *Exceptional Children Quarterly.* 2:4.

Bergin, V. D. (1980). *Special education needs in bilingual programs.* Rosslyn, VA: National Clearinghouse for Bilingual Education.

Brown v. Board of Education of Topeka (1954). 347 U.S. 483, 74 S.Ct. 686, 91 L.Ed. 873.

Carey, H. L. (1971, August). Education services for the handicapped: The federal role. *Compact.* 5:4.

Casso, H. (1973). *A descriptive study of three legal challenges for placing Mexican American and other linguistically and culturally different children into educably mentally retarded classes.* Doctoral dissertation. University of Massachusetts, Amherst, MA.

Casteneda v. Pickard (1981). 48 F.2d 989 (5th Cir.).

Center for Applied Linguistics (1981). *Papers in applied linguistics, bilingual education series: 9. The current status of bilingual education legislation: An update.* Washington, DC. Author.

Cordasco, F. (1976). *Bilingual schooling in the United States: A sourcebook for educational personnel.* New York: McGraw-Hill.

Covarrubias v. San Diego Unified School District (1971). No. 70394-T (S.D. Calif.).

Diana v. California State Board of Education (1970). No. C-70, RFT, Dis. Ct. No. Cal.

Dyrcia S. et al. v. Board of Education of the City of New York (1979). 79 C. 2562 (E.D.N.Y.).

Jose P. v. Ambach (1983). 557 F. Supp. 11230 (E.D.N.Y.).

Keyes v. Denver School District No. 1 (1976). 480 F. Supp. 673 (D. Colo.).

Lau v. Nichols (1974). 414 U.S. 563.

Leibowitz, A. H. (1980). *The Bilingual Education Act: A legislative analysis.* Rosslyn, VA: National Clearinghouse for Bilingual Education.

Lora v. Board of Education of the City of New York (1984). 587 F. Supp. 1572 (E.D.N.Y.).

Meyer v. Nebraska (1923). 262 U.S. 390.

Mills v. D.C. Board of Education (1972). 348 F. Supp. 866 (D.D.C.)

Moran, D. (1981). Educational malpractice suit filed. *NOLPE Notes,* Topeka, KS. vol 16, no. 12, National Organization on Legal Problems of Education.

Otero v. Mesa County Valley School District No. 51 (1975). 408 F. Supp. 162 (D. Colo.).

Pennsylvania Association for Retarded Citizens (PARC) v. Pennsylvania (1971). 334 F. Supp. 1257 (E.D. Pa.).

Rios v. Reed (1977). 75 C. 296 (E.D.N.Y.).

Serna v. Portales Municipal Schools (1974). 351 F. Supp. Supp. 1279 (D.N.M.).

Stein, C. B. (1984). *The 1984 Bilingual Education Act.* Rosslyn, VA: National Clearinghouse for Bilingual Education.

Teitelbaum, H., & Hiller, R. (1977). The legal perspective. In *Center for applied linguistics, bilingual education: Current perspectives/law.* Arlington, VA: Center for Applied Linguistics.

Teitelbaum, H., & Hiller, R. J. (1979). Bilingual education: The legal mandate. In H. T. Trueba & C. Barnette-Mizrahi (Eds.), *Bilingual multicultural education and the professional: From theory to practice,* Rowley, MA: Newbury House.

United Cerebral Palsy (UCP) of New York v. Board of Education of the City of New York (1979). 79 C. 560 (E.D.N.Y.).

U.S. Office of Education, Office of Bilingual Education (1980). Manual for application for grants under bilingual education, 1974. In A. H. Leibowitz, *The Bilingual Education Act: A legislative analysis.* Rosslyn, VA: National Clearinghouse for Bilingual Education.

Weintraub, F. J. (1971). *The encyclopedia of education.* New York: Macmillan.

Wyatt v. Aderholt (1974). 503 F.2d 1305 (8th Cir.).

Yu Cong v. Trinidad (1925).

CHAPTER FIVE

Development of the Bilingual Special Education Interface

Leonard M. Baca
Rose M. Payan

- Conceptual Framework for Bilingual Education
- Operational Definition for Bilingual Education
- Conceptual Framework for Special Education
- Operational Definition of Special Education
- Interface Design for Bilingual Special Education
- A Theoretical Framework for Bilingual Special Education
- Operational Guidelines for Bilingual Special Education
- Interface Requisites
- Summary

Objectives

- To describe the conceptual underpinnings of bilingual and special education
- To develop a theoretical framework for Bilingual Special Education
- To describe the operational implementation of both programs
- To explore models for interfacing bilingual and special education instruction
- To develop a clearer understanding of program and instructional requirements essential to the development of a Bilingual Special Education interface

A challenge before educators is the shaping of what seem to be two separate educational programs and philosophies into variable methods of instruction for a unique student population: bilingual exceptional individuals. The mingling of Bilingual Education and special education is at best in its beginning stages (Fradd & Tickunoff, 1987). There remains the need for empirical validation and fine tuning of this new educational program. Preliminary reports, however, are claiming success and additional programs are being developed and implemented throughout the country.

This chapter presents a redefinition of Bilingual Education and special education and discusses factors that impede their interface. Philosophical and theoretical frameworks for both programs, along with specific program components, are discussed. Also presented in the chapter is an operational design for the interaction between bilingual and special education for each area of exceptionality, including the variety of language functioning found among limited English proficient (LEP) students. Instructional methodologies and an array of student placements are recommended. Lastly, the chapter addresses the requisites for the establishment of a Bilingual Special Education program.

Conceptual Framework for Bilingual Education

Common theoretical constructs exist for Bilingual Education. A surface view of bilingual programs, however, may lead one to believe that familiar program components are nonexistent and that Bilingual Education is variably defined. In studying the contiguity of program definition and intent, it is essential first to differentiate between the meanings of *program* and *instruction.* Instruction can be defined as the teacher behaviors employed to facilitate learning, while program is the manner in which the instruction is packaged. Instruction is the manner and degree to which the content is presented, while program would include content and materials.

There is general agreement that educational programs for the language minority student should assist the student to:

- Acquire academic concepts and learning skills
- Acquire and develop English language skills
- Develop primary language skills

The degree to which these goals are addressed and in what manner depend on the political beliefs and educational philosophies of the program implementers. How these goals translate to school programs is addressed in the section regarding the operational definitions of Bilingual Education (p. 83).

Key components to Bilingual Education programs can be classified by instructional, teacher, and school administration areas. Again, the extent to which each component is emphasized yields the operational variations among Bilingual Education and exemplifies various program foci. Instructional components include cognitive development, primary language development, second language acquisition, and multicultural education.

Cognitive Development

The primary purpose of schooling for the LEP student is not the mere acquisition of English but includes the acquisition and development of cognitive skills. The acquisition of academic concepts and skills vital to cognitive development is best achieved when the student's primary language is used as a vehicle for instruction. Concept acquisition includes learning abstract ideas, such as the meaning of state and county, or quantitative concepts, such as more, less, sum, and division. Development of basic academic skills includes the acquisition of skills such as reading, writing, and organizing.

Primary Language Development

When concepts are introduced and reinforced in the student's primary language, linguistic ability in that language is enhanced. Growth in linguistic ability is interrelated with intellectual growth because language is viewed not only as a means of representing thought but also as a vehicle for thinking.

Second Language Acquisition

As previously stated, it is imperative that the limited English proficient student fluently command English language skills. Not only should this linguistic command be demonstrated in verbal fluency, but it should also be exhibited by achieving academically in English.

Multicultural Education

The bilingual instructional program is sensitive to the diverse cultural backgrounds of students, including monolingual English students, in the classroom. Students' cultural experiences are considered, and instruction is provided within the students' cultural framework. The students' self-concepts are enhanced as their cultural backgrounds are valued. Students are taught to value cultural diversity. Common to all Bilingual Education programs are the effects of teacher or instructional staff competencies. The degree to which such competencies are present reflects the nature of the program implemented.

The California Office of Bilingual Bicultural Education (OBBE, 1982) has identified four major objectives for instructional programs serving ethnolinguistic populations. Regardless of the approach taken, at the end of the treatment, language minority students should exhibit:

- High levels of English language proficiency
- Appropriate levels of cognitive/academic achievement
- Sufficient levels of primary language development, and
- Adequate psychosocial and cultural adjustment

OBBE further summarized research evidence and outlined major principles and standards for implementing Bilingual Education programs at the elementary school levels K–6. These standards constitute a theoretical framework for program implementation based upon five major principles that are substantially supported by empirical evidence.

1. If language minority students are to gain maximum academic benefits from their schooling, they must develop high levels of language proficiency both in English and in their native language (Cummins, 1979, 1981; Development Associates, 1980; Duncan & De Avila, 1979; Kessler & Quinn, 1980).

Therefore, bilingual programs should not only focus on the enhancement of English proficiency but include the continued development of native language proficiency. Research cited indicates that students with high levels of language proficiency in both languages were most likely to obtain academic success.

2. Language proficiency can be classified in two dimensions: Basic Interpersonal Communicative Skills (BICS) and Cognitive/Academic Language Proficiency (CALP). Basic Interpersonal Communicative Skills refer to the aspects of language proficiency normally acquired by native speakers of a language, skills that are essential in socialization and in communicating needs, desires, and ideas. Such skills are not necessarily those demonstrated in the use of language for the heuristic function. Cognitive/ Academic Language Proficiency refers to those universal skills associated with literacy and cognitive development that are acquired through formal instruction (Carmazza & Brones, 1980; Cummins, 1980, 1981; Dulay & Burt, 1978; Hammill & McNutt, 1980).

Children may demonstrate a high level of relative language proficiency on an instrument that assesses basic communicative skills in English, but not have an equally highly developed or demonstrated level of proficiency in English in the academic areas.

3. For language minority students, the development of high levels of Cognitive/Academic Language Proficiency forms the basis for similar proficiency in the second language, allows for normal academic progress, and assists in the acquisition of the second language (Cummins, 1979, 1980, 1981; Development Associates, 1980).

4. When meaningful opportunities are provided for comprehensive second language input along with positive motivation to learn English, language minority students will acquire the basic communicative skills of English (Dulay & Burt, 1973, 1976; Krashen, 1981; Legaretta, 1979; Saville-Troike, 1978; Terrell, 1981).

5. The perceived status of students affects the interactions between teachers and students and among the students themselves. In turn, student outcomes are affected.

These five principles on the education of language minority students provide standard guidelines for program implementation. Operational implementation of these principles would mean that the student's native language development should not be ignored. Bilingual instruction implies the provision of information in the language the student best comprehends. However, based on available research evidence, the student's native language should not be ignored once the student comprehends English if indeed the student is to obtain academic success. A higher level of language proficiency in both languages would ensure such success.

A second implication of these principles centers on the view of language proficiency. This theoretical framework identifies research to support two levels of language functioning. A student can demonstrate social communicative abilities in the second language while not being able to use that language effectively for acquiring formal learning skills. This would imply the inclusion of assessing academic performance in a language when judging overall proficiency. Whether the student can read the language and how well the child can perform academic skills using that language in various contexts are among the additional factors to be considered.

Last, research supports that the language minority child will learn English, given meaningful contextual experiences and the proper motivation. The level of English proficiency will initially be at the basic communicative stage, and a higher development of cognitive and academic proficiency in the native language would facilitate the acquisition of these skills in English.

Based on the five theoretical principles outlined, the California Office of Bilingual Bicultural Education (OBBE, 1982) developed implementation standards as advisory to local school districts.

Language minority students should:

- Receive instruction in and through their primary language on a consistent basis throughout kindergarten to sixth grade

- Receive formal reading instruction in the primary language
- Have available a variety of reading materials in their primary language at all grade levels and in various subject areas
- Acquire a second language (English) within comprehensible and meaningful contextual situations
- Receive second language instruction that focuses on communicating content rather than the memorization of language forms
- Be allowed to respond in either the first language (L_1) or the second language (L_2) during initial second language instruction

Teachers of language minority students should:

- Have native or near-native proficiency in the student's primary language
- Be sensitive to and accepting of varieties of the minority language
- Be knowledgeable in the primary language development process
- Be knowledgeable in the secondary language acquisition process
- Receive language, methodology, and cultural training to develop the skills necessary for implementing instructional programs

Parents of language minority students should:

- Be given sufficient information regarding instructional programs
- Be encouraged to use the primary language in the home, especially in literary activities
- Be provided with opportunities to participate in classrooms and on school advisory committees, and to suggest school improvements

Based on currently available research information, it is believed that an adherence to these implementation standards would lead to an improvement in the acquisition of English language skills and to the general academic achievement of language minority students. The proposed theoretical framework is summarized in Table 5–1.

Subsequent theoretical frameworks and implementation standards will emerge as the field of Bilingual Education continues to evolve. The presentation of this framework is not meant to present the end to implementation designs, but rather a conceptual understanding upon which to build operational descriptions of Bilingual Education Programs. These theoretical and operational descriptions would subsequently form a base for conceptualizing a design and operational framework on how actually to implement a Bilingual Special Education program. It is expected and hoped that the material presented in this chapter will lead to the adaptation, modification, and creation of subsequent program designs.

Operational Definition for Bilingual Education

Given any theoretical construct upon which to build practice, it is important to be aware that actual practice may not reflect the theoretical design, as is the case with many bilingual programs. School districts may verbalize that they subscribe to a specific program philosophy, that is, transitional or maintenance, but in reality the instructional program provided might not support their premise.

This section will present operational definitions of Bilingual Education by describing various bilingual program placement options, by describing what the student may receive given program goals and staff capabilities, and finally by providing an operational description based on the theoretical framework presented in the previous section. It is our intention to clarify the "hows" of bilingual program implementation so

Table 5–1
Summary of Theoretical Framework for Bilingual Multicultural Programs

Instructional goals for LEP students:	Goals are best accomplished by providing:	Program strategies are based on the following theoretical constructs:
Develop high levels of English language proficiency Achieve appropriate levels of cognitive/academic success Develop sufficient levels of primary language development Achieve adequate levels of psychological adjustment	Instruction in the primary language through grade six Formal reading instruction in the primary language Second language/English language instruction in a meaningful context that focuses on content Instruction sensitive to students' cultural differences Opportunities for parent/community input	High levels of language proficiency in both English and the native language ensure maximum academic gains. Language proficiency is manifested in two forms: basic interpersonal communication competence and cognitive/academic language proficiency. A high level of cognitive/academic language proficiency in the native language will allow for academic progress and will form the basis for similar proficiency in English. Language minority students will acquire English skills when motivation and meaningful opportunities are provided.

as to establish a basis for developing a Bilingual Special Education Program interface.

The four general goals of Bilingual Education as described in the previous section encompass the development of high levels of English language proficiency, appropriate levels of cognitive/academic achievement, sufficient levels of primary language development, and adequate levels of psychological/social adjustment. In other words, the educational goals for limited English proficient students are that they acquire the cognitive and academic skills necessary to promote future learning, that they enhance the native language so as to provide a base for second language development, and that they acquire high levels of English language skills. These educational goals translate into four general instructional program components for Bilingual Education:

- Acquisition of concepts and learning skills
- Development of the primary language (i.e., native language reading instruction)
- Acquisition of a second language
- Multicultural education

Organizational components include:

- Management support
- Articulation between bilingual and general education programs
- Integrated staff training
- Community involvement

These instructional and organizational components represent basic necessary elements that must be present for effective implementation of Bilingual Education programs (Cervantes, 1981). The degree to which these components are implemented vary depending on the philosophy, sociopolitical conditions, community requirements, staff resources, and nature of the educational leadership provided at the school setting.

To make sense of the multiplicity of bilingual implementation models that currently exist, the implementation design for a program based on the theoretical framework previously described should be understood. In fact, the standards of implementation proposed by this framework and based on empirical evidence do improve second language acquisition and cognitive/academic achievement for language minority students; it is assumed that such an operational framework, when applied to special education program constructs, would in turn provide meaningful educational experiences for the handicapped, limited English proficient student. The following section will describe the implementation of a model Bilingual Education program based on the theoretical constructs provided. This model will then be adapted for the instruction of an LEP special education student, thus producing a design for interface.

Ideally, a Bilingual Education program designed to consider implementation standards outlined by the California State Department of Education (OBBE, 1982) and based on the theoretical framework described would provide the language minority student with cognitive and academic instruction in and through the primary language. Thus LEP students would receive instruction in subjects such as math, science, language arts, and social studies in their primary language. Instruction in the primary language in the academic areas would result in the enhancement and development of the primary language. For example, the Spanish-speaking kindergarten child may not know the terms for geometric shapes in Spanish. Math instruction on geometric shapes in Spanish would not only lead to a conceptual understanding of shapes but also to vocabulary development in the primary language. Academic instruction provided in the student's primary language develops the student's academic language proficiency and ensures that the student does not develop two vernaculars: a school-based vocabulary in English and primary language vocabulary that lacks academic content.

A second factor in the implementation of a bilingual program based on the proposed theoretical model is the inclusion of primary language development. LEP students would receive instruction to develop their primary language so as to build a base for second language learning. As previously described, the primary language is enhanced when academic subjects are taught in that language. Critical to that enhancement is reading instruction in the primary language. It is assumed that the skill of reading is more readily acquired when students are taught to read in a language they more proficiently command.

A third program aspect of Bilingual Education is the second-language component. This component is considered most critical to bilingual program implementation because much anxiety is produced over the mastery of English and the eventual sole instruction in English. Ideally, second language instruction should be provided in an environment in which contextual meaning is emphasized. The focus of the second language instruction should be on building communicative competence rather than an understanding of mere grammatical forms. The learning environment should provide opportunities for natural communication in the second language to occur. Second language instruction in the language arts areas of reading and writing occurs once the student has acquired these skills in the primary language.

A fourth bilingual program component is the multicultural component. Because educational curriculum reflects customs, values, and life-styles, it is essential that a bilingual curriculum incorporate the cultures of the students involved. The families, communities, and backgrounds of all students in the program should be reflected in the curriculum. A multicultural curriculum that reflects the student's culture assists in developing pride in cultural heritage and thus enhances the student's self-concept.

Essential to the implementation of a "model" Bilingual Education program based on the prescribed theoretical framework are two noninstructional components: staff involvement and parent/community involvement. A prerequisite to the implementation of this bilingual program model is the presence of trained bilingual staff. The staff skills prescribed by this framework require the teacher to command the primary language to native or near-native fluency. The teacher's ability to speak the student's primary language influences both the student's development of the primary language and the acquisition of the second language (OBBE, 1982). To implement the proposed program design, the teacher must be able to teach reading in the primary language, to acknowledge and accept the varieties of minority languages that can exist, and to be knowledgeable and sensitive to the student's cultural background.

A final but equally important bilingual program component is the meaningful participation of parents and community. Meaningful participation is evidenced when minority language parents are involved in the classroom and when they are able and encouraged to suggest improvements to the school program. The six program components are summarized in Table 5–2.

The first area of discussion when implementing Bilingual Education is the variable of language use. Because Bilingual Education is the use of two languages as a means for instruction, the manner in which the languages are actually employed should be carefully considered. One cannot assume that the primary language is actually being used for classroom instruction just because the teaching staff is bilingual. In fact, descriptive research on Bilingual Education programs has documented that English is often the language used in instruction while the primary language is used for behavioral control. The primary language must be used at least 50% of the instructional time to produce positive academic benefits for the language minority child. The educational practitioner must be cognizant of the manner in which the two languages will be used in instruction. This is especially critical to the implementation of Bilingual Special Education programs. The practitioner must identify in what language the academic content will be presented, how the concepts will be reinforced, and when and how the other language will be introduced.

In summary, this section has described a framework within which bilingual instructional models can exist without prescribing one form of delivery. It is necessary to move beyond the expounding of theory to a description of actual program practice. However, such descriptions may lead to the description of one design that does not lend itself to the idiosyncrasies of situations and settings. The instructional needs of the LEP student, along with the level of English proficiency, should predict the techniques, tactics, and strategies used in program implementation. We now have available information upon which to base program practice. Theoretical assumptions, supported by research and systematic observations, can now form a basis for bilingual program implementation. This framework is pliable enough to include bilingual program implementation with various placement offerings, staff configurations, and modes of language use. The principles and implementation standards outlined by this framework will be used to define a Bilingual Special Education framework. (For a summary of Bilingual Education program options, see Table 5–3.)

Conceptual Framework for Special Education

Special education, like general education, is based on the premise that all students in America's society have a right to and should receive

Table 5–2
Implementation Design for Bilingual Education Programs

Bilingual Program Components	
Instructional	**Language minority students receive:**
1. Concept acquisition/learning skills	Instruction on general concepts in academic areas in and through the primary language throughout kindergarten to grade six
2. Primary language development	Instruction in and through the primary language at least 50% of the school day
	Instruction in primary language development to enhance receptive and expressive skills
	Instruction in reading in the primary language
3. Second language acquisition	Exposure to the use of English in natural settings
	Instruction in English focuses on communicative content rather than on language forms
	Opportunities to express themselves in English in low-anxiety situations
4. Multicultural education	Instruction within the cultural context that is most familiar
	Exposure to other cultures
	Instruction on the acceptance and value of diverse cultures
	Instruction in the value of their culture
Noninstructional	**Bilingual program teachers:**
5. Teachers and staff	Have native or near-native proficiency in the primary language
	Are sensitive to and accepting of varieties of minority languages
	Are knowledgeable of the primary language development process
	Are knowledgeable of the second language acquisition process
	Are provided with language, methodology, and cultural training necessary to implementing a bilingual program
	Parents and community:
6. Parent and community involvement	Are provided opportunities to participate in school advisory programs and to suggest improvements in the school program
	Are encouraged and provided opportunities to participate in the classroom on meaningful instructional activities
	Are encouraged and provided instructional materials to foster primary language reading in the home

an adequate, meaningful education. Exceptional children, like other students, must be provided opportunities to develop their abilities fully. The educational system must be pliable enough to allow for the individual differences that exist among the student population. This general philosophy of the exceptional student's right to a meaningful, appropriate education is the fundamental principle upon which local program guidelines and practices are established.

Although a philosophical base for special education is implied through the legal framework established in current legislation, common theoretical constructs are evidenced throughout

Table 5–3
Bilingual Education Program Options

Placements	Instructions provided by	Comments
Self-contained bilingual classroom (single grade/combination grades)	Bilingual teacher/bilingual aide	Most advantageous placement because student can receive instruction in primary language while acquiring English
Bilingual classroom—team teaching (single grade/combination grades)	Bilingual teacher/monolingual aide: monolingual teacher/bilingual aide	Provides student with separate language models
Regular classroom placement with monolingual teacher trained in Bilingual Education philosophy and methodology	Monolingual English teacher/bilingual aide	Teacher conducts planning and supervises aide who provides instruction in the primary language
Regular classroom placement with designated instructional services	Bilingual resource teacher	Bilingual resource teacher provides special instruction within the classroom setting or student is pulled out into a resource center concept
Regular classroom placement with designated services formally outlined in a bilingual individual learning plan (BILP)	Bilingual resource teacher	LEP student receives instructional services as outlined in BILP
Magnet school	Bilingual teachers/bilingual aides	LEP student attends a special school that offers Bilingual Education

the special education field. Consensus exists surrounding the type of educational planning, the setting, and the provider of special instruction. Generally, educational planning emphasizes the learning strengths and abilities of the handicapped student, and labeling the student according to the handicap is avoided (Gearheart, 1980). However, all handicapped students should receive specific assistance that relates directly to the area of disability.

A second common goal for special education relates to the location where instruction is received. Whenever possible, exceptional children should be served in the regular classroom. Special assistance should be provided in a normal instructional setting and efforts should be made to keep the exceptional student in the regular classroom setting or to return the child to that setting as soon as possible. A third construct involves the delivery of special instruction. Because of the unusual and special needs the handicapped child may possess, instruction should be provided by a specially trained teacher. Special education personnel should provide direct instructional services to the student and provide supportive services to the regular classroom teacher. Last, as in Bilingual Education, special education emphasizes the importance of parent involvement in the areas of assessment, planning, and program implementation.

Table 5–4 summarizes the educational principles that undergird special education programs.

In summary, the focus of special education is to provide proper services to exceptional chil-

Table 5–4
Summary of Theoretical Framework for Special Education

Adapted from *Special education for the '80s* by B. Gearheart, 1980, St. Louis: Mosby. Copyright 1980 by Mosby. Reprinted by permission of author.

Instructional goal for special education students:	Goal is best accomplished by providing:	Program strategies are based on the following theoretical constructs:
Develop conceptual, academic, and social abilities	Instruction in the least restrictive environment Individual planning of instruction Instruction that focuses on students' abilities Specific assistance related directly to the area of disability Instruction through specially trained special education personnel Necessary involvement in the assessment, planning, and program implementation from parents	Assessment must be broadly based, flexible, and ongoing Regular classroom teachers are highly important members of instructional team and should be included in the planning and program implementation Early intervention is desirable and most beneficial Special education services for a broad age range, preschool to adult, are essential Prevention should be viewed as priority Some disabilities are best viewed as symptoms rather than disorders Special education services may vary in the amount and duration required depending on the nature of the disability Providing a maximum amount of information to parents is essential

dren, including those students with special language needs, and fully develop their conceptual, academic, and social abilities. Individual instructional programs tailored to the particular needs of students are developed to reflect the special education principles outlined.

Operational Definition of Special Education

A description of common program guidelines will be presented to provide an operational definition of special education. With the passage of the Education for All Handicapped Children Act, P.L. 94–142, program components essential to the implementation of special education have been defined and clarified. Although school districts may vary in the format by which these guildelines are implemented, similar program components can be traced throughout special education programs.

A quick review of these elements will be presented; they are dealt with in greater depth in subsequent chapters. The focus of this section is to identify instructional components essential to the operation of special education programs so as to include them in a design for interface of Bilingual Education and special education.

Evidenced across all special education programs are the following key program elements (Gearheart, 1980):

Screening. Broad-scale testing procedures are employed to identify students who may require more intensive assessment.

Referral. Appropriate specialists are consulted about a student who may require further assessment and special education services.

Assessment. Information is systematically collected regarding the student's mental, social, academic, and psychological performance to identify specific abilities and weaknesses.

Staffing. An official meeting involves all concerned persons, for example, teacher and speech therapist, concerning the education and placement of a particular student. The student's primary handicap, need for specialized services, and type of intervention required are discussed during the staffing phase.

Placement. Special education programs offer a variety of placement configurations that will be discussed later in this section. Placement offerings reflect the variety of types of assistance that students may require.

Regardless of the types of exceptional students served in local programs, the implementation of special education would include a form of these key program elements or components. An additional program component is the development of an individualized educational plan for each exceptional student.

Essential to the implementation of special education programs that adhere to key elements of an appropriate education for all students is the provision of a full array of educational services. Program alternatives must be available if the ideology of a least restrictive environment is to be operationalized. Because different combinations of assistance may be required, the school district must be prepared to offer more than a self-contained special class setting.

P.L. 94–142 has outlined special education operational policies for the implementation of programs. The operational framework prescribed by this legislation is flexible enough to allow diversity in local program implementation while maintaining continuity among program principles. Each element that contributes to the functioning of a special education program is applied to the distinctive educational needs of students. Remaining to be discussed are the common axioms for instructing students with specific exceptionalities.

Agreement exists as to the nature of the instruction to be provided to students with handicaps, such as visual impairments and hearing loss. The specific instructional elements for each exceptionality will be discussed under the Bilingual Special Education programmatic interface.

Special education program implementation components are summarized in Table 5–5.

Interface Design for Bilingual Special Education

The review of the basic premises and implementation designs for both Bilingual Education and special education sets a foundation for conceptualizing a design for interface. The connection of both programs must be accomplished at an ideological and operational level. It is essential to interweave theories, philosophies, and program strategies and to move the concept of interface from abstraction to implementation. Subsequent chapters address programmatic designs for interface currently enacted at local school districts. This section will present a structure for interface at the theoretical and operational level.

The interface of bilingual and special education services does not simply occur by the teaming of personnel from both disciplines. Ed-

Table 5–5
Special Education Program Implementation Components

Adapted from *The handicapped student in the regular classroom,* 2nd ed. by B. Gearheart and M. Weishahn, 1980, St. Louis: Mosby. Copyright 1980 by Mosby. Reprinted with permission.

Key program elements	Instructional components	Instructional placement
Screening Referral Assessment Staffing Individual instructional planning Placement	Each student must have an individualized education program that includes the following: Statement of the student's present levels of educational performance Statement of annual goals, including short-term instructional objectives Projected date for initiation and the anticipated duration of services Appropriate objective criteria, schedules, and procedures for evaluating the attainment of instructional goals	Regular class placement with consultation from special education personnel Regular class placement with consultation and special materials from special education Regular class placement plus itinerant services Regular class placement plus assistance in resource room Part-time regular class, part-time special class Special class in regular school Special class in separate special day school Hospital and homebound services Residential or boarding school

ucational staff must be aware of the definition and intent of both programs, common misconceptions of program role and function, and remaining unresolved issues in both program areas. Only by dealing with such programmatic areas can staff then begin to define and articulate an educational program for the bilingual exceptional student. Educational staff must identify the student's strengths as well as the primary disability, the level and nature of the instruction to be provided, the means by which it will be provided, the setting for the instruction, and the duration of the instruction. Such curriculum planning is best accomplished when the philosophy, goal, and purpose for the instruction are clearly understood.

The philosophical foundation for an interface design for Bilingual Special Education would include philosophical understandings from both disciplines. Philosophical statements for Bilingual Special Education should not vary greatly from general education goals. The problem with establishing educational goals for the bilingual exceptional student has been the tendency to change the focus of educational intent. A goal for monolingual exceptional students would be to assist the students in developing social, emotional, and academic abilities to their fullest potential. When the exceptional student speaks a language other than English, educators are prone to state that this student's primary educational goal is to learn English. Granted, assisting in the fullest development of the bilingual exceptional student's social, emotional, cognitive, and academic skills would most definitely include the acquisition of English. The danger that exists in making the learning of English the primary educational goal is that the focus and concentration on the teaching of English language skills will produce an English-speaking exceptional student who drastically requires development in the academic areas.

Focusing the goal on the acquisition of English language skills may defer the enhancement of abilities in other areas. Precious learning time is lost if it is stipulated that the bilingual exceptional student must learn English before instruction in other areas can occur. Opportunities to develop cognitively and academically can be provided alongside opportunities that lead to the acquisition of English. Active teaching of academic and cognitive skills in the student's primary language does not mean that teaching English skills will be excluded. These two educational goals are not mutually exclusive or incompatible; however, both goals must be connected in a systematic instructional design for each student.

Major goals for bilingual and special education programs were previously stated in this chapter in the following manner:

Special Education Goals	**Bilingual Education Goals**
To develop conceptual, academic, and social abilities to fullest potential	To develop: ▪ High levels of English language proficiency ▪ Appropriate levels of cognitive academic achievement ▪ Sufficient levels of primary language development ▪ Adequate psychosocial and cultural adjustment

The goals for a Bilingual Special Education program would require the intermeshing of these two separate statements. A philosophical statement for Bilingual Special Education could read as follows:

> A Bilingual Special Education program would provide special instruction to enhance the cognitive/academic and social abilities of the bilingual exceptional student to the child's fullest potential. Instruction is provided through the primary language while providing opportunities for learning English.

Philosophically, a Bilingual Special Education interface design should reflect the importance of providing special tailored instruction by employing the student's primary language and enhancing the acquisition of English proficiency. The importance of the cultural context and instructional setting in which learning occurs should also be reflected.

A Theoretical Framework for Bilingual Special Education

Because Bilingual Special Education is an interdisciplinary field, it is only reasonable to expect that its theoretical framework should also be interdisciplinary. This framework should be based on principles and research findings from each of the three parent disciplines of regular education, Bilingual Education and special education.

The first part of the theoretical framework is taken from the effective schools research of regular education. The field of regular education has been concerned with how to best educate high-risk students for many years. When Coleman (1968) conducted his well-known study on schooling in the United States, he reported that family background was the key variable for predicting school success. His research painted a very pessimistic picture of schooling in poverty areas. He and other researchers from the period thought that very little could be done to improve schools in poverty areas.

In the late 1970s this picture began to change. A few inner-city school districts began to report achievement at or above national norms. Researchers decided to go into those schools and document everything they did that might account for the improved results. This effort became known as the effective schools research movement. Edmonds (1979) summarized much of this research. He stated that the characteristics of effective schools are:

1. Strong administrative leadership
2. High positive expectations for all students and staff
3. Orderly but not rigid environment
4. Academic skill acquisition given first priority
5. School energy and resources organized for first priority
6. Frequent monitoring of student progress

In a similar summary of research findings on school effectiveness, Lazotte (1984) stated that schools are effective when the following conditions are met:

1. A clear sense of mission is shared.
2. Students can learn and teachers can teach.
3. Effective leadership is present.
4. Effective use of class time is made.
5. Effective home-school support systems are in place.

Moving beyond effective schools in general and looking specifically at effective classrooms, a National Institute of Education (1982) study documented what constitute effective classroom management practices:

1. Using a systematic approach
2. Preparing in advance
3. Planning before the school year starts
4. Establishing procedures and routines at the start of the school year and maintaining them
5. Focusing student attention on group lessons and independent work times
6. Establishing procedures during the first two weeks of school
7. Preventing problems from arising, rather than developing responses after they have occurred
8. Maximizing student time on task for the improved learning of the basic skills

In the area of instruction the National Institute of Education (1982) documented the following in effective classrooms:

1. Checking previous day's work and reteaching when necessary
2. Presenting new content/skills, proceeding rapidly but in small steps, giving detailed instructions and explanations
3. Having students practice with considerable teacher involvement until they understand 80% or more of the materials
4. Giving feedback and correctives, recycling when necessary
5. Providing for independent practice, after which students should obtain mastery at the 95% level
6. Reviewing skills and information weekly and monthly

Other researchers have applied the effective schools research model to bilingual schools. Carter and Maestas (1982), for example, have reported that teachers and administrators in effective bilingual schools do the following:

1. Teach English as the primary objective.
2. Treat the two languages as equally important.
3. Stress basic skills in both Spanish and English.
4. Maintain high expectations for academic achievement.
5. Demand diligent study.
6. Organize programs that detail goals and objectives.
7. Monitor individual academic achievement.
8. Have planned measures to correct weaknesses.

9. Include cultural and experiential realities drawn from the community.

10. Employ teachers who are excellent language models in one or both languages.

11. Believe bilingual education is effective in raising academic achievement.

Tikunoff (1982) in a longitudinal study of effective bilingual programs also documented effective bilingual teacher behaviors. According to his research, effective bilingual teachers do the following:

1. Emphasize basic skills.
2. Focus on developing L_1 and L_2 skills.
3. Respond to cultural clues.
4. Communicate clearly (provide comprehensible input).
5. Mediate instruction using L_1 and L_2.
6. Engage students in task completion.
7. Monitor student progress.
8. Provide frequent, immediate feedback.
9. Communicate task and instructional demands.

According to Tikunoff (1987), the person most responsible for bringing about an effective school environment is the principal.

The second part of the theoretical framework is taken from the empirical principles that guide Bilingual Education. These principles have been carefully summarized by the California State Department of Education (OBBE, 1982). They are as follows:

1. For bilingual students the degree to which proficiencies in both L_1 and L_2 are developed is positively associated with academic achievement.

2. Language proficiency is the ability to use language for both academic purposes and basic communicative tasks.

3. For language minority students the development of the primary language skills necessary to complete academic tasks forms the basis for similar proficiency in English.

4. Acquisition of basic communicative competency in a second language is a function of comprehensible second language input and a supportive affective environment.

5. The perceived status of students affects the interactions between teachers and students and among the students themselves. In turn, student outcomes are affected.

Finally, the theoretical framework incorporates some of the proven principles from special education. A review of the special education literature shows that the following strategies and principles have proven themselves effective in working with handicapped students:

1. Instruction in the least restrictive environment
2. Individual planning of instruction
3. Instruction that focuses on student abilities
4. Use of a learning strategies approach to remediation
5. Instruction through specially trained special education personnel
6. Parental involvement in all aspects of the program

Operational Guidelines for Bilingual Special Education

By summarizing the information presented in the theoretical framework, operational guidelines can be established for the implementation of Bilingual Special Education. Among these are the following:

1. A clear sense of mission regarding Bilingual Special Education is shared by all staff members.

2. Strong and effective leadership is provided for the Bilingual Special Education program.

3. High expectations are established for all teachers and students in the program.

4. Effective home-school support systems are established.

5. Native language instruction as well as English as a Second Language (ESL) instruction are included in all IEPs as appropriate.

6. Teachers mediate instruction, monitor student progress, and provide frequent feedback using both L_1 and L_2, as appropriate.

7. Instruction focuses on the student's abilities and needed learning strategies.

8. Special instruction considers the student's cultural background by using experiences drawn from the community.

9. The student's primary language skills are developed up to the cognitive and academic level to attain similar advanced English language skills.

10. Special instruction is provided by appropriately trained Bilingual Special Education staff.

11. Time on task and task completion are encouraged in the least restrictive environment.

12. All students, all languages, and all cultures are treated with equal respect.

13. All staff must believe that Bilingual Special Education is effective in raising the achievement level of LEP handicapped students.

The stated guidelines for operationalizing a Bilingual Special Education program are further defined when molded to specific areas of disability. The ingredients for a Bilingual Special Education program need to be combined with instructional techniques tailored to each area of disability. General guidelines for instructing students who are visually impaired, hearing impaired, learning impaired, speech handicapped, or emotionally disturbed should be taken into consideration.

There exist common factors to consider in combining special and Bilingual Education Program principles into an interface design. The developer of a Bilingual Special Education program for each individual student needs to weigh not only the degree of disability but also the level of language proficiency in both English and the primary language, as well as the student's intellectual capacity. The student's placement on each of these three continuums will determine the nature of instruction and the educational placement. Figure 5–1 depicts these three essential criteria.

The students' disabilities must be considered for program design, along with their intellectual capacities and their proficiencies in English and the other languages. For example, a student of average intelligence who has a high level of language proficiency in Spanish, a minimal level of ability in English, and limited visual acuity will require curricular services and placement different than a student who is linguistically limited in both languages, exhibits lower intellectual performance, and is severely language delayed. The degree of disability, the level of intelligence, and the level of linguistic ability in both English and the other language should be considered.

Placement configurations can be numerous and should reflect the diversity that exists among students and local school sites. There are, however, common placement options, some of which are preferred. Those preferred would more directly adhere to the proposed theory for instructing bilingual handicapped students. In addition to cultural and linguistic considerations, other factors would apply in deciding placement for bilingual students. The students' level of relative language proficiency, amount of language input, and cultural environment should be considered. The following combination of special education placement decision variables and bilingual factors need to be addressed in identifying placements:

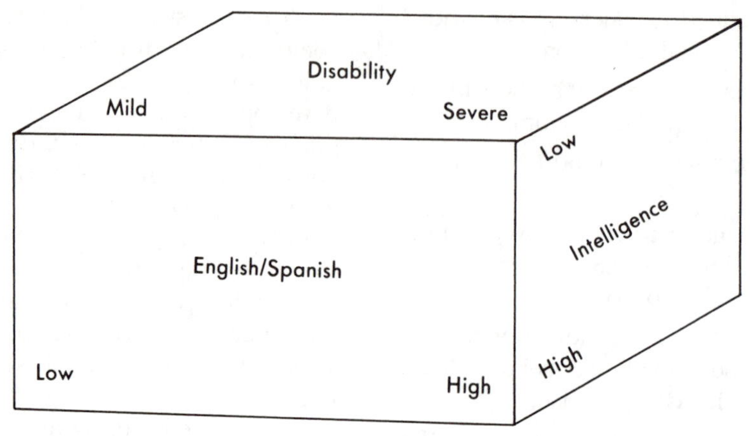

Figure 5–1
Student functioning level on three critical variables.

1. Student's age
2. Type and degree of impairment or disability
3. Age at which disability occurred
4. Level of language involvement because of the disability
5. Level of academic achievement
6. Entry level language skills (upon entering school)
7. Measured intellectual ability
8. Method and language used in measuring academic achievement and intellectual ability
9. Level of adaptive behavior
10. Time spent in United States
11. Current cultural home setting
12. Social maturity
13. Level of language proficiency in English and other language
14. Amount and type of language input received in the home environment
15. Speech and language capabilities in both languages
16. Presence of multiple handicaps
17. Ambulation or mobility
18. Success in past and present placements
19. Wishes of students and parents

The program placement must be the best fit between the student's needs and the available resources. Placement decisions for the bilingual exceptional student need to reflect the thinking on the type and nature of the instruction to be provided, the language of instruction, the conveyor of instruction, the duration of instruction, and the student's learning needs and style.

Operationalizing Bilingual Special Education requires the creation of an instructional social system that involves active teaching of cognitive skills and includes the development of language skills while focusing on the acquisition of English skills. All instruction is prescribed in a manner that accommodates and remediates the student's exceptionality. Productive participation of students in any instructional setting requires their understanding of directions and the nature of tasks. Instruction must be provided within a relevant cultural context so that expectations can be understood by the student. Because language is the primary conveyor of instruction, the student's stronger language must be employed in instruction to ensure understanding the intent of instructional tasks. When the intent of instructional tasks is understood, the student can more meaningfully participate and interact in the instruction.

Bilingual Special Education is operationalized at each local level with each individual student in mind. It is the operation of the philosophy that students learn best in a language they understand best. There are varying degrees to the implementation of Bilingual Special Education, which reflect the varying degrees and types of exceptionality. The common thread, however, is to provide for all students educational experiences that develop lifelong learning skills.

Interface Requisites

Certain requisites are necessary to the enactment of a Bilingual Special Education program at the local school level. First, local school districts and education agencies must recognize the problem. Limited English speaking students with handicaps require special instruction in the language they best understand while acquiring English language skills. Decision makers need to understand the nature and complexity of instructing LEP handicapped students. Once the problem is recognized, the school district must develop a formal policy to address the problem. Such policy will direct program development, definition, and implementation. A subsequent step is to know how many LEP special education students are enrolled and require special services.

Bilingual Special Education program planning should include personnel from both Bilingual Education and special education. Articulation among programs is necessary and, most importantly, both programs should be mainstreamed into the general education offering. Bilingual Special Education requires the use of resources from all education areas. This educational offering cannot be viewed as separate and so removed from the general education offering that it is considered foreign and estranged from the total school functioning. Bilingual Special Education, like Bilingual Education and special education, should be viewed as an integral arm of general education, a needed extension to meet the distinctive needs of some students. These responsive arms of general education should not be viewed as fractionary but as part of the makeup of general education.

Requisites to the enactment of Bilingual Special Education include:

- The realization by policy makers and decision makers of the need for a Bilingual Special Education offering
- A formal policy by the school district to address the needs of LEP-handicapped students
- Local administrative support for Bilingual Special Education
- The involvement of bilingual and special education staff and administrative staff in the conceptualization, design, and implementation of Bilingual Special Education
- The training of Bilingual Special Education staff on special education philosophy and instructional techniques
- The training of special education staff on Bilingual Education content, definition, and implementation techniques
- The training of general education staff, including administrative and support staff, on Bilingual Special Education definition, design, and implementation
- The monitoring of program implementation through such means as administrative support and staff meetings
- The involvement of parents and community in program design and implementation

- The evaluation of actual program implementation and its effectiveness

If Bilingual Special Education is to be a reality in local school districts, it is vital that both administrators and practitioners have a conceptual and operational understanding of its intended purpose. It cannot be assumed that this understanding is automatic because practitioners are involved in a bilingual or special education area. The understanding is an evolving, interacting process that is designed to reflect increasing insight on students' needs and methodologies to mediate those needs.

Summary

The interface of bilingual and special education requires the conceptual and operational understanding of both programs. A design for Bilingual Special Education is based on basic premises for each separate educational offering. The marriage of these two programs requires an understanding of the reasons for program success and failure. Like a marriage, the interface of bilingual and special education is an evolving relationship, a relationship developed for the sole purpose of meeting the educational needs of limited English proficient students with handicaps. The essential elements for this union have been described and a theoretical framework for the enactment of a meaningful relationship has been presented.

Discussion Questions

1. Explain the conceptual underpinnings of Bilingual Education.

2. Explain the conceptual underpinnings of special education.

3. Describe the operational implementation of Bilingual Education.

4. Describe the operational implementation of special education.

5. Discuss the critical elements of the Bilingual Special Education theoretical framework.

6. Discuss models for interfacing bilingual and special education instruction.

7. Explain the program and instructional requirements essential to the development of a Bilingual Special Education interface.

References

Caramazza, A., & Brones, I. (1980, March). Semantic classification by bilinguals. *Canadian Journal of Psychology.* 34(1):77–81.

Carter, T. P., & Maestas, L. L. (1982). *Effective bilingual schools serving Spanish speaking children.* Unpublished manuscript.

Cervantes, R. A. (1981). Bilingual education: The best of times, the worst of times. In K. Coles-Circincione (Ed.), *The future of education: Policy issues and challenges.* Los Angeles: Sage.

Coleman, J. S. (1968, Winter). The concept of equality of educational opportunity. *Harvard Educational Review.* 38:1.

Cummins, J. (1979). Linguistic interdependence and the educational development of bilingual children. *Review of Educational Research.* 49:222–251.

Cummins, J. (1980). The exit and entry fallacy in bilingual education. *NABE Journal.* 4:25–60.

Cummins, J. (1981). The role of primary language development in promoting educational success for language minority students. In *Schooling and language minority students: A theoretical framework.* Los Angeles: Evaluation, Dissemination and Assessment Center, California State University.

Development Associates (1980). *Evaluation of California's educational services to limited- and non-English speaking students. Final report.* San Francisco: Author.

Dulay, H. C., & Burt, M. K. (1973, December). Should we teach children syntax? *Language Learning.* 23(2):245–258.

Dulay, H. C., & Burt, J. K. (1976, January). Creative construction in second language learning and teaching. *Language Learning.* Special issue no. 4.

Dulay, H. C., & Burt, M. K. (1978). From research to method in bilingual education. In J. D. Alatis (Ed.), *International dimensions of bilingual education.* Washington, DC: Georgetown University Press.

Duncan, S. E., & De Avila, E. A. (1979, Fall). Bilingualism and cognition: Some recent findings. *NABE Journal.* 4:15–50.

Edmonds, R. R. (1979). Effective schools for the urban poor. *Educational Leadership.* 37:15–27.

Fradd, S. H., & Tickunoff, W. J. (1987). *Bilingual education and bilingual special education: A guide for administrators.* Boston: College Hill Press.

Gearheart, B. (1980). *Special education for the '80s.* St. Louis: Mosby.

Gearheart, B., & Weishahn, M. (1980). *The handicapped student in the regular classroom,* 2nd ed. St. Louis: Mosby.

Hammill, D. D. & McNutt, G. (1980, May). Language abilities and reading: A review of the literature on their relationship. *Elementary School Journal.* 80(5):269–277.

Kessler, C., & Quinn, M. E. (1980, August). Bilingualism and problem-solving abilities. *Bilingual Education Paper Series,* vol. 4, no. 1. Los Angeles: National Dissemination and Assessment Center, California State University.

Krashen, S. D. (1981). Bilingual education and second language acquisition theory. In *Schooling and language minority students: A theoretical framework.* Los Angeles: Evaluation, Dissemination and Assessment Center, California State University.

Lazotte, E. (1984). Policy prospects for improving urban education. In R. Lindsey (Ed.), *Effective schools.* California State University, Los Angeles. Class syllabus.

Legaretta, D. (1979). The effects of program models on language acquisition by Spanish-speaking children. *TESOL Quarterly.* 13:521–534.

National Institute of Education (1982). *Research on teaching: Implications for practice.* Conference proceedings. Washington, DC: Author.

Office of Bilingual Bicultural Education, California State Department of Education (1982). *Schooling and language minority students: A theoretical framework.* Los Angeles: Evaluation, Dissemination and Assessment Center, California State University.

Saville-Troike, M. (1978). Implications of research on adult second-language acquisition for teaching foreign languages to children. In R. C. Gringas (Ed.), *Second language acquisition and foreign language teaching* (pp. 68–77). Arlington, VA: Center for Applied Linguistics.

Terrell, T. D. (1981). The natural approach in bilingual education. In *Schooling and language minority students: A theoretical framework.* Los Angeles: Evaluation, Dissemination and Assessment Center, California State University.

Tickunoff, W. J. (1982). *Descriptive study of significant bilingual instructional features.* San Francisco: Far West Laboratory for Educational Research and Development.

Tickunoff, W. J. (1987). Providing instructional leadership: The key to effectiveness. In S. H. Fradd & W. J. Tikunoff *Bilingual education and bilingual special education: A guide for administrators.* Boston: College Hill Press.

CHAPTER SIX

Language Acquisition and the Bilingual Exceptional Child

Sister Phyllis Supancheck

- Communicative and Cognitive Demands and Required Competencies
- Language Acquisition
- Importance of Culture in Language Acquisition
- Importance of Age in Second Language Acquisition
- Differences Between Second Language Acquisition and Learning
- Approaches to Second Language Acquisition and Learning
- Second Language Acquisition Suggestions for Culturally and Linguistically Different Exceptional Students
- Summary

Objectives

- To present information on first and second language acquisition
- To compare first and second language acquisition
- To present models of second language acquisition and learning
- To apply knowledge of second language acquisition and learning to culturally and linguistically different exceptional students

Children from culturally and linguistically different backgrounds are failing to achieve in most of their academic subjects and are dropping out of school (California State Department of Education, 1981; Cummins, 1981, 1984). Among the many reasons is that these children do not have the linguistic competencies necessary to meet the communicative and cognitive demands of school. Educators and researchers who have studied this problem have described conditions necessary for second language acquisition and designed various approaches to second language development.

The complexity of the problem increases as one attempts to find the most appropriate program for children who are not only culturally and linguistically different, but also have exceptional needs such as learning disabilities, language disorders, or mental retardation. The teacher of the culturally and linguistically different exceptional (CLDE) child needs to understand school-related demands and to have the knowledge and the competency required to implement appropriate programs in developing cognitive strategies and communication skills.

Communication is a process involving an exchange of clearly understandable messages between a sender and a receiver (Rivers, 1987a). These messages are frequently transmitted by *language,* a system of symbols and codes (Owens, 1988). Through language, persons express ideas, solve problems, discuss daily events, share experiences, and gain an understanding of their world (Kessler, 1984). In the United States, communication in school, at home, in the neighborhood, and on the job requires a certain level of fluency in English, depending on the demands of the situation. Within the daily functional demands placed on language learners, both formal and informal learning takes place. Maintaining the integrity of this communication process and developing communicative competence are imperative for learning. Therefore, learning is affected when communication breaks down.

Academic difficulty in communication for culturally and linguistically different exceptional students may be due to an unfamiliarity with the language, a language disorder, or both. The special educator involved in the assessment, placement, and programming of such students must be able to distinguish between these causes of communication breakdown and design a program to meet the particular needs of CLDE children (Maldonado-Colon, 1984). To do this, teachers must (1) understand the nature of communicative and cognitive demands in their classroom, (2) know basic principles of first and second language acquisition, (3) know the approaches to learning and acquiring a second language and the strengths and limitations of these approaches, and (4) apply the most effective methods of second language learning/acquisition with their students.

Therefore, this chapter will discuss the nature of communicative and cognitive demands and the competencies necessary to meet these demands; first and second language acquisition and the conditions necessary for optimal language acquisition; differences between language acquisition and language learning; approaches to second language acquisition and learning and their strengths and weaknesses; types of language disorders; and the application of this knowledge in designing appropriate instructional programs.

This discussion pertains to children who have acquired a primary language other than English and who are considered limited English speakers when they enter school. Their proficiency, although classified as limited, will differ. Dulay and Burt (1980) describe three subpopulations of limited English proficient (LEP) students based on their English competency as compared to their fluency in their primary language: English-superior, equally limited, and non-English superior. The first group, English-superior, includes students who, though limited in English, are more proficient in English than in their home language. On the language assessment instruments such as the Language Assessment Scale (LAS) or the Bilingual Syntax Measure (BSM), these students may score 4 in English and 3, 2, or 1 in their primary language. Those who are equally limited in English and in their home language have the same score between 1 and 4. The final group, the non-English superior, are students who are more proficient in their home language than in English. (See Figures 6–1, 6–2, 6–3, and 6–4.) In any of the above categories, if a score in both languages falls at 3 or below the child may require further assessment to probe speech, hearing, or language disorders, mental retardation, or emotional disturbance to determine the student's needs (Dulay & Burt, 1980; Maldonado-Colon, 1984).

Cummins (1979) has further suggested that children must reach a certain proficiency in one language before they can master a second language. Research (Pacheco, 1983) seems to support this notion, as many children continue to code switch and never develop either language.

Communicative and Cognitive Demands and Required Competencies

Communication has many functions. It is used in two major situations: in daily, casual conversation and in formal academic discourse. These situations require two levels of language proficiency. The degree of competence required in different settings will vary depending on the communicative and cognitive demands of the situation.

Communicative Demands

Communicative demands are the skills necessary to give and receive understandable information in a particular situation. Kessler (1984) suggests that these demands require the following types of communicative competence: (1) grammatical or linguistic competence (i.e., recognizing and using the phonological, syntactic, and lexical features of language); (2) sociolinguistic competence (i.e., knowing the cultural rules determining appropriate use of the language); (3) discourse competence (i.e., being able to connect utterances to form a meaningful entity); (4) strategic competence (i.e., being able to use paraphrase, repetition, circumlocution, message modification, hesitation, and avoidance).

The demands change as a function of the purpose of communication. Level of vocabulary, complexity of sentence structure, and specific tasks required of the student affect how much change will occur. The levels of competence for demands in an informal conversation would differ from those necessary for discussing issues, reading a textbook, or writing paragraphs.

Cognitive Demands

Cognitive demands are the competencies required to solve problems. They are determined by the complexity of the task relative to the student's ability. What may be easy for one person may be difficult for another. Moreover, what may be a hard task for a person one day may be simple the next day. Therefore, the cognitive demand depends on the relative difficulty of the task, which changes over time.

In a conversational setting, when the purpose of the communication may be to express needs, desires, feelings, or experiences, children will use whatever skills they have to convey

FIGURE A. LIMITED ENGLISH PROFICIENCY CLASSIFICATION

English proficiency levels	Classification
5: Proficient	Proficient or fluent in English
4: Intermediate 3: Survival 2: Comprehension only 1: Beginning	Limited English Proficient (LEP)

FIGURE B. SPANISH-SUPERIOR CLASSIFICATION

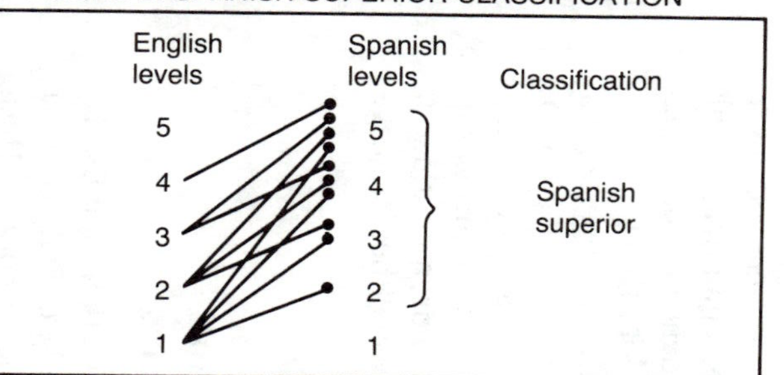

FIGURE C. ENGLISH-SURPERIOR CLASSIFICATION

English levels
5
4
3
2
1
Spanish levels
5
4
3
2
1
Classifications
English superior

FIGURE D. EQUALLY-LIMITED CLASSIFICATION

English levels
5
4
3
2
1
Spanish levels
5
4
3
2
1
Classification
Equally limited

Figures 6–1 to 6–4 (Figures A–D)

From "The relative proficiency of limited English proficient students" by H. Dulay and M. Burt, 1980. *NABE Journal* 4(3):1–23. Copyright © 1980 by *NABE Journal*. Reprinted by permission.

messages. After watching and listening to adults and peers in their surroundings over a period of time, they learn the competencies necessary to communicate effectively (Naremore, 1985). Children gradually learn when and how to use words, gestures, and facial expressions, and how to begin, maintain, and end a conversation appropriately (Kessler, 1984). Although adults may ask children to wait for their turn before speaking or may reprimand them for interrupting a conversation, there is no formalized training to learn these casual conversational skills.

In a formal classroom situation the purpose of communication is to learn new concepts or to share knowledge already attained (Dulay & Burt, 1980). Although some of the same conversational competencies are required in this situation, further communicative and cognitive demands are placed on the student.

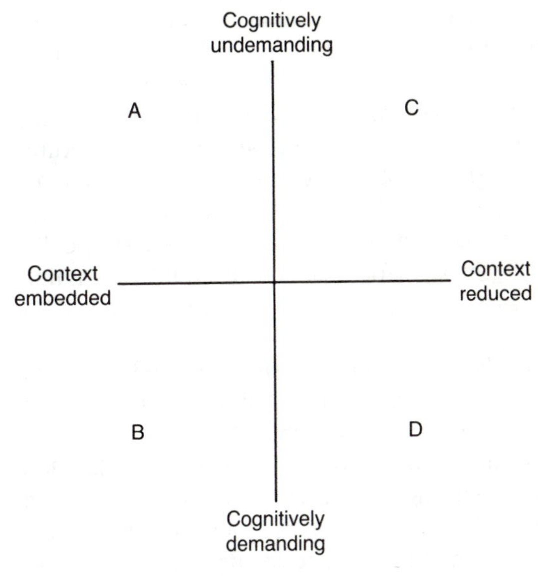

Figure 6–5
Range of Contextual Support and Degree of Cognitive Involvement in Communicative Activities

From *Bilingualism and special education: Issues in assessment and pedagogy* by J. Cummins, 1984, San Diego: College-Hill Press. Copyright © 1984 by College-Hill Press. Reprinted by permission.

Interaction of Communicative and Cognitive Demands

Communicative and cognitive demands interact. Cummins (1981) explains these demands and their interaction by diagramming two continuums, each perpendicular to the other, as shown in Figure 6–5.

Context-Embedded/Context-Reduced. The first continuum extends horizontally from *context-embedded* tasks to *context-reduced* tasks. Context-embedded tasks are those that use a set of tools and techniques such as gestures, facial expressions, movements, objects, pictures, and other hands-on materials to assist the student to understand the meaning of the language used in the task. The most simple case: informal or casual conversation focused on concrete topics in the immediate environment. Such context-embedded tasks may also be found in classroom setings. For example, in the domain of science, a student may be studying the importance of light within a photosynthesis process. In a context-embedded situation the student could perform an experiment. Plants would be put in rooms or on ledges that had different sources (i.e., fluorescent artificial light, natural sunlight) and amounts of light (i.e., light for half a day, 24 hours of light). The student would discuss observations with the teacher and/or peers. All the context tools mentioned would be available to the student and the teacher to help clarify the concept studied.

On the other hand, in a context-reduced situation the student is forced to rely exclusively on language to convey and derive meaning. The student would read about an experiment or would be told in abstract terms about the theory and then would arrive at some conclusion. No context tools such as pictures or objects (plants) would assist him in understanding the concepts. In such context-reduced situations the student must have already developed an understanding of the terminology used to explain the new concepts. The task involves abstractions and depends on comprehension of vocabulary specifically chosen for that task as well as meaning conveyed in syntax and narrative structure.

Levels of Proficiency. Cummins (1981) calls the first level of proficiency, that which is important for casual conversations, Basic Interpersonal Communicative Skills (BICS). Students labeled as fluent English speakers may be proficient in English at this level. A BICS level of proficiency, however, is inadequate for understanding cognitively demanding concepts without the assistance of context tools (Cummins, 1981; Oller, 1983).

The language proficiency needed to comprehend the more challenging tasks is called Cognitive/Academic Language Proficiency (CALP). Cummins (1981) suggests that those who are proficient in a language at this level are able to use abstractions and deal with information in a decontextualized setting. It generally takes a second language learner at least five to seven years to arrive at this level of proficiency. A student who has developed language to this degree is not as dependent on context-embedded situations to understand concepts.

Considerations for Culturally and Linguistically Different Exceptional Children. When considering instruction for the culturally and linguistically different exceptional child the context continuum shown in Figure 6–5 should be kept in mind. Students who have difficulty learning concepts may become more confused as the tasks given them become more abstract. However, when language is couched in contextual clues, the meaning becomes more apparent and the student has a better chance to comprehend and master the concept. This principle applies when the concept is taught in the student's primary language, and to even greater extent when it is taught in the second language. Cummins (1981) suggested that many students for whom English is a second language will need context-embedded tasks to understand the difficult concepts being taught in the classroom.

Cognitively Demanding/Cognitively Undemanding. The second continuum presented by Cummins (1981) and shown in Figure 6–5 ranges in a vertical direction from tasks that are cognitively undemanding to those that are cognitively demanding. The cognitively undemanding tasks are those that the student can do without thinking; they have become automatized. For example, students who can already read do not have to sound out each letter in a word before saying the word. They are able to read the passage easily and concentrate more on comprehending the meaning of the paragraph.

At the other end of the continuum is the cognitively demanding task. The concepts at this point require more active thinking on the part of the student, who must plan a solution to the problem, monitor its progress, and evaluate the outcome. The level of difficulty and the demand on the student will be different for each student. What may be cognitively demanding for one person may be undemanding for another. For example, a normally developing seventh grader will have mastered the basic skills of addition, subtraction, multiplication, and division so that the processes will be performed automatically without much thought. A child with learning problems in this area, however, may have such difficulty with both addition and multiplication that the process of working arithmetic problems becomes an overwhelming struggle. The cognitive demands of the task, therefore, are relative. Moreover, as persons learn a concept, the demand may change. What was once cognitively demanding for them may at another time be undemanding. For example, some young children may, at first, find an addition fact problem such as $2 + 3 = 5$ to be difficult. However, after studying mathematics for a few months, they may have extended their knowledge so much that the answer to this math fact comes automatically to them, requiring little thinking skills. It is no longer cognitively demanding.

All learning tasks fit somewhere on those two intersecting continuums. Those that are context-embedded and cognitively undemanding will be relatively easy, requiring a minimal understanding of the language and few thinking skills, whereas those that are context-reduced and cognitively demanding will be more difficult, requiring cognitive/academic proficiency in the language and good thinking skills.

Many children are placed in learning situations in which the teacher talks a lot about abstract concepts and uses few if any contextual cues. These classrooms exist on the elementary level but are even more consistently present on the secondary level. Teachers lecture to "get the material covered." A student who does not respond correctly on exams or begins to behave inappropriately in the classroom is labeled "lazy" (Cummins, 1984), "stupid," "a clown," or "a child who doesn't make an effort." Often the possibility that the student does not understand the teacher because the communicative and cognitive demands are too great is not considered.

The most important factors in children's education are that the students are cognitively challenged and that the material being taught is comprehensible. It is important, therefore, for persons with a primary language other than English to acquire proficiency in English, for educators to be aware of the communicative and cognitive demands placed on their students, and for educational systems to provide an instructional program that maintains a cognitive challenge while making the content understandable.

Language Acquisition

Proficiency in English is important for the culturally and linguistically different child attending school in the United States. Researchers have studied the process of acquiring a second language to assist teachers in using optimal settings and appropriate methods. Because the acquisition of a first language (L_1) is similar to that of a second language (L_2), it is helpful to know the process of first language acquisiton.

Communicatively Based Context with Sufficient Input

First Language Acquisition. Children learn their first language in communicatively based settings where there is comprehensible input in sufficient amounts. First communication experiences usually take place at home in the interaction with parents. These communicative acts may be initiated by either the parent or the baby. Often newborns express their discomfort or hunger through crying or other vocalizations (Owens, 1988; Kessler, 1984). The parent responds to this message by meeting the needs of the baby. Very often the parent accompanies this physical care with gentle cooing or talking. A *conversation* between the parent and the child ensues. The children's language gradually evolves into one-word sentences, two-word sentences, and eventually into more complex structures (Clark & Clark, 1977). When children become more aware of the world around them they ask questions. Caretakers respond with explanations, simple one-word answers, or gestures such as nodding, shrugging their shoulders, or shaking their heads. As the child, the parents, and other caretakers continue to communicate in meaningful, natural settings such as the home and the neighborhood, the child acquires language (Owens, 1988). Vocabulary, syntax, intonation, rhythm, pronunciation, and appropriate use are learned not from a book or formal training but from constant use in conversation in meaningful contexts.

Krashen (1981) proposes that children acquire language by receiving input *(i)* that is just a little beyond what they are able to understand ($i + 1$). New vocabulary or structures are presented in context-embedded situations, with paralinguistic and nonlinguistic cues such as gestures, facial expressions, pictures, and objects to supplement the meaning. In the home this often takes place in informal learning situations. For example, a mother talking with her child may give the direction, "Put your socks in the drawer." Because the child may not yet know the full meaning of this direction, the mother would first model the desired behavior as she says it. She may then give a pair of socks to the child and touch the socks and the drawer as she again gives the direction. In the conversation that follows, the mother continues to clarify the meaning as necessary and the child gives her feedback on understanding the message.

Finally, this comprehensible input must be in sufficient amounts. Although researchers have not defined what is meant by *sufficient input,* it seems that children develop their primary language in communication-based situations in which they have opportunities to converse with caretakers, other adults, and peers.

Second Language Acquisition. The person acquiring English as a second language also develops language in communication-based settings that provide sufficient comprehensible input (Krashen, 1985). For the school-age child these communication-based settings include the school and the neighborhood churches, stores, and playgrounds. Home is generally not a place where the second language would be developed, because the child's primary language is usually the language of communication at home. The culturally and linguistically different child may encounter problems in developing language if neither the primary nor the second language is developed due to insufficient input in either language.

Comprehension is enhanced in the communication-based settings by use of gestures, diagrams, maps, pictures, and objects. In school the student who is limited in English may depend on these contextual clues to receive comprehensible input on the playground or in the classroom. Not only is it important that students receive comprehensible input, but it is also necessary for them to have adequate and meaningful input in the second language (Esquivel & Yoshida, 1985). Situations in which communication (i.e., interaction between two persons) is optimal will provide second language learners with sufficient input and give them experiences that are interesting to them and relevant to their daily lives. These types of opportunities may be provided for a child acquiring English as a Second Language by encouraging conversation and allowing for times of cooperative learning. Various approaches to provide this input will be discussed in a later section.

Natural Order

First Language Acquisition. First languages are acquired in a natural order that is predictable (Krashen, 1981, 1982; Owens, 1988). Children acquiring their first language progress through various stages of language development. The structural order of every language is not known, but it is assumed that children acquiring languages will proceed through the same steps as other children in their cultural group. Minor individual differences will naturally occur because of some variation due to the particular phonemic, grammatical, and cultural differences.

Second Language Acquisition. The first stages of babbling, cooing, and imitating sound are not repeated in the development of the second language, but other stages are very similar and develop as the child seems ready. Brown (1973), for example, has outlined the order of acquiring morphemes in English when it is the child's first language. Although second language acquisition of English may not occur in exactly the same order, it is similar (Dulay & Burt, 1974, 1975; Krashen, 1977).

Krashen (1981) is careful to point out that because there does seem to be this natural order of acquisition, educators may be tempted to teach the student English as a Second Language in this order. Cautioning against this strategy, Krashen emphasizes that language should not be forced artificially, but rather acquired naturally. In secondary foreign language classes instructors often teach to the natural order in their numerous and meaningless sentence drills. The teachers using this method assume that the students are all at the same level of learning. A student who happens to miss the day that one form is taught may miss out on it completely. When a language acquisition approach is used, however, structures come up repeatedly in natural conversation.

Anxiety-Free Atmosphere

First Language Acquisition. Most children learn their primary language in a nonthreatening, anxiety-free atmosphere. There is generally no pressure to acquire language because parents and other caretakers seem aware of the gradual progression of language development and easily accept the amount of time it takes. Moreover, language is acquired through conversation in meaningful contexts where the focus is not on the learning of the language but on the message given and received.

Second Language Acquisition. In his discussion of the Affective Filter Hypothesis, Krashen (1981, 1985) emphasizes the importance of affect in second language acquisition. Three components of affect influence the acquisition of language: the level of anxiety (Dulay, Burt & Krashen, 1982), the motivation for acquiring a second language (Krashen, 1982), and the amount of self-confidence and self-esteem (Krashen, 1981). First, if anxiety is at a level that the person feels incapacitated, all information received, no matter how comprehensible the input, and all possible output will be blocked (Krashen, 1981). Persons learning English as a Second Language should feel comfortable in the communication settings, whether these be at home, at school, or in the neighborhood. Pressure from peers ridiculing different pronunciation or incorrect idiom use, pressure from teachers unable to make content material covered in class comprehensible, or pressure from societal expectations for employment may add to the anxiety.

Secondly, motivation for acquiring English as a Second Language may be low. Some families have come to the United States as refugees with the hope of someday returning to their country; others want to maintain their culture and believe that the only way to do this is to maintain their primary language and not learn English (Cummins, 1981); and still others are migrant workers who know they are in the United States only temporarily. For these people and others who resist acquiring a second language, English is not important. This lack of motivation, although it may be seen more in adults, will also affect students in school. Their resistance may be interpreted as laziness or as a sign of retardation by their teachers. It is difficult to convince culturally and linguistically different exceptional students who are influenced by these attitudes and are content in their ghettoed situation that acquiring English will benefit them.

Finally, a lack of self-confidence or self-esteem will prevent students from acquiring a second language. They need to feel confident enough to take the risk of making mistakes. This factor has a strong influence on the language acquisition of the CLDE student. Often these students have already failed so much in school, there seems to be no area in which they feel confident. For optimal input to be effective, persons must have low anxiety about learning the language, strong motivation and interest, and confidence that they can learn the language. The language minority child, often affected by conditions that tend to raise the affective filter—such as poverty, quick cultural changes, and school failure—may be delayed in second language acquisition.

In conclusion, the acquisition of the second language is very similar to that of the first language (McLaughlin, 1978). They are both acquired in a communicatively based setting, should occur in a natural order, and develop best in a low-anxiety situation.

Importance of Culture in Language Acquisition

First Language Acquisition. Payne (1986) emphasizes that language, which is acquired within a cultural context, is socially conditioned. He suggests four other features of first language acquisition. First, *society teaches its young members its form of communication* (Iglesias, 1985). This is not done in a formal class where the student studies phonology (sounds), morphology (basic unit of meaning), syntax (grammar), semantics (meaning), or pragmatics (function). Neither is the language learned by watching television or listening to the radio. The child learns by listening and conversing with adults and peers in the give and take of daily living.

Second, *language is the means through which the culture is communicated* (Bilingual Education Office, 1986). For many peoples this has been an oral tradition, but as print has entered our societies, it too has been a medium for conveying concepts, history, and values.

Third, *language is an important vehicle for cultural identification and solidarity.* Cultures commonly resist change of language or dialect. This protection of one's language is presently happening in the United States. The residents of some states that have had a large increase in language minority people have declared English to be the *official* language of the state. Similarly, various cultural groups continue to encourage the use of their native languages at home and in the community to preserve their cultural identification.

Finally, *language cannot be studied properly except in its cultural context.* In recent years, a greater interest has arisen in the area of *pragmatics,* the use or function of language. How a language is used within a culture is just as important, if not more so, than the correct verb forms and pronunciation.

Brantlinger and Guskin (1985) define language as having a dual role as both a part of culture and the medium through which that culture in all its many aspects is expressed (Payne, 1986; Erickson, 1985). Children learning their own language are learning their own culture (Saville-Troike, 1986; Taylor, 1986).

Second Language Acquisition. Second language learning requires the child to learn a second culture as well (Saville-Troike, 1986). Because language is a part of culture, decisions about its use or nonuse in the classroom, neighborhood, and home will have a psychological and social effect on the child and the family (Siguan & Mackey, 1987). This effect may be positive or detrimental depending on how the language and the culture of the child are viewed by the people in the child's environment. When the language and culture are respected and their expression encouraged, the effect is generally positive. All other factors being equal, the child may have a good self-concept. If, however, value is not given to the child's cultural background or to the primary language, the effect on self-concept may be detrimental, as is often seen when an acculturation process is the means chosen to teach a second language. Because acculturation is the process of learning a second culture and language that rejects the primary culture and language, the child and the family are also rejected. This process often leaves the child feeling a part of no culture (Cummins, 1981).

Moreover, differences in language and culture can cause conflict between the home and the school (Saville-Troike, 1986; Westby & Rouse, 1985; Brantlinger & Guskin, 1985). Language use and behavior may be interpreted differently by different cultural groups. Unknowing teachers may not realize that the values they hold as exemplary may be thought of as rudeness by others. Harris (1985) describes a particular setting in which a teacher related the behavior of her students to a group of Navajo and Anglo parents. Many of the Navajo mothers tended to perceive the extremely active speech behavior of the students as discourteous, restless, self-centered, and undisciplined, whereas the majority of the Anglo mothers interpreted the same behavior as self-disciplined, exciting to observe, evidence of active learning, and advantageous to the child's development. What was appropriate for the Anglo culture was considered rude and inappropriate for the Navajo culture represented in this school. The Native American children who did not readily participate in school activities and discussions may have been penalized by the school system that seemed to picture them as standoffish, dull, or unsocial.

Educators have had to recognize the importance of the cultural background of their students as well as their language acquisition needs; the two cannot be separated. Methods of assisting students in acquiring a second language incorporate aspects of the new culture while acknowledging the value of the child's first language and culture.

Importance of Age in Second Language Acquisition

Children acquire primary language in a process that begins at birth and reaches its virtual completion at about five years of age. It is interesting to note that it is not until children enter a formal school setting, however, that *study* of language begins. During the five or six years that precede entry to school, children acquire language merely by using it. Without formalized training they have learned how to say the sounds with the correct intonation, how to put sounds together to form basic units of speech, how to put the proper prefixes and suffixes on roots to formulate words, how to put words in the correct order in a sentence and in the correct form of the word, how to make the utterance meaningful to the listener, and how to use language appropriately.

Although children acquire a second language in much the same way as they acquire their first language, the acquisition proceeds at different rates depending on the age of the person (Cummins, 1981; Krashen, Long & Scarcella, 1982). The following summarizes Krashen's (1981) findings of age difference in second language acquisition:

1. Older acquirers are faster in the early stages of second language acquisition because (a) they are better at obtaining comprehensible input (conversational management); (b) they have superior knowledge of the world, which helps to make input comprehensible; and (c) they can participate in conversation earlier, via use of first language syntax.

2. Younger acquirers tend to attain higher levels of proficiency in second languages than adults in the long run because of a lower affective filter.

In conclusion, language acquisition is influenced by the age of the person. Older persons are quicker in being able to use the language than younger persons, although the young child may have better pronunciation and facility in the long run.

Differences Between Second Language Acquisition and Learning

Proficiency in a second language can be facilitated in a variety of ways. Krashen (1981, 1982, 1985), in an attempt to understand the processes involved in the development of second language proficiency, differentiated between second language acquisition and second language learning. Second language acquisition is the process of gaining proficiency in a second language with little or no formal instruction. This process does require meaningful, natural interaction in the new language. Acquisition takes place in communication-based settings that are rich in comprehensible input. Native speakers modify their speech to aid the acquirer and use whatever contextual cues are necessary to make the message meaningful. The focus in language acquisition is on understanding the message rather than on the form of the message. Correct grammatical structure is gradually understood and used as one practices the language in actual conversations and discussions. Instead of correcting spoken or written errors, persons model correct usage while continuing to provide more input.

On the other hand, second language learning is a more formal process of gaining proficiency in another language. It is a conscious process wherein one tries to learn the grammatical structures of the new language and apply them in verbal discourse and written form. Instructors use textbooks containing prepared dialogues, practice drills, and vocabulary lists usually written in a form that is meant to teach a particular grammatical structure. Error correction occurs often for both the spoken and written assignments within a formal instructional setting. Rules are taught and practiced.

According to Krashen's Monitor Hypothesis (1981), the purpose of language learning is to monitor the use of language. To effectively monitor the learning of a second language, *the learner must have the time* to evaluate what is said in conversations and then prepare how to say something correctly in response. In most conversations this time is not available. All meaning, if there was any, is lost. In the natural flow of conversation there is no time for figuring out the correct tense of a verb or the noun-verb agreement. Secondly, *the learner must focus on form.* When the focus of the language moves from meaning to form, the prime purpose of language—the communication of a message—is overshadowed. Thirdly, *the learner must know the rules.* This is a formidable requirement, as every language has many rules. Moreover, the person learning the second language must also know all the exceptions to the rules (Krashen, 1981).

In summary, second language acquisition approaches the gaining of proficiency in a new language in a different way than second language learning. *Acquiring* a language occurs in natural, conversational settings where the emphasis is on the message communicated. *Learning* a language focuses on the understanding and use of correct grammatical structures in predesigned instructional formats.

Approaches to Second Language Acquisition and Learning

The approaches or methodologies designed to assist a person in reaching proficiency in a second language may be divided into three categories: (1) acquisition approaches, (2) learning approaches, and (3) integration of acquisition and learning approaches. These methodologies differ in terms of the level of a person's consciousness while learning grammatical rules and the types of settings in which they occur.

Acquisition Approaches

In general, the acquisition approaches parallel natural language acquisition. Sufficient comprehensible input is provided in a low-anxiety atmosphere. Terrell (1981) suggested the following to obtain comprehensible input: "(1) create a necessity for communication of some message, (2) communicate a message, and (3) modify (simplify) their speech until the students understand the message" (p. 123). Modification can include talking more slowly, articulating more clearly, increasing the volume on key words, and using exaggerated intonation accompanied by appropriate body language and movement. He further suggested having more awareness of vocabulary, using fewer idioms and less slang, and clarifying the meaning of unfamiliar terms by using paralinguistic and nonlinguistic cues.

Without a low affective filter all comprehensible input would be blocked. Terrell (1981) also suggested that the teachers create an atmosphere that is low in anxiety. "(1) The emphasis should be on the use of language in interpersonal communication, i.e., the focus is on the students and their needs and desires as individuals; (2) all attempts at language use should be accepted and encouraged without overt correction of form; and (3) no attempt should be made to force production before acquirers are ready" (p. 125).

Natural Approach. The Natural Approach (Terrell, 1981); Krashen, 1985) is an acquisition approach that follows the conditions of second language acquisition as outlined previously. Other acquisition approaches seem to integrate aspects of learning with acquisition. There are two basic principles of the Natural Approach to second language acquisition: (1) speech is not taught directly, but is acquired through sufficient comprehensible input in a low-anxiety environment; and (2) speech emerges in natural stages (Terrell, 1981).

The first principle reemphasizes the need for comprehensible input in natural settings. Both the classroom and the playground can be natural settings for language development. Although teachers may not be giving direct instruction in second language learning, communication opportunities can be provided for the student within the classroom. Lessons incorporating peer and cross-age tutoring and cooperative learning situations give students classroom time to converse in a nonthreatening way with their peers. Respect for one another's ideas and contributions is a key aspect of cooperative learning. Students are encouraged to listen, to share their thoughts about the topic being discussed or the problem being solved, and to give appropriate feedback and reinforcement. The focus is always on the message, never on the form. This technique is being used effectively in classrooms with culturally and linguistically different exceptional students. Teachers will often mix native speakers into each group so that modeling rather than error correction will occur. Moreover, the instructors have the time to go from group to group giving necessary prompts, assisting students to discover the answers with the whole group's help and to build listening and speaking skills.

The playground at school provides numerous formal and informal opportunities for children to develop a second language. When the teacher either organizes games in which English-speaking students are integrated with native language speakers or encourages this integration in informal conversational situations, the linguistically different children pick up the vocabulary and the idiomatic phrases used by the other children. They also learn what language style is appropriate in a variety of settings. Because culturally and linguistically different students often feel insecure and incompetent, the teacher plays a key role in ensuring that they are not isolated either in the classroom or on the playground.

Terrell's (1981) second principle states that this second language acquisition will occur in a natural order. If one were to separate language acquisition into stages of development there would be three main stages: (1) the Conversation/Survival Communication Stage (similar to the BICS level of language acquisition); (2) the Transition/Extended Communication Stage (transition between conversation and more cognitive/academic language); and, (3) the Cognitive/Academic Proficiency Stage (language used in academic tasks).

During the Conversation/Survival Communication Stage, a person acquiring a second language progresses naturally through three levels: preproduction, early production, and later production. During preproduction children may experience a *silent* period. Although they may not be saying anything, they will respond physically to commands (Asher, 1969) and listen intently to the sounds and rhythms of the language (Terrell, 1981). In early production children begin to use some single words (nouns and verbs) and common phrases such as "Thank you," "How are you?" "I need a . . ." These words and phrases are connected with objects and experiences that are meaningful and important to daily survival. Gradually children progress to using two words and then short sentences, while continually increasing their vocabulary. In later production fluency and confidence in conversational techniques develop.

Terrell's (1981) Natural Approach is generally concerned with gaining a BICS level of language acquisition. The Transition/Extended Communication Stage and the Cognitive/Academic Proficiency Stage of language development are not emphasized by this approach. It appears that these stages are incorporated under traditional learning situations, just as they are for the native speakers who begin formal language development as they enter school.

Affective-Humanistic Methods. In addition to Terrell's Natural Approach to second language acquisition, several other approaches emphasize discussion of affect. The students and teachers using these methods are encouraged to share personal experiences, values, feelings, opinions, interests, and fantasies. Three popular methods include Christensen's Affective Learning Activities (Christensen, 1975), Moscowitz's Humanistic Activities (Moscowitz, 1978), and Galyean's Confluent Education (Galyean, 1976). These approaches do not generally develop cognitive/academic language proficiency but focus primarily on the message being communicated and secondarily on developing basic communication skills such as listening, turn taking, and initiating and maintaining conversation.

In summary, the second language acquisition methods have been designed to encourage a BICS level of language proficiency. These form the base upon which other approaches may be used to provide the cognitive/academic level of language proficiency needed to participate effectively in academic learning situations.

Learning Approaches

Grammar-Based Approaches. In general, grammar-based approaches focus on direct instruction in language structure. For many years theoreticians insisted that using dialogue and pattern drill was the way to teach language (Krashen, 1982). In this method emphasis was placed on phonologically and syntactically correct words, phrases, and sentences. There was little importance placed on comprehensible input and meaningful communication. Many students using only this approach, which included such methods as grammar translation or audio-lingualism, did not acquire a second language (Krashen, 1985). There was a need for practitioners and theorists to work together more closely to devise theories of second language acquisition and to formulate strategies based on those theories.

Integration of Acquisition and Learning Approaches

In general, integrated approaches blend natural acquisition features with direct instruction. Schools seem to use both acquisition and learning principles in their methodologies for teaching students a second language. Each of the methodologies discussed subsequently emphasizes the learning of language as well as the natural acquisition of language through meaningful comprehensible input. They are communicative-based approaches with a primary focus on communication rather than on learning grammatical structures and rules.

Although Terrell (1981) lists the following as acquisition approaches, they are categorized in this section because they are conducted in formal situations that have as their purpose the teaching of language. These approaches include Lozanov's Suggestopedia (Bancroft, 1978; Lozanov, 1978), Curran's Community Counseling-Learning (Curran, 1976; LaForge, 1983; Stevick, 1973, 1980), Galyean's Confluent Education (Galyean, 1976, 1977), and Asher's Total Physical Response (Asher, 1977). The following section will discuss two of these approaches: Suggestopedia and Total Physical Response. Sheltered English (Northcutt & Watson, 1986), Language Experience (Van Allen & Allen, 1976), and Notional/Functional/Situations Syllabus (Van Ek, 1977; Wilkins, 1976; Matreyek, 1983a, 1987) will also be discussed.

Suggestopedia. Suggestopedia is a method not easily used in elementary and secondary schools in the United States. In Suggestopedia, a method begun in Sofia, Bulgaria, small groups of people meet for four hours a day for one month. Bancroft (1978) explains that this procedure consists of three parts: (1) review, which includes traditional conversations and games; (2) presentation of new material consisting of extensive dialogues based on situations familiar to the students; and (3) an active and a passive seance. During the active seance the teacher reads the dialogue while students follow the text and engage in deep and rhythmic Yoga breathing. The passive seance includes music that is played while the students meditate on the text. This method seems to have been successful for second language learners as they are placed in a low-anxiety situation where there is much intense comprehensible input.

Total Physical Response. Asher (1969, 1977) introduced an approach called Total Physical Response (TPR), in which the instructor gives a command that the students execute in class as a group. The teacher models the response for the students and uses whatever gestures and objects are necessary to make the message clear. Later, when confidence grows, individual students are given commands, first by the instructor and then by other students (e.g., "sit down," "touch your nose"). This method involves repetition, body movement, and sufficient practice, all of which assist in building a wide range of practical vocabulary.

Sheltered English. Another common technique used in many classrooms with limited English speakers is Sheltered English (Northcutt & Watson, 1986), a process wherein one teaches both content material for each of the subject areas (i.e., mathematics, social studies, science) and the English vocabulary or technical terminology necessary to understand the concepts being taught. Sheltered English uses props, visuals, media, and body language as clues to clarify the meanings of new words and ideas.

Researchers (Wong Fillmore & Swain, 1984) suggested that persons may acquire English as a Second Language by using this approach as long as the following conditions are present: (1) learners must be motivated to learn, (2) native speakers must be involved as models and co-learners, and (3) there must be the opportunity for native speakers and second language learners to communicate.

Within this framework, educators may focus on different components. Chamot (1985), for example, emphasizes the teaching of modified subject matter and the development of academic competence. She proposes that this is best accomplished by clarifying the vocabulary associated with each subject area, by teaching specific language functions necessary for academic communication (e.g., informing explaining, classifying, and evaluating), by differentiating the language structures and discourse features associated with various academic disciplines, and by developing language skills used in different academic functions such as listening comprehension, reading, speaking, and writing.

De Avila (1985) extended this notion further by focusing on the importance of having sufficient access to meaningful and interesting content. He suggested that many culturally and linguistically different children continue to fail because they are merely required to memorize meaningless facts that are unconnected to concepts. This type of learning is uninteresting and leads quickly to a lack of motivation and poor attitudes toward learning. De Avila encouraged teachers to design programs that provide opportunities and training for students to work cooperatively in groups. In this way they learn the social skills of communication and develop an understanding of the concepts being taught and discussed.

Wong Fillmore (1985) and O'Malley (1985) focused on the need to develop learning strategies. Within their models they suggest that modified content instruction incorporates the learning of metacognitive skills (planning, monitoring, and self-evaluation); cognitive skills (inference, grouping, imagery, auditory representation, note taking, and elaboration); and social/affective skills (peer cooperation and questioning for clarification).

Language Experience. Language Experience is a technique that uses the student's own vocabulary language patterns and background of experiences to create the reading text. Reading becomes a meaningful process for the student (Dixon & Nessel, 1983). As the teacher and student discuss the topic that the student has chosen, language is being developed. The teacher writes the dictated story that the group has created and together they read it. This approach allows the student to acquire language in an informal, real-life setting in which the student is freely interacting with fluent speakers of the target language. The cognitive demands of this approach are within the student's ability level because the reading material matches the oral language patterns already developed.

Notional/Functional/Situations Syllabus. This set of syllabi are designed to assist the English learner in understanding and using notion, function, and situation words and phrases in both their daily conversations and academic tasks. Notions refer to terms about time ("before," "since"), space ("close to," "just outside of"), classification ("sort," "kind"), comparison ("equally," "different from"), cause-effect ("due to," "consequently"), quantity ("few," "enough"), and relationship ("quickly," "rather") (Matreyek, 1983b). Functions are those ways of using language that meet the needs of a particular situation. They include such practical language uses as asking or offering help, expressing anger or impatience, and apologizing or forgiving (Matreyek, 1987). Finally, situations refer to conversation techniques that can be used to begin, continue, change, and end conversations. Some of the techniques discussed are asking about and expressing opinions, providing reflections, offering commentaries, and clearing up misunderstandings (Matreyek, 1983a).

The preceding discussion only skims the surface of the many approaches that have developed for teaching English as a second language. These approaches use the formal school situation to help students acquire English without an overemphasis on grammatical structure. Teachers provide opportunities for students to interact with native language speakers in meaningful contexts. Which of these approaches is best depends on the particular needs of the students (Dulay & Burt, 1980).

Second Language Acquisition Suggestions for Culturally and Linguistically Different Exceptional Students

Based on the foregoing discussion of first language acquisition and second language learning, a number of suggestions can be made for facilitating English as a second language in CLDE students. These suggestions will enable sequential development of BICS and CALP, moving children to function under conditions from low to high cognitive demand. Suggestions also emphasize instruction that parallels natural acquisition processes.

- *Provide sufficient comprehensible input* (Krashen, 1982). Teachers can use any of the communicative-based approaches that appeal to them and to their students to provide enough comprehensible input in the school and on the playground.
- *Provide simplified input* (Krashen, 1982). Persons speaking with those acquiring a second language can speak more slowly and clearly, using less slang, fewer idioms, and shorter sentences.
- *Focus on comprehension and communication* (Krashen, 1982; Seymour, 1986; Cummins, 1984). The importance of language lies in communication. This requires that both the input and the output be understood and meaningful. Context-embedded, cognitively demanding tasks within the student's abilities seem to be the most challenging and beneficial combination (Cummins, 1984).
- *Provide nonlinguistic means of encouraging comprehension* (Krashen, 1982). Gestures, pictures, audiovisual materials, and facial expressions are all helpful in providing an environment conducive to understanding verbalized or written language.
- *Take advantage of the world around the person acquiring a second language* (Krashen, 1982; Dukes, 1981). By using the materials and events within the child's own experience, the child will better be able to comprehend messages communicated in a second language.
- *Provide frequent comprehension checks* (Krashen, 1982). An adult can check for comprehension by asking questions. In the beginning yes/no questions that require little response are easier and present no threat to the student. Later, more difficult questions such as "Why?" may be asked. These would require more complex answers and a greater feeling of self-confidence.
- *Adults provide language models for the students* (Heath, 1986). Institutions such as schools, churches, scouts, and youth groups can provide both adult and peer language models for the person acquiring a second language. Modeling occurs naturally when persons are working on joint tasks such as making things, entertaining others, and preparing materials (Rivers, 1987b).

- *Do not restrict use of first language by second language students* (California State Department of Education, 1984). The student acquiring a second language will sometimes incorporate the first language into the conversation. This may be due to several reasons, including insufficient vocabulary in the second language.
- *Create motivational situations* (California State Department of Education, 1984). A student is more easily motivated when language situations and forms are drawn from the student's current needs, desires, and interests; when language is practiced in the context of real-life situations; and when lessons incorporate real needs to communicate information, feelings, desires, and opinions.
- *Be flexible with approaches in second language acquisition* (Rivers, 1987b). Teachers need to be familiar with the various methods of assisting a person in acquiring a second language. Then, with a repertoire of methodologies and materials, teachers can choose what is best for their students.
- *Encourage students to expand appropriate responses* (Westby & Rouse, 1985). After teachers acknowledge incorrect or incomplete responses made by students or accept and praise correct responses, they then request further information from the students.
- *Do not do error correction* (Krashen, 1982). Error correction places the focus on grammatical and phonetical structures instead of on communication. The more students engage in conversation with good language models, the more they are likely subconsciously to incorporate those rules into their language.
- *Provide tools to help students obtain more input* (Krashen, 1982). Krashen (1982) suggests that students need to learn the skills of how to start, maintain, and end conversations; how to ask native speakers for help in the conversation; how to let the native speaker know the conversation is understood (head nods, "uh-huh"); and how to change the subject.
- *Develop metacognitive skills* (Wong, 1982). The language learning disabled child from a language minority group often lacks the metacognitive skills necessary to participate in the daily academic tasks required in American schools (Wong, 1982). To develop the skills, the teacher needs to help the student (1) determine what the task is, (2) reflect on what the child knows or needs to know to do the task, (3) devise a plan for dealing with the task, (4) monitor progress, and (5) evaluate the outcome (Wong, 1982).
- *Encourage peer conversation* (Westby & Rouse, 1985; Muma & Pierce, 1981; Saville-Troike, 1984; Rivers, 1987a). Peer conversation can occur in whole- or small-group discussions. This is a technique often employed by those using cooperative learning methods.
- *Maintain on-target behavior* (Westby & Rouse, 1985). An important area of second language acquisition is learning how to use language in particular situations. Chaining (stringing related sentences together) in conversations and in group discussions is one of those skills. A teacher can assist a student with this skill by redirecting the student to the topic.
- *Have a combination of high-context activities and low-context activities* (Westby & Rouse, 1985; Rivers, 1987a; Cummins, 1984). Language development occurs as one uses manipulative materials and objects in coordination with oral and written language. These activities would include such tasks as making cookies from a recipe and talking about the calendar, weather, and events of the day.

- *Have a family member help with low-context activities at home* (Westby & Rouse, 1985; Muma & Pierce, 1981; Linares, 1983). Family members can read a library book with the student. Teachers can teach family members how to ask appropriate questions and how to talk about the story with the student as they read together. If the family members cannot read, pictures and events can be discussed.
- *Guide the students through reading and writing skills* (Krashen, 1984). Students learning to read and to write in a second language will need the same kinds of skills that first language learners need. This follows from Cummins's (1984) theory of common underlying proficiency: whatever one learns in one language can be transferred to a second language.
- *Provide culturally and linguistically valid therapy* (Taylor, 1986a; Linares, 1983; Saville-Troike, 1986; Westby & Rouse, 1985). Treatment must be in the context of the values, attitudes, and wishes of the indigenous culture relative to communicative disorders and what to do about them.
- *Use preferred learning style and social interaction* (Taylor, 1986b; Johnson, 1981). Take into consideration the preferred learning style and the rules of social and communicative interaction as defined by the student's indigenous cultural or linguistic group.
- *Provide an affective, low-anxiety climate* (Taenzer, Cermak, & Hanlon, 1981). Provide a low-anxiety environment that is warm, caring, and accepting.

Summary

The planning and implementation of appropriate educational programs for linguistically different exceptional students requires that teachers (1) understand the nature of language and communication processes, (2) understand first and second language acquisition processes, (3) know the cognitive and language demands of their classroom, (4) know various approaches to second language learning and acquisition, and (5) be able to apply the principles of these approaches in their classrooms.

Children acquire their first language in natural settings where there is sufficient comprehensible input. Although a second language might be acquired best in a similar atmosphere, many culturally and linguistically different children learn their second language in a limited number of settings. For some children, the classroom is one of the few settings where the second language is heard and spoken. Aware of the need to provide meaningful and comprehensible input, educators and researchers have developed various approaches to learning a second language. Teachers of culturally and linguistically different exceptional children must choose methods most appropriate to the needs of their students.

Discussion Questions

1. How is first language acquisition similar to second language learning?
2. What suggestions can you make to a regular education teacher who has a CLDE child mainstreamed into the class?
3. What criteria would you use to ascertain the *best* approach to second language learning for a special day class of learning handicapped students who represent various cultural and language groups?
4. What could you do to get the parents of a CLDE student involved in a home program? Outline a possible plan of language development.
5. What information would you include when giving a half-hour presentation to regular education teachers about the needs of CLDE students?
6. You are a principal of an elementary or secondary school. What steps can you take to assist your teachers in working with CLDE students?

7. Your school board is concerned about the heavy dropout rate of language minority students. Prepare a presentation suggesting steps the school or school district might take to meet the needs of culturally and linguistically different students.

References

Asher, J. J. (1969). The total physical approach to second language learning. *Modern Language Journal.* 8(1):3–18.

Asher, J. J. (1977). *Learning another language through actions: The complete teacher's guide.* Los Gatos, CA: Sky Oaks Productions.

Bancroft, W. J. (1978). The Lozanov method and its American adaptations. *Modern Language Journal.* 62(4):167–175.

Bilingual Education Office, California State Department of Education. (1986). *Beyond language: Social and cultural factors in schooling language minority students.* Los Angeles: Evaluation, Dissemination and Assessment Center, California State University.

Brantlinger, E. A. & Guskin, S. L. (1985). Implications of social and cultural differences for special education with specific recommendations. *Focus on Exceptional Children.* 18(1):1–12.

Brown, R. (1973). *A first language.* Cambridge, MA: Harvard University Press.

California State Department of Education. (1984). *Individual learning programs for limited-English-proficient students: A handbook for school personnel.* Sacramento, CA: Author.

California State Department of Education, Office of Bilingual Bicultural Education (1981). *Schooling and language minority students: A theoretical framework.* Los Angeles: Evaluation, Dissemination, and Assessment Center, California State University.

Chamot, A. U. (1985). English language development through a content-based approach. In *Proceedings of the Information Exchange co-sponsored by the National Clearinghouse for Bilingual Education and the Georgetown University Bilingual Education Service Center* (pp. 49–56). Rosslyn, VA: National Clearinghouse for Bilingual Education.

Christensen, C. B. (1975). Affective learning activities. *Foreign Language Annals.* 8(3):211–219.

Clark, H. H., & Clark, E. V. (1977). *Psychology and language: An introduction to psycholinguistics.* San Diego: Harcourt Brace Jovanovich.

Cummins, J. (1979). Linguistic interdependence and the educational development of bilingual children. *Review of Educational Research.* 49(2):222–251.

Cummins, J. (1981). The role of primary language development in promoting educational success for language minority students. In *Schooling and language minority students: A theoretical framework.* Los Angeles: Evaluation, Dissemination and Assessment Center, California State University.

Cummins, J. (1984). *Bilingualism and special education: Issues in assessment and pedagogy.* San Diego: College-Hill Press.

Curran, C. A. (1976). *Counseling-learning in second languages.* Apple River, Illinois: Apple River Press.

De Avila, E. (1985). Motivation, intelligence, and access: A theoretical framework for the education of minority language students. In *Proceedings of the Information Exchange co-sponsored by the National Clearinghouse for Bilingual Education and the Georgetown University Bilingual Education Service Center* (pp. 21–32). Rosslyn, VA: national Clearinghouse for Bilingual Education.

Dixon, C. N., & Nessel, D. (1983). *Language experience approach to reading (and writing): Language experience reading for second language learners.* Hayward, CA: Alemany Press.

Dukes, P. J. (1981). Developing social prerequisites to oral communication. *Topics in Learning & Learning Disabilities.* 1(2):47–58.

Dulay, H., & Burt, M. (1974). Natural sequences in child second language acquisition. *Language Learning.* 24(1):37–53.

Dulay, H., & Burt, M. (1975). A new approach to discovering universal strategies of child second-language acquisition. In D. Dato (Ed.), *Developmental psycholinguistics: Theory and applica-*

tions. Washington, DC: Georgetown University Press.

Dulay, H., & Burt, M. (1980). The relative proficiency of limited English proficient students. *NABE Journal.* 4(3):1–23.

Dulay, H., Burt, M., & Krashen, S. (1982). *Language two.* New York: Oxford University Press.

Erickson, J. G. (1985). How many languages do you speak? An overview of bilingual education. *Topics in Language Disorders.* 5(4):1–14.

Esquivel, G. B., & Yoshida, R. K. (1985). Special education for language minority students. *Focus on Exceptional Children.* 18(3):1–8.

Galyean, B. (1976). Humanistic education: A mosaic just begun. In G. A. Jarvis (Ed.), *Perspective: A new freedom.* ACTFL Foreign Language Education Series, Vol. 7. Lincolnwood, IL: National Textbook.

Galyean, B. (1977). A confluent design for language teaching. *TESOL Quarterly.* 11:143–156.

Harris, G. A. (1985). Considerations in assessing English language performance of Native American children. *Topics in Language Disorders.* 5(4): 42–52.

Heath, S. B. (1986). Sociocultural contexts of language development. In Bilingual Education Office, *Beyond language: Social and cultural factors in schooling language minority students* (pp. 143–186). Los Angeles: Evaluation, Dissemination and Assessment Center, California State University.

Iglesias, A. (1985). Communication in the home and classroom: Match or mismatch. *Topics in Language Disorders.* 5(4):29–41.

Johnson, D. J. (1981). Factors to consider in programming for children with language disorders. *Topics in Learning & Learning Disabilities.* 1(2):13–28.

Kessler, C. (1984). *Language acquisition processes in bilingual children.* Los Angeles: Evaluation, Dissemination and Assessment Center, California State University.

Krashen, S. D. (1981). Bilingual education and second language acquisition theory. In *Schooling and language minority students: A theoretical framework* (pp. 51–82). Los Angeles: Evaluation, Dissemination and Assessment Center, California State University.

Krashen, S. D. (1977). Some issues relating to the Monitor Model. In H. D. Brown, C. Yorio, & R. Crymes (Eds.), *On TESOL '77: Teaching and learning English as a second language: Trends in research and practice* (pp. 144–158). Washington: TESOL.

Krashen, S. D. (1982). *Principles and practice in second language acquisition.* New York: Pergamon.

Krashen, S. D. (1985). *Inquiries and insights: Second language teaching: Immersion and bilingual education: Literacy.* Hayward, CA: Janus.

Krashen, S. D., Long, M. H., & Scarcella, R. C. (1982). Age, rate, and eventual attainment in second language acquisition. In S. D. Krashen, R C. Scarcella, & M. H. Long (Eds.). *Child-adult differences in second language acquisition* (pp. 161–172). Rowley, MA: Newbury House.

La Forge, P. G. (1983). *Counseling and culture in second language acquisition.* Elmsford, NY: Pergamon.

Linares, N. (1983). Management of communicatively handicapped Hispanic American children. In D. R. Omark & J. G. Erickson (Eds.), *The bilingual exceptional child* (pp. 145–162). San Diego: College-Hill Press.

Lozanov, G. (1978). *Suggestology and outlines of suggestopedy.* New York: Gordon and Breach.

Maldonado-Colon, E. (1984, May). Serving the limited- and non-limited English speakers in programs for the speech/language handicapped: Implications for personnel. In *Workshop on communicative disorders and language proficiency: Assessment, intervention, and curriculum implementation,* Los Alamitos, CA.

Matreyek, W. (1983a). *Communicating in English: Examples and models: Notions.* New York: Pergamon.

Matreyek, W. (1983b). *Communicating in English: Examples and models: Situations.* New York: Pergamon.

Matreyek, W. (1987). *Communicating in English: Examples and models: Functions.* Englewood Cliffs, NJ: Prentice-Hall.

McLaughlin, B. (1978). *Second language acquisition in childhood.* Hillsdale, NJ: Lawrence Erlbaum Associates.

Moskowitz, B. A. (1978). The acquisition of language. *Scientific American.* 239:92–108.

Muma, J. R. & Pierce, S. (1981). Language intervention data or evidence. *Topics in Learning Disabilities.* 1(2):1–11.

Naremore, R. C. (1985). Explorations of language use: Pragmatic mapping in L_1 and L_2. *Topics in Language Disorders.* 5(4):66–79.

Northcutt, L., & Watson, D. (1986). *Sheltered English teaching handbook.* Carlsbad, CA: Northcutt, Watson, Gonzales.

Oller, J. W. (1983). Testing proficiencies and diagnosing language disorders in bilingual children. In D. R. Omark & J. G. Erickson (Eds.), *The bilingual exceptional child* (pp. 78–88). San Diego: College-Hill Press.

O'Malley, J. M. (1985). Learning strategy applications to content instruction in second language development. In *Proceedings of the Information Exchange co-sponsored by the National Clearinghouse for Bilingual Education and the Georgetown University Bilingual Education Service Center* (pp. 69–76). Rosslyn, VA: National Clearinghouse for Bilingual Education.

Owens, R. E. (1988). *Language development: An introduction.* 2nd ed. Columbus, OH: Merrill Publishing Company.

Pacheco, R. (1983). Bilingual mentally retarded children: Language confusion or real deficits? In D. R. Omark & J. G. Erickson (Eds.), *The bilingual exceptional child* (pp. 233–253). San Diego: College-Hill Press.

Payne, K. T. (1986). Cultural and linguistic groups in the United States. In O. L. Taylor (Ed.), *Nature of communication disorders in culturally and linguistically diverse populations* (pp. 19–46). San Diego: College-Hill Press.

Rivers, W. M. (1987a). Interaction as the key to teaching language for communication. In W. M. Rivers (Ed.), *Interactive language teaching* (pp. 3–16). Cambridge: Cambridge University Press.

Rivers, W. M. (Ed.). (1987b). *Interactive language teaching. Cambridge: Cambridge University Press.*

Saville-Troike, M. (1984). *What really matters in second language learning for academic achievement?* Forum lecture, TESOL Summer Institute, Toronto.

Saville-Troike, M. (1986). Anthropological considerations in the study of communication. In O. L. Taylor (Ed.), *Nature of communication disorders in culturally and linguistically diverse populations* (pp. 47–72). San Diego: College-Hill Press.

Seymour, H. N. (1986). Clinical principles for language intervention among nonstandard speakers of English. In O. L. Taylor (Ed.), *Treatment of communication disorders in culturally and linguistically diverse populations* (pp. 115–134). San Diego: College-Hill Press.

Siguan, M., & Mackey, W. F. (1987). *Education and bilingualism.* London: Kogan Page.

Stevick, E. W. (1973). Review of Curran 1972. *Language Learning.* 23:259–271.

Stevick, E. W. (1980). *Teaching languages: A way and ways.* Rowley, MA: Newbury House.

Taenzer, S. F., Cermak, C., & Hanlon, R. C. (1981). Outside the therapy room: A naturalistic approach to language intervention. *Topics in Learning & Learning Disabilities.* 1(2):41–46.

Taylor O. L. (1986a). Historical perspectives and conceptual framework. In O. L. Taylor (Ed.), *Nature of communication disorders in culturally and linguistically diverse populations* (pp. 1–17). San Diego: College-Hill Press.

Taylor, O. L. (Ed.) (1986b). *Treatment of communication disorders in culturally and linguistically diverse populations.* San Diego: College-Hill Press.

Terrell, T. D. (1981). The natural approach in bilingual education. In *Schooling and language minority students: A theoretical framework* (pp. 117–146). Los Angeles: Evaluation, Dissemination and Assessment Center, California State University.

Van Allen, R., & Allen, C. (1976). *Language experience activities.* Boston: Houghton Mifflin.

Van Ek, J. A. (1977). *The threshold level for modern language learning in schools.* London: Council of Europe, Longman.

Westby, C. E., & Rouse, G. R. (1985). Culture in education and the instruction of language learning-disabled students. *Topics in Language Disorders.* 5(4):29–41.

Wilkins, D. A. (1976). *Notional syllabuses.* Oxford: Oxford University Press.

Wong, B. L. (Ed.) (1982). Metacognition and learning disabilities. *Topics in Learning & Learning Disabilities.* 1(2):vii.

Wong Fillmore, L. (1985). Second language learning in children: A proposed model. In *Proceedings of the Information Exchange co-sponsored by the National Clearinghouse for Bilingual Education and the Georgetown University Bilingual Education Service Center* (pp. 33–44). Rosslyn, VA: National Clearinghouse for bilingual Education.

Wong Fillmore, L., & Swain, M. (1984, March). Child second language development: Views from the field on theory and research. Paper presented at the TESOL Conference, Houston TX.

CHAPTER SEVEN

Language Assessment for the Bilingual Exceptional Child

Rose M. Payan

- Determining Language Proficiency
- Language Screening
- Background and Problematic Issues Related to Language Screening
- Language Background Questionnaire
- In-Depth Speech and Language Assessment
- Definition of Speech and Language Disorders
- Criteria for Selecting Standardized Tests
- Testing the LEP Student in English
- A Language Assessment Procedure
- Language Assessment Tests
- Summary

Objectives

- To stress the importance of language assessment with LEP exceptional children
- To show the distinction between language dominance and language proficiency
- To define and explain the process for language screening
- To discuss problem areas associated with language screening
- To explain procedures for determining the home language profile
- To review and explain the process of in-depth language assessment
- To review definitions of speech and language disorders
- To establish criteria for selective standardized tests
- To describe procedures for testing the LEP student in English

The analysis of linguistic abilities is implicit in the proper assessment of the limited English proficient (LEP) exceptional child. If sound educational decisions are to be made regarding this particular student's eligibility for special education programs, a formal assessment of both primary language capabilities and English language abilities must be obtained. A comprehensive assessment process assists the practitioner in determining the student's primary instructional need. The objective of this assessment is the identification of the student's cognitive, linguistic, physical, and social abilities to ensure a meaningful and appropriate educational plan. This plan should allow for instruction that assists in the mastery of basic concepts and skills on which future learning is based. Special instruction for the LEP child is matched to the specific area of need and presented in the language the child understands best, while providing for the learning of English (Cummins, 1984).

The first and perhaps most critical step in the assessment process is the initial screening of the child's language abilities in English and in the primary language to determine which language should be used for assessment (Mattes & Omark, 1984). The practitioner must decide if a comprehensive assessment will be performed in English or the primary language. This initial screening does not replace, although it contributes to, the more in-depth language assessment included in a comprehensive assessment.

Once language screening has been completed, the next step in the language assessment process is the in-depth evaluation of the student's entire range of communicative abilities. The assessment of speech and language helps to evaluate the child's receptive and expressive command of the particular elements of language and their use in discourse. Speech and language evaluations are essential to identify or eliminate suspected communication disorders. For the limited English proficient child, it is important that the speech and language evaluation be completed in the language the child is most exposed to and understands best (Mattes & Omark, 1984).

The third component of the linguistic assessment of the LEP student is the evaluation of the child's linguistic abilities in English. Society expects children eventually to function in English; therefore the assessment of abilities in English provides information in determining the type and nature of English instruction.However, English instruction would not replace instruction in the native language that is appropriate to the bilingual handicapped child's primary instructional need.

This chapter outlines and discusses the steps to language screening and the terms associated with language screening, such as *language dominance* and *language proficiency*. Elements of a comprehensive speech and language evaluation are presented.

Determining Language Proficiency

Determining the student's language proficiency in English and in the native language is essential for assessment. This information will assist the practitioner in deciding the language in which further assessments are made. These assessments include psychological, linguistic, and socioemotional evaluations and collection of preliminary information on the student's language background and communicative competencies. In determining language proficiency, it is essential to first understand the term and how it relates to assessment (Miller, 1984).

The term *language proficiency* refers to the degree to which the student exhibits control over the use of language, including the measurement of *expressive* and *receptive* language skills in the areas of phonology, syntax, vocabulary, and semantics and including the area of pragmatics or language use within various domains or social circumstances. Proficiency in a language is judged independently and does not imply a lack of proficiency in another language (Burt, Dulay, & McKeon, 1980).

The measurement of language proficiency differs from the measurement of *language dominance*. Language dominance assessment refers to the measurement of the degree of bilingualism, which implies a comparison of the proficiencies in two or more languages (Burt, Dulay, & McKeon, 1980). This comparison provides an indication of the individual's bilingual abilities and identifies the stronger language. Thus the dominant language is reflected in the higher of two proficiency scores (Bernal & Tucker, 1981).

However, this estimate of dominance is suspect because it may be influenced by the social environment, the instrument used in measurement, the criteria used to compare proficiency information, and the social context in which the language assessment was made. Language dominance means that when performance in two languages is compared, proficiency will be higher in one language than the other. Some students will exhibit equal levels of proficiency in both languages and these levels will be equally low, as may be the case of a student with suspected language disabilities (i.e., language delay in the native language). This condition may also be a function of inherent psychometric limitations of the test (Bernal & Tucker, 1981).

A third term commonly associated with language screening is *language preference*. Language preference is the individual's preferred language without regard to proficiency in that language. A distinction between language preference and its effects on measured language proficiency is not usually included in the screening process, nor have procedures for making these judgments been developed. Observing the student's interaction with peers, siblings, and parents gives the practitioner clues to the student's preferred language use for certain functions of language. Perhaps this preference may have been hampered by the testing situation (Miller, 1984; Mattes & Omark, 1984).

Language proficiency is best assessed by instruments that evaluate proficiency through a wide variety of language skills and rank performance and classify students by linguistic categories. It is important not to make judgments on proficiency based on the individual's performance in one linguistic skill (for example, vocabulary comprehension or the comprehension of antonyms). Proficiency measures should be selected to test the range of the student's receptive and expressive skills, for the soundness of its psychometric qualities, and for the utility of scores for making judgments on the language best used in assessment.

The minority student's language proficiency in English may have been determined before referral for a special education evaluation. The practitioner should obtain test results and determine just how the level of proficiency was obtained. Was the instrument used designed specifically for proficiency assessment? What were the modes of responses required by the child? What language skills were assessed? Who performed the assessment and when? Has the student's language proficiency been reevaluated? The practitioner should obtain the level of proficiency in the native language if the information is not available. To form a more objective and useful understanding of proficiency in both languaged, a reassessment may be required and advisable for the practitioner.

Before the 1960s, language testing focused on testing discrete surface elements of speech production (phonology, morphology, syntax). The approaches then taken with testing language may have been consistent with the body of knowledge and definition of language at that time. Since then, however, increased research and knowledge about the construct of language and the meaning of language proficiency have led to an emergence of a broader perspective of language. More integrative perspectives about language have been pursued in the 1970s and 1980s (Oller & Perkins, 1980).

The notion of what constitutes language proficiency can be viewed from a variety of perspectives. On one extreme are researches that have postulated a global language proficiency (Oller, 1978) that underlies all language abilities.

Oller (1978) contended that language proficiency could not be defined in discrete elements but rather must be conceptualized and assessed holistically. Other researchers (Berko, 1958; Leopold, 1949) have viewed language proficiency as composed of discrete constituent elements that can be individually defined and evaluated. Proficiency in speech aspects of language related to the specific language's phonology, syntax, and lexical and semantic systems have been a focus of much research in this area in the past. Comparisons of linguistic features between languages have received primary attention under these models. Today most language specialists acknowledge and include both the discrete point and more holistic integrative definition in the discussion of language (Adolph, 1988).

Cummins (1980) has focused his research on language proficiency into two basic theoretical constructs. He distinguishes Basic Interpersonal Communicative Skills (BICS), which includes face-to-face communication in daily discourse situations, from Cognitive/Academic Language Proficiency (CALP), which he defines as language proficiency used in the development of literacy skills in the first (L_1) and second languages (L_2). Cummins's work suggests that it may take one to two years for an individual to become proficient in a language in BICS, but that development of CALP may take as long as seven years.

In 1981 Cummins proposed his Threshold Hypothesis and the Development Interdependence Hypothesis as he investigated the development of CALP in bilingual populations. Briefly summarized, the Threshold Hypothesis stated that the development of cognitive and academic processes in bilingual learning is a function of the level of language competence demonstrated by the individual in both languages.

Where a minimal threshold level exists in L_1, normal cognitive development would result. Where the threshold level exceeded minimal levels, an accelerated cognitive development was found. However, in studies involving subtractive bilingual approaches where L_1 is immediately replaced by L_2 as the child enters school, and where L_1 does not attain the minimal threshold, both cognitive development and acquisition of L_2 are adversely affected.

Cummins's Development Interdependence Hypothesis postulates that the level of L_2 competence that a bilingual child attains is a function of the level of the child's L_1 competencies at the time when L_2 development resulting from intensive exposure to L_2 occurs without a loss of L_1 competence. As one relates oral language proficiencies of CALP to reading and written language in both L_1 and L_2, the question of how to evaluate these processes arises.

The development of tests designed to assess language proficiency in bilingual populations has been heavily skewed to the development of instruments that assess oral language linguistic features. Phonology, morphology, syntax, and lexicon are the primary skills assessed by the Language Assessment Scale (LAS), Bilingual Syntax Measure (BSM), and Bilingual Inventory of Natural Language (BINL), the three most commonly used measures of language proficiency in the United States (Wald, 1981). Each of these tests focuses on different oral language features. Thus, determination of language proficiency becomes a function of each of the test's specific forms.

A study conducted by Gillmore and Dickenson (1979) found little comparability between the LAS, BMS, and BINL. It is not surprising, then, because of the different criterion focus of each test, that judgments regarding the determination of proficiency varies as a function of the specific test used.

The Woodcock Language Proficiency Battery (WLPB) is a test that goes beyond the measurement of oral language. It also measures academic language (reading and writing). A recent study by Adolph (1988) found that the WLPB distinguishes handicapped from nonhandicapped LEP Hispanic students.

Another test that measures academic language proficiency has recently been published by CTB/McGraw Hill (1988). This test is called the Language Assessment Scales Reading/Writing (LASR/W). This test was developed by Duncan and De Avila, who are also the developers of the original Language Assessment Scales. The new test is available in two alternate forms and may be used for students in grades second through ninth. The LASR/W includes multiple choice assessment of vocabulary, language fluency, reading comprehension, mechanics, and usage. The LASR/W is designed as a screening device to produce placement and reclassification information for language minority students. It may be used as a pre- and post-test for determining entry and exit information. The test was developed on a sample of 4,000 Hispanic, Asian, Native American, Anglo American, and Pacific Island students in more than 15 cities across the United States. A new scoring procedure has been developed using the results of both the LAS and the LASR/W. This procedure yields a language proficiency index (LPI), which provides a method for distinguishing among students who are limited English proficient. This ability to better differentiate between types of LEP students will allow for better planning and instruction (Duncan, 1988).

Once the student's language proficiency has been determined, the practitioner should have the information necessary to identify the appropriate language for assessment and further instruction. Some proficiency measures provide clearer criteria by which to make these determinations than other measures. The absence or presence of this type of information in the technical manual should be considered when selecting a proficiency measure.

Language Screening

Language screening, in this context, refers to the initial identification of the child's overall linguistic abilities in English and in the primary language. The purpose of this evaluation is to identify those children best assessed in their primary language, because it cannot be assumed that the language minority child would be able to understand and speak enough English to comprehend test directions and stimuli presented in English. The child's home language and a general indication of language proficiency in English and in the primary language may be obtained through the language screening process. The term *language screening* and the process outlined in this chapter differ from the type of language screening routinely performed by speech and language clinicians to identify students suspected of having speech and language disorders. The recommended language screening process does not solely determine eligibility for special education programs but assists in establishing the language in which the child is best equipped to function.

Background and Problematic Issues Related to Language Screening

The need to establish the language minority student's ability in English and in the primary language was given great impetus through the increase of federal- and state-funded bilingual education programs. The Supreme Court decision in *Lau v. Nichols,* (1974) mandated meaningful education to limited and non-English-speaking students. Procedures for providing meaningful educational opportunities were developed by the U.S. Office for Civil Rights and called for the identification of students whose home language differed from English and the classification of students on the basis of language skills (Office for Civil Rights, 1975).

Consequently, LEP students who could not benefit from instruction in English had to be identified. This requirement for student selection to Bilingual Education programs led to the development of numerous methods for language screening. Although this area of assessment within the Bilingual Education arena is still in an embryonic stage, some techniques and instruments have direct application to the assessment of the LEP exceptional children and are the only resources for objectively and systematically evaluating the performance of these students.

Problematic issues surrounding the language screening process occur because of the lack of clarity regarding the purpose and expected outcomes of the process; the lack of understanding by special education practitioners regarding the heterogeneity of the population, specifically the Hispanic population; and the questions surrounding the psychometric properties of existing measures and the contribution of test results identifying students for special education programs. Identification and placement decisions cannot be based solely on the information obtained through the initial language screening process.

The intent of this process is to identify the language of the home and to obtain an estimate of language capabilities in English and in the native language. When this is done, particular attention should be given to social status and social language use. LEP and Bilingual Special Education (BSE) students may be hindered in their learning because of complex reasons that stem from inabilities other than their command of English. Learning problems may stem from sensorimotor delays, auditory-vocal processing, visual-perception difficulties, and/or noncognitive behaviors (Thonis, 1981). Therefore an attempt to identify student performance of these skills must be made in addition to language screening.

It is erroneous to assume that the linguistic abilities of Hispanic students are homogeneous. It is also wrong to assume that there is no dialectical variation in different parts of the United States. The heterogeneity existing in linguistic ability among Hispanic students is expansive. It cannot be assumed that a Hispanic student is bilingual or monolingual or that Spanish is understood or spoken, irrespective of surname. It is also erroneous to assume that these children all use the same variety of English. The formal screening process describes the linguistic characteristics of the population. The degree to which students exhibit nativelike control in two languages within the various demands and references of each language and in defined social domains may yield extensive classification of distinct linguistic abilities. It is essential to differentiate among (1) students who are of limited English proficiency and (2) students who demonstrate a high proficiency in their native language from (3) LEP students who are also limited in the native language and from (4) students who exhibit a high proficiency in both languages.

The measures and procedures used in making these determinations have been questioned. An array of measures purporting to identify a degree of linguistic competence have been based on the assessment of a single aspect of language and do not include an assessment of receptive and expressive language performance skills, nor do they give an estimate of communicative competency (Garcia & Acosta, 1980). Criticism has also been voiced concerning the measures that do provide a level of proficiency through an assessment of an array of linguistic skills. The concerns surround the validity of the instruments when the student's relative linguistic standing was compared to external criteria. The question of whether the obtained ranking by proficiency instruments truly represents the student's communicative competence in the academic classroom setting has not yet been solved. Irrespective of criticism, the use of language proficiency measures is defensible because of the need to make educational decisions that are not based totally on subjective judgment and because alternative measures are not available. Decisions concerning language proficiency should be made using instruments that assess a wide array of skills and measure language proficiency rather than language dominance (Mattes & Omark, 1984).

The linguistic evaluation of language minority students should include an understanding of the student's linguistic environment—language usage, including the direct measurement of linguistic skills in both languages. The evaluation should consider the pragmatic level of the student's language. Because of the various kinds of information required to make informed judgments about a student's linguistic abilities, three types of measures have emerged for assessing linguistic skills. Direct, indirect, or a combination of these two types of assessments are used depending upon what information is sought by the practitioner.

Direct measures refer to an objective assessment of performance in one or more of the four linguistic skills of listening, speaking, reading, or writing and across one or more linguistic levels of phonology, lexicon, morphology, and syntax (De Avila & Duncan, 1980; Garcia & Acosta, 1980). Language proficiency is evaluated by direct measures, while indirect measures are used to assess language usage and to obtain information on language background. Indirect measures are valuable because they afford the opportunity of sampling the child's natural language in a variety of contexts.

Language Background Questionnaire

The language background questionnaire is an indirect measure to determine which languages are used in the child's home environment, by whom they are used, for what purposes, and with what frequency. This information is surveyed through the use of self-report questionnaires: rating scales based on knowledge of the child or on an interview with the child's family or through questionnaires completed by a member of the child's family (De Avila & Duncan, 1980). Judgment about the child's command of either English or about the primary language cannot be made exclusively from information provided by language background questionnaires because the accuracy of such procedures is speculative. Self-report questionnaires and parent ratings are subject to social acceptance, and teacher ratings depend on the teacher's own linguistic background and familiarity with the child. The types of questions commonly presented in language background questionnaires will not directly identify the language the child commands readily but will describe the child's linguistic environment, the amount of language input received, and impressions of the child's communicative abilities.

The identification of the *home language* will supplement information on the student's language usage but will not determine language proficiency. It may be possible for the student to exhibit greater proficiency in English than in the home language (Ramirez & Politzer, 1976). (See the Language Background Questionnaire, pp. 142–143).

In-Depth Speech and Language Assessment

An in-depth assessment of a student's speech and language abilities is an integral part of a thorough special education evaluation. The purpose of this assessment describes the student's communicative abilities to determine if communication disorders exist and to recommend strategies and activities for remediation. The in-depth speech and language assessment for LEP students should be conducted in the language understood best. A child with a language disorder may not demonstrate a high degree of proficiency in either the native or English language. The speech and language assessment for LEP students is critical because the detailed information on which to base judgments of language difference or disorder will be acquired through this assessment. The valid speech and language assessment of LEP students may be hampered by lack of trained personnel who can perform this assessment in a language other than English, by lack of resources, or by unfamiliarity with valid and reliable instruments or procedures developed for non-English speakers.

Although language tests are available in some languages, the application of these instruments may not result in an accurate assessment. Speech and language assessments for LEP students are often conducted through informal testing procedures by clinicians who are not skilled in a language other than English. Some clinicians prefer the use of informal procedures over the use of formal tests with nonminority students, because standardized tests provide normative data based on a sample of limited responses (Hewett, 1977). This preference, however, offers greater informality in the assessment of LEP students because the clinician must depend on the impressions of an interpreter or bilingual personnel not skilled in the area of speech and language diagnosis. Yet other clinicians will use standardized instruments because they can be administered quickly and provide normative data for performance comparisons. Even when the most or least appropriate procedures are used, the final determination of a language disorder is based on the judgment of the clinician (Taylor, 1984).

Definition of Speech and Language Disorders

The traditional role of the speech clinician involves working with disorders of speech, including problems of articulation, voice, and fluency, and disorders of hearing and language comprehension. Speech defects are noted when the speech of the child deviates so far from the speech of others that it calls attention to itself, interferes with communication, or causes the individual to be maladjusted (Van Riper, 1971). Speech disorders have been traditionally grouped in the following categories: disorders of articulation, disorders of voice, and disorders of fluency (for example, stuttering) (Hewett, 1977; Miller, 1984).

An articulation disorder exists when a phoneme is incorrectly produced so that it sounds different from the sound expected. Disorders of articulation occur in four forms: omission, substitution, distortion, and addition.

An omission is characterized by the exclusion of the target phoneme, while in a substitution, the phoneme is replaced by another recognizable phoneme. A sound is distorted when its production is cluttered by nonrecognizable phonemes. The frequent addition of an extra phoneme to a word is referred to as an addition. Severity of an articulation disorder depends on the child's overall comprehension. Although omissions are considered among the more severe disorders, the number and type of phonemes misarticulated and the frequency of misarticulation may identify the speaker's comprehension abilities.

Articulation tests are designed in numerous ways. They may assess phoneme production within words, within sentences, and in many phonetic contexts. Diagnostic tests include all the phonemes of the language tested in all the possible positions in words—initial, medial, and final. Screening tests are abbreviated articulation tests to analyze the production of a limited number of phonemes in a sample (Lynch, 1978). Regional or dialectical variations of phoneme production should not be considered as articulation disorders.

Voice disorders include problems with vocal quality, pitch, and intensity. A vocal disorder occurs when the voice is not sufficiently loud for the communicative circumstances or when it has an inappropriate pitch level for the individual's size and is not flexible enough to satisfy social or occupational needs (Emerick, 1981). Defects in vocal quality appear in the production of sound in a breathy, hoarse, harsh, and nasal manner. Pitch breaks, monopitch, and odd inflections are examples of voice disorders related to pitch. A soft or weak voice and an extremely loud voice typify disorders of intensity (Emerick, 1981).

Some LEP students may exhibit true voice disorders and such disorders would seem to be detected easily. The clinician, however, must be aware of inflection patterns typical of the student's native language. What would seem to be a voice disorder in pitch or intensity may be the normal communication pattern of the student's language.

A disorder of fluency is a disturbance in the smoothness or flow of speech. Stuttering is a dysfluency of speech through the prolongation of sounds or syllables and the repetition of words noticeable to the listener and irritating to the speaker (Van Riper, 1971). Another fluency disorder is cluttering. Cluttering is characterized by a rapid, jumbled, and slurred speech pattern. The speaker may be unaware of the communication breakdown (Emerick, 1981). Fluency disorders may be found among LEP students. It is important to assess fluency in both languages spoken by the student. Dysfluencies may occur in one language and not the other. Such information would be useful to the clinician in developing a plan of treatment.

A second type of communication disorder used by speech clinicians to diagnose and provide services is disorders of language. In 1975 the American Speech, Language and Hearing Association (ASHA) Committee on Language defined language disorders as mild, moderate, or severe impairments in the normal ability to comprehend or produce spoken or written language. Children with linguistic disorders fail to comprehend or speak their native language appropriately for their chronological age (Lynch, 1978). Such inabilities revealed themselves as difficulties in processing language at the levels of phonology, morphology, syntax, and semantics. Therefore a language-disoriented child would not be able to function within the norms of any speech community.

A consensus of the terms used to describe children who are not learning language normally does not exist at this time. *Deviant language, language disorders, language disability,* and *delayed language* are among the terms most commonly used (Bloom & Lahey, 1978). The term *language disorder* is used most often to describe specific behaviors or the absence of language behaviors that would be expected considering the student's chronological age.

When language is defined as a code of communication where ideas are represented through a conventional system of words, sentences, and larger units of meaning, a language disorder can be seen as an inability in conceptualizing ideas or representing these ideas in a linguistic code. Language delays occur when the conventional code is developed at a rate later than when it is acquired by peers (Bloom & Lahey, 1978).

Children who have disorders of form will be unable to use the conventional system of signals, words, and sentences for communicating. For the LEP student from a Spanish-speaking environment, the conventional system consists of Spanish phonemes and sentences. An LEP student who speaks a native language as well as other students but does not have the same command of form in English could not be properly identified as language disordered.

The LEP student's ability to form concepts and to use language appropriately may not be known. If the student exhibits the inability to form ideas in the native language and also to represent those ideas in words to communicate, then a language disorder would be suspected. Activities to facilitate language learning would be meaningful only when offered in the individual's native language. The presentation of language activities in English compounds the learner's language inabilities.

Language minority students may possess speech and language disorders. It is important to maintain the same criteria when evaluating LEP students as when evaluating the language behavior of minority English-speaking students. A language minority child is not language disordered simply because of a reluctance to speak English. The objective of the speech and language assessment should remain the same for the LEP student—the evaluation of the student's overall linguistic performance to determine if the student has problems in articulation, voice, fluency, comprehension, or expression in the child's native language (Mattes & Omark, 1984).

Criteria for Selecting Standardized Tests

Completing an in-depth speech and language evaluation on limited English proficient students requires procedures and measures in the student's native language. Although standardized language tests have been developed for the Spanish speaker, a limited number are available in other languages. This applies to both norm- and criterion-referenced tests (Omark & Erickson, 1983). The practitioner needs to select the most appropriate measures for the purpose of evaluation. A selection between the use of norm-referenced or criterion-referenced tests depends on the purpose for testing, the practitioner's reporting requirements and the language skill to be measured. For example, criterion-referenced instruments developed for particular groups may be appropriate in measuring vocabulary comprehension because the measurement of vocabulary often includes a student's social and cultural background. The use of vocabulary as an indication of language development often penalizes students who have not been exposed to the "right language" (De Avila & Duncan, 1978).

The special education practitioner cannot assume that tests available in a minority language will automatically be reliable and valid for use in language assessment. Several questions remain to be asked and selection criteria need to be developed. Test selection should begin with a review of the content. This review should include an examination of the difficulty of the test items and its propriety for the population to which it would be administered (Walsh & Loret, 1979). The test content should not be outside the student's social, cultural, or learning environment (Cervantes, 1976). A minority language test should not be a direct translation of an English test because the constructions measured and the difficulty of particular items are often not carried through the translation (Omark & Erickson, 1983). Direct translation produces constructions not used with the same frequency in other languages (De Avila & Havassy, 1974). Too often tests are translated into standard forms of a language without regard for dialectical and regional differences, thus implying ethnic homogeneity. Another problem with some translated tests is that they have no norms of their own, so the practitioner is left to assume English norms are applicable (Bernal, 1977).

Test format should also be considered in test selection (Watson, 1980). The time required to administer the test and the method of student response (for example, nonverbal or paper-pencil) should be weighed. The mode of presentation and responses required by children on language tests should focus on normal discourse and not on rare or uncommon variations.

A review of a test's technical manual is critical before a test is selected. Technical information regarding test use, purpose and intent of the test, and the test's psychometric properties should be available to the practitioner.

The test's reliability and validity are usually provided in the manual. Reliability refers to the consistency of the scores obtained. Validity refers to the quality of the scores —whether the test measures what it is designed to measure. Content validity and criterion validity are important to examine for the measurement of language. The content should represent an array of linguistic skills within the language tested. Criterion validity refers to the degree to which scores on one measure relate to scores on an external criterion (Anderson et al., 1975). Another way to look at criterion validity is to ask how well the linguistic performance obtained on the test compares with a student's linguistic abilities when judged by a teacher or by another measure. If the test content does not validly reflect the skills the examiner wishes to assess, the test should not be used. In addition, the technical manual should stipulate the norms for a norm-referenced language test. Also, consideration must be given to how norms were derived and the language characteristics of the students from whom they were derived.

Score interpretation is another factor to consider in test selection. For what purpose will the score be used? Are comparative or normative data available for similar populations? Does the test distinguish between the quality and quantity of the linguistic responses given? (Is *how much* was produced judged differently from *what* was produced?) Are the test results useful for decisions regarding the identification, placement, and instructional approaches for the LEP student?

In summary, speech and comprehension tests in minority languages should be used in the evaluation of language skills of LEP children. However, these tests should not be used indiscriminately by the practitioner simply because they are available. Tests should be screened for the validity of content, format appropriateness, test quality, and usefulness for offering sound judgments regarding the LEP student's need for speech and language services.

Testing the LEP Student in English

A valid assessment of the LEP student is an assessment of the student's native language. A determination of the LEP student's need for speech and language therapy would not be made from an assessment of the student's linguistic abilities in English. An assessment of English skills, however, would provide an overall indication of the types of skills possessed by the LEP student (Miller, 1984; Mattes & Omark, 1984; Omark & Erickson, 1983). Care must be taken by the reader not to interpret assessment of English skills as an affirmation of the role of the teacher of English as a Second Language (ESL).

The primary objective of the speech clinician should be the diagnosis of speech and language disorders as previously defined in this chapter and the selection of activities to improve language development in the student's native language. However, the linguistic abilities mastered in the native language could be reinforced in English by the clinician. The teaching of English should not be used as an alternative to instruct in the student's area of need in the native language.

A major obstacle to the assessment of the LEP student's English skills is the lack of instruments designed to measure the acquisition of English as a Second Language (Omark & Erickson, 1983). English language tests are usually not developed for LEP populations. Therefore any test selected must be used with caution. Efforts should be made to begin evaluation using tests in English designed for LEP students. If standardized language tests are used, the determination must be made first as to what the English test is eliciting from the student with respect to what it claims to test. Also, the test user should determine the types of responses considered appropriate in terms of the LEP student's linguistic community (Wolfram, 1979) and decide from the outset if credit will be given for these responses, thus altering the test results.

If standardized tests are used and altered in any way from the procedures outlined in the test manual, the test results are invalid (Taylor, 1984). Scores on altered administrations should not be repeated or integrated in the same manner as if tests were administered to standard English speakers. The LEP student's score on an altered administration should not be compared to the norm group; rather, the information obtained would add to the practitioner's informal observation of the student's abilities. An alternative to the use of standardized tests is the gathering of speech and language data from natural contexts. An important element to assess in this evaluation is the amount of input the student receives in English. Important questions to ask are: To whom does the student speak English? In what contexts?

Preliminary information about the LEP student's skills and abilities in English may be obtained from the language proficiency test used in the initial language screening. A wider array of English-language skills assessment yields a greater amount of information regarding the ability to function in English.

A Language Assessment Procedure

Seven steps are essential for language assessment of LEP students referred for special education evaluation. These steps are depicted in Figure 7–1.

Step 1: The Referral

Figure 7–2 provides information obtained through the referral. The thorough, lengthy, and rather complicated form has a twofold purpose. First, inappropriate referrals may be discouraged because considerable time is needed to complete the form. Secondly, and more importantly, specific questions are asked about the referred student to assist in the decision for continued evaluation.

Additional strategies might be discussed and considered. Alternatives to continued evaluation might be explored. If the parent and the other members present decide to terminate the referral, then the process is stopped and assistance is provided to the child as necessary.

If they agree that additional information is necessary, then they proceed to the next step.

Step 2: The Parent Interview

The parent interview (see Figure 7–3) is an important step in the process for identifying LEP students with speech and language disorders.

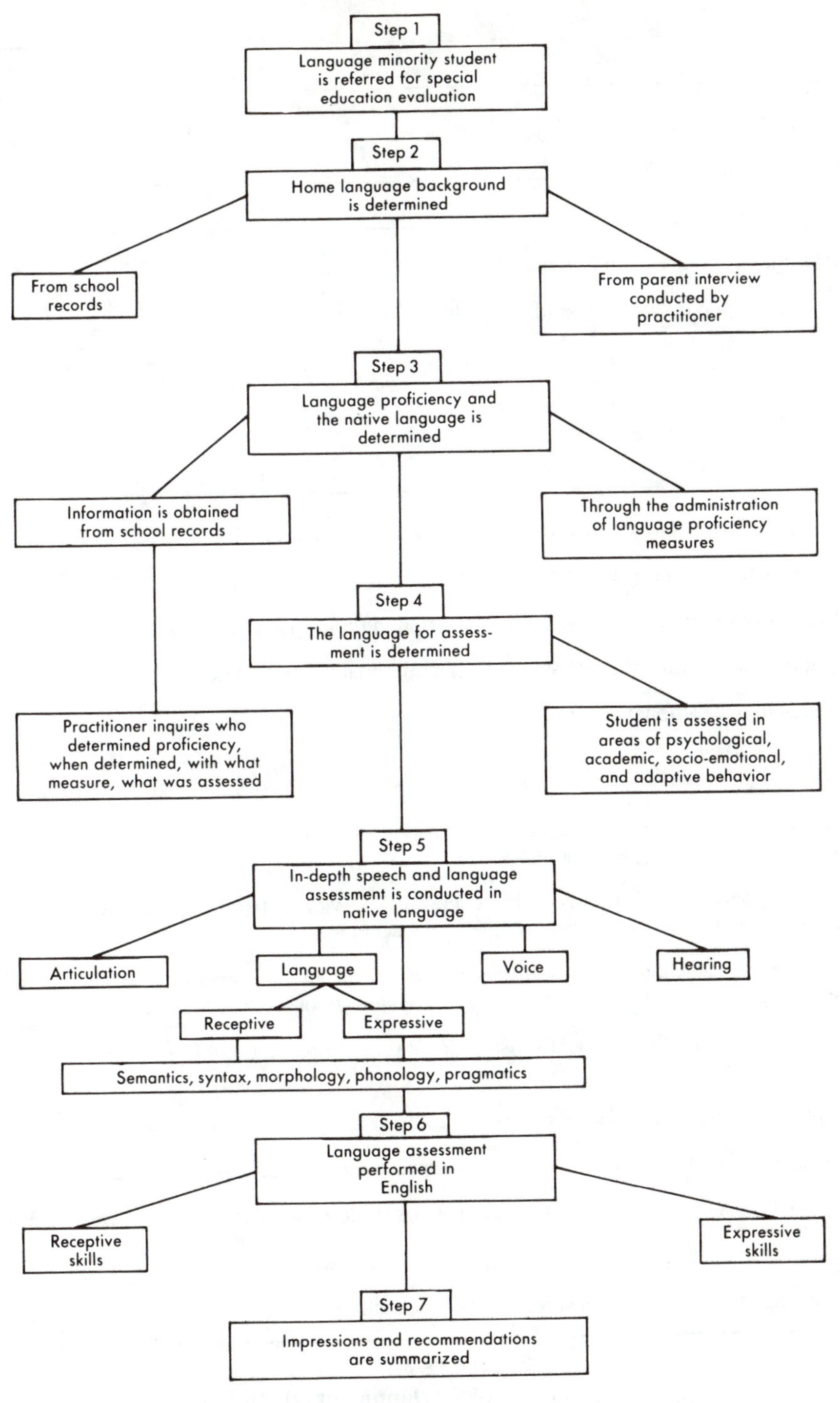

Figure 7–1
Language Assessment of LEP Students

Student's name ______________________ School ______________

Grade ________ Teacher ______________________

Referral

1. The student was referred by: ______________________
2. Relationship to student: ______________________
3. Is the person making the referral bilingual? Yes ______ No ______
4. How familiar is the person with the student's culture?

1	2	3	4
Limited familiarity			Very familiar

5. What were the primary reasons for referral?

____

____

6. What type of instructional program is the student receiving?

   ______ Regular classroom with no special instruction in the primary language

   ______ Regular classroom with the assistance of a bilingual teacher's aide

   ______ Bilingual instructional program

7. If the student is in a bilingual program, what type of instruction is provided and by whom?

   ______ Bilingual teacher and a bilingual aide provide instruction in the student's primary language and in English throughout the school day.

   ______ Monolingual teacher and bilingual teacher's aide provide instruction primarily in English with clarification and tutorial assistance given by teacher's aide.

   ______ Monolingual teacher provides instruction primarily in English with a bilingual resource teacher providing instruction in the primary language for a portion of the school day.

8. Approximately how much of the student's instructional time is provided in his/her primary language? ________ %.

   What percentage of time is provided in English? ________ %.

9. In what language is the student receiving reading instruction? ______________________
10. Have the student's English as a Second Language (ESL) abilities been assessed? Are results available?

    ____

11. What was the language of the student when he/she first entered school? ______________________

Figure 7–2

Linguistic Assessment of LEP Handicapped Students

Figures 7–2 to 7–8 adapted from forms used in the Los Angeles County Schools.

12. Rate the student's comprehension abilities:

	1	2	3	4
In English	Extremely poor	Poor	Adequate	Normal
In other language	Extremely poor	Poor	Adequate	Normal

13. Rate the student's expressive abilities:

	1	2	3	4
In English	Extremely poor	Poor	Adequate	Normal
In other language	Extremely poor	Poor	Adequate	Normal

14. Do you think the student's communication difficulties are caused by an inability to understand and speak English? Explain.

15. Compared to other limited English-proficient students in your class does this student

	Yes	**No**	**Non-applicable**
Respond to individual instruction but not to group instruction?			
Have difficulty listening?			
Have difficulty in responding appropriately to verbal instruction?			
Begin to act before you finish the instructions?			
Take longer than most children to respond to questions or instructions?			
Have trouble with common sequences (e.g., days of week, months of year, counting) in either English or other language?			
Tend to demonstrate (gesture or "act out") what he/she wants or means rather than communicate verbally?			
Repeat verbal instructions to self or out loud?			

Figure 7–2
Continuing

Continued

	Yes	No	Non-applicable
Ask that verbal instructions be repeated before responding?			
Participate in general conversations but have difficulty responding when asked for specific information?			
Remember more about short stories presented with pictures than stories presented without pictures?			
Have difficulty listening to verbal instructions when other sounds or noises are present?			
Appear reluctant to participate in activities with other children?			
Require and obtain assistance from peers?			
Have trouble completing a task?			
Need step-by-step instructions to complete a task?			
Give responses that are peculiar or "don't make sense"?			
Have speech that is difficult to understand?			

16. What language does the student prefer to use when
    - interacting informally with friends ____________________
    - asking questions of bilingual adults ____________________
    - working alone ____________________
    - presenting information to peers or adults ____________________

17. How would you compare this student's academic performance to that of the other LEP students in your class?

    ____
    Lowest 25% 50% 75% Highest

18. Please indicate the titles and levels of books presently used with this student:

    Reading ____________________

    Math ____________________

    ESL ____________________

19. Comments: ____________________

    ____

Figure 7–2
Continuing

The background information obtained from the parent may shed light on the child's language difficulties. In particular, a communicative difference rather than a communicative disorder might explain the child's language problems.

The parent interview also allows the parent to assist in the identification of voice, fluency, articulation or language disorders in the child.

A subsequent meeting is scheduled with the parent and the school staff to examine additional information. If these data do not continue to suggest a language disorder, then the process is stopped. If a language disorder is indicated, and there is agreement of the members present, then the next step is followed.

Step 3: Language Proficiency

Figure 7–4 provides 15 questions regarding language proficiency of the referred student. The purpose of this step is to determine if the student has been previously evaluated and found to be limited English proficient.

Answers to this questionnaire are valuable in helping the bilingual assessment personnel to determine the language in which the student should be evaluated. These questions would generally be directed by the bilingual speech and language assessor toward the bilingual resource teacher involved with the student.

If the data are insufficient or inadequate, then additional information regarding language proficiency in English and native language should be obtained before proceeding to the next step.

Step 4: Language for Assessment

Questions regarding the student's primary language are included in step 4 (see Figure 7–5). The purpose of this step is to ascertain whether the student was evaluated in a variety of areas in the primary language.

If these important questions cannot be adequately addressed, additional data must be obtained before attempting the next step.

Step 5: Speech and Language Assessment

Figure 7–6 includes questions that assess the speech and language skills of the student in the native language.

How clearly and precisely these questions can be answered will be directly related to how well the student will be remediated or assisted in the primary language.

Step 6: English Language Assessment

In addition to assessing the language skills of the student in the primary language, educators should evaluate the student's English language skills (see Figure 7–7).

Figure 7–7 provides what areas need to be addressed when the student's English language skills are considered. Accuracy in both steps 5 and 6 is critical because these steps help to determine whether the student will receive remediation in the native language, English, or some combination of both.

Step 7: Summary and Recommendations

The final step involves a discussion of all the steps as well as a decision as to how the remediation might be provided (see Figure 7–8).

At this point, the bilingual classroom teacher, bilingual evaluation team, and the parent would summarize the data and discuss possible solutions and recommendations. For the student to be placed in a bilingual speech and language program, the parent would need to give signed permission.

However, once the child is assigned to the bilingual speech and language program, the process has not ended. The student's progress must be closely monitored and reviewed periodically with the parent.

Date ______________________

Student's name ____

Birthdate ____________________ Birthplace ______________________

Parent or guardian ______________________________

Address ______________________________ Phone ______________

1. What languages are spoken in your home? ______________________

2. Which language is used most frequently in your home? ______________

3. Which language did your child first learn to speak? ______________

4. Which language do you speak to your child? ______________________

5. Which language does your child use to communicate at home? __________

6. Persons in the home:

Names	Languages spoken	Languages understood

7. Do you have any concerns over your child's language abilities? Explain.

8. Do you ever have trouble understanding your child's speech? Explain.

Figure 7–3
Language Background Questionnaire
Parent Interview

9. Is your child's language development progressing as rapidly as the language development of your other children? Explain.

10. Do other people find it difficult to understand your child's speech?

11. Does your child have difficulty answering questions or following directions?

12. Did any of your other children have speech and language difficulties?

____

Signature of interviewer

Figure 7–3
Continuing

1. Has the student been formally identified as being limited English proficient? Yes _____ No _____
(If no, skip to question 9.)

2. If yes, when was the identification performed? ______________________________

3. What is the student's home language? ______________________________

4. Who provided home language information? ______________________________

5. What instruments were used in determining the student's language proficiency in English? What information was obtained?

6. Did these instruments assess a variety of language skills? If so, which ones, and how did the student perform?

7. Was the student's language proficiency in the primary language assessed? Is a profile of abilities available? Describe:

8. Has the student's language status been reevaluated? If so, when, by whom, and with what results?

9. If language proficiency information has currently been collected by practitioner, what was the information obtained regarding the student's home language environment? Include language used in parent-child-sibling interactions.

Figure 7–4
Language Proficiency

10. What was the teacher's rating of student's proficiency in English and in the primary language?

11. What were the results of the language proficiency assessment in English when measured by standardized proficiency assessment instruments?

12. Which language would you judge the student as most proficient in? Why?

13. Was an assessment of general linguistic abilities performed in the student's primary language? What results and impressions were obtained?

14. Do you suspect the student has a communication disorder in the primary language?

15. Should the multifacted assessment of the student's abilities be performed in English, the primary language, or a combination of both? Why?

Figure 7–4
Continuing

1. What is the student's primary language?

2. What instruments or procedures were used to assess psychological functioning in the primary language?

3. What instruments or procedures were used to assess academic functioning in the primary language? Reading? Math? Written language?

4. What instruments or procedures were used to assess socioemotional functioning in the primary language?

5. What instruments or procedures were used to assess adaptive behavior in the primary language?

Figure 7–5
Language for Assessment

Speech

1. Judge the student's overall intelligibility in connected speech:
   In primary language:

1	2	3	4
Extremely unintelligible	Poor	Mildly distorted	Normal

   In English:

1	2	3	4
Extremely unintelligible	Poor	Mildly distorted	Normal

2. Were any abnormalities in the voice quality detected? Describe.

3. What results were attained from administering articulation tests in English? (problem sounds)

   Primary language? (problem sounds)

Figure 7–6
Speech and Language Assessment

Continued

Language

4. What instruments or procedures were used to assess receptive, expressive, and nonverbal language skills in the student's primary language?

5. What was the nature of the instruments used? (e.g., developed in the primary language, spontaneous direct translations)

6. How were the concepts of time, space, and quantity assessed, yielding what results?

7. How was a language sample obtained? How was it scored, yielding what results?

8. How can the subtests for the language proficiency measured used in language screening contribute to describing specific language skills?

9. Was the student observed actually using the language? What impressions were obtained?

10. Does this student require speech and/or language services in the primary language? If yes, of what type?

Figure 7–6
Continuing

1. What language measures were administered in English?

2. Were any measures designed to specifically assess English as a Second Language acquisition administered?

3. How were English language measures administered?

4. Was the prescribed test administered for these instruments modified in any way? If so, how? (i.e., Were items omitted that were judged to be culturally inappropriate?)

5. Was a language sample in English obtained? How was it scored and what were the results?

6. What impressions were obtained by observing the student's use of English in various settings?

7. Does the student have a language disorder in English that is not related to the fact that the student is acquiring English as a Second Language?

Additional comments:

Figure 7–7
English Language Assessment

1. What were the primary reasons for referral? ______________________________

____

2. What is primary language spoken in the home? ______________________________

3. Has the student been formally identified as being limited English proficient? Yes _____ No _____

4. Was the student's language proficiency in the primary language assessed? Is a profile of abilities available? Describe ______________________________

____

5. Was the student's psychological, academic, socioemotional functioning, and adaptive behavior assessed in the primary language? If not, explain ______________________________

____

6. Were any deficiencies noted in the speech or language of the student's primary language? If yes, explain

____

7. Were any deficiencies noted in the speech or language of the student's English? If yes, explain _____

____

8. Does the student have a language disorder in English that could be related to the fact that the child is acquiring English as a Second Language? Explain ______________________________

____

9. Is speech and/or language assistance required in the student's primary language? Explain _________

____

10. Is speech and/or language assistance required in English for this student? Explain _____________

____

Figure 7–8
Summary and Recommendations

Summary

This chapter has outlined and recommended steps for the valid language assessment of the limited English proficient student. The background for and the problematic issues surrounding language screening were presented, as were the definitions of terms regarding language proficiency testing. Procedures for completing an in-depth speech and language assessment were provided and the criteria for judging the presence of a speech and language disorder were defined. A discussion on the selection of Spanish speech and language measures and the assessment of the LEP student's English language abilities was given as well.

Discussion Questions

1. Describe how the language screening process defined in this chapter differs from the language screening performed by speech and language clinicians.

2. Describe how language proficiency differs from language dominance.

3. Explain how a child whose home language has been identified as Spanish can have a higher proficiency in English.

4. Explain why language screening is important to the overall special education assesssment process.

5. Outline the positive and negative effects of testing an LEP child in English. Is it necessary? If so, why? What are the drawbacks?

6. Write a fictitious report using the forms found in Figures 7–2 to 7–8.

7. Review three language proficiency instruments. Describe and compare the skills assessed, how they are assessed, and the instrument's psychometric properties. Select the test that appeals most to you and provide reasons for your selection.

References

Adolph, C. H. (1988). The application of the Woodcock Language Proficiency Battery as an assessment tool for bilingual students referred for special education. Unpublished doctoral dissertation, University of Colorado.

Anderson, S., et al. (1975). *Encyclopedia of educational evaluation.* San Francisco: Jossey-Bass.

Berko, S. (1958). The child's learning of English morphology. *Word.* 14:150–177.

Bernal, E. (1977). *Adapting assessment procedures to specific population characteristics: The Chicano child.* ERIC Document Reproduction Service No. ED145–943, San Antonio, TX: University of Texas.

Bernal, E., & Tucker, J. A. (1981). *A manual for screening and assessing students of limited English proficiency.* Paper presented at the Council for Exceptional Children's Conference on the Exceptional Bilingual Child, New Orleans.

Bloom, L., & Lahey, M. (1978). *Language development and language disorders.* New York: Wiley.

Burt, M., Dulay, H., & McKeon, D. (1980, October). *Testing and teaching communicatively handicapped Hispanic children, the state of the art.* Prepared for the California Department of Education, Grant #38–B161–Ho–B293–7100.

Cervantes, R. A. (1976). Language dominance assessment: Formal and informal procedures. In R. Cervantes, et al., *Language dominance test development and instructional placement: A case study.* Washington, DC: National Institute of Education.

Cummins, J. (1980). The cross-lingual dimensions of language proficiency: Implications for bilingual education and the optimal age issue. *TESOL Quarterly.* 4(2):171–174.

Cummins, J. (1984). *Bilingualism and special education: Issues in assessment and pedagogy.* San Diego: College-Hill Press.

De Avila, E., & Duncan, S. (1978). A few thoughts about language assessment: The Lau decision reconsidered. *Bilingual Education Paper Series, 1*(8). Los Angeles: National Dissemination and Assessment Center, California State University.

De Avila, E., & Duncan, S. (1980). Definition and measurement of bilingual students. In R. Cervantes (ed.), *Bilingual program policy and assessment issues.* Sacramento: State of California, Bureau of Publications.

De Avila, E. & Duncan, S. (1987). LAS, reading and writing. Monterey, CA: CTB/McGraw-Hill.

De Avila, E. & Havassy, B. (1974). *I.Q. tests and minority children.* Austin, TX: Dissemination Center for Bilingual Bicultural Education.

Duncan, S. (1988, April). Language testing news. Linguametrics Group. Special NABE Edition.

Emerick, L. (1981). A casebook of diagnoses and evaluation in speech pathology and audiology. Englewood Cliffs, NJ: Prentice-Hall.

Garcia, E., & Acosta, C. (1980). *Language assessment measures for bilingual children: why and why not.* Paper presented at the Ninth Annual International Bilingual/Bicultural Education Conference, Anaheim, CA.

Gillmore, G., & Dickenson, A. (1979). *The relationship between instruments used for identifying children of limited English speaking ability in Texas.* Houston: Region IV Education Service Center.

Hewett, F. (1977). *Education for exceptional learners.* 2d ed. Boston: Allyn & Bacon.

Lau v. Nichols (1974). 414 U.S. 563.

Leopold, W. F. (1949). *Speech development of a bilingual child: A linguist's record.* Evanston, IL: Northwestern University Press.

Lynch, J. (1978). Evaluation of linguistic disorders in children. In S. Singh & J. Lynch (Eds.), *Diagnostic procedures in hearing, language, and speech.* Baltimore: University Park Press.

Mattes, L. J. & Omark, D. R. (1984). *Speech and language assessment for the bilingual handicapped.* San Diego: College-Hill Press.

Miller, N. (Ed.) (1981). *Bilingual and language disability: Assessment and remediation.* San Diego: College-Hill Press.

Office for Civil Rights, U.S. Department of Health, Education and Welfare (1975). *Task force findings specifying remedies for eliminating past education practices ruled unlawful under Lau v. Nichols.* Washington, DC: Government Printing Office.

Oller, J. (1978). The language factor in the evaluation of bilingual education. In J. E. Alatis (Ed.), *Georgetown University round table on languages and linguistics.* Washington, DC: Georgetown University Press.

Oller, J. & Perkins, K. (1980). *Research in language testing.* Rowley, MA: Newbury House.

Omark, D. R. & Erickson, J. G. (1983). *The bilingual exceptional child.* San Diego: College-Hill Press.

Ramirez, A., & Politzer, R. (1976). The acquisition of English and the maintenance of Spanish in bilingual education programs. *TESOL Quarterly.* 9:113–124.

Taylor, R. L. (1984). *Assessment of exceptional students: Educational and psychological procedures.* Englewood Cliffs, NJ: Prentice-Hall.

Thonis, E. (1981). Reading instruction for language minority students. In *Schooling and language minority students: A theoretical framework.* Los Angeles: California State University.

Van Riper, C. (1971). *The nature of stuttering.* Englewood Cliffs, NJ: Prentice-Hall.

Wald, M. (1981). *Handbook for proficiency assessment.* Sacramento, CA: California State Department of Education.

Walsh, M., & Loret, P. (1979). *Assessing language proficiency.* Sacramento, CA: California State Department of Education.

Watson, D. (1980). *Non-discriminatory assessment handbook.* Vols. 1 and 2. Sacramento, CA: California State Department of Education.

Wolfram, W. (1979). *Dialects and educational equity: Speech pathology and dialect difference.* Arlington, VA: Center for Applied Linguistics.

CHAPTER EIGHT

Assessment Procedures for the Exceptional Child

- Norm-Referenced versus Criterion-Referenced Tests
- Assessment and Legislative Requirements According to P.L. 94–142
- Models of Assessment for the Bilingual Exceptional Child
- Implementing an Assessment Procedure for the Bilingual Exceptional Child
- Obtaining Relevant Data
- Determination of a Specific Learning Disability
- Summary

Objectives

- To understand what special education professionals recommend with respect to assessment
- To describe the legislative requirement for assessment according to P.L. 94–142
- To describe the components of a diagnostic-intervention process model
- To explore appropriate measures within the diagnostic-intervention process model
- To develop an understanding of the step-by-step procedures in a bilingual assessment with the diagnostic-intervention process

As shown in Chapter 7, the issue of assessment is filled with misconceptions, inconsistencies, confusion, and considerable controversy, as well as cultural, linguistic, and ethnic variables. The research clearly indicates that many assessment instruments are limited with respect to language minorities.

How should culturally, linguistically, and ethnically different children be evaluated? This question is frequently asked of educators confronted with diverse populations within the school setting. How can educators be sure that the bilingual child just evaluated is truly learning disabled?

An examination of texts in the field of Bilingual Education, special education, and Bilingual Special Education does not offer clear answers to these questions (Haring & McCormick, 1986; Taylor, 1984; Cummins, 1984; Mattes & Omark, 1984; Miller, 1984; Omark & Erickson, 1983).

The limitations and disadvantages of traditional assessment procedures with bilingual exceptional children were discussed at length in Chapter 7. What procedures should be used?

Norm-Referenced versus Criterion-Referenced Tests

Some educators, after examining the history of traditional formal assessment and bilingual exceptional children, believe that formal testing—norm-referenced tests—should be eliminated completely and substituted with criterion-referenced assessment. Educators, however, appear divided on the issue.

In norm-referenced assessment, a student's performance is compared with the scores of a specific reference group. The scores from the reference group provide an indication of average performance that becomes the norm for individual comparison. This reference group methodology generates criticism of norm-referenced tests.

A major issue is the representativeness of the reference group. How characteristic is the normed group to a particular population? The normed group should be similarly matched with the population as a whole on various demographic variables such as age, sex, ethnicity, geographic region, socioeconomic status, community size, and grade level. These data should be based on current U.S. Census, National Center for Education Statistics, or U.S. Office of Civil Rights figures.

Another issue revolves around the number of students in the normative group. For example, because minorities make up 27% of the U.S. population according to 1980 census figures, minorities should make up 27% of the normative sample. In addition, the number of students in the normative group must be large enough to provide statistically for the stability of test scores.

How relevant the norms are for the student evaluated is another consideration. It is critically important that an individual student's test score be compared with the proper normative group for adequate test interpretation.

Criterion-referenced testing, on the other hand, refers to testing that compares the student's score with some established standard or criterion. Students are not compared to one another or to some norm but to an expected level of performance.

Criterion-referenced tests appear particularly useful within the classroom setting. They can assist the classroom teacher in determining whether the child is ready for another level of instructional activities. When a child can compute math problems at 90% efficiency, for example, the child has passed the criterion and is ready for the next level of math activity.

Norm-referenced tests differ from criterion-referenced tests in the area of scale of measurement. In norm-referenced assessment, a particular normative group is used for comparative purposes and an index of average performance. In criterion-referenced tests, a score is used to indicate percent mastery of some ability or concept.

Though it has been demonstrated that traditional norm-referenced tests have numerous limitations, criterion-referenced tests also have disadvantages. What will be selected for the student to learn and be evaluated on? Who will make the selections?

Another issue is the level of performance that indicates successful completion of the activity. Should it be 75% correct? Why not 80% or 95% correct? Who will judge whether the objective was obtained?

In addition, using criterion-referenced tests does not eliminate the comparison of children because children scoring at low levels are more likely to be identified as "slow" or "retarded" while children scoring at higher levels are more likely to be identified as "advanced" or "smart."

Both norm-referenced and criterion-referenced testing have their role in the education of bilingual exceptional children. Norm-referenced tests are particularly useful in comparing individual differences between children. Criterion-referenced assessments, on the other hand, are useful in determining whether children have attained various instructional objectives.

Local Norms

Some educators feel that the solution to the problems with traditional norm-referenced assessment instruments is the development and use of local norms (Archuleta & Cervantes, 1981; Baca & Cervantes, 1978; Cervantes & Baca, 1979; Mercer, 1981). They believe that when local comparison groups are developed, the limitations and disadvantages typically associated with norm-referenced tests can be diminished.

In particular, the issue of the representativeness of the reference group would be more appropriately addressed. Thus, with local norms one could feel more confident that the characteristics of the normed group were similar to the characteristics of the student being assessed.

Unfortunately, despite the obvious benefits of establishing local norms, few educators appear either interested or willing to develop adequate local norms. Most respond that they lack the expertise to develop a valid and reliable test with appropriate local norms.

Others, however, disagree with the establishment of local norms for other reasons.

> A second malpractice involves simple renorming, i.e., the computation of ethnic norms, often locally. Renorming accomplishes what adding points does but the numbers are determined empirically. The only real advantage of renorming is that it provides good descriptive statistics for a particular ethnic population and a better distribution of scores. But renorming appears to the uninitiated to do more, to somehow make the test better. It does not (Bernal, 1977).

Assessment and Legislative Requirements According to P.L. 94–142

Procedures for the assessment of bilingual handicapped children must conform to the letter of the law. Archuleta and Cervantes (1981) discuss a five-phase assessment and evaluation model for nondiscriminatory assessment. Phase III discusses the identification of instruments with the following requirements according to P.L. 94–142:

> State and local educational agencies shall ensure, at a minimum that:
>
> a. Testing and evaluation materials and procedures used for the purposes of evaluation and placement of handicapped children must be selected and administered so as not to be racially or culturally discriminatory.
>
> b. Testing and evaluation materials and procedures must be provided and administered in the language or other mode of communication in which the child is most proficient, unless it is clearly not feasible to do so.
>
> c. Tests must be administered to a child with a motor, speech, hearing, visual or other communication disability, or to a bilingual child, so as to reflect accurately the child's ability in the area tested rather than the child's impaired communication skill or limited English language skill unless those are the factors the test purports to measure.
>
> d. Tests and other materials used for placement must be properly and professionally evaluated for the specific purpose for which they are used, and administered by qualified personnel in conformance with instructions provided by the producers of the tests and materials.
>
> e. Tests and other evaluation procedures must include assessment of specific areas of educational need.
>
> f. No single test, type of test, or procedure may be used as the sole criterion for determining an appropriate educational program for a child.
>
> g. Evaluation procedures must include—
>
> 1. An assessment that is sufficiently comprehensive to diagnose and appraise the child's suspected impairment; and
> 2. A multidisciplinary approach for children suspected of having severe, multiple, or complex disorders, including a specific learning disability.
>
> h. All relevant information with regard to the functional abilities of the child must be used in making a placement determination. (*Federal Register*, Aug. 4, 1984, 300.158)

Models of Assessment for the Bilingual Exceptional Child

Glaser (1963) suggests that tests should be used primarily for educational and instructional purposes regarding the student's progress. Acquiring information used to develop more appropriate methods for instruction should be a purpose of instruction regardless of a child's sociocultural, ethnic, or linguistic background. Rather than emphasizing labeling, categorizing, and sorting of students for program placement, information from assessment should enhance the development and evaluation of programs and students.

Cromwell, Blashfield, and Strauss (1975) argue that assessment, diagnosis, and evaluation must lead to instructional planning and define a diagnostic-intervention process to include four components:

A. Historical-etiological information
B. Assessment of present behavior
C. Defined treatments or interventions
D. Predictive outcomes or prognosis

The authors emphasize that the situational and cultural context must be taken into account in obtaining A and B information, and that components C and D actually determine the usefulness and validity of diagnosis. Thus the diagnostic or assessment component consists of A, B, or AB, and the intervention component consists of

C, D, or CD. The complete diagnostic intervention process would have an ABCD profile.

Educational assessment should be examined as a process that is continuous and that provides the rationale for specific planning instruction. Measures of pupil growth and change determine the validity of the student's educational plan and the accuracy of the assessment. Sabatino (1972) states:

> The handicapped child's education is dependent upon a continuously changing instructional pattern, based upon his needs and functions. There is no one diagnostic statement that can cover any more than one educational planning period. In short, then, the term diagnostic-prescriptive implies that diagnosis should have an immediate relationship to teaching if it is to have any instructional value. The problem is that educational diagnosis is dynamic, continuous. The one-shot approach to psychoeducational child study sadly lacks the capability to validly sample behaviors leading directly to the instructional management of handicapped children.

Cartwright and Cartwright (1972) have developed a diagnostic teaching model designed to correct learning problems and enhance learning assets. This model provides a framework for decision making in assessment as well as the steps involved in instructional planning. These steps include:

> Step 1: Identifying the relevant attributes or characteristics of the student; focus on those which are related to the behaviors of most concern to the teacher and on those which indicate a need for special teaching or management techniques.
>
> Step 2. Specifying teaching goals; translate these goals into instructional objectives.
>
> Step 3. Selecting instructional strategies which will ensure accomplishment of stated objectives and which will be appropriate to the known attributes of the learner.
>
> Step 4. Making and/or selecting appropriate materials related to specific strategies for instruction.
>
> Step 5. Testing the strategies and materials; the ultimate test is, "Does it work with the child?" If the objective is reached, the next objective is specified; if not, Steps 1–4 are repeated in sequence.

This section is primarily concerned with the extension assessment activities that are a part of Step 1. Other sources examine Steps 2 through 5 much more thoroughly (Cartwright & Cartwright, 1972, 1974; Georgrades & Clark, 1974; Hammill & Bartel, 1975; Mills & Mills, 1972).

The Pasanella and Volkmor Model

One model that has considerable applicability for the bilingual exceptional student is the Pasanella and Volkmor (1977) model. Their assessment model includes (1) observation, (2) interviewing, (3) examining school records, and (4) testing. These activities may or may not occur in this order. Also, depending on the needs of the child, not all the activities may be required. In all cases, due process procedures must be followed (see Chapter 4) and parents must be notified before the school begins any assessment related to special educational programming.

Basically, observation is an organized and systematic assessment technique for examining a student's behavior to facilitate instruction. The student's behavior is observed in a variety of different situations at school and, if possible, away from school. Teacher-pupil and pupil-pupil interactions are noted, as well as the learning environment.

Interviewing is an important, efficient, and valuable informal method of data collection. Interviews provide information regarding the teacher's concerns about the student, how the student deviates from the teacher's expectations, how the parents see the situation, the parents' concerns, and the student's perception of the situation.

School records can provide important information for the assessment process. Depending on what is available in the student's cumulative folder, the records might provide some historical or chronological perspective on the student's behavior. Careful examination of school records can be quite enlightening.

With respect to testing, Pasanella and Volkmor (1977) point out that there is growing support for skill testing. More and more professionals are increasingly dissatisfied with process tests (visual motor, psycholinguistic, intelligence) and the suspect reliability and validity of these tests. Skill testing in reading, writing, and mathematics, on the other hand, shows rather clearly the strengths and weaknesses in a variety of academic areas.

The model provided by Pasanella and Volkmor has considerable usefulness and validity. Although it was not designed specifically for assessment of culturally or linguistically different students, it does have application to these groups. For example, valuable and oftentimes crucial data can be obtained through observation, interviewing, and examination of school records. Indeed, these procedures are incorporated in the assessment procedure recommended for bilingual exceptional children. Background information about a student is essential for any evaluation.

The Bilingual Assessment Model

The bilingual assessment model, which takes into account socioeconomic, linguistic, and ethnic factors, would be measurably more valuable than the Pasanella and Volkmor (1977) model. Mercer and Ysseldyke (1977) have provided a framework from which to examine such a process based on the works of others (Cromwell, Blashfield, & Strauss, 1975; Mercer, 1979; Ysseldyke, 1973; Ysseldyke & Salvia, 1974, 1975). Their assessment model has considerable application for bilingual exceptional children. The following section is based on their pioneering work.

As mentioned earlier in the chapter, Cromwell, Blashfield, and Strauss (1975) indicate that if a diagnostic-intervention program includes (A) historical-etiological information, (B) assessment of present behavior, (C) defined treatments or interventions, and (D) predictive outcomes or prognosis, then the greater is its validity and usefulness, particularly in assessment of bilingual children suspected of having learning handicaps. To rule out effects due to culture, linguistic background, and test bias as much as possible, Ysseldyke (1977) and his associates have described an assessment process based on five conceptual models: (1) the medical model, (2) the social system model, (3) the psychoeducational process model, (4) the task analysis model, and (5) the pluralistic model.

The Medical Model. The medical model has also been called the clinical model, the disease model, and the pathological model. It is a model developed in medicine to understand and combat human diseases. Basically, this model is designed to identify biological dysfunctions, disease processes, physiomotor impairments, or other pathological conditions in individuals.

As a school staff begins to evaluate students suspected of having some handicap, excluding biological or health problems becomes quite important. The assumption of course is that the symptoms exhibited by the child are related directly to some biological condition in the child. In addition, this biological condition is thought to be diagnosable and treatable regardless of the child's cultural, linguistic, socioeconomic, or racial background. That is, the medical model assumes that the sociocultural characteristics of the individual are not directly producing the symptomatic behavior; hence the person's sociocultural background is not relevant to diagnosis. However, situations of poverty, malnutrition, inadequate child rearing, and socioeconomic deprivation could be related to pathological symptoms (Hallahan and Kauffman, 1986). For the most part, if the medical model is used appropriately and prudently, culturally, linguistically, or racially discriminatory results should not be observed.

Appropriate Measures. Measurement instruments used in the medical model focus on the assessment of biologically determined symptoms. That is, they typically focus on deficits, measuring the extent of the pathological condition. More specifically, these measures focus on the assessment of errors made when performing physical tasks or on the extent of pathological signs. In practical terms, this means that behavioral measures within the medical model usually count the number of errors a child makes while performing a particular task. The higher the number of errors, the more the deficit. These instruments are valid insofar as they relate to other biological information about a child. Specifically, a child with "physical" disability would be expected to have high scores (numerous errors) on tests of physical dexterity. On the other hand, because the medical model is not culture bound, measures should not be correlated with the sociocultural background characteristics of the child being measured.

Meier (1975) lists numerous screening tests and procedures for determining biological factors, such as measures of nutritional status, vision, and hearing. Among them are the Automated Multiphasic Health Testing and Service procedures, amniocentesis, metabolic measures, measures of nutritional status, vision, Apgar rating, hearing screening, and the behavioral and neurological assessment scale. Connor and others (1975) also provide a summary of current classification systems and screening procedures for physical and sensory handicaps such as visual impairment, hearing impairment, and physical and neurological disorders.

Mercer (1979) includes a medical model measure in her System of Multicultural Pluralistic Assessment (SOMPA), which examines visual acuity, auditory acuity, health history, physical dexterity tasks, weight by height, and visual motor coordination.

The Social System Model. The social system model is also called the social adaptivity or social deviance model. It is based on the social deviance model in sociology. Though this model has not been typically used in assessment, such a model is implicit in most present psychological assessment procedures. The social system model examines a child's social behavior and compares it to the expectations of other members of the child's socioeconomic group. Deviant or unusual behavior would be behavior beyond the expectations of others within the group. Normal behavior, on the other hand, is behavior that conforms to the expectations of the group members. However, it is entirely possible for a child to be judged normal in one role and abnormal in another. There is no assumption of biological causation.

Appropriate Measures. Social system model measurement instruments assess how well children can perform their social roles. Does the behavior of this child meet the social norms of the groups in which the child is participating? Measures are designed to assess particular roles in particular social systems. The validity of these measures is determined by the correlation of scores on the measure and judgments about the child's behavior made by other group members. The determination of which behaviors are socially valued is made by those groups in the social system that have the power to make and enforce the rules by which others will live.

Another validation question is whether a particular direct measure of a child's performance in a specific social system accurately represents the evaluations of other members of the social system. Does a particular teacher's rating of a child's performance in the student role reflect the rating that would be given by other teachers? The judgments of persons who are nonmembers of the social system cannot be used to determine the validity of the assessments made by system members, because nonmembers are outside the normative structure of the group.

Measures of social competence have been identified (Lambert, Wilcox, & Gleason, 1974) to assess the child's role in the family, neighborhood, peer group, and community. Hobbs (1975) has described ecological strategies in program planning for individual children that are based on profiles of the strengths and weaknesses of the child in particular settings. Mercer (1974) suggests that children have a right to have their social role performance or adaptive behavior evaluated when special education diagnoses are being made. This recommendation was based on research findings that indicated that the social role performance of students labeled significantly learning disabled tended to be indistinguishable from that of other individuals in the community (Mercer, 1973).

Cervantes and Baca (1978) have indicated that adaptive behavior scales have had a long history dating back to Sequin in 1837, Voisin in 1843, Howe in 1858, and Goddard in 1912. According to Cervantes and Baca (1978), adaptive behavior is defined as "the effectiveness with which an individual copes with the natural and social demands of his environment."

Several scales to measure social competency within the school and community are available. The American Association on Mental Deficiency Adaptive Behavior Scale, Public School Version (Lambert et al., 1975) is one. The scale provides a profile of adaptive behavior strengths and weaknesses and appears to have adequate reliability, but there are some questions regarding the validity of the test. Other measures are the Vineland Adaptive Behavior Scales and the Scales of Independent Behavior.

The Psychoeducational Process Model. The psychoeducational process model is frequently referred to as the ability training model. It is based on the belief that different children benefit differentially from different instructional strategies. Particularly since the rise of the learning disabilities movement, interest has focused on this model, which basically is designed to identify process or ability strengths and weaknesses to prescribe instruction. Assessment batteries are generally administered and designed to identify psychoeducational process deficits or disabilities within the child.

An assumption of the psychoeducational process model is that academic problems are directly related to psychoeducational process deficits or disabilities within the child. That is, a necessary requirement to the adequate development of academic skills is the adequate development of cognitive, perceptual, and psycholinguistic processes or abilities. Along with this assumption is the idea that children's academic problems are not related to inadequate teaching or inadequate educational experiences.

Another assumption within the psychoeducational process model is that the processes evaluated are tied to academic success and must be stimulated processes within a child, and can be reliably and validly determined with test batteries.

However, the assumptions underlying the psychoeducational process model have not withstood the rigors of empirical verification. Few measures of psychoeducational processes have significantly high levels of reliability and validity to be useful in making educational decisions about children (Coles, 1978). In a comprehensive examination of the learning disabilities test battery, Coles concluded:

> The evidence appears, therefore, to point to the conclusion that the tests do not measure neurological dysfunction in learning disabled children, but that methodological inadequacies prevent us from drawing this conclusion with certainty. These same methodological problems do, however, provide support for the position that we do not know what these tests measure. Even if all of the tests were significantly correlated with academic achievement, we would still not have much evidence to demonstrate that the etiology of the test performance was neurological, emotional, pedagogical, developmental, or attributable to any number of other factors. Controlling for and identifying these factors is clearly a difficult undertaking, but this undertaking should be within the scope of our present investigatory skill. Unfortunately, few of the studies reported here have acknowledged the complexity of their task, and fewer still have used procedures that adequately take it into account.

Appropriate Measures. Good judgment is needed in selecting, administering, and evaluating psychoeducational process model assessment batteries for culturally, linguistically, and ethnically different students. Educators and psychologists, aware of some of the technical and theoretical limitations of certain tests with minority populations, continue to use some of the more traditional nonlanguage measures (for example, Bender Visual Motor Gestalt Test, Columbia Mental Maturity Scale, Leiter International Performance Scale, and Rulon's Semantic Test of Intelligence), as well as measures of psycholinguistic ability (Illinois Test of Psycholinguistic Ability and Peabody Preline Vocabulary Test), often with strong reservations (Laosa, 1977).

Measures of processes or abilities are, for the most part, norm-referenced measures that interpret a child's performance to the performance of other similar children. Oakland (1977), Laosa (1977), Mercer (1979), and Ysseldyke (1973, 1977) argue that localized norms of these measures may in many cases be more appropriate standards by which to compare a child's performance. These authors point out that such norms could be developed for a region, state, district, or community and enhance the meaningfulness of psychoeducational process assessment instruments.

However, concerns over technical features of these instruments' particularity, reliability, and validity, as well as item and language bias, continue to distort the appropriateness of these tests with culturally, linguistically, and ethnically different children.

Glass (1983), in a review of the research on the effectiveness of perceptual motor training, found absolutely no positive effect. Similar results have been reported on psycholinguistic training and academic performance (Kavale, 1981).

The Task Analysis Model. Similar to the psychoeducational process model, the task analysis model has also been applied in the field of special education. Educators such as Bijou (1970), Gold (1972), and Resnick, Wang, and Kaplan (1973) have advocated the assessment of academic skill development and differential instruction designed to move children from one academic skill level to another, more advanced level.

An important assumption in the task analysis model is that successful academic performance is related to the interaction between the mastery of the behaviors necessary to complete the task successfully and the characteristics of the task. It is also assumed that examining the psychophysical causes of academic difficulties is useless and unnecessary. However, an additional assumption is that skills are developed upon a system of hierarchies such that the development of more complex and abstract skills depends on the successful development of less complex lower-level skills.

In assessing why children fail academically, no attempt is made to identify medical, social, or psychoeducational process deficits. Supporters of this model believe that identifying such deficits is unnecessary and, indeed, the existence of deficits appears to be questionable (Archuleta & Cervantes, 1981; Coles, 1978; Mann, 1971).

It is also believed that within the task analysis model, skill development is significantly influenced by the linguistic, economic, and sociocultural background of the child. Weaknesses in skill development can result from inadequate experience, difficulties understanding English, insufficient opportunities to learn, or inadequate teaching.

Appropriate Measures. Norm-referenced tests are generally not used within the task analysis model because this model focuses on skill development and on assessment of particular skill levels of children. Criterion-referenced assessment instruments are more generally used within this model. These tests measure the level to which a child exhibits the skills necessary to complete the stated specific objectives successfully. The children evaluated with this model are not compared to other similar children.

Because children are treated as individuals and not compared to others, racial and cultural bias as well as discrimination are absent.

The Woodcock Reading Mastery Test is an example of a criterion-referenced measure of skill development in reading. Key Math is an example of a similar measure in mathematics. Other examples include Criterion Reading, Diagnosis, The Fountain Valley Teacher Support System, and the Wisconsin Design, which are designed to assess how well a child demonstrates specific reading or mathematic skills (Mercer, 1979; Ysseldyke & Salvia, 1974, 1975).

Other available tests rely on normative data for comparison of student profiles. The Wide Range Achievement Test, Peabody Individual Achievement Test, California Achievement Test, Boehm Test of Basic Concept, Kaufman Test of Educational Achievement, and the Woodcock-Johnson Psychoeducational Battery are current examples. The Woodcock-Johnson Psychoeducational Battery (Woodcock & Johnson, 1977) is currently receiving a favorable response from the educational community and is available in both an English and a Spanish version, as are many others. Although there do appear to be some questions regarding the validity of the Cognitive Abilities Full Scale score, the Tests of Achievement appear quite satisfactory in the measurement of academic achievement.

The Pluralistic Model. The pluralistic model is similar to the task analysis model in that it is an attempt to use testing procedures that are responsive to linguistic, ethnic, and cultural aspects of American society and thus lessen the impact of linguistic, racial, and cultural bias in assessment. Tests within this model include sociocultural information as a base for test score interpretation as an attempt to control for these factors within a test.

An important assumption within the pluralistic model is that all children, regardless of their linguistic, ethnic, or cultural background, have the potential for learning and that differences in test scores across cultural groups are related to bias within the testing procedures. Another assumption states that tests evaluate what a child has learned within a specific sociocultural environment and that all tests are linguistically, racially, and culturally biased. Thus those children whose sociocultural environment is similar to those in the test's standardization sample will more likely perform better on the test than those not reared in that sociocultural environment.

Appropriate Measures. Of these approaches in the pluralistic model, SOMPA (Mercer, 1979) is interesting in its use of a multiple normative framework for various sociocultural, socioeconomic, or ethnic groups. Mercer and her associate Lewis, used multiple regressions to predict the average scores for children from different sociocultural environments. The economic, social, cultural, and linguistic characteristics of the child's family are inserted into the multiple regression equation and the child's Estimated Learning Potential (ELP) is generated, which is a prediction of the child's ability, given the particular background.

However, SOMPA remains considerably controversial. There are questions about the appropriateness of the pluralistic model, the lack of adequate national norms, and insufficient validation in practical assessment. It should be used with caution and attention should be paid to its limitations.

Comparison of Models. Each of these five assessment models provides a dissimilar view of a child. Attempts to develop diagnostic-intervention programs for culturally, linguistically, and ethnically diverse groups might include using such a multimodel approach that incorporates information from all five perspectives.

The medical model provides an ABCD profile and is useful in diagnosing and treating physical problems. The social system model provides a BD profile and is useful in evaluating social role performance in a variety of social situations. The psychoeducational process model also provides a BD profile, though its usefulness in making prognoses remains uncertain. The task analysis model highlights a BC configuration and is considerably useful in educational programming. The pluralistic model suggests an ABD profile and is significantly useful because it provides a basis for estimating the learning potential of culturally, linguistically, and ethnically different children in a manner that is potentially less racially and culturally discriminatory.

The use of each model and appropriate measures within each model would be in a child's best interest in providing a comprehensive view of that child's total functioning.

In addition, and perhaps much more importantly, using these procedures would remove considerable bias and discrimination that is frequently present when culturally, linguistically, and ethnically different children are evaluated.

Implementing an Assessment Procedure for the Bilingual Exceptional Child

As discussed in the previous section, a comprehensive assessment process consists of (A) historical-etiological information, (B) currently assessable characteristics, (C) specific treatments or interventions, and (D) a specific prognosis. This section attempts to describe a culturally, linguistically, and ethnically appropriate assessment process. It is based on the educational research of Bernal (1977), Mercer (1979), Tucker (1977), Ysseldyke (1973, 1977), and Ysseldyke and Salvia (1974, 1975).

In any form of assessment and particularly with language minorities, a comprehensive assessment program should involve a team effort throughout. Such a team must include the student's parents or guardians, the student's teachers, a school administrative representative, and the individuals involved in other aspects of the assessment.

The child's parents are an integral part of this process and the school staff should never make decisions about special education placement and programming without involving the parents in each step of the process.

That process is depicted in Figure 8–1 and shows one form such an assessment process might take. This model highlights the importance of parent involvement and emphasizes retention in the regular classroom, with intervention strategies as ongoing and continuous options. Placement in a special education program is considered only when no other options remain.

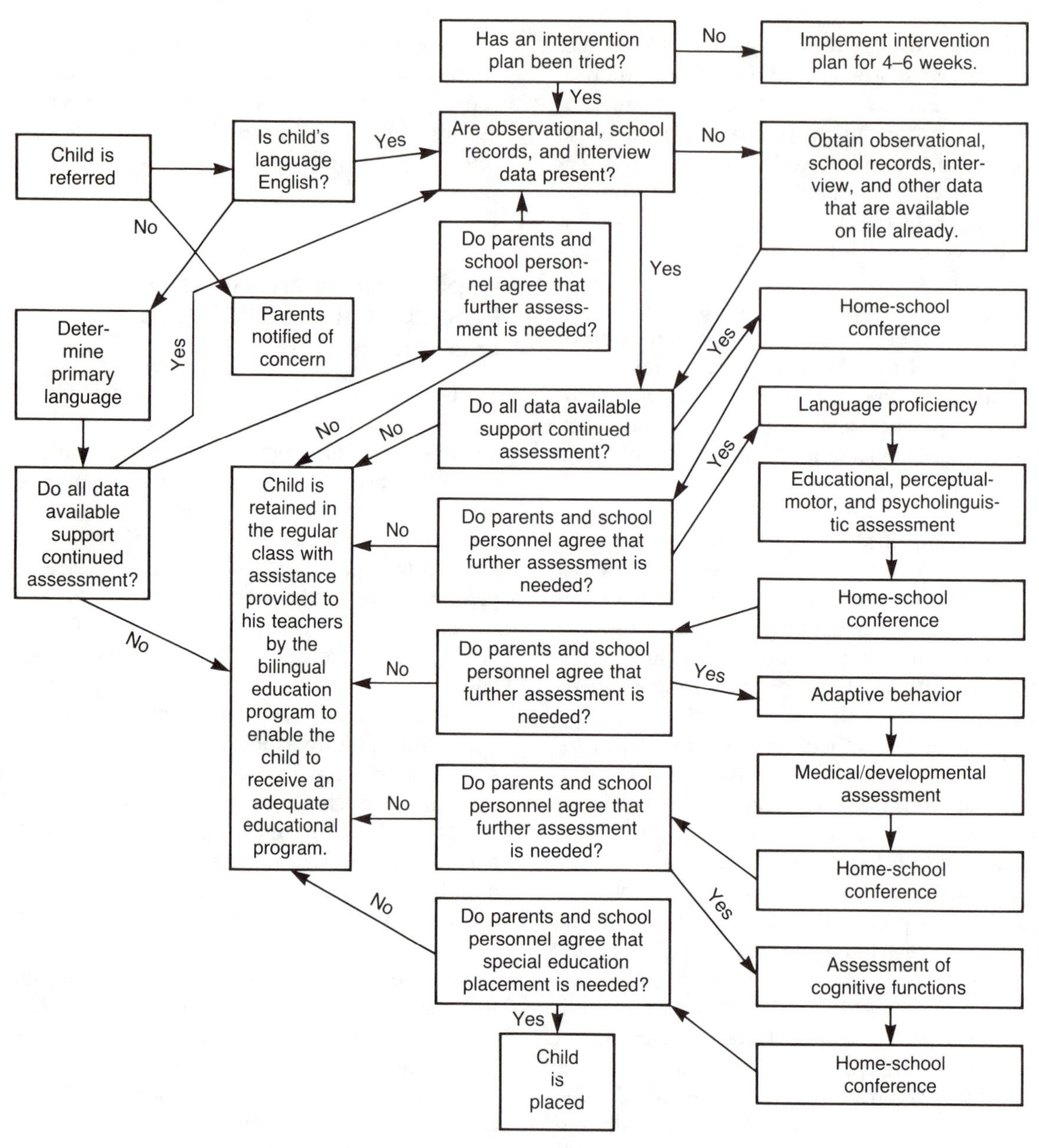

Figure 8–1

An Assessment Procedure for Bilingual Exceptional Children.

(Modeled after "Operationalizing the Diagnostic Intervention Process" by J. A. Tucker. In T. M. Oakland, (Ed.), 1977, *Psychological and Educational Assessment of Minority Children*. New York: Brunner/Mazel.

Obtaining Relevant Data

The relevant data that are essential to the assessment process include information in the following areas:

1. Referral data
2. Primary language data
3. Observational and interview data
4. Other available data, including school records
5. Language proficiency data
6. Educational assessment data
7. Perceptual-motor and/or psycholinguistic assessment data
8. Adaptive behavior data
9. Medical and/or developmental data
10. Cognitive assessment data

Referral Data

The first step in any assessment is the referral of a student for special education program consideration. There are basically two general reasons for a child to be referred. The first is that the child's behavior deviates significantly from what is considered average for children of that age or grade level. For example, a child in the third grade unable to identify the alphabet, when classmates are reading at a third grade level, might be suspected of having a learning problem and thus be referred by the teacher. In a second case the teacher might be unable to provide adequate educational programming for the student with significant behavioral and academic differences. The teacher might feel unable to provide the student with kindergarten and first grade reading instruction plus work with the rest of the third grade level reading groups in the class.

The referral form should represent a statement of concern from the classroom teacher, or referring individual, about the student's learning or behavior. This form should be clear, concise, easy to complete, and not too demanding of the teacher in terms of assessment skills or time needed to complete.

The following five items are basic to the referral form:

1. Accurate identifying information. Information regarding a student's age, birth date, grade level, date of referral, or date of any testing may seem obvious but is frequently overlooked or incomplete.

2. Primary language spoken in the home. Information regarding the child's primary language is extremely critical and frequently overlooked. Accurate knowledge regarding the language spoken in the home could alert the assessment staff to possible learning difficulties related to second language acquisition.

3. The child's presenting problem. This part should be precisely stated. Such terms as "below grade level" and "has social problems" are general, vague, and useless. Statements must focus directly on the problem. More accurate statements might be: "He is currently reading at the first grade level and can identify all letters of the alphabet." "She fights with students in her reading group when they tease her about reading."

4. Specific comments on learner strengths. All students have some positive points or strengths. However, when there are numerous problems they are frequently overlooked, and justifiably so. Identifying the student's strengths could provide valuable ideas for planning remediation.

5. Specific measures taken to solve the problem. An important point here is what alternatives the teacher has tried to remediate the problem. Some problems that students are exhibiting could possibly be resolved with a consultation with a staff member at the school.

Figure 8–2 provides an example of a referral form that illustrates many of the points discussed above. Once the referral data are completed they should be returned to the assessment team for consideration. Data should be examined to be sure that all sections have been completed and second that specific responses have been provided where necessary. Careful scrutiny should be given to the question regarding home language usage. If the primary language spoken in the home is one other than English, then the possibility of difficulty related to second language learning should be considered. Also, the referral should be flagged for careful scrutiny by team members.

It is important that the parents or guardians of the child be notified of a concern about the child's learning or behavior. Generally, such notification should come from the referring person, usually the teacher. The reassurance basically is to avoid reactions such as "No one ever told me my child was having any problems!" Second, the parents would be made aware of possible special education intervention. The due process procedures would be explained to them.

There is evidence that students are not referred in a representative manner and that ethnic, linguistic, cultural, and sex variables are frequently encountered (Cervantes, 1988). As a result, educators, particularly Bilingual Special Education personnel, are carefully examining the student referral and emphasizing interventions and curriculum modifications over a period of time, and proceeding with a comprehensive evaluation after numerous interventions have proved inadequate.

As school districts have become increasingly concerned about the representativeness of their special education programs, specific intervention activities are becoming mandatory in some cases. Thus, referred students are receiving assistance within the school setting from the resources available and are not being automatically evaluated for some type of learning disability.

Though interventions have always been an integral part of the initial referral, there appears to be a greater emphasis now on increasing these activities in a much more specific and accountable manner.

Jones (1988) suggests that focusing on the intervention aspect of the student referral will significantly decrease the number of student evaluations and Bilingual Special Education program placements.

Primary Language Data

Information regarding the primary language spoken in the home should be obtained. This can be obtained either informally through an interview with a parent or guardian or formally through the administration of a structured interview with possibly the use of a questionnaire.

However, what is important is the determination of which language is spoken most consistently within the home between the child and the various family members. This information will assist in determining what language should be used when evaluating the child.

Observational and Interview Data

Intervention strategies following the referral should be implemented for at least a month, but preferably for six weeks. However, if these activities appear insufficient, then observational and interview data are obtained. These data can assist with intervention activities as they contribute additional information about the referred child. The purpose here is to obtain systematic and objective information regarding the student's behavior from someone other than the referring person. The purpose clearly is not to question a teacher's competence or ability to

Student Referral Form

Student's Name ____________ Birthdate: ________ Age ____________

Referring person ____________ Position ________ Date ____________

Parent/Guardian ____________ Phone: Home ________ Work ________

Address ____________

____________ Reachable by: ________ day ________ evening

School ____________ Grade ____ Room # ____ Teacher ____________

Primary language spoken in the home ________ Is student bilingual? Yes ____ No ____

Basis for determination of bilingualism ____________

Health problems known ____________

Academic history (include schools attended, grade levels, and most recent grades earned).

Academic functioning level (be specific)

Student's strengths (be specific and examine academic, social, emotional, and other areas)

Behavioral functioning level (be specific)

Describe the presenting problem (be specific and include information when it was first observed, the situation in which it occurs, and how classmates respond).

Describe the measures you have taken to solve this problem (be specific examining possibly: changes in seating, assignments, classes; tutoring by peers, adults, or paraprofessional; conferences with pupil, parent, or support staff; alternative programs).

Interventions	*Date Started/Ended*	*Person(s) Responsible*	*Results*
________	________	________	________
________	________	________	________
________	________	________	________

Has a prior comprehensive evaluation ever been completed? Yes ____ No ____

If yes, please state information including date, place and person(s) responsible ____________

____

____

Has student ever been in special education? ________ If so, what program? ____________

Parent contacted by ____________ Position ________ Date: ____/____/____

Interpreter needed for parent? Yes ________ No ________ Type ____________

Is student to be referred for special education evaluation? Yes ________ No ________

Parent notified of results of meeting by ____________

Figure 8–2
Student Referral Form

identify a problem but objectively and precisely to define the factors that surround the student's difficulty in the classroom.

Sometimes teachers are so close to the problem that they cannot see the forest for the trees. But basically the purpose of classroom observation is to obtain some indication of the problem and the extent to which the problem deviates from the average performance in the classroom.

Information obtained by observational data should include data about such variables as:

1. Peer dynamics
2. Group participation
3. Classroom structure and organization
4. Learning environment
5. Student-teacher interactions

Figure 8–3 presents a possible observation form that could be used in a school setting. The observer should be specific.

Information obtained by interview should be as comprehensive as possible and include data about teacher, student, and parent concerns. A significant advantage of the interview is its almost unlimited scope and ability to shed light on a situation without necessitating extensive assessment. The function of the interview is distinct from that of an in-depth sociological case history.

An important distinction is that the interview should emphasize the student's perception of what is occurring and what might be contributing to the situation.

Figure 8–4 provides one example of an interview. Interviews can take many forms, from structured to unstructured. This one takes a combination of both.

A major limitation of the interview is its subjective and interpretive nature. That is, a person's memory of recent or past events and situations could be fuzzy and inaccurate. Also, the interviewee is likely to be biased and emphasize an interpretation that is self-complimentary.

However, interviewing different sources may provide a more accurate picture of what is actually occurring; thus interviews with at least the teacher, parent, and student are required.

Once the observational and interview data have been obtained, they should be analyzed along with the referral by designated members of the assessment team.

State or district policies may determine which designated professionals may be involved. For example, the question of state certification or licensing by staff members might rule out some school staff members from this phase.

The questions to be answered are threefold: (1) Could these learning difficulties be remediated with specific intervention strategies that could be provided outside of special education? (2) With the additional data, are there any indications of a possible learning disability that might require special education intervention? (3) Are these difficulties related to the student's bilinguality?

If the answer to the first question is no, then the assessment procedure continues and the teacher is provided with strategies and ideas to assist the student. If the answer is yes, then the process continues.

A positive answer to the second question would continue the process whereas a negative answer would end the assessment procedure. The teacher would continue to receive resource assistance in working with the child.

With respect to the third question, a no answer would allow the process to continue to gather data. A yes answer here would stop the assessment process and alternate assistance would be recommended, such as referral to the Bilingual Education program, English as a Second Language program, or other district programs for linguistically different pupils.

However, if the student is bilingual but it is not certain whether the suspected learning difficulties exist, it probably would be in the student's best interest to recommend both a referral to a program for linguistically different pupils

Classroom Observation

Student's name ________________ School ________________ Grade ________ Room # ________
Teacher's name ________________
Student's needs as seen by referring person ____
____
____

Time of day ________________ Length of observation in minutes ________________

Classroom setting (be specific, including approximate number of students, seating, organization of classroom, daily schedule, etc.).

Specific activity (reading, math, etc., size of group, etc.).

Management and instructional techniques of teacher (be specific, including use of positive or negative reinforcement, verbal and nonverbal cues, etc., Note teacher-child interaction. How does teacher present materials, use of questioning, student answering, etc.).

Observation of student's behavior with independent seat work assignments (be specific, including how well student completes work, attending to tasks, etc.).

Observation of student's behavior in group situation (be specific, including group size, types of interactions between student and group members).

Observation of student's interactions with peers as they relate to the classroom or other education setting (be specific, including how conversations are initiated, who initiates, how student responds, etc.).

Additional comments:

Does the classroom teacher believe that the student's behavior during the observation period was typical of student's everyday school performance?

Yes ______ No ______

Observer ________________ Title ________________
Date ________________

Figure 8–3
Classroom Observation Form

and to continue the assessment process with a cautious note.

Other Available Data, Including School Records

Observational and interview data can provide an invaluable profile of a student. However, the student's cumulative folder can provide additional valuable information that may give some historical perspective on the student's current problem.

The school records can further assist the intervention process by providing critical data about a child's background.

For example, some behaviors that a child is exhibiting could be related to absences from school if the child has attendance problems.

Referral Interview Summary

Student's name ______________ School ______________ Grade ________ Room # ________
Teacher's name ______________
Interviewer for teacher ______________ Student ______________ Parent ______________
Date of interview of teacher ______________ Student ______________ Parent ______________

Teacher interview (ask general open-ended questions such as, what is your major concern about the student? What could be done to help the student?, etc.).

Student interview (ask general open-ended questions such as, what do you enjoy doing at school, on the playground, at home? What subjects are most fun or enjoyable? What makes them enjoyable or fun? What subjects are most difficult? What makes them enjoyable?, etc.).

Parent interview (ask general open-ended questions such as, how do you see you child's progress at school? What subjects do you think your child enjoys most? Least? How does your child get along at home? School? Neighborhood?, etc.).

Figure 8–4
Referral Interview Summary Form

Also, a student's frequent transfers from different schools could account for problems in establishing friendships.

Students who have arrived from a foreign country typically undergo adjustment problems to a new environment that may take anywhere from one day to several years (Lambert, 1972).

Data from medical records, such as hearing and vision screening, may be on record and be related to the current behavior. Other medical data might best be interpreted by the school nurse or staff member designated by the department of health services.

In any event, state and district policies clearly indicate who has access to the available data in a child's cumulative folder. Questions of certification and licensing occur generally with those school staff members who make judgments regarding this data.

The question to answer here is whether these additional data corroborate indications of learning difficulties that might justify a special education intervention. If the answer is no, then possibly no further assessment would be required. The student's teacher, however, would need additional assistance in working with the student.

If the answer is yes, then the process should continue. Again, should there be indications of bilingualism, then it probably would be in the student's best interest to continue the assessment process and to refer the student to the Bilingual Education program.

A parent-school conference is essential at this point. The parents would have been informed of the referral and the special education program placement possibility. This information would have been provided in the primary language of the parents. The conference is held to discuss the nature of the referral as well as the observational, interview, and school record data with the parents. If the parents do not understand English, an interpreter should be provided for them. Their approval is necessary for the assessment to proceed. If the parents should disapprove or disagree about continuing the assessment, then the process is terminated and the teacher is given assistance to meet the educational needs of the child.

Language Proficiency Data

Once the parents and school staff members have agreed that further assessment is necessary, data regarding language proficiency are obtained.

Determining children's primary language, their proficiency in that language, and the degree to which the primary language is consistent and compatible with the language used in the school is critical in determining whether the symptoms exhibited by the student are related to a handicap or just to common problems related to learning a second language.

Basically, the purpose of administering a language proficiency instrument is to determine the extent to which language may be an intervening variable on the other data collected. For example, it may be difficult to determine that a student has a significant learning disorder if that student is proficient in Vietnamese but judged to be nonproficient in English.

The first question to be answered is: In which language is the child most proficient? If the answer is that the child is proficient in Chinese, for example, then continued assessment should be in that language if possible. As has been pointed out in previous sections, continuing the assessment process of this child in English would be meaningless, inappropriate, and invalid.

If the child is equally proficient in both English and the native language, then decisions become more difficult. As the student exhibits competencies in the English language, the decision must be made whether to proceed with assessment in English, the primary language, or both. Overall, it would be in the student's best interest to have as much data as possible regarding functioning in both languages to determine strengths and weaknesses, as well as to aid in the development of prescriptive measures for remediation.

The second and critically important question becomes: Is there any indication that the child's primary language proficiency could be the causal factor with respect to academic difficulties? The answer must be no for assessment to continue. That is, even in the primary language the difficulty is noted and supports the referral, observation, and interview data as well as the school records. A Laotian-speaking child, for example, may be mentally deficient, but this diagnosis would need to be consistent across all data areas up to this point for assessment to continue.

Again, if the child is bilingual and the data are not consistent, then assessment should not continue. At this point, it would be in the student's best interest to stop the assessment process and look at alternate forms of assistance.

Educational Assessment Data

If assessment is to continue, the next part of the process is a determination of the student's educational skills. Parents must be informed and documented parent permission for testing must be obtained.

The purpose is to gather additional educational data about the student's functional educational skills in specific subject matter areas. An important determination here is whether a discrepancy exists between the student's reported classroom achievement and the level of performance on individual tests.

In assessing the academic skills of referred students, one should consider the curriculum of the educational program within the classroom, school, and district. If students are eventually to succeed in a regular classroom, they must acquire the basic skills consistent for their grade levels. What those skills are should be reflected in the educational assessment instruments used.

How well the assessment shows the child's academic strengths and weaknesses in math, reading, and other language areas will affect the degree to which the results can be translated into prescriptive intervention strategies. Unless the test results are directly related to instruction, then the effort has been useless and wasted.

Figure 8–5 provides an example of a form that could be used to include educational assessment data. On this form language is broken down into oral and written components. Other skill areas include reading, spelling, speech production, and math. To present the data in a positive frame of reference, current levels of performance are broken down into strengths and weaknesses.

A question to be answered once the educational assessment data have been obtained is whether the strengths and weaknesses noted are consistent with a profile of a significant handicap. For example, the question—Could the child's limited English proficiency account for the present level of academic performance?—becomes important.

If the answer is related to those factors, then it probably would be best to refer the student for assistance through the Bilingual Education program. On the other hand, the educational assessment data may provide additional support for the position that the student does indeed have a significant handicap.

Perceptual-Motor and/or Psycholinguistic Assessment Data

The concerns about the inadequacies of psychoeducational tests as well as tests in general with linguistically different populations have been repeatedly documented (Archuleta & Cervantes, 1981; Baca & Cervantes, 1978; Cervantes, 1988; Cervantes & Baca, 1979; Cervantes & Bieber, 1981; Laosa, 1977; Mercer, 1973).

As a result, test developers have flooded the market with a variety of tests described as appropriate for linguistic minorities. It has thus become increasingly important for educators to develop some statistical skills, particularly with norm-referenced tests. Understanding and evaluating the standardization sample, reliability and validity of a test can help to eliminate inappropriate tests.

Standardization Sample. The importance of the standardization sample was discussed in some detail at the beginning of this chapter. Representatives of the normative group, number of students in the normative group, and appropriateness of the normative group are three critical factors. If student profiles are compared, the normative sample must reflect the characteristics of the population, particularly with respect to age, sex, ethnicity, grade level, socioeconomic status, and geographic region.

Reliability. Reliability is a measure of the consistency of the test; a reliable test should give similar scores when readministered. Reliability is most frequently expressed by a reliability coefficient and is represented as a score between 0 and 1.00. A test with a low reliability coefficient would be .25. A test with a high reliability coefficient would be .95. With respect to educational and intelligence tests, reliability coefficients of .85 are generally expected.

Validity. The validity of a test refers to how well a test measures what it is supposed to measure. The more valid the test the more one can generalize and make inferences from the standardization sample to the student profile.

Validity is most frequently expressed as a correlation coefficient between two or more factors. For example, a test with high predictive

Student's name ______________ Birth date ______________ Age ______________
Address ______________
Parent/guardian ______________
School ______________ Grade ______ Room # ______ Teacher ______________
Primary language spoken in the home ______________
Is student bilingual? Yes ______ No ______
Basis for determination of bilingualism ______________
Date of educational assessment ______________
Administered by ______________ Title ______________

Area assessed	Present level of performance Strengths	Weaknesses
Language		
1. Oral language		
2. Written language		
Reading		
Spelling		
Speech production		
Math		

Figure 8–5
Educational Assessment Survey

validity would indicate that a student scoring high on a test would score equally high on some other criterion measure. On the other hand, a student scoring low would be expected to score low on another criterion if the predictive validity was .95.

With the factors of standardization sample, reliability, and validity in mind, the following tests of educational achievement are considered adequate and in some cases are available in languages other than English:

Boehm Test of Basic Concepts—Revised

Kaufman Test of Educational Achievement

Key Math Diagnostic Arithmetic Test

Peabody Picture Vocabulary Test—Revised

Test of Auditory Comprehension of Language—Revised

Woodcock-Johnson Psychoeducational Battery

In evaluating linguistically different students with achievement tests it is important to match the test to their bilingual ability. Children who are monolingual Vietnamese should be evaluated in Vietnamese. If an achievement test is not available in that language, it may be necessary to rely on a language proficiency test. However, a language proficiency test should never be used in isolation but in conjunction with a nonverbal test such as the Leiter International Performance Scale on Raven's Progressive Matrices.

Adaptive Behavior Data

An important consideration in the assessment process is whether the behavior observed in the classroom is consistent with the behavior observed in other environments, for example, the playground, the home, the neighborhood, and the community. Indeed, a sad joke heard frequently is that the student is only mentally retarded or emotionally disturbed in school! At home the child is perfectly average in every way. Such comments have been reported in numerous studies (Laosa, 1977; Mercer, 1973, 1979; Oakland, 1977).

Essentially an assessment of adaptive behavior determines if a student's social skills are consistent with those of other students of the same age, sex, and socioeconomic, linguistic, and ethnic background.

Does the student's adaptive behavior away from the school setting appear consistent with the data thus far obtained, and does it continue to suggest special education intervention? If the answer is yes in both cases, then the assessment process would continue to obtain the necessary data.

If the answer is no, termination of further assessment should be carefully considered. In this case the child's teacher would be assisted in meeting the educational needs of the child. Another alternative might be to continue the assessment and to compare the data from other sources.

Medical and/or Developmental Data

A student could appear to the classroom teacher or other school staff member as having numerous symptoms of a significant handicap when, in actuality, the student could be suffering from a medical condition that could be medically remedied. For example, a student suffering from diabetes or epilepsy could appear to have significant behavior or learning difficulties that are directly attributable to physical condition. Thus it is important to know the medical and developmental history of the child when decisions about educational programming are being considered.

Basically, the purpose of such data is to rule out a physical or medical condition as a contributing factor to the underlying symptoms of a disability. On the other hand, medical and developmental data could confirm a diagnosis of a significant disability, such as a brain injury or birth trauma.

Interpretation of medical and developmental data should be limited to staff members with the necessary school district and state requirements of training, certification, and licensure.

Can the child's present behavior be explained in terms of the child's medical and/or developmental history? If the answer is yes, referral to a medical center might be considered in lieu of, or in addition to, special education intervention.

If the answer is no, one possibility would be to stop the assessment process and refer the student to assistance elsewhere. A second alternative would be to continue assessment and obtain data from other sources.

Once data have been obtained regarding the student's adaptive behavior as well as the medical and/or developmental history, a home-school conference is held to discuss the results. A decision is reached about whether assessment should continue or terminate.

Cognitive Assessment Data

Assessment of cognitive functioning is recommended as the last step in the assessment procedure for bilingual exceptional children. This assessment has been the most controversial and damaging to linguistically different students. As a result, educators must proceed with caution.

As with ability and achievement tests, cognitive tests must be administered in the student's primary language, the language in which the child is most proficient.

Currently, several instruments can be used to determine the student's ability to learn. The Learning Potential Assessment (Budoff, 1987) has shown that students of ethnically diverse populations can improve their performance as a result of specific training.

Budoff (1987) points out that the intent of learning potential assessment is to obtain an estimate of intelligence by seeing how the child reasons out problems of varying difficulty. If, following training, the child can solve problems at an average peer level, this indicates that the child is not mentally retarded. Intelligence, according to Budoff, is the ability to profit from experience.

However, one significant limitation of the learning potential procedure is its usefulness for the classroom teacher. More specifically, Budoff and his colleagues have been unable to translate the procedures into some type of prescriptive measure for each child. Until that occurs, the Budoff training-based procedure remains just another method of reclassifying misclassified mentally retarded children.

Similarly, the Learning Potential Assessment Device (LPAD, Feuerstein et al., 1987) has been described as a possible substitute for the IQ test (Lidz, 1987). It also uses a test-train-retest paradigm. The LPAD battery attempts to:

1. Assess how much an individual level of intellectual linguistic functioning can be modified
2. Determine the amount of investment of teaching effort required to produce the specified degree of modification
3. Ascertain the extent to which the student is able to apply new patterns of functioning to other areas
4. Identify the individual's preferential learning style

Feuerstein's position is that retarded academic performance is primarily related to a lack of appropriate mediated learning experiences. Thus this environmental deficiency may cloud a student's true learning potential. With respect to linguistically and culturally different children, one cannot assume that they have had the same opportunities to learn the content domains of standard IQ tests as have other children. Therefore, he believes, it is inappropriate to use such achievement-oriented tests to estimate a child's future learning potential. A more appropriate procedure, according to Feuerstein, is to give such children new learning tasks that have not been encountered before, observe their learning processes, teach them some principles of learning and problem solving, observe how easily they learn given teaching, and then require them to apply the principles to the solution of new problems. Feuerstein et al. (1981) have modified existing tests (Raven's Colored Progressive Matrices, Rey's Organization of Dots, and Arthur's Stencil Design Test) and selected new tests (Rey's Plateaux Test) to produce a clinical battery that attempts to determine the degree to which the effects of "cultural deprivation" could be reversed by appropriate experience.

Lidz (1987) suggested that the continued interest in dynamic assessment may eventually substitute for the IQ test. It certainly appeared more appropriate when compared to IQ instruments that evaluated children on culturally and linguistically loaded items and required experience with standardized tests.

Feuerstein et al. (1987), however, pointed out that the LPAD does have limitations and disadvantages. One significant limitation was the personality characteristic requirements of the examiner. The evaluators must have the ability to be active, stimulating, and encouraging during the assessment.

Other disadvantages are the length of time required to administer the LPAD (several hours) and the accompanying financial burden.

The LPAD as well as Budoff's (1987) learning potential procedure do appear to have considerable promise for culturally and linguistically different students. Some investigators, on the other hand, are taking a different approach. They are developing cross-cultural assessment procedures based on the developmental stages of children as described by Jean Piaget (Bernal, 1977; De Avila & Havassy, 1974).

The results of a field study were reported by De Avila and Havassy (1974). Approximately 1300 Mexican-American and White-American children from New Mexico, Colorado, Texas, and California were used to test the interrelations among the four neo-Piagetian measures (Cartoon Conservation Scales, Water Level Task, Figural Intersection Test, and Serial Task).

The investigators found that the Cartoon Conservation Scales, the Water Level Task, and the Figural Intersection Test possessed high reliability and validity and exhibited developmental stage progression across age consistent with Piaget's theory of cognitive development. De Avila and Havassy (1974) concluded:

> The findings of the present research reveal that when these methods and procedures are employed, Mexican-American children perform at cognitive levels appropriate for their chronological age. Even though there is statistically significant variation of performance across sites, all performance is well within the normal range of appropriate levels of cognitive functioning. A related and equally important finding of this research is that it failed to find differences in level of cognitive developmental performance between Anglo and Mexican-American children. The data show the same developmental curves for both ethnic groups. These findings are supportive of Piagetian Theory. From these findings, the authors conclude that Mexican-American children develop cognitively the same as, and at basically the same rate as, Anglo-American children.

The Cartoon Conservation Scales developed by De Avila and Havassy (1974) appear to have validity for use with bilingual exceptional children. The authors indicate that it is appropriate and fair for use with both Anglo and minority populations.

However, one limitation of the Cartoon Conservation Scales is the lack of information about the student's verbal skills that are prerequisite to academic achievement.

The Kaufman Assessment Battery for Children (Kaufman & Kaufman, 1982) is described as a recent assessment tool appropriate for use with bilingual exceptional children. The K-ABC provides standard scores in four areas of functioning: Sequential Processing, Simultaneous Processing, Mental Processing and Composite (Sequential plus Simultaneous and Achievement). It is designed for children between the ages of $2\frac{1}{2}$ and $12\frac{1}{2}$ years.

Kaufman and Kaufman view intelligence as based on the distinction between sequential and simultaneous mental processes and the K-ABC was derived primarily from the fields of neuropsychology and cognitive psychology.

The authors developed the standardization sample based on 1980 census data that was stratified by geographic region, sex, race and ethnic group.

The K-ABC is described as being more culturally fair when compared to traditional IQ tests. A comparison of Anglo versus Hispanic scores showed that Anglo students scored only 3.1 points higher than Hispanic students on the Mental Composite Scale of the K-ABC compared to 11.2 points higher on the Full Scale WISC-R.

A limitation of the K-ABC includes the standardization sample, which does not appear to be representative of the population of Hispanic and Black children in the United States. Thus the K-ABC may not be as culturally fair as the authors indicate.

Another limitation of the K-ABC is its heavy reliance on visual stimuli, which make it unsuitable for children with visual impairments.

The question to answer is: Are the results of the cognitive assessment consistent with all the data previously obtained? If the answer is no, then the test score should be considered invalid and not usable as a part of the decision-making process.

If the answer is yes or maybe, careful judgment is necessary regarding decisions about the student's intellectual functioning according to the test.

Finally, a home-school conference is held to discuss results of the cognitive assessment. The test scores are examined in light of all the previous data and a decision is made about placing the child in a special education program. Only after the data have consistently indicated that a handicap is the primary cause of the student's classroom difficulties can the student be placed in a special education program. Placement on questionable or incomplete data denies the child civil rights as an individual.

Determination of a Specific Learning Disability

Within the field of special education, no program other than the program for the mild mentally retarded has been more controversial than the learning disabilities program. Because large numbers of students (nearly 2 million according to 1983 population estimates) are placed in this program, we will highlight it here.

Linguistically and culturally different children make up a large percentage of this program. As a result, the U.S. Office of Education has provided regulations in the diagnosis of learning disabilities.

> A team may determine that a child has a specific learning disability if:
>
> 1. The child does not achieve commensurate with his or her age and ability levels in one or more of the areas listed below and
>
> 2. The team finds that a child has a severe discrepancy between achievement and intellectual ability in one or more of the following areas:
>
> a. oral expression
>
> b. listening comprehension
>
> c. written expression
>
> d. basic reading skills
>
> e. reading comprehension
>
> f. mathematics calculation or
>
> g. mathematics reasoning
>
> The team may not identify a child as having a specific learning disability if the severe discrepancy between ability and achievement is primarily the result of:
>
> a. a visual, hearing or motor handicap
>
> b. mental retardation
>
> c. emotional disturbance, or
>
> d. environmental, cultural, or economic disadvantage (*Federal Register,* December 29, 1977, p. 65083).

Thus, for a linguistically different child to be identified as learning disabled, a significant discrepancy between achievement and cognitive ability is required. Most school districts now interpret a significant discrepancy from 1.5 to 2.0 or more standard deviations from the mean. In addition, environmental, cultural, or economic disadvantage are not the cause of the significant discrepancy. The net effect is that many school districts are seeing significant decreases in the number of bilingual learning disabled children.

Summary

Because assessment in special education has been fraught with inconsistencies, inadequacies, and controversy, developing an assessment procedure for bilingual exceptional children appears impossible. It is valuable to see what educators in the field of special education are recommending with respect to the assessment of language minority children.

An examination of texts on the topic of exceptional children revealed that assessment procedures for culturally, linguistically, and ethnically different children are not available.

Legislative guidelines were examined to determine what legal requirements were necessary in the assessment of language minority students. P.L. 94–142 has provided a base from which an assessment procedure could be developed for language minorities.

Diagnostic, assessment, and evaluation models were examined in light of their appropriateness for culturally, linguistically, and ethnically different children. Models discussed included the assessment, diagnosis, and evaluation model (Cromwell, Blashfield, & Strauss, 1975); the diagnostic teaching model (Cartwright & Cartwright, 1972); and the assessment models of Pasanella and Volkmor (1977), Mercer (1979), Ysseldyke (1973), and Ysseldyke and Salvia (1974, 1975).

Of these, an assessment model for culturally and linguistically diverse populations was examined in detail. This model was based on assessment data from five conceptual models: (1) the medical model, (2) the social system model, (3) the psychoeducational process model, (4) the task analysis model, and (5) the pluralistic model.

The medical model is based in medicine and is designed to identify biological dysfunctions. The social system model examines the student's social behavior and compares it to the behavior of similar students in that socioeconomic group. The psychoeducational process model assumes that a child's academic problems are related to cognitive, perceptual, and psycholinguistic processes.

The task analysis model emphasizes the assessment of academic skill areas and uses criterion-referenced assessment instruments. These tests measure the student's skill level within a specific subject area and do not compare performance with that of other children.

The pluralistic model recommends the inclusion of the sociocultural, linguistic, and ethnic information when interpreting IQ test scores. The scale developed by Mercer (1979) uses this type of framework for students from Black and Hispanic backgrounds.

The next section discussed the implementation of the assessment procedure for bilingual exceptional children in a step-by-step manner. The process involves the following areas: (1) referral data, (2) primary language data, (3) observational and interview data, (4) other available data, including school records, (5) language proficiency data, (6) educational assessment data, (7) perceptual-motor and/or psycholinguistic assessment data, (8) adaptive behavior data, (9) medical and/or developmental data, and (10) cognitive assessment data.

Discussion Questions

1. Explain two ways in which norm-referenced tests differ from criterion-referenced tests.

2. With respect to assessment, what requirements are included under P.L. 94–142? Discuss five requirements.

3. What 10 components are included in the recommended assessment model for bilingual exceptional children?

4. Discuss what is obtained for language proficiency data.

5. Discuss what is obtained for adaptive behavior data.

References

Archuleta, K., & Cervantes, H. T. (1981). The misplaced child: Does linguistically different mean learning disabled? In P. C. Gonzales (Ed.), *Proceedings of the eighth annual international bilingual bicultural education conference.* Rosslyn, VA: National Clearinghouse for Bilingual Education.

Baca, L., & Cervantes, H. T. (1978). The assessment of minority students: Are adaptive behavior scales the answer? *Psychology in the Schools.* 15:366–370.

Bernal, E. M. (1977). Assessment procedures for Chicano children: The sad state of the art. *International Journal of Chicano Studies Research.* 8:69–81.

Bijou, S. W. (1970). What psychology has to offer education now. *Journal of Applied Behavior Analysis.* 3:65–71.

Budoff, M. (1987). The validity of learning potential assessment. In C. S. Lidz (Ed.), *Dynamic assessment: An interactional approach for evaluating learning potential.* New York: Guilford Press.

Cartwright, C. A., & Cartwright, G. P. (1974). Developing observation skills. New York: McGraw-Hill.

Cartwright, G. P., & Cartwright, C. A. (1972). Gilding the lily: Comments on the training based model. *Exceptional Children.* 39:231–234.

Cervantes, H. T. (1988). Nondiscriminatory assessment and informal data gathering: The case of Gonzaldo L. In R. L. Jones (Ed.), *Psychoeducational assessment of minority group children: A casebook. (pp. 239–256). Berkeley, CA: Cobb and Henry.*

Cervantes, H. T., & Baca, L. (1978). Assessing minority students: The role of adaptive behavior scales. *Journal of Non-White Concerns.* 7:122–127.

Cervantes, H. T., & Bieber, B. J. (1981). Non-discriminatory assessment: One school district's response. In R. G. Maya, (Ed.), BUENO Center for Multicultural Education Monograph Series, vol. 2, no. 2 (pp. 39–49). Boulder, CO: University of Colorado.

Coles, G. (1978). The learning disabilities test battery: Empirical and social issues. *Harvard Educational Review.* 48:313–340.

Cromwell, R. L., Blashfield, R. K., & Strauss, J. S. (1975). Criteria for classification systems. In N. Hobbs (Ed.), *Issues in the classification of children,* vol. 1. San Francisco: Jossey-Bass.

Cummins, J. (1984). *Bilingualism and special education: Issues in assessment and pedagogy.* San Diego: College-Hill Press.

De Avila, E. A., & Havassy, B. E. (1974). *Intelligence of Mexican American children: A field study comparing neo-Piagetian and traditional capacity and achievement measures.* Austin, TX: Dissemination Center for Bilingual Bicultural Education.

Federal Register, Dec. 29, 1977, p. 65083.

Federal Register: Part II (1982, August 4). Department of Health Education. Education of handicapped children: Assistance to states for education of handicapped children, proposed rules, 47:33836–33860.

Feuerstein, R., et al. (1981). *Examiner manuals for the learning potential assessment device.* Jerusalem: Hadassah-WIZO, Canada Research Institute.

Feuerstein, R., Vaacou, R., Jensen, M. R., Kaniel, S., & Tzuriel, D. Prerequisites for assessment of learning potential: The LPAD model. In C. S. Lidz (Ed.), *Dynamic assessment: An interactional approach to evaluating learning potential.* New York: Guilford Press.

Georgrades, W., & Clark, D. C. (Eds.) (1974). *Models for individualized instruction.* New York: MSS Information Corp.

Glaser, R. (1963). Instructional technology and the measurement of learning outcomes: Some questions. *American Psychologist.* 18:519–521.

Glass, G. Effectiveness of special education. *Policy Studies Review.* 2:65–78.

Gold, M. W. (1972). Stimulus factors in skill training of the retarded on a complex assembly task: Acquisition, transfer, and retention. *American Journal of Mental Deficiency.* 76:517–526.

Hallahan, D. P., & Kauffman, J. M. (1986). Exceptional children: Introduction to special education. Englewood Cliffs, N.J.: Prentice-Hall.

Hammill, D. D., & Bartel, N. R. (Eds.) (1975). *Teaching children with learning and behavior problems.* Boston: Allyn & Bacon.

Haring, N. G. & McCormick, L. (1986). *Exceptional children and youth: An introduction to special education.* Columbus, OH: Merrill Publishing Co.

Hobbs, N. (1975). The futures of children. San Francisco: Jossey-Bass.

Jones, R. L. (Ed.) (1988). *Psychoeducational assessment of minority group children: A casebook.* Berkeley, CA: Cobb and Henry.

Kaufman, A. S., & Kaufman, N. L. (1982). *Kaufman assessment battery for children: Interpretive Manual.* Circle Pines, MN: American Guidance Service.

Kavale, K. (1981). Functions of the Illinois test of psycholinguistic abilities: Are they trainable? *Exceptional Children.* 47:496–510.

Lambert, N., Wilcox, M., & Gleason, W. (1974). *The educationally retarded child.* New York: Grune & Stratton.

Lambert, N., et al. (1975). *AAMD adaptive behavior scale: Public school version.* Washington, DC: American Association on Mental Deficiency.

Lambert, W. E. (1972). A social psychology of bilingualism. In R. D. Abrahams, and R. C. Troike (Eds.), *Language and cultural diversity in American education.* Englewood Cliffs, NJ: Prentice-Hall.

Laosa, L. M. (1977). Nonbiased assessment of children's abilities: Historical antecedents and current issues. In T. M. Oakland (Ed.), *Psychological and educational assessment of minority children.* New York: Brunner/Mazel.

Lidz, C. S. (Ed.) (1987). *Dynamic assessment: An interactional approach for evaluating learning potential.* New York: Guilford Press.

Mann, L. (1971). Psychometric phrenology and the new faculty psychology: The case against ability assessment and training. *Journal of Special Education.* 5:3–14.

Mattes, L. J. & Omark, D. R. *Speech and language assessment for the bilingual handicapped.* San Diego: College-Hill Press.

Meier, J. H. (1975). Assessment and intervention for young children at developmental risk. In N. Hobbs (Ed.), *Issues in the classification of children,* vol. 2. San Francisco: Jossey-Bass.

Mercer, J. R. (1973). *Labeling the mentally retarded.* Berkeley, CA: University of California Press.

Mercer, J. R. (1974). A policy statement on assessment procedures and the rights of children. *Harvard Educational Review.* 44:125–141.

Mercer, J. R. (1979). *System of multicultural pluralistic assessment.* New York: Psychological Corp.

Mercer, J. R. (1981, May). Personal communication.

Miller, N. (Ed.) (1984). *Bilingualism and language disability: Assessment and remediation.* San Diego: College-Hill Press.

Mills, B. C., & Mills, R. A. (Eds.) (1972). *Designing instructional strategies for young children.* Dubuque, IA: William C. Brown Co.

Oakland, T. M. (1977). *Psychological and educational assessment of minority children.* New York: Brunner/Mazel.

Omark, D. R., & Erickson, J. G. (1983). *The bilingual exceptional child.* San Diego: College-Hill Press.

Pasanella, A. L., & Volkmor, C. B. (1977). *Coming back . . . or never leaving: Instructional programming for handicapped students in the mainstream.* Columbus, OH: Merrill Publishing Co.

Resnick, L. B., Wang, M. C., & Kaplan, J. (1973). Task analysis in curriculum design: A hierarchically sequenced introductory mathematics curriculum. *Journal of Applied Behavior Analysis.* 6:670–710.

Sabatino, D. (1972). Resource rooms: The renaissance in special education. *Journal of Special Education.* 6(4):335–347.

Taylor, R. L. (1984). *Assessment of exceptional students: Educational and psychological procedures.* Englewood Cliffs, NJ: Prentice-Hall.

Tucker, J. A. (1977). Operationalizing the diagnostic intervention process. In, T. M. Oakland, (Ed.), *Psychological and educational assessment of minority children.* New York: Brunner/Mazel.

Woodcock, R. W., & Johnson, M. B. (1977). *The Woodcock-Johnson psycho-educational battery.* New York: Teaching Resources.

Ysseldyke, J. E. (1973). Diagnostic-prescriptive teaching: The search for aptitude-treatment interactions. In L. Mann & D. Sabatino (Eds.), *The first review of special education*. Philadelphia: Buttonwood Farms.

Ysseldyke, J. E. (1977). Aptitude treatment interaction with first grade children. *Contemporary Education Psychology*. 2:1–9.

Ysseldyke, J. E., & Salvia, J. (1974). Diagnostic-prescriptive teaching: Two models. *Exceptional Children*. 41:181–186.

Ysseldyke, J. E., & Salvia, J. (1975). *Methodological considerations in aptitude treatment interaction research with intact groups*. Unpublished paper, Pennsylvania State University, University Park, PA.

CHAPTER NINE

Staffing and the Development of Individualized Educational Programs for the Bilingual Exceptional Student

Alba A. Ortiz
James R. Yates

- Variables Affecting Services for LEP Handicapped Students
- Admission, Review, and Dismissal Committee
- Parental Participation
- Placement Alternatives
- Individual Educational Programs (IEPs)
- Instructional Goals and Priorities
- Variables Affecting Individualized Planning for LEP Handicapped Students
- Promising Instructional Strategies
- Classroom Management
- Example of Educational Planning for LEP Handicapped Students
- Summary

Objectives

- To understand the critical variables that affect the provision of services to the LEP handicapped student
- To become aware of the major responsibilities of the ARD committee as applied to the LEP handicapped student
- To become knowledgeable about the unique role of parents in the LEP process
- To comprehend the broad range of student placement alternatives
- To learn how to develop IEPs for the LEP handicapped student

Probably no aspect of special education in the schools today has generated as much comment and controversy as the individualized education program (IEP) that is required to be written for all handicapped children. The current national emphasis on instructional planning for exceptional children is directly related to requirements of P.L. 94–142, the Education for All Handicapped Children Act. The law does not specify the planning process to be followed, but it does set forth detailed requirements on what should be included in an IEP and the conditions under which the plan should be developed. The law's intent is not to standardize instructional planning or to promote a particular teaching methodology. The goal is to establish use of the IEP to bring about quality education for exceptional children and youth.

P.L. 94–142 defines an individualized education program as:

> A written statement for each handicapped child developed in any meeting by a representative of the local educational agency or an intermediate educational unit who shall be qualified to provide, or supervise the provision of, specially designed instruction to meet the unique needs of handicapped children, the teacher, the parents or guardian of such child, and, whenever appropriate, such child.

At present school districts are finding themselves at a loss in tailoring IEPs to unique populations of handicapped individuals such as bilingual exceptional children. For such children, programs must be appropriate not only in terms of special education needs but also in terms of linguistic, cultural, and other background characteristics. The complexity of this task has made schools reluctant to provide special education services for fear they will not be able to defend diagnostic procedures, placement decisions, and educational plans (Ortiz & Yates, 1983). Such fears may be the result of increased litigation and a growing trend toward malpractice suits directed at professional individuals who have participated in identification, placement, and instructional process decisions. Efforts to avoid litigation may actually result in minority children being deprived of a free, appropriate education (Reynolds, 1978).

Variables Affecting Services for LEP Handicapped Students

The development of appropriate individual educational programs and implementation of such plans for limited English proficient (LEP) handicapped children is further complicated by a lack of trained personnel, appropriate procedures, adequate information, and available instructional strategies and materials. Along these lines it is important to make the following points:

1. Lack of assessment personnel. Because of the scarcity of assessment personnel who can test children in their native language and who are qualified to interpret performance in light of the child's linguistic and cultural characteristics, modifications in assessment procedures may occur. For example, an interpreter may be introduced into the testing environment. Such modifications often significantly affect standardization.

2. Inadequate procedures. Inadequacies in assessment instruments and procedures for identifying handicaps among LEP children are often not considered when decisions are made related to school problems and suggested educational programming.

3. Lack of trained personnel. Many LEP exceptional children cannot be provided an appropriate education because of the lack of special educational personnel uniquely trained to serve this population. Of particular concern is the lack of personnel who can provide instruction in the child's native language (Ortiz & Yates, 1982).

4. Limited knowledge base. Research in the area of special education for bilingual exceptional children is almost nonexistent. Existent evidence is basically deductive or generalized from studies completed in Bilingual Education, special education, or general theories of learning. Without legitimate data and knowledge specific to this population, efforts to provide appropriate services will continue to be based on assumptions and intuitions.

5. Lack of instructional materials. Few materials are specifically designed for handicapped children from linguistically and culturally diverse backgrounds. Instructional personnel most frequently adapt materials or create their own, a difficult task given the absence of a theoretical basis for modification, adaptation, or creation.

6. Bilingual Education. There is growing concern that Bilingual Education has become an alternative to special education placement. Education personnel making placement decisions may hope that putting a child in a class with a teacher who speaks the child's native language may alleviate the child's handicap. Bilingual educators often lack necessary training to determine whether a child is handicapped or to provide educational interventions that help exceptional children. Further, bilingual teachers are at a loss in preventing inappropriate placement of exceptional children in their class.

7. Policy/law. School districts are aware of the need to serve all handicapped children and of sanctions that can be imposed for failure to do so. Existing safeguards in law, for example, P.L. 94–142, if appropriately implemented, greatly improve the services for linguistically and culturally diverse exceptional children.

8. Bilingual Education resources. The development of Bilingual Education programs has resulted in an increased availability of personnel whose training and experiences can be a valuable resource in instructional planning for exceptional children. Additionally, Bilingual Education offers an array of instructional materials and identified strategies that can be adapted for special education.

9. Other resources. Related programs such as migrant education, early childhood education, and social, welfare, and health services can be brought to bear on the education of linguistically and culturally diverse exceptional children. Sufficient resources may currently exist for adequately serving such children, but awareness and coordination of such resources are vital.

10. Training programs. The Office of Special Education and the Office of Bilingual Education and Minority Languages Affairs of the U.S. Department of Education have provided funds to develop training programs to meet the needs of Bilingual Special Education personnel. Such programs are designed specifically to train individuals to provide the specialized services required by linguistically and culturally diverse exceptional children.

Given the complex variables that must be addressed in providing special education services to linguistically and culturally diverse exceptional children, a logical question to ask is: Where does one begin? For students who are indeed handicapped, developing and implementing individual educational programs that provide linguistic and culturally relevant interventions appropriate to their special education needs is necessary.

Admission, Review, and Dismissal Committee

Law and procedure require that the interpretation of assessment data and the determination of a child's program and placement in special education be made by a team of persons knowledgeable about the student, competent in interpretation of evaluation results, aware of placement options, and responsible for assignment of personnel to provide services necessary to meet the unique needs of the child. This team has three major responsibilites:

1. Determining eligibility for initial assignment to special education (admission)

2. Reviewing the child's individual educational plan, evaluating progress, and determining whether the child should continue to be enrolled in special education (review)

3. Determining when special education services should be terminated (dismissal)

The admission, review, and dismissal (ARD) committee includes, at a minimum, a representative of appraisal, instruction, administration, the parent, and, if appropriate, the child. LEP handicapped children may require a wider array of services resulting in the need for more representation and expertise on the ARD committee than the minimum representatives required under law or policy. For example, the team must have the expertise of someone who can interpret performance and make suggestions of intervention congruent with the child's language, culture, and background characteristics. The ARD team might very well include the principal, a regular classroom teacher, a special education teacher or supervisor, a Bilingual Education specialist, and other support personnel such as a bilingual counselor, community liaison, or a teacher of English as a Second Language.

A representative of administration definitely should be present, and this representative must have the power to provide or to supervise provision of special education as well as other support services. Because the child is likely to be eligible for several programs, the administrator must have the authority to ensure that the ARD team's recommendations are implemented and that resources and personnel are assigned across programs to meet the child's education needs. Under ideal circumstances, the administrative representative would be the building principal ultimately responsible for personnel and provision of services to the child. The primary responsibility of such a principal would be to achieve cooperation among the instructional personnel and integration of resources and services.

Parental Participation

Historically, parents have simply given consent for their children to receive special education services after placement decisions have been made by educational personnel. P.L. 94–142 establishes procedures requiring parental participation. Under this law parents must be provided information, assistance, and/or counsel to ensure that they understand the various proceedings, deliberations, and decisions that may result. Written prior notice in the native language of the parents is required in matters relating to identification, evaluation, and placement of a handicapped child. Parental consent forms must include all information relevant to the activity, including a description of any evaluation procedures, tests, records, or other reports that the school will use as a basis for decision making. Parents must also be informed that their consent is voluntary and can be withdrawn at any time. In addition, parents must be advised that they have the right to bring to meetings and deliberations someone who can serve as their advocate. The advocate present during these deliberations should be familiar with special education and able to assist the parents in understanding and interpreting various information and language used.

School personnel commonly complain that parents of minority children do not care about their children and fail to take interest in them. These views are erroneous. School personnel complain that parents are not involved, supportive, or helpful to the school or education professionals. The problem may actually be a conflict between the values and perceptions of school personnel and those of parents. For example, parents in lower socioeconomic classes may have priorities that supersede their children's education, such as finding ways to provide adequate nutrition, shelter, and clothing. Parents may perceive participation in school conferences as very important but may not have the flexibility or control over their environments to allow them to attend such meetings. As a result, conferences may be a luxury parents can ill afford. Interpreting lack of attendance as lack of interest may well be an injustice to parents.

Some parents of minority children have a profound respect for authority. Teachers, like clergy, are considered professionals to be revered. Among some traditional Hispanics there is a transfer of authority to the teacher, who becomes the primary caretaker and is considered a substitute parent. Parents perceive teachers and other school personnel as experts in academic matters and, once they have transferred their responsibility to the educational expert, they feel it is not their prerogative as a parent to interfere or to question decisions or actions of school authorities. The following true story illustrates that, contrary to the perception of school personnel that parents are nonsupportive and do not assume responsibility for the children's education, an exact level of support is likely to exist.

A Mexican-American child attending a primary school across the street from the intermediate school where one of her brothers was a student was given a five-dollar bill for lunch. Her mother instructed her to give the change to her brother so he might also purchase lunch. When the girl reached the intermediate school campus, she was accosted by the principal, who, without asking questions, spanked the girl's hands for disobeying the school rule prohibiting children from leaving their own school campus. At home, the girl explained to her mother what had happened. The mother spanked her again for the same reason—disobeying the school rule—despite the fact that the child was trying to do what the mother had directed. The message that the mother was conveying to the child was that during school hours, school personnel are the only authority to whom the child should answer, and the school rule outweighed the mother's directive. In addition to punishment received at the school, and at home from her mother, the girl was also punished by her older brother because he had had to go hungry.

Parents, be they minority or Anglo, want the best possible education for their children but may feel they should not be involved in the educational processes or decision making because they lack skill, training, or information. They may very well perceive schooling to be totally the realm of the professional. In addition, their own experiences with school may not have been particularly satisfying and they may resist returning to the school environment, which holds uncomfortable memories. These variables and others may make it extremely difficult for parents to participate meaningfully in the decision-making process associated with special education.

Schools may need to provide training programs whereby parents of handicapped children can become aware of and obtain skills needed to be effective participants in the ARD committee process. Any attempt to provide parental educational programs must be appropriate to the parent, just as such requirements exist for the child's program. Training programs should be consistent with the parents' language, culture, and other background characteristics. If training is not provided in the language of the parent, it will be ineffective though well intentioned. In addition, even if the parents speak English, they may be reluctant to express thoughts, concerns, or doubts. Requiring interaction with the school representative in a language other than their native language may inhibit their acquisition of the skills that are the goal of parent training.

If increased parental participation is a desired outcome for schools, schools must be willing to invest the time, personnel, and resources to achieve that involvement and identify other agencies that can assist in such change processes. If parental support, at-home reinforcement, and at-home continued development are desired, as is so common particularly in special education programming, schools must develop appropriate mechanisms to communicate, train, and facilitate the behavior of parents.

Placement Alternatives

Based on the interpretation of assessment data, the ARD committee must determine whether the child meets eligibility criteria for legally defined handicaps. If the child does meet criteria for special education placement, a decision must be made as to the placements or programs in which the child will receive the most appropriate education. In reaching such a decision, there must be a determination of the "least restrictive environment," ensuring that:

> (1) to the maximum extent appropriate, handicapped children . . . are educated with children who are not handicapped, and
> (2) that special classes, separate schooling or other removal of handicapped children from the regular educational environment occurs only when the nature or severity of the handicap is such that education in regular classes with the use of supplementary aids and services cannot be achieved satisfactorily. (P.L. 94–142 , Final Regulations, Section 121a.550)

Frequently the concept of "least restrictive environment" is ignored when the placement decision is made for children who have limited English-speaking abilities. These students are placed in bilingual programs full-time in the hope that teachers who speak their native language will be able to remediate deficit conditions. This is not the case for children who are indeed handicapped.

Exceptional bilingual children should have access to a continuum of placement alternatives, including:

- Full-time regular education placements such as Bilingual Education or English as a Second Language classes in which teachers adapt instruction to accommodate students' handicaps
- Mainstream placements with assistance from special educators who serve as consultants to regular educators in instructional planning for mainstreamed pupils
- Placement in Bilingual Education or English as a Second Language programs along with special education instruction in resource room settings
- Full-time special education placements in which instruction not only addresses students' handicaps but is also adapted to fit students' linguistic, cultural, or other background characteristics

It is critical that the child be placed in the program or programs that provide the highest likelihood of success. According to Reynolds (1962), there are two critical concepts in educational programming for handicapped children:

1. The most severely or profoundly handicapped students will be furthest removed from Bilingual Education programs; mild to moderate handicapped children are most likely to be found in Bilingual Education classrooms on a partial or full-time basis.

2. The goal of the educational programs should be to return the handicapped child to the Bilingual Education classroom on a partial or full-time basis as soon as possible, but only as appropriate.

Although it may seem obvious, handicapped minority children who have adequate English language skills can be mainstreamed in regular classrooms, but they should be provided the same range of placement alternatives.

If children are mainstreamed into Bilingual Education programs, bilingual teachers must be provided assistance by special educators and training to provide educational interventions that will help handicapped students achieve their potential. Teachers must be trained to adapt or modify aspects of Bilingual Education curriculum such that the handicapped child will be successfully integrated into the classroom program. This is an important but not awesome task, given the typical range and student abilities found in Bilingual Education classes. Conversely, given the dearth of special education teachers with bilingual training, Bilingual Education personnel must assist special education teachers in adapting curriculum, instruction, and materials in terms of language, culture, and life-style. Special education intervention is likely to require such a team approach.

Individual Educational Programs (IEPs)

If a child is to receive special education services, a written statement must be developed that documents decisions reached, content, implementation, and evaluation procedures, relative to the child's educational program. This is the IEP, which includes:

1. A statement of the child's present level of educational performance
2. A statement of annual goals describing the educational performance to be achieved
3. Short-term instructional objectives, which must be measurable intermediate steps between the present level of educational performance and annual goals
4. Statement of specific educational services needed by the child, determined without regard to cost or availability of services
5. A description of all special education and related services that are needed to meet the child's unique needs, including any special instructional media or materials
6. A description of the extent to which the child will participate in the regular education program
7. The date when services will begin and the length of time they will be given
8. A list of the individuals responsible for implementing the child's program
9. Criteria and procedures for annual review of the IEP

Although ARD committees and educational personnel may have the prior experience of making placement decisions for handicapped children that encompass one or two specialized services, the situation may be quite different for decisions related to linguistically and culturally diverse exceptional children. A child, for example, may be mainstreamed into a Bilingual Education classroom, may leave that class for instruction in English as a Second Language, may also have periods of instruction in a special education resource room, and may perhaps be the recipient of speech therapy. In this hypothetical case, at least four highly specialized instructional personnel are involved in the implementation of this particular child's educational program. Given the potential for larger numbers of highly specialized personnel to be involved in the provision of services, it becomes extremely critical for school districts to recognize that coordination and sequencing of instruction are a primary concern. Therefore participants in the IEP and ARD committees' processes must each have clear understanding of the educational needs of the child so that adequate information can be shared to facilitate this extensive coordination.

Instructional Goals and Priorities

Once the specialized instruction and services necessary to meet the needs of the linguistically and culturally diverse exceptional child have been identified, it may not be possible or educationally sound to attempt to address all these needs or concerns simultaneously. Therefore the decisioning committee needs to implement procedures that will prioritize goals and services. At this point it is clear that the ideal decision-making team would include the administrative representative, particularly the building principal, who will ultimately have responsibility for coordinating and assuring implementation of the various IEPs. As such, the building principal then plays a critical role in achieving the coordination and cooperation that are essential for serving children requiring many integrated services.

Once the decision-making team reaches an initial agreement on the priorities for instructional goals and services, they should specify the time line and individuals responsible for maintaining the IEP, monitoring progress, and synthesizing information to be fed into the monitoring process. Although coordination and sequencing of instruction seem complex, certain straightforward procedures could be implemented that would enhance the possibility of success. For example, specific forms could be used at the time of the placement decisions and IEP development whereby specific responsibilities and the person responsible could be delineated, with information such as time lines and names of professionals inserted on the form. In addition, as instructional programs are implemented, given the large number of specialized personnel who could potentially be involved in serving linguistically and culturally diverse exceptional children, photocopies of evaluation materials could be made. In this way, as instruction is implemented and evaluation completed, observations relative to the child can be noted quickly and efficiently by the person involved and shared immediately with other instructional personnel working with the student.

Variables Affecting Individualized Planning for LEP Handicapped Students

Educators frequently fail to address significant learner traits and their effects on the teaching-learning process because decisions are predicated on an assumption that all handicapped children are monolingual, majority group members. To counteract this, Ambert and Dew (1982) suggest that IEPs for exceptional bilingual students specify (1) instructional strategies that take into account linguistic facility, academic skill levels, modality, and cognitive style preferences; (2) the language or languages of instruction; (3) curricula and materials designed specifically for linguistically and culturally diverse populations; and (4) motivators and reinforcers that are compatible with the learner's cultural and experiential background. Figure 9–1 suggests areas that should be considered in adapting IEPs for exceptional language minority students.

Language

Children learn the language spoken by those around them. That language is the vehicle through which basic needs, including food, clothing, and shelter, are communicated and by which the environment and those in the environment, particularly parents, are manipulated.

Comprehensive Language Assessment
- Language dominance
- Language proficiency
  - Conversational skills
  - Academic language proficiency

Type of Language Intervention Required
- Language enrichment
  - Native language or English
- Language development
  - Native language or English
- English as a Second Language
- Language remediation
  - Native language
  - English as a Second Language

Language Use Plan
- Who?
- Why?
- When?

Recommended Instructional Strategies or Procedures
- Holistic language approaches
- Cultural relevance
- Collaborative learning
- Peer tutoring
- Intrinsic motivation
- Learning to learn strategies
- Attribution retraining

Figure 9–1
Additional Components of IEPs for Exceptional Language Minority Students

The child perceives membership in the group sharing language, and this membership affords a sense of security and safety. Language communicates group values, beliefs, orientation, and life-style, further reinforcing group identity.

Children's sense of security and well-being is easily shattered when they are immersed in an environment in which the language spoken is not their native language. They are threatened because of an inability to communicate needs, to manipulate the new environment, or to understand the expectations held by peers and significant others in this setting. Before the advent of Bilingual Education and other programs for linguistic minorities, children who came to school with little or no knowledge of English were almost always destined to fail. Such children were required to meet two expectations simultaneously: (1) to learn English without benefit of sequenced instruction and (2) at the same time, from day one of the school experience, to perform school tasks and learn basic skills in a language foreign to them.

Fortunately, legislation and litigation such as the Bilingual Education Act of 1968 and *Lau v. Nichols* (1974) mandate that schools offer programs for limited English speakers so that they are not excluded from school activities and can learn English in a logical, sequential manner. Under Bilingual Education, children learn basic skills in the native language so they do not fall behind English-speaking peers in academic areas. In addition, English as a Second Language programs provide sequential instruction to teach children English as quickly and effectively as possible. Children move into full English language curriculum when they are proficient in English.

Limited English proficient students do not lose their right to Bilingual Education when they are found to be eligible for special education services. On the contrary, these students have the right to pedagogically sound programs that not only meet needs associated with their handicap but that also accommodate their language status by providing instruction in a language that is comprehensible to them.

Choosing the Language of Instruction

One of the complexities of language planning involves the great diversity in the communication skills of linguistic minorities. The continuum presented in Figure 9–2 illustrates that language dominance varies as a result of the speech and language community in which children are reared. These variations must be considered in planning instructional programs.

Language Assessment. Assessment processes should determine the child's relative language proficiency, that is, they should provide data that allow skill levels in the native language and in English to be compared. Assessments should focus not only on describing students' conversational skills but should also measure mastery of the more complex, abstract dimensions of language uses that are related to literacy development. The dominant language should be the language of instruction. As a rule of thumb, children dominant in a language other than English should receive instruction in that language; children dominant in English should be instructed in English. If no clear dominance can be established, other variables may be considered, including (1) the child's age, (2) the child's language preference, (3) motivation, (4) previous language experiences, and (5) attitudes or wishes of the parent. The language of instruction, however, should be the language through which the child learns best.

Limited English Proficient Students. A common misconception is that because exceptional LEP children are likely to experience difficulty in mastering language skills, the language of instruction should be English to ensure that children can communicate in the language of this country. The literature on language acquisition and Bilingual Education does not support such a rationale. Unless children master their native or primary language, they will have difficulty developing second language skills and will in all likelihood experience difficulty developing cognitive skills. Contrary to popular belief, increased exposure to English does not improve or hasten second language acquisition (Krashen, 1982). Consequently, submersion or "sink or swim" programs in which children are placed in the same classroom with native English speakers, without native language or ESL support, will not be successful. The fact that "sink or swim" has been their most common experience may explain why Hispanics continue to leave school in such high numbers.

Language Handicapped Students. Children at the extremes of the language continuum have serious language problems because their language skills are not consistent with chronological age or developmental norms for native speakers of the language. Children reared in homes where English is predominant should receive instruction in English. Unless there are intervening variables, the child reared in a family or speech community where a language other than English is predominant should receive special education in that language. Too often, educators assume that if a student has not acquired language, it will not matter whether English or the native language is used for instruction, and, consequently, opt for instruction in English. Such reasoning, however, ignores the language stimulation that has been provided by parents. If students have not acquired the language of their parents, there is little likelihood that they will be able to acquire English skills. Moreover, it is much easier for professionals to acquire basic communication skills in the students' native language than for a severely handicapped student to acquire English.

Bilingual Students. Children who are classified as bilingual (i.e., not eligible for Bilingual Education or English as a Second Language programs), are usually placed in regular classroom programs in which instruction is provided entirely in English. Because these children have managed to acquire rapidly the surface structures of English, they impress professionals as having the linguistic abilities necessary to handle the complex, context-reduced language that is used by teachers and found in textbooks and other instructional materials. When they begin

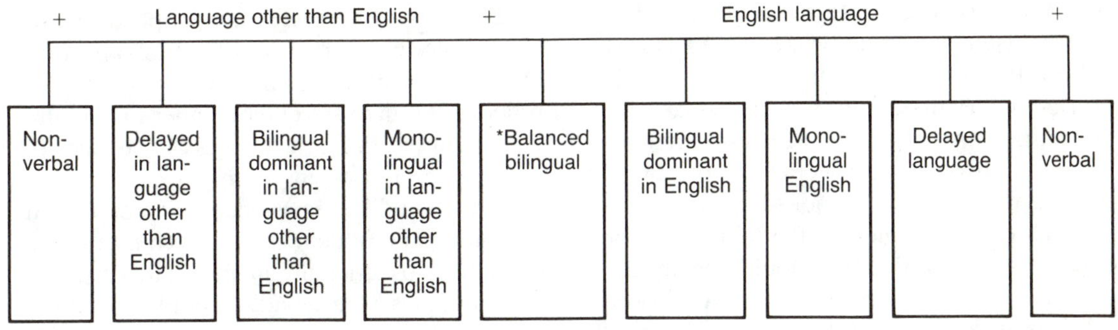

Figure 9–2

Continuum of language. Balanced bilingual is defined by Saville and Troike as being equally skilled in the use of two languages (Saville & Troike, 1975).

to experience difficulty, lack of English proficiency is ruled out as a possible cause of the problem because these students appear to have no difficulty understanding or communicating in English with teachers or peers. While they demonstrate good interpersonal communication skills, bilingual children may need more time to obtain cognitive academic language proficiency required for mastery of literacy skills (Cummins, 1984). It is likely that bilingual students will require a language development program to assure that their English skills are commensurate with those of Anglo peers.

Type of Language Intervention Required. Beyond choosing the language of intervention, the IEP should also specify the type of language intervention required. Figure 9–1 suggests several categories of language intervention. Some students will have intact language skills and will simply require that teachers help them refine and expand their linguistic abilities. This type of language intervention can be characterized as *language enrichment,* in that a decision has been made that the student's language proficiency is adequate for academic instruction. Other students will require *language development* programs. For example, students from lower socioeconomic status environments sometimes experience difficulty because their language skills, although adequate for communication in the home and community, do not match the type of language spoken by teachers and found in schoolbooks. The task of teachers in such cases is to provide a language development program that allows students to handle the language demands of the classroom. Still other students will require *English as a Second Language* instruction because they do not speak English. For these students, ESL lessons are provided in English, with English development based on students' experiential background and on native language skills they already possess. Finally, students with communication disorders will need *language remediation.* As indicated previously, it is critical that these students receive special education services in their native language. In some circumstances, usually because of lack of bilingual special educators, the only option available will be to teach handicapped students in English. In such cases special education instruction must be modified using English as a Second Language strategies.

Language Use Plan. Because handicapped students are likely to receive services from several instructional or related services personnel, a language use plan should be developed as part of the IEP. The language use plan essentially describes who will be using which language, for what purpose (why), and in which skill or subject. For each objective specified in the IEP, a person is designated as responsible for instruction leading to attainment of that objective. For bilingual students, the IEP should specify the language in which instruction or other services will be provided, not only by special education and regular classroom teachers, but also by speech pathologists, counselors, occupational and physical therapists, and others. Specifying the language of instruction will assure that instruction is consistent with the student's language status.

Cultural Relevance of Instruction

While educators generally agree that adapting curricula and materials to reflect a multicultural perspective will help reduce incompatibilities between student characteristics and school program characteristics, they disagree about the nature of cultural differences that must be considered and about how instruction should be adapted (Henderson, 1980). Educators frequently seek to compensate for deficiencies in home background, but this compensation is offered without knowledge of precisely what, if anything, is lacking in the home (Benson, Medrich, & Buckley, 1980).

Unfortunately, much of the literature that describes minority individuals reinforces existing stereotypes. If educational programs are tailored to the stereotype, they are likely to be inappropriate. For example, in an effort to develop culturally relevant food units for school-age children, commercial materials may incorporate pictures of breakfast foods depicting Mexican American children eating *chorizo* (Mexican sausage) and tortillas. The reality may be that Mexican American children, like many Anglo children more commonly eat cold cereals for breakfast. While intentions to produce culturally relevant instructional materials are good, the results may still be irrelevant because they reflect a common stereotype rather than reality.

No one set of characteristics can be ascribed to all members of any ethnic group. Instead, culture should be envisioned as a continuum, with individuals demonstrating traits ranging from those traditionally attributed to a group to those that describe a totally assimilated individual who does not reflect ethnic minority group membership (Ramirez & Castaneda, 1974). It is appropriate to incorporate history, heritage, traditions, and life-styles of diverse cultural groups when developing or adapting instructional materials or curricula. However, when traditional aspects of culture are accented, teachers may inadvertently reinforce the very stereotypes they wish to eliminate. In addition to a focus on traditional aspects, educators should learn as much as possible about students' *contemporary* culture so that learning environments and curricula are compatible with and build on their daily experiences. This underscores the importance of involving parents and community members in the educational process. A critical analysis of the characteristics of the home and community as they presently exist provides a more viable foundation for curriculum development that will be relevant to and meet the needs of culturally and linguistically different members of the school population.

Socioeconomic Status

According to Cardenas (1974), developmental patterns of children growing up in poverty environments differ from developmental patterns of middle-class children. Teachers expect children to come to school with a set of experiences that they feel will facilitate learning, including exposure to books, academic orientation, exposure to success models and educational toys and materials, and educational interactions with parents. When children lack such experiences, teachers attribute school problems to their "deficient environment." Frequently teachers determine that they will not be able to help such children because the children are culturally deprived or disadvantaged (although these terms are no longer commonly used, the values or attitudes expressed by them seem to persist). Rather than being deficient or limited, the environment has provided such children a wealth of experiences that are different from those of middle-class children. To ask children to identify with and learn from a curriculum based on experiences that they have not had is to predispose them to failure.

Locus of Control. Some students continuously encounter academic failure because of incompatibilities between the way they learn and the way teachers teach. Various terms have been used to discuss behaviors of these students, including internal versus external locus of control (Vasquez, 1975), learned helplessness (Henderson, 1980), field independence versus field sensitivity (Ramirez & Castaneda, 1974), and cultural deprivation (Feuerstein, 1980). These authors suggested that for a variety of reasons, including socioeconomic status, certain students exhibit behaviors that predispose them to school failure.

The concept of loci of control originally formulated by Rotter (1966) describes a person's perception of the relationship between one's actions and outcomes. "Internals" believe they are in control of their lives and that work and effort result in reward. "Externals," on the other hand, believe that outcomes are determined by luck, chance, fate, or powerful others (such as teachers) who control their destinies in random fashion. Vasquez (1975) summarized the effects of external locus of control on learning:

1. Self-reliance. Externals depend on others regarding completion of assigned tasks. They constantly seek teacher guidance and feedback because they lack confidence in their ability to complete assignments correctly.

2. Achievement motivation. Internals are better able to plan and implement strategies that yield desired outcomes, thus enhancing the possibility of successful achievement of goals. Externals see no relationship between their actions and outcomes and thus fail to plan or strategize how to accomplish goals. In a classroom, therefore, externals are more likely to wait passively for directions or instructions from the teacher instead of implementing or beginning activities independently.

3. Expectations of success. Internals attribute success to their own behavior, ability, skill, and effort. When failure is determined to be related to lack of effort, internals develop ways to change the level of effort or the strategy and therefore more actions in directions more likely to ensure success. On the other hand, externals do not appear to profit from experience and have a narrow ability to generalize from one task to another similar task to increase the likelihood of success.

4. Intensity of effort. The self-concept of internals is enhanced by success and by the analytical ability to determine the consequences of failure. Because the external individual is unlikely to reflect upon experiences as either successful or unsuccessful, their behavior exhibits little ego involvement. Consequently, these students are characterized as lacking motivation, a trait that is likely to produce frustration and irritation for the teacher who probably has an internal locus of control.

5. Performance under skill conditions. Internals are challenged and enjoy working under conditions that require a display of skill. Under conditions of testing, for example, the internal individual is likely to analyze systematically the levels of difficulty of test items and to move to complete easier items first. The external individual may not recognize differences in item difficulty and thus is more likely to begin with the first item

and work steadily until time is exhausted, usually before all items are completed. The external is therefore more likely to be judged as deficient or "below grade level" because the lack of organizational skills in test taking or task completion results in incomplete products that then receive low grades.

An external locus of control can have devastating effects on achievement of language minority children. These students do not demonstrate the learning style preferred by the school system and therefore have difficulty within that system. How often do teachers (regular and special education), principals, and other education professionals say that their major goal is to produce independent thinkers and independent learners? If such a goal exists within the system, individuals who clearly deviate or have difficulty moving toward such a major goal will more likely be judged deficient or abnormal. Because it is unlikely that these students can interpret their environment and adapt to meet the expectations of the system, it is unrealistic to place the major burden or responsibility for such adaptations on them. The major responsibility for adaptation must be placed on professionals within the school system.

Teacher Perceptions and Expectations

Some studies emphasize that when teachers hold positive perceptions and expectations, they are more likely to provide increased quality of educational opportunity (Rist, 1970; Good & Brophy, 1973; Brophy & Good, 1986). Conversely, because the quality of instruction is diminished over time for some children, specifically minority children, the decreasing quality of instruction alone could explain differences in achievement level of such children.

Adelman (1970) hypothesized that some children have school difficulties primarily because school programs do not accommodate individual differences. He stressed that some children experience school failure as a result of variables such as pupil characteristics, teacher characteristics, and teacher-pupil interaction patterns—quite different interpretations than the ones frequently provided, which center on lack of support in the home, the child's insufficient capabilities, and inadequate resources within the educational system.

Teachers' stereotypes about poverty environments influence their perceptions of children and their behavior as teachers. The following excerpts from a case study prepared by a regular classroom teacher, who incidentally was pursuing a master's degree in special education, illustrate how misconceptions and biases are reflected in observations and evaluations of student performance.

Child: J. E. **Sex:** Female **Age:** 12 years, 1 month
Grade: 5 and in EMR class on part-time basis.

Reason for referral: The child was referred to special education for academic slowness, personal hygiene problems, and poor peer relations. There is no record of the person referring. I have not had access to the child's parents and can only go on what the present resource teacher says.

Parents: The father is not home. The mother is not well educated and does not seem responsible. She collects welfare checks.

Siblings: There are two older sisters, both pregnant and not married. J. E. has a younger brother who has a serious kidney illness and is hospitalized in another city. Consequently, J. E. frequently lives with her aunt.

Home: Her home is like the projects but not that nice. There is no water or electricity in the home.

Behavior: J. E. is aggressive but that behavior is appropriate to her environment. Punishment at home is physical and I assume inconsistent. J. E. does not like school and her attendance is erratic. Because her mother is away so frequently, J. E. seems to be left to her own devices to solve problems.

Cultural Status of the Family: Poor, no cultural advantages.

Physical: Eye exam shows that J. E. should be wearing glasses all the time, but she does not have them or does not wear them; I'm not sure which.

Language: Poor.

Conclusions:

1. J. E.'s social home life has definitely led to her social problems.
2. I do not think J. E. has any great future hidden academic potential. I do not feel she has a great future but I think she can be made aware of her feelings and possibilities and realities as far as her social status when she grows up. I really don't think she kids herself about such things.
3. I do feel if she does not get teachers that are helpful and understanding later in her school career, there is a very good chance that she will end up in correction facilities or pregnant.
4. With luck she will get through high school and find a job. Birth control information may be vital for this to happen.
5. With the right people, J. E.'s future could be bright.

Promising Instructional Strategies

The preceding discussion alerts teachers to student variables that will influence the teaching-learning process. The first step in educational planning is to personalize the instructional environment so compatibility between student characteristics and teacher/teaching characteristics is accomplished. The second step is to select instructional strategies that complement student characteristics and increase the likelihood that learning will occur.

Common Stereotypes Presented in the Case Study. A number of biases are reflected in the preceding evaluation:

1. People from poverty environments are considered culturally disadvantaged, the characteristics of the individual are assumed to be characteristics of an ethnic group as opposed to an economic class. This is, in part, because minorities are overrepresented at the lower ends of the socioeconomic index. The term *economic disadvantage* is more appropriate; *cultural disadvantage* communicates a lack of valuing of the ethnic group.

2. There is an implication that people who are on welfare are not responsible. In this case, the mother was attending to a sick son and might therefore have been unable to work. The teacher, although aware of this, placed a higher value on achievement than on the well-being of a family member. Additionally, the mother's absences precluded spending time with J. E., yet the mother was characterized as lacking interest in her daughter.

3. Statements are not substantiated by fact. The child is said to be the recipient of physical punishment, which is assumed to be inconsistent. The perception that individuals from poverty environments have violent dispositions is reflected in descriptions of interpersonal relationships and in the statement that the child's aggressive behavior is "appropriate to her environment."

4. The most devastating observations made about the child are statements that communicate that the teacher holds no expectations for the child to succeed. Such perceptions can become self-fulfilling prophecies and a child, despite potential and ability, can be doomed to lowered levels of education achievement, economic status, and vocation.

Unless teachers are made aware of biases or errors in judgment, children from poverty environments will be likely candidates for special education. Because teachers feel that such children will not learn, they do not teach them; because they are not taught, they fail; because they fail, they are referred to special education.

The child must be placed in a school environment that stimulates development and rapidly produces accelerated development in those areas critical to educational success in typical school situations (Cardenas, 1974).

Mobility

Cardenas (1974) suggests that mobility, a variable closely related to socioeconomic status, is also a frequent reason why children fail in school. Mobility refers to lack of consistency in school attendance. When the child is in and out of school, gaps begin to develop in learning and in skills mastery. Such mobility can be attributed to several factors:

1. The child's parents are migrant laborers and pursue agriculturally related work in different parts of the state or country. The child therefore may begin school late in the year and leave school before the academic year is completed. The child may therefore only be in school a few months per year.

2. The child may stay out of school to work and help parents meet basic needs, or the child may stay home to take care of younger children so that parents can work.

3. If the parents are non-English speakers, the child may frequently be absent because the parents require the child to act as an interpreter, for example, in business-related matters.

4. Sometimes the child changes schools several times a year because parents are unable to pay rent and thus are forced to move.

5. The child may not attend school and may ultimately drop out because school programs may lack relevance.

Mobility interrupts a child's education to the extent that the child is unable to meet the demands of the school environment. As gaps in skills widen, children may begin to act out their frustrations related to poor achievement; such students are likely to be referred to special education. Alternative interventions that could be provided are individualized instructional programs in the regular school program and programs such as bilingual education and migrant education. Children are often expected to catch up on their own, and teachers feel that they cannot provide individualization. As a result, such children do not remain in school or may be placed in special education.

Reciprocal Interaction

Cummins (1984) suggests that the nature of instruction provided in special education classrooms serves to maintain students' low functioning. According to Cummins, instruction is characterized by an emphasis on transmission teaching models that emphasize task analysis and sequence instruction from simple to more complex activities, with content transmitted by means of direct instruction and highly structured drills and independent seatwork. Transmission-oriented teaching presents difficulty for limited English proficient students because activities are frequently stripped of context and therefore lose meaning and purpose. Of particular concern is that language lessons, which emphasize sentence patterns or drills and focus on linguistic structures, may actually interfere with the second language acquisition process.

Reciprocal interaction teaching models are more effective than transmission models for exceptional minority language students. Reciprocal interaction teaching is characterized by genuine dialogue between student and teacher, in both oral and written communication, and focuses on development of higher levels of cognitive skills rather than on basic skills. For example, reading is taught using bottom-up approaches that emphasize comprehension rather than top-down approaches that emphasize word recognition. Literacy skills are taught using approaches such as language experience stories, dialogue journals, shared book experiences, and creative writing tasks, with an emphasis on developing high levels of competence in the native language. Moreover, teachers do not teach language as a *subject* but instead consciously integrate language use and development into all curricular content.

Direct Instruction

For direct instruction to be effective with limited English proficient students, teachers must assure that sufficient contextual cues are provided to make the task meaningful and must guard against segmenting tasks into simpler but decontextualized units. In his study of significant bilingual instructional features, Tikunoff (1982) found that during effective bilingual instruction, teachers communicated clearly and engaged students in task completion with a high degree of accuracy. Effective teachers organized instructional activities that created, reinforced, and communicated task demands, monitored students' work, and provided frequent and immediate feedback. Beyond that, though, teachers mediated instruction using both English and the native language and responded to and used cultural clues in teaching. This mediation helped assure that direct instruction was both linguistically and culturally relevant. Willig, Swedo, and Ortiz (1987) found that direct instruction was most effective when provided in the native language.

ESL Instruction

For minority students who are academically at risk, strong promotion of native language conceptual skills will be more effective in providing a basis for the acquisition of English oral language and literacy skills (Cummins, 1984). Instruction in English academic skills should not be initiated if the child is experiencing difficulty mastering such skills in the native language. This indicates that the child is not ready to make the transition from native language instruction to second language instruction. Making the transition prematurely will create additional learning difficulties for the student.

One of the dilemmas of recommending native language instruction is the lack of bilingual special educators to provide such teaching. Given the shortage of such personnel, it is critical that monolingual special educators recognize that LEP students will not profit from specially designed instruction until they develop adequate English language proficiency. It is therefore important that English as a Second Language instruction be a part of students' IEPs and that special educators become familiar with the most current practices and research on second language teaching.

According to Krashen (1982), language acquisition takes place best when input is provided that is comprehensible, interesting, relevant, not grammatically sequenced, and provided in sufficient quantity. Methods such as the Total Physical Response Approach (Asher, 1979) or the Natural Approach (Krashen & Terrell, 1983) seem to be more effective because they allow students to develop comprehension skills, attempt to reduce student anxiety, and provide comprehensible input. An advantage for many handicapped students is that these methods offer simplified language codes and active involvement in the learning process.

Learning to Learn

Motivation problems in academic learning situations are usually linked to poor learning histories, cognitive deficits, and negative attributional states (Borkowski, Weyhing, & Turner, 1986). Underachieving students fail to see that their own intellectual efforts may contribute to solving the problem and instead see themselves as passive recipients of information. Henderson (1980) suggests that teachers provide opportunities for students to set goals and to help determine their own activities. Students can be taught to evaluate tasks, plan various options, select appropriate strategies to achieve goals, and modify their own behavior as they encounter problems (Paris & Oka, 1986). Teaching students problem-solving strategies increases the likelihood of academic success. In turn, success enhances the student's own perception of competence and helps maintain on-task behaviors. Moreover, success helps foster intrinsic motivation and appreciation of learning for learning's sake. IEPs should recommend reinforcement systems that emphasize task engagement and performance in relation to a standard, rather than systems that focus on tangible rewards and maintain external motivation.

Collaborative Learning

Collaborative learning provides excellent opportunities for students to develop leadership, to learn how to make decisions, to resolve conflicts, and to enhance communication skills, all critical to independent functioning. Teachers can foster positive interdependence by establishing that the goal of the group is to ensure the learning of all group members, giving rewards based on the overall achievement of the group, structuring tasks so they require cooperation and coordination among group members to achieve the goal and giving complementary roles, sequenced for successful completion, for all members of the groups. Cooperative learning strategies are particularly effective for learners who have difficulty operating from a framework of independence and intrinsic motivation. An additional benefit for limited English proficient students is that collaborative learning groups offer natural contexts for development of both conversational and academic language proficiency.

Classroom Management

Brophy and Good (1986) suggests that to maximize learning, teachers must install procedures that ensure that students know what work they are responsible for, how to get help when they need it, and what to do when they finish. Effective managers give thorough explanations of assignments and provide guided practice before they ask students to work independently. They then monitor work for completion and accuracy and provide timely and specific feedback. If students experience difficulty, effective teachers reteach or teach prerequisite skills to assure mastery of content. So that students need not wait for long periods for teacher assistance, good managers appoint certain students—or paraprofessionals if they are available—to act as resource persons and establish buddy or peer tutoring systems or other approaches to collaborative learning; these measures maintain task engagement and prevent students from becoming confused or engaging in activities with low accuracy.

Use of such procedures will increase students' involvement in instruction and assure higher success rates, factors that are critical to achievement. These procedures are especially important for special education teachers who serve language minority students in that, in addition to diverse handicaps and academic levels, these teachers must also accommodate diverse linguistic abilities and sociocultural backgrounds, factors that also influence the nature and type of instruction provided (e.g., native language instruction versus instruction in English using ESL strategies versus English-only instruction).

Example of Educational Planning for LEP Handicapped Students

Unless educational planning considerations discussed in the previous sections are incorporated into IEPs, the child will continue to experience school failure and may not profit from special education services. The following case study illustrates how information about a child's language, culture, and learning style can be used to develop instructional programs appropriate to the child's unique needs.

Instruction for F. T. should be coordinated across programs and personnel. Care should be taken that strategies being used by the Bilingual Education teacher and by special education personnel are congruent and that the language of instruction in academic areas is consistent to avoid confusing the student.

Child: F. T. **Sex:** Male **Age:** 8 years, 4 months
Grade: 2
Language: Spanish-dominant

Present level of performance: F. T. has been in a Bilingual Education classroom for three years. He is Spanish dominant. Both Spanish and English language skills are characterized by errors in vocabulary, syntax, and grammar. He does not make articulation errors in Spanish. His English errors are characteristic of Spanish speakers learning English as a Second Language (e.g., *sh* for *ch* substitution as in *sh*air for *ch*air). F. T.'s reading comprehension is at the first-grade level. He has difficulty with comprehension questions requiring prediction or inference. He is classified as learning disabled and is receiving special education instruction in reading.

Learning style: F. T.'s cognitive style is characteristic of a student with an external locus of control. A strong orientation toward family and peers is present, influencing behavior and decision making. He is motivated to do well so "my family will be proud of me." He prefers working with others and his teacher is concerned about his inability to complete tasks that require individual effort.

Instructional Recommendations

1. Use collaborative learning strategies that tap into F. T.'s preference for group effort. To increase independence, however, assign tasks that are within his capability level and that will contribute to the completion of the group project. Gradually increase the difficulty level of assigned tasks and responsibilities.
2. Priority should be given to native language development, with language lessons focusing on development of cognitive academic language proficiency in Spanish. F. T. should be given an opportunity to communicate ideas without having to worry about mechanics. He should be given an opportunity to read and write every day. Approaches such as those recommended by Graves (1983) can be used to develop both writing and reading skills. Teachers may wish to use a dialogue journal in which F. T. writes a message to which teachers then respond as a way of reinforcing meaningful communication. Language experience approaches to reading can also be used to develop both decoding and encoding skills. Comprehension questions should focus on higher-order skills including sequencing, inference, and evaluation.
3. Because he is already conversant in English, language development activities (as opposed to basic ESL instruction) would be appropriate. English language lessons should focus on meaningful communication, and drills and patterns should be minimized. Teachers should incorporate language lessons into subject matter instruction by reviewing important vocabulary and concepts F. T. will encounter in presentations, textbooks, workbooks, and other instructional materials. Opportunities for extended discussions (as for example, in the collaborative learning activities) and natural dialogues should also be incorporated into lessons.
4. Initially, teachers should provide structure and frequent feedback to facilitate task completion. However, F. T. should also be taught learning-to-learn strategies to improve problem-solving skills.

Summary

The 1980 census confirms the magnitude of obligation of educators to focus, adjust, and adapt educational programs for linguistic minorities. The mission of adequately providing services to bilingual exceptional students is a difficult task for schools. It is clear, however, that schools must successfully provide services to these children to meet humanistic, legal, and educational mandates. Implementing the requirements of P.L. 94–142 would make a significant contribution toward accomplishing this mission.

Discussion Questions

1. Name and discuss at least three variables that negatively affect the provision of quality service to bilingual exceptional students.

2. Name and discuss at least three variables that positively affect the provision of quality service to bilingual exceptional students.

3. Describe the composition and individual roles of the members of an ARD committee for a bilingual exceptional student.

4. Conduct simulations of a parent conference wherein you, the teacher, explain to the parents their role in the IEP planning meetings.

5. Develop IEPs for LEP handicapped students based on real or simulated case studies.

References

Adelman, H. (1970). An interactive view of causality. *Academic Therapy.* 6:43–52.

Ambert, A., & Dew, N. (1982). *Special education for exceptional bilingual students: A handbook for educators.* Milwaukee: Midwest National Origin Desegregation Assistance Center.

Asher, J. (1979). *Learning another language through actions: The complete teacher's guidebook.* Los Gatos, CA: Skyoak Productions.

Benson, C. S., Medrich, E. A., & Buckley, S. (1980). A new view of school efficiency: Household time contributions to school achievement. In J. W. Guthrie (Ed.), *School finance policies and practices. The 1980's: A decade of conflict* (pp. 169–204). Cambridge, MA: Ballinger.

Borkowski, J. G., Weyhing, R. S., & Turner, L. A. (1986). Attributional retraining and the teaching of strategies. *Exceptional Children.* 53(2):130–137.

Brophy, J. & Good, T. (1986). Teacher behavior and student achievement. In M. C. Wittrock (Ed.), *Handbook of research on teaching* (pp. 328–375). New York: Macmillan.

Cardenas, J. A. (1974, January 21). *An education plan for the Denver Public Schools,* San Antonio, TX: National Educational Task Force de la Raza.

Cummins, J. (1984). *Bilingualism and special education: Issues in assessment and pedagogy.* Clevedon, Avon, England: Multilingual Matters.

Feuerstein, R. (1980). *Instrumental enrichment: An intervention program for cognitive modifiability.* Baltimore: University Park Press.

Good, T. L., and Brophy, J. E. (1973). *Looking in classrooms.* New York: Harper & Row.

Graves, D. (1983). *Writing: Teachers and children at work.* Exeter, NH: Heinemann.

Henderson, R. (1980). Social and emotional needs of culturally diverse children. *Exceptional Children.* 46:598–605.

Krashen, S. (1982). Bilingual education and second language acquisition theory. In *Schooling and language minority students: A theoretical framework.* Los Angeles: Bilingual Education Evaluation, Dissemination, and Assessment Center.

Krashen, S., & Terrell, T. (1983). *The natural approach: Language acquisition in the classroom.* Oxford, England: Pergamon Press.

Lau v. Nichols (1974). 414 U.S. 563.

Ortiz, A. A. & Yates, J. R. (1983). Incidence among Hispanic exceptionals: Implications for manpower planning. *Journal of the National Association for Bilingual Education.* 7(3):41–53.

Ortiz, A. A. & Yates, J. R. (1982). Teacher training associated with serving bilingual exceptional students. *Teacher Education and Special Education.* 5(3):61–68.

Paris, S. G. & Oka, E. R. (1986). Self-regulated learning among exceptional children. *Exceptional Children.* 53(2):103–108.

Public Law 94–142 (1977, August 23). Rules and regulations for implementing Public Law 94–142, *Federal Register,* Washington, DC: U.S. Government Printing Office.

Ramirez, M., III, & Castaneda, A. (1974). *Cultural democracy: Bicognitive development and education.* New York: Academic Press.

Reynolds, M. (1962). A framework for considering some issues in special education. *Exceptional Children.* 28:367–370.

Reynolds, M. (1978). Staying out of jail. *Teaching Exceptional Children.* 10:60–63.

Rist, R. C. (1970). Student social class and teacher expectations: The self-fulfilling prophecy in ghetto education. *Harvard Educational Review.* 40:411–450.

Rotter, J. (1966). Generalized expectancies for internal versus external control of reinforcement. *Psychological Monographs* 80:1–28.

Saville, M. R., Troike, R. C. (1975). *A handbook of bilingual education.* Washington, DC: Teachers of English to Speakers of Other Languages.

Tikunoff, W. (1982). *The significant bilingual instructional features descriptive study: Progress and issues from Part I.* Paper presented at the meeting of the American Educational Research Association, New York.

Vasquez, J. A. (1975). Locus of control: Learning and implications for educators. In *School desegregation and cultural pluralism: Perspectives on progress,* San Francisco: Far West Laboratory for Education Research and Development.

Willig, A. C., Swedo, J. J., & Ortiz, A. A. (1987). *Characteristics of teaching strategies which result in high task engagement for exceptional limited English proficient Hispanic students.* Austin, TX: University of Texas at Austin Handicapped Minority Research Institute on Language Proficiency.

CHAPTER TEN

Bilingual Special Education Curriculum Development

Catherine Collier
Michael Kalk

- Step 1: Planning
- Step 2: Becoming Familiar with the Child's Culture and Language Background
- Step 3: Becoming Familiar with the Child's Special Learning Style and Education Needs
- Step 4: Preparing an Individual Instructional Plan
- Step 5: Developing Individualized Lessons and Materials Appropriate to the Child's Exceptionality
- Step 6: Modifying Individualized Lessons and Materials Using a "Cultural Screen" and Sensitivity
- Step 7: Using Resource People for Assistance and Cooperation in Instruction and Coordinating Services
- Step 8: Evaluating the Child's Progress and Developing a New Individual Plan and Materials as Needed
- Summary

Objectives

- To describe the curriculum development process for Bilingual Special Education
- To develop a clearer understanding of the special learning needs of bilingual exceptional children, especially as they relate to curriculum development
- To describe the unique cultural and linguistic considerations the curriculum developer must integrate into the curriculum
- To describe the development of individual instructional plans for bilingual exceptional children
- To provide brief descriptions of and educational prescriptions for specific exceptionalities
- To provide guidelines for the selection of and adaptation of curricular materials
- To provide information about multicultural resources available to the curriculum developer
- To provide guidelines for communicating with and coordinating services among resource people
- To offer appropriate suggestions for teaching in the culturally diverse classroom

The integration of Bilingual Education and special education is a recent phenomenon. What does this mean as far as curricular materials are concerned? It means that few teachers are trained to work with bilingual exceptional children and that a curriculum for this group has not been conceptualized. There is a dearth of curricular materials specifically geared to Bilingual Special Education and teachers must develop new curricula and adapt existing ones.

A survey by Bland et al. (1979) found an urgent need for language arts and social learning materials to meet the unique cultural needs of Hispanic handicapped; the materials available were seen as being culturally and linguistically unsuited. In a study conducted by McLean (1981), lack of curricular materials and trained personnel were cited as the greatest needs in providing service to bilingual exceptional children. The continuing need for curricular adaptation for culturally and linguistically different exceptional (CLDE) children is also discussed in Hoover and Collier (1986).

Bilingual Education and special education curriculum guides may indicate how to prepare the bilingual special student to assume a responsible role and to function effectively in a pluralistic society. However, these materials must be integrated; it is not enough to place the child in the bilingual class and then in the special education class. Neither would provide comprehensive instruction to meet the child's special needs. The bilingual teacher does not usually have the training to provide for exceptional children, and the special education teacher is rarely trained to deal with acculturation and second language acquisition.

The eight essential steps in developing and implementing a comprehensive curriculum for bilingual exceptional children are:

1. Planning
2. Becoming familiar with linguistic and cultural considerations
3. Becoming familiar with special learning needs
4. Developing an individualized instructional plan
5. Individualizing lessons for exceptionality
6. Individualizing lessons for culture and language
7. Using resource people and coordinating services
8. Conducting ongoing evaluation

These eight steps are shown in Table 10–1. This chart also illustrates the interaction and

Table 10–1

Eight Steps in the Curriculum Development Process for Bilingual Exceptional Children

The four major partners in Bilingual Special Education (BSE) curriculum development are (1) the parents, (2) the mainstream teacher, (3) the bilingual teacher, and (4) the special education teacher. These four coordinate their efforts as resources (R) and participants (X) in the preparation and implementation of the BSE child's instruction. (From *Curriculum development for bilingual exceptional children* by C. Collier, 1982. Unpublished paper. University of Colorado.)

	Who Participates = X Who Is Consulted = R			
Steps	Parents and Family	Mainstream Teacher	Bilingual Specialist	Special Education Specialist
1. Meet as a team to begin the planning process. Outline planning steps.	X	X	X	X
2. Become familiar with the culture and language background of the child.	R	X	R	X
3. Become familiar with the special learning style and education needs of the child.	X(R)	X	X	R
4. Prepare an individual instructional plan with short- and long-term goals (in some cases this may be an IEP).	X	X	X	X
5. Develop individualized lessons and materials appropriate to child's exceptionality.	R	X	X	R
6. Modify individualized lessons and materials using a "cultural screen" and sensitivity.	R	X	R	X
7. Refer to resource people for assistance and cooperation in instruction; coordinate services.	RX	XR	RX	RX
8. Evaluate child's ongoing progress and develop new individual plan (IEP), materials, etc., as needed.	RX	RX	RX	RX
Start cycle over.				

coordination of the four team members—parent, mainstream teacher, bilingual specialist, and special education teacher.

Step 1: Planning

To meet the needs of the students, all four team members—parent, teacher, bilingual specialist, and special education specialist—must be involved in planning. In some circumstances it may also be desirable to include the child. According to Clark and Yinger (1980):

> Practice in planning and organizing the first weeks of school becomes especially important if the notion that the school and its programs should reflect and be responsive to the values, cultural background, and social milieu of the community of which it is a part is taken seriously. This suggests that new teachers at a school should spend at least some part of the late summer getting to know the community, visiting the

homes of their prospective students, and grounding their instructional and social system decisions in the reality of the larger community in which their students live.

The research done by Clark and Yinger about teacher planning may be summarized as seven preliminary findings:

1. Planning is important to teachers and generally invisible to everyone else.
2. Planning in practice differs from traditional prescriptions for planning.
3. Planning during the first weeks of school has long-term effects.
4. Teacher planning transforms curriculum into instruction.
5. Routines can increase teacher efficiency and flexibility.
6. Communicating plans puts thoughts into actions.
7. Teacher reflection aids teacher development.

Formal planning is a must when developing the individual instructional plan, usually in short- and long-range goals that need to be converted to workable objectives and finally to lesson plans and tasks. Planning ought to begin with the specific learning objectives, developed from an assessment of the child's exceptionality and specific linguistic needs; next, alternate ways to meeting the objectives should be developed, building on the special cultural and linguistic background of the child; and finally, the best should be selected for maintaining and developing mastery of the objective.

Planning is necessary for converting the curriculum into instruction, especially to prepare and acquire needed curricular materials and for adapting special education classroom materials to the student language and culture. Teachers should run through the task and think aloud while performing the task so that decisions can be made about the content, scope and sequence, and pace and learnability of the materials. This tells the teacher what is available to work with and how best to present the task to the students. This think aloud method is also called process tracing (Shavelson & Stern, 1981) and is also useful in studying the operations involved in students' performance on the task.

Farnham-Diggory's version (1972) for the student is protocol analysis, which is based on what the student is actually doing during the task, that is, thinking out loud. Another version is stimulated recall (Shavelson & Stern, 1981), which is used when the process tracing would interfere with the student's performance on the task. After the task is completed the student is helped (cued) in recalling the covert mental activities that accompanied the performance on the task, that is, the cognitive processes and the operations on the task. Active processing is another name for this cognitive learning strategy of having the student "self-talk" through a lesson (Collier & Hoover 1987).

Another recommendation made by Clark and Yinger (1980) is that routines can increase teacher efficiency and flexibility and can lead to structure in the student's environment. Routines for teachers lead to a style that reduces the need for planning each activity and lead to increased student time on the task, which is a central variable in school learning.

Finally, the teacher's communication to the student of a plan of what to do and how to do it leads to a commitment of cooperation and interaction in the teacher-learning process. Discussion of specific application of planning follows throughout the chapter.

Step 2: Becoming Familiar with the Child's Culture and Language Background

Before and during planning with the parents and special education and Bilingual Education staff members, the teachers need to familiarize themselves with the linguistic and cultural heritage of the child. The parents and bilingual staff are excellent resources for this information. In addition, the teachers should get in touch with national and state organizations serving culturally diverse populations. Some of these are:

1. Tribal councils such as the Navajo Tribal Council, Window Rock, AZ, or the Zuni Tribal Council, Zuni People, NM.

2. Culture and language study centers such as Alaska Native Language Center, Fairbanks, AK; Language and Intercultural Research Center, Brigham Young University, Provo, UT; or Information Center on Children's Cultures, 331 East 38th Street, New York, NY 10016.

3. National Association for Bilingual Education, Room 405, 1201 16th Street, N.W., Washington, DC 20036.

4. National Clearinghouse for Bilingual Education, 11501 Georgia Avenue, Wheaton, MD 20902.

Teachers should look specifically for information and materials that will aid instruction and the preparation of the individualized lessons. Teachers can ask for instructional aids such as pictures, photographs, and publications that could be used in the classroom.

If teachers do not speak the students' language, they should at least identify significant linguistic and cultural differences that will affect the student's learning. Some of the linguistic factors may be:

1. Phonemes (sounds) that exist in English and not in the native language. These will be more difficult for the children to learn to hear and speak when they learn English. An example of this is the *th* sound.

2. Phonemes that exist in the native language and not in English and that may appear in utterances in place of similar English phonemes. An example of this is the way Yupik Eskimo children pronounce words beginning or ending with *g* or *k*. Their pronunciation reflects a phoneme in their language (an uvular consonant) that does not appear in English but that occurs in the same position as *g* and *k* in words. These utterances are not to be treated as resulting from physical speech or hearing impediments but identified as belonging in one language context and not appropriate for use in another. Other examples are the discrimination of *s* and *sh* for Yupik Eskimo children or the *sh* and *ch* for Hispanic children.

3. Linguistic or syntactical structures of the native language and of English that are "incompatible" in effecting communication. There are many acceptable and compatible variations of English and native language combinations. "Incompatible" is to be used only for areas where miscommunication or dyscommunication may result in serious misunderstandings. An example of this would be in the use of tenses, gender, or number.

The box on pp. 212–213 contains an article that further illustrates the need for the teacher to become familiar with the language of the child and the need to identify possible areas of linguistic difficulty in going from the native language to English.

In addition to becoming knowledgeable about the language of the child, the teacher should become familiar with the child's culture. The teacher should learn as much as possible from the parents, bilingual specialist, and the previously noted organizations, and become sensitive to potential individual cultural differences that may affect the child's learning. The teacher may wish to introduce cultural materials into the classroom, such as some of the books, films, and pictures that are available from the various organizations.

However, although materials are helpful, their presence alone cannot meet the exceptional bilingual child's special learning needs (Jones, 1976). Feuerstein (1979) concludes that enriching the child's visual environment is of little benefit to learning and achievement unless the child's interaction with these materials is mediated (instruction or explication is provided) by the teacher. Also, various problems arise with the introduction of materials developed for use in one context being used in another cultural context. Relevance is more than simply "looking appropriate." As in any curriculum development, the instruction must be based on knowledge of the specific culture and specific learning needs of the child, as well as the goals and expectations of the specific community. When using materials from particular resources and adapting materials from another cultural context, the teacher should be sensitive to the difficulties inherent in linguistic and cultural transference. Language and culture are closely related; language is the medium through which the culture is transmitted.

The two cannot be separated without creating and aggravating learning problems. Suppose the teacher wishes to teach a lesson about homes as part of a social studies unit. The teacher has many pictures of various styles of shelter from cultures around the Americas, including pictures of a Navajo hooghan and a casita from rural Mexico. Using the native language vocabulary for these dwellings, rather than only calling them homes, houses, or shelters enhances the lesson. In addition, none of these terms can convey the deeper meaning of "shaghan" to a Navajo or of "hogar" to a Spanish-speaking child, nor would children as readily grasp the essence that a hooghan is a "shaghan" to a Navajo or an apartment to an urban Hispanic or a frame house to an Anglo. Lessons such as this are not uncommon in primary and special education classes and, because the pictures are usually general stereotypes of cultural groups, the teacher must be careful to use accurate cultural/linguistic terms and to explain that although common at one time to the culture, not all modern Navajos, for example, live like this. Nothing makes modern Eskimos groan more than being asked if they live in an igloo and eat raw meat.

The teacher must not assume that what is true in the teacher's own culture is necessarily true in another. Even seemingly universal perceptions should be closely examined in the teacher's search for cultural and linguistic relevance (Cazden, John, & Hymes, 1972; Hoover & Collier, 1986). For example, lessons about color recognition and discrimination are common in regular primary classrooms. In these lessons children learn the names and characteristics of the colors in their crayon boxes and the colors around them in the room. They learn to discriminate. This lesson is usually seen as basic to reading readiness and to developing perceptual and visual acuity. However, this lesson is not readily adaptable to children from various diverse cultures, for example, Native American or Asian cultures, especially if the child is entering school speaking only the native language. Many cultures do not perceive colors the same way that Western European cultures do (Collier & Hoover 1987b). The words for several of the eight crayon box colors do not exist in the language of the children, nor do they discriminate colors in the same cultural ways as Western European cultures. In Eskimo culture, for example, "orange" and "purple" do not exist. In modern bilingual programs in western Alaska, children are taught to use either "uulincaaq" or "perpelaaq," words borrowed from English (orange and purple) and given a Yupik Eskimo pronunciation and postbase, or they use "qalleryak" and "quisgaq," words created or "coined" by linguists in the 1970s from items in the cultural environment with a similar hue (Reed et al., 1977). In Navajo, for example, colors are "Łichii" (reddish hues), "Łitso" (yellowish hues), "dootlizh" (bluish greenish), "Łikizh" (spotted), and "Łiba" (gray). Both Navajo and Yupik have words for "white," "black," and "brown." However, they do not use them in reference to human beings as is true with many Western European cultures.*

Children from these non-Western European cultures would not see any or much difference between hues of red and orange or between blue and purple without extensive instruction. These examples are brought up as reminders that teachers must not assume anything about the children they work with, even that children will perceive color and objects in the environment in the same way as other children. Whether it is important to train children to see and identify eight basic colors (red, orange, yellow, green, blue, purple, brown, and black) as found in their crayon boxes, is up to the individual teachers and programs.

Another problem with transference of materials and programs from one cultural/linguistic context to another is the difference in underlying conceptual structures (Cazden, John, & Hymes, 1972; Fromkin & Rodman, 1978; Collier & Hoover, 1987a). This applies to both culture and language, though it is often more obvious in language. Two simple examples are gender and time reference. Most Western European cultures have many terms that distinguish gender in the language, for example, *la, las, el, los, she, he, his.* Many Native American and other non-Western European cultures do not have any discrimination in this regard. Words are sexless, and activities in the third person singular, for example, "X is building a boat," are spoken of as being done by either sex. Knowledge of the particular culture would tell which sex is likely to be doing the activity (Neithammer, 1977; Spindler & Spindler, 1978). Because many cultures are sensitive to different sex roles, teachers should become familiar with this distinction. When teaching children "he/she," for example, the teacher should incorporate culturally appropriate activities, otherwise the children are likely to be as confused as ever about gender differences in English. After some understanding of the concept of male/female in "he/she" is established, the teacher can move the children away from the sexually stereotyped activities into nondiscriminatory use of the terms.

Time reference is another area in which children from different cultures may have trouble resulting from differences in conceptual structures. The concept of time is different. Western cultures tend to view time as having a reality of its own, as though hours and minutes exist physically rather than as arbitrary culturally defined units used to divide up the periods such as sunrise until sunset or moon phases. Most people of non-Western European heritage do not divide up "time" in this arbitrary way, and when they do, it is not in the same "scientific" units as Western cultures (Pepper, 1976; Hall, 1984). The same is true for measurements of distance and space and for quantities (Hall, 1966). As more children are given public school educations and television is broadcast into their homes, they are exposed to the use of hours, minutes, inches, feet, clocks, rulers, and pluralization in English and certainly need to learn to use these objects and terms. However, the teacher must teach these lessons with sensitivity to the underlying conceptual structures in the culture of the particular child.

Some of the underlying cultural structure is not readily revealed through language (Hall, 1959; 1976), and teachers should make themselves as knowledgeable about their children's cultures as possible through associating with local community and staff members of these cultures. Differences in cultural values can in-

*Navajos and some other groups discriminate diverse cultural groups by cultural descriptors, not by race or color. Some modern Navajos will sometimes use "Łizhinii" as a slang translation for "Black." But in general it is confusing for Native American children to learn color as applied to humans, and it also seems to encourage the development of negative attitudes toward other cultures.

HELLOP YOURSELLEF TO SOME MILLEK:

Breaking Through the Language Barrier*

A Yup'ik Eskimo youngster accepts learning to speak English as a part of life. Isn't that what going to school is all about? However, as he grows older and becomes a more proficient English speaker, which usually happens when he starts having to communicate in English, he becomes or is made aware of the differences between his natural and secondary languages.

One way he becomes aware is when a non-Yup'ik speaker asks, "How do you say 'I'm hot' in Yup'ik?" He answers in one word, "kiiryugtua." The Yup'ik speaker is fine until the questioner asks, "Which part is 'I'?" At that point, he draws a blank. The youngster is usually made aware when his non-Yup'ik speaking listener doesn't understand what he says or ridicules his pronunciation of an English word or his sentence structure.

How do the two languages differ? First of all, in the English language, each idea is usually expressed by a single word, whereas in the Yup'ik language one word can be a complete sentence. This is because Yup'ik utilizes suffixes or postbases, which are attached to a root, or base or stem. Take the Yup'ik word for "boat": "angyaq." To make the sentence, "I am making a boat," Yup'ik adds the suffixes "-li-" (meaning "to make") and "-nga," the first person ending, to produce "angyaliunga," where "-u-" is the intransitive marker. To say "I will make a boat," add the postbase "-ciq-" (meaning "will") after "-li-" to produce "angyaliciqua." (The "ng" drops when it is between two single vowels.) If I'm not sure about whether or not I will make a boat, I add the postbase "-sugnarq-" (meaning "probably") after "-ciq-" to make "angyaliciqsugnarqua." If our final word were broken up into the base or stem and postbases (angya-li-ciq-sugnarq-ua), it would translate into English as "boat-make-will-probably-I," which is the reverse of the word order in English. This sentence also shows that Yup'ik does not make use of articles—"a," "the" and "an"—as does English.

If I expressed the above sentence using the third person singular ending ("angyaliciqsugnarquq"), my listener would most likely be correct in guessing that a male "will probably make a boat," but he would have to gather that information from the context of our conversation. This is to say that Yup'ik simply does not concern itself with gender, which in English exists only in the third person singular. You now know why a Yup'ik speaking person may refer to the same person as "he" or "she" when conversing in English.

If a Yup'ik speaker says "see" when he means "she," "duck" when he means "dug," "clup" when he means "club," or doesn't pronounce the "ch" in "church" or the "j" in "job" quite right, he is telling you that some of the sounds in the English language are absent from the Yup'ik language and that he is substituting a sound in Yup'ik which comes closest to the English sound he wishes to make. When he tells you to "hellop yoursellef to some millek" (Help yourself to some milk), he's saying that in Yup'ik words don't end in a consonant cluster.

Instead of merely expressing our sentence as "I will probably make a boat," Yup'ik speakers say, "I," "We two" or "We (three or more) will probably make a boat." However, when you engage a Yup'ik in a conversation in which you use verbs requiring objects (transitive verbs), the singular, dual and plural feature becomes suddenly complex. Take the verb "to see," whose base is "tangrr-" in Yup'ik. English uses

terfere with the effectiveness of certain curriculum materials and teaching techniques, which may work well with children of one culture but not of another (Cazden, John, & Hymes, 1972). Examples of this can be seen in typical English as a Second Language (ESL) lessons when children are looked in the eye and asked, "What is your name? How are you?" It is considered very impolite, aggressive, and threatening in many traditional cultures to ask these questions directly of the person and to look a person in the eye for a prolonged period (Woodward, 1981).

first person to second person: I see you (singular or plural); first to third person: I see him, her, it, them; perhaps, first to first person: I see me, us; second to first person: You see me, us; second to third person: You see him, her, it, them; and third to first and second persons: He see me, you, and so on. In Yup'ik both the number of the subject (singular, dual or plural) and that of the object are included in a transitive verb, which amounts to a one-word sentence. Thus, I, we (two), we (three or more); he, she, it, they (two), they (three or more); you (one), you (two), you (three or more) see(s) me, us (two), us (three or more); him, her, it, them (two), them (three or more); you (one), you (two), you (three or more). There are, however, no first person to first person nor second person to second person forms in Yup'ik, as in the English "I see me."

In "Tangrraa"--"he, she, it sees him, her or it," the subject and object can be supplied with separate words. Perhaps, you want to say, "The child sees a dog." Using the transitive verb, the sentence would translate into Yup'ik as follows: "Mikelnguum tangrraa quimugta." Unlike English, the order of the words does not matter. Combine the words in any order you wish, and the sentence still has the same meaning. This is because the subject and the object each take a different form and are easily identified. Though the order of the words is not important, the order of the postbases within a word matters very much.

Not only does a Yup'ik speaker say "That bug (insect)" or "This bug," but he will also tell you where the bug is and whether or not it's moving. Is it lying still near the speaker? If so, is it on the same level with him, visible below him, not visible below him, visible on the ceiling above him, not visible above him, visible beyond him, not visible beyond him? Is it stationary or moving near, above, below, on the level or are there one, two, three-or-more bugs? Is it crawling toward the speaker, away from him, toward his companion? All of these terms can be expressed in one word and in the singular, dual or plural form.

Have you ever heard a Yup'ik speaker say in English, "Where is my combs?" or "They're long," when referring to someone's hair? This is because Yup'ik pluralizes some words. Words for "sled" (because of two runners), "glasses" (eyeglasses) and other things that come in twos--excluding hands and feet--are expressed in dual form. But the problem reverses itself, too. After a Yup'ik youngster has spoken English for a while, particularly in places where English is the predominant language, he no longer wants to wash his hair using the Yup'ik word which means precisely that. He now wants to wash his hair using two Yup'ik words which are a translation of the English expression. However, when he chooses the Yup'ik translation for English, "Close your eyes," instead of the single Yup'ik word, he wants you to close your eyes in the same way you close the door, put a lid on a pot, or hide yourself under a blanket. Also, after he gets used to answering "No" to a question such as "Aren't you hungry?" if he truly wasn't hungry, and "yes" if he was, he has to remember that in Yup'ik he must say, "No (I am not hungry)" or "Yes (I am not hungry)" or else he eats or starves whether he wants to or not.

In Yup'ik people, animals and things "want to" or "keep wanting to." In English only people and animals "want to," while things "tend to" or "keep (verbing)." Also, a Yup'ik child may tell you to "Let him stop" when he wants you to "Make him stop." This is because the postbase for a person's or animal's "wanting to eat" and a ball's "tending to roll" are expressed by the same postbase and so are "letting" and "making."

Now you know why a Yup'ik speaker may produce absurd English. He's most likely translating Yup'ik expressions into English. Likewise a non-Yup'ik speaker produces absurd Yup'ik when he translates English expressions into Yup'ik.

*From "Hellop yoursellef to some millek: Breaking through the language barrier," by L. Coolidge, February 25, 1982. *Tundra Drums,* p. 8. Reprinted by permission.

In Navajo, Apache, and Eskimo cultures, the repeated use of a person's formal name, constant eye contact, and repeated asking of the same personal questions are seen as signs of ill-wishing, impoliteness, or even witchcraft (Kluckhohn & Leighton, 1962).

The following is summarized from Woodward (1981), illustrating these underlying behavior differences, in this case with Indochinese students (although many of these points are also applicable to other non-Western European cultures).

1. There is no direct eye contact. By not making any direct eye contact, the students show their respect. Some teachers in the United States interpret such behavior as undesirable and insist that these students look at them when the teachers are talking. It will only take a few weeks before Indochinese students adopt American students' behavior and look their teacher in the eye.

2. They do not initiate conversation. Indochinese children are always taught to wait until they are spoken to. Teachers are advised to start a conversation every day to elicit students' oral responses.

3. Indochinese students feel that volunteering to answer is a kind of showing off. The teachers should ask questions provoking the students' oral responses.

4. Indochinese students are not accustomed to body contact by a teacher. However, later they seem to like to be touched by the teacher. Nevertheless, Laotian children do not enjoy a pat on the head; Laotians consider the head as the place where their highest spirit resides.

5. To Asian children, a loud voice is a sign of anger. Some American teachers tend to use a louder voice when communication is difficult. Instead, they should use simpler sentences and repeat slowly rather than loudly.

6. Indochinese children are used to the teacher-centered approach and are not used to the problem-solving approach or self-directed studying. Thus, initial participation in a group for such study is more effective than individual assignment.

A child of a culture that values such politeness and indirectness may not respond very well to such aggressively Western curricula as Science Research Associates' Direct Instruction Systems for Teaching and Remediation (DISTAR). The culturally sensitive teacher using DISTAR (which has very useful learning sequences) should modify those elements of the presentation technique that are counterproductive for the particular cultural context. This is also true of many other "Western" curricula besides DISTAR.

Finally, the teacher should find out how the particular culture deals with the particular exceptionalities of the children. This knowledge may be useful in curriculum development, either as something to include in the lessons or as a caution to the teacher that the child may be unusually sensitive or insensitive to various aspects of the exceptionality. For example, in a curriculum planning meeting between teacher and community members, a Navajo medicine man mentioned that he traditionally treated children who did not speak by using bird feathers and bird songs. The teacher located appropriate bird feathers and songs and pictures of the birds and incorporated them into her oral/aural language lessons for three children who had been referred for language development. This enlivened the language lessons in both English and Navajo and appeared to aid in their effectiveness. It also bolstered the parents' and community's feeling of involvement in the instruction of their children.

Step 3: Becoming Familiar with the Child's Special Learning Style and Education Needs

Learning styles differ within both the cultural and individual context (Kagan, 1965; Cornett, 1983). Some children appear to learn better from aural rather than visual cues and vice versa. Some seem to learn better in shorter time spans than in long concentrated periods of study or repetition. The ability or inability to distinguish a specific object as a discrete entity within a general pattern may also be a matter of learning style (Collier & Hoover, 1987a). Some children appear to learn better from a global approach rather than from an analytical approach (Mosley & Spicker, 1975). An example of this is use of the whole-word "sight" approach as opposed to the word-analysis "phonics" approach in teaching reading (Chall, 1967). Children may need to be taught how to think analytically before such skills as the "phonics" approach are possible (Almanza & Mosley, 1980). However, an initial inability to distinguish particular phonemes of English may be a sign of the non-English-speaking students' second language development and not necessarily an indication of global versus analytical learning style. Woodward (1981) notes that many LEP students from non-Western European cultures learn better from a visual approach.

> The majority of LEP students are visually oriented and are accustomed to rote learnings. Thus the "look and say" approach is more effective than the phonetic approach during the beginning stage. During the initial period their auditory discrimination skill is not at a sufficient level to identify some sound differences in English which do not exist in their primary language.

Major perceptual modalities, as well as cultural and linguistic factors, may affect learning style. The perceptual modes usually considered in special education are visual, auditory, kinesthetic, and tactile (Bolander, Lamb, & Ramirez, 1981). The *visual* and *auditory* modes are the most frequently used in the classroom today. Students are constantly required to use these as they "look and listen" to classroom instruction. The *kinesthetic* mode involves adding movement to the learning process. An example of kinesthetic learning is tracing a letter or word over and over again so that the student feels the motion required to make that letter or word. *tactile* means touching. Beaded alphabet cards are an example of a material that makes use of tactile cues to teach letter discrimination.

A particular perceptual cue or modality may not work well with a particular student. Just as there are variations in abilities within any classroom, there are also variations in perceptual styles. Students with perceptual problems may have 20/20 vision and not understand what they see. Students may have normal hearing but be unable to understand or remember all that they hear. Students with limited English proficiency (LEP) may have difficulty relying on the auditory modality for learning because of the phonetic differences discussed earlier.

Cultural learning styles should also be considered in assessing the best teaching style with a particular student (Collier & Hoover, 1987). Does the culture emphasize group achievement and conformity? Does the child react negatively to individual praise and positively to praise as a member of a successful group? Does the child respond better to adult-directed instruction than to individualized seatwork or peer tutoring? Is it more culturally appropriate to use physical demonstrations and experience activities rather than diagrams and verbal/visual directions? These and other considerations discussed in this chapter must become part of the teacher's assessment of the culturally and linguistically different students' learning needs.

The teacher should teach to the student's strength to maximize the student's chances for success in the classroom. The teacher should teach to strengths in a group setting and to areas that need strengthening in an individual setting. Assessment is the first step in determining strengths and needs. The teacher can make an informal assessment through observation of a student's classroom performance and behaviors. The teacher should determine which types of tasks the student does best and which present the most difficulty. Because most classroom instruction is either visual or auditory or both, the teacher can begin by assessing these types of tasks. If the student is low in visual and/or auditory skills, the teacher could then facilitate the student's learning by making greater use of tactile and kinesthetic approaches. The teacher should also consider perceptual approaches such as these in their cultural contexts: group versus individual situations, peer versus teacher-guided, individual discovery/experience versus directed/mediated experience (Hoover & Collier, 1986).

After identifying the student's strengths and weaknesses, the teacher should determine how well the instructional program being used in the classroom meets the student's learning styles by reviewing methods and materials to determine whether they provide for learning through the student's strengths. Many times the teacher can adapt an instructional program to a student's needs. If the student is a strong visual learner, the teacher could perhaps supplement an instructional program that does not emphasize visual perception with visual aids necessary for the student to progress in that program. If the student is strongly group oriented, the teacher could be sure always to have a small group work together on the seatwork portion of the lessons.

Many educators of exceptional children recommend using a multisensory approach. The following is an excerpt from Bolander, Lamb, & Ramirez (1981) that describes this approach in the LEP classroom.

> A multisensory approach makes use of several modalities. It is a very effective approach with handicapped students because it provides for variation in learning styles. In selecting or developing multisensory methods and materials, the teacher should remember to teach to the student's strength first. For example in teaching a visual learner, the teacher would address the visual modality first and then involve the auditory, kinesthetic, and tactile modalities.
>
> There are times when the teacher may not be able to adapt an instructional program well enough to meet the student's needs. For example, if the teacher is using a reading program that employs a phonetic approach, a visual learner with severe auditory discrimination problems will have much difficulty learning to read even if the teacher makes use of visual aids. The student would be more successful with the Look-Say approach to reading. Therefore, the teacher in this situation should use a different reading program.
>
> All the learning modalities are naturally interrelated to help the student learn. Therefore, in teaching to the student's strengths, the teacher should not ignore the student's weaknesses. The weaknesses should be remediated where possible. In teaching to the student's strength and remediating the student's weaknesses, the teacher is providing opportunities for more integrated learning.
>
> The teacher who lacks language skills in the native language of handicapped LEP students should make greater use of the visual, kinesthetic, and tactile modalities. The auditory modality should not be stressed with students who lack sufficient competency in English to be able to comprehend auditory information. The auditory modality is the modality that is most important in the acquisition of language and as such, cannot be ignored. However, the handicapped LEP student should not be kept from progressing in other areas while he/she is working on acquiring competent second language skills.*

The use of multisensory approaches coupled with multicultural materials and crosscultural techniques is a good beginning in bridging the bilingual/bicultural and special learning needs of the culturally and linguistically different exceptional child. In addition to differences in learning styles, the educational needs of these children also differ in regard to exceptionality. Brief guidelines for working with specific handicapping conditions, culturally and linguistically different exceptional children, and the use of teaching specific strategies are discussed elsewhere in this book.

---

*From *Coordinated services for handicapped LEP students* by M. Bolander, E. Lamb, and J. L. Ramirez, 1981. Program developed for the Houston Independent School District. Reprinted by permission.

Step 4: Preparing an Individual Instructional Plan

As shown in Table 10–1, parents, teachers, and specialists must work together to prepare the individual instructional plan. There are four general parts to developing an individual instruction plan and nine specific considerations. The four areas are assessment, objectives, methods, and evaluation.

Assessment

Formal assessment may already have occurred, usually before a child is referred to the special program. This is usually done by formal achievement, IQ, developmental, language, and other tests. The teacher receiving such a child should be familiar with these assessments and what they imply regarding developing an appropriate program for the child. A discussion of formal assessment of bilingual exceptional children is in Chapter 8 in more detail. A diagnostic intervention plan and prereferral evaluation of special needs should have been completed. This is described in Chapter 11. However, it is generally preferable to conduct some informal evaluations also, especially specific to preskills the child will need for particular areas of instruction. Teachers should not assume anything! They should check by giving the child small informal tests. For example, teachers could ask children to group colored objects or toys by shape (triangle, square, rectangle, circle), by color (keeping in mind the previous cultural discussion), and then by use or other category. Children can be asked to explain their sorting patterns. This simple exercise will identify children with differences in perceptual cognition style and aid in choosing the correct instructional approach and possible areas for compensatory instruction (Collier & Hoover, 1987a).

Another sample informal assessment is to ask children to identify sounds (for example, by clapping when they hear such sounds as *th, b,* and *s* within random words or sentences). This can be done with the teacher facing the students, with clearly visible lip and tongue movements, or with picture cues and then with the teacher behind or out of sight (Gearheart & Weishahn, 1984). This is an informal way to determine if visual cues would enhance aural lessons or if children need lessons in aural discrimination. This type of informal assessment can be made into games useful in easing the culturally and linguistically different child's acculturation.

In addition, the two specific areas that must be assessed both formally and informally are:

1. Language ability
What is the child's dominant receptive mode?
What is the child's dominant expressive mode?
What level of proficiency does the child have in the native or second language?

2. Achievement level
Do achievement and instructional levels vary in different subject areas?

Objectives

Once the specific need and some indication of learning style is determined, the teacher should develop specific objectives and lesson plans.

It is important to be very clear in describing objectives. If the teacher is unclear about what is expected from the students or what will be done in a lesson, then it will also be unclear to the children and interfere with their learning. One method of describing objectives in curriculum and lesson planning is to use "behavioral" objectives. This is a way of describing exactly what outcomes are expected. The planning team decides what the student needs to learn and describes it in terms of what the student will be able to do as a result of each particular lesson.

The teacher may have broader goals and objectives that have been used in developing the general scope and sequence of the curriculum but then use specific behavioral objectives for the individual lessons.

A concise way to separate specific task objectives from broader objectives is task analysis. The steps of task analysis as outlined by the Center for Innovation in Teaching the Handicapped (CITH, 1974) are as follows:

1. Specify main task, consider conditions and standards. How accurate do children have to be? What form should children use? Example: Telling time. Use of wall clock as standard. Children accurate to five minutes.

2. Identify subtasks at preceding levels of complexity. What simpler tasks must the child be able to do to perform the main task? Example: Child needs to be able to tell hour and minutes correct to five minutes, but does not need to be able to discriminate a watch from a clock to tell time.

3. Treat each subtask as a main task and repeat procedure for finding simpler subtasks. Example: Being able to tell hour involves knowing that the short hand points to the hour. The hour is the first number you say when telling time. If short hand is on or after the number, you say that number. The short hand goes around "clockwise" (so "after" means to the right of the number, and the child must be able to discriminate between short and long hands).

4. Determine entry level of students. The entry level is what the learners can already do.

Methods

After determining the general and specific objectives of the curriculum and individual lessons, the team needs to determine the sequence of the lessons, the scope of the curriculum, and realistic time lines for the units. To do this, many teachers use lesson planning books or month/year calendars, which allow them to lay out the whole curriculum over the time periods available. This takes extra planning time but is valuable in determining points in the curriculum where special events and people may be built into the lessons, for example, relevant historical dates or events, (such as Cinco de Mayo, Martin Luther King Day, or the 1968 Navajo Treaty), harvest or hunting seasons relevant to the particular culture, or cultural beliefs associated with seasons or moon phases. It is also beneficial for the teachers to determine how much time is available to achieve a particular goal, especially if the child is to be mainstreamed by a certain date or upon completion of a particular skill. The teachers need to work closely together to assure that the exceptional bilingual child receives the time necessary for the acquisition of the needed skill or therapy.

It is also important to include time for developing preskills, evaluating progress, and teaching review/remedial lessons when planning the sequence and scope of the curriculum. The individualized curriculum must be coordinated with the scope and sequence of the regular programs as well as the bilingual and special education programs. All this planning takes time but makes classroom life, teaching, and learning much easier for both teachers and students.

In selecting the appropriate method of instruction, after determining the specific objectives, the teacher may use the techniques suggested in the curricular materials being adapted, while keeping in mind the earlier discussion of cultural relevance and transference problems. Other suggestions for techniques and strategies are provided in Chapter 11. The appropriateness and effectiveness of materials and methodology often become apparent only after trial and error, although this selection process can be enhanced and speeded up by discussing the adapted curriculum with other teachers, parents, or cultural consultants. One method of instruction, which has proved to be useful in exceptional cross-cultural instruction, is the integrated curriculum (Collier, 1979).

In the integrated curriculum, the teacher selects focal topics drawn from the lives of the students and develops specific skills and lessons around these general topics, integrating many specific skills and subject lessons into the central topic. For example, the teacher may develop an integrated curriculum around the general unit topic "The Family at Home." The students work on bilingual lessons that develop their skills in various subject areas.

1. Math and science skills (How does your father measure the logs for the corral? How is adobe made? How does your grandfather [or uncle] determine the proper time and season to tell stories? To shear the sheep? To plant the crops or harvest? What about the treatment of illness? Let's make some fry bread, sopapillas, or rice.).
2. Language arts skills (Tell us about when you helped your grandmother. Tell or write about where your home is located. How does your mother teach you about what to do in the morning? Let's all read Kee's story about taking the lambs to water.).
3. Motor/visual development (drawing pictures of family, home, maps of the area; building models of hooghans or wickiups; dioramas of the environments. Traditional games and activities that build coordination, such as dancing or drama).
4. Other individualized lessons and activities designed to meet specific needs.

In considering method, remember to (1) proceed from the easiest to the most difficult tasks and (2) begin with the most frequently used tasks and move to the unique tasks.

Some specific considerations to keep in mind under the area of method are:

1. The language of instruction. The child's performance on language proficiency tests is the basis of this decision. Both basic interpersonal communication skills and cognitive/academic language proficiency should be assessed in both languages. Until children achieve cognitive/academic proficiency in English, they should not receive instruction relying heavily on English. Until children achieve some receptive proficiency in English, they should not receive English-only instruction in academic subject areas. Once they have developed substantial receptive English skills, children's development of English skills may benefit by their participation in English instruction while they receive concurrent review or alternate instruction in their native languages. ESL can be effectively integrated into bilingual instruction.
2. Which teacher is responsible for which instruction. This may vary for different instructional objectives and will probably change over time as the student gains proficiency in English or different skill areas.
3. The phase of instruction. Different teachers may be responsible for different phases of instruction, that is, initiation, application, remediation, and maintenance. For example, an educable mentally retarded LEP child may be introduced to a new concept by the bilingual specialist in Spanish. After the child understands the general concept, the special education consultant may be able to provide broadening application instruction and assist the regular teacher in maintaining competency in the application of the concept or skill. The special education specialist would also be available for remediation if necessary.
4. Learning Style. Teachers should consider the student's strengths and weaknesses in various cognitive learning styles. For example, the teacher could consider whether the student approaches tasks analytically or globally and with field independence or field sensitivity.
5. Time on task. The planning team must consider the optimal time for each objective. This

includes the consideration of attention span, classroom time available, and student's cultural time frame.

6. Methodology. The planning team should consider the student's cultural/linguistic background, exceptionality, instructional level, and learning style and integrate these into the plan.

It is also important to identify what preskills are needed for each objective. In addition, the teacher should consider the mode of reinforcement to be used. There are many means of motivating students and reinforcing learning. The key for the bilingual exceptional student, as with all students, is to find out what is especially rewarding to that particular student. Some of these rewards may be praise, a smile, touching, being a student helper (for other students or teacher), free time, or cooperative or group success.

Evaluation

Evaluation of the objectives must be part of each lesson. To determine how closely the children have met the objectives and to decide how extensive a review lesson is needed, the students' performance must be evaluated. This can be through formal assessment via tests, sometimes required by school administration, and through informal methods such as in-class quizzes or summation activities.

The teacher responsible for the specific area of instruction should be responsible for the evaluation of that objective. General ongoing evaluation of performance should come from meetings of the planning team.

The objective lesson plan on pp. 222–223 includes the four parts of the individualized plan: assessment, objective, method, and evaluation as already discussed. This lesson was developed by a teacher to teach Yupik Eskimo as a second language to mentally retarded Yupik children who had been removed from their villages and placed temporarily in residential programs in an urban area. The lesson comes after units on body parts and other preliminary lessons.

The nine considerations for the planning team to keep in mind while developing the individual instructional plan are:

1. Individualize the problem. Consider what the child can and cannot do in particular situations, level of functioning, relevant medical data, cultural/linguistic background, and educational history. Modify curricular materials as necessary.

2. Remember that comprehension precedes demonstration. If the child is unable to perform at a certain level as expected, the child may not have correctly understood and assimilated the concept. It may be advantageous to maintain the use of the native language for additional instruction.

3. Use appropriate cognitive learning strategies.

4. Control the environment. Eliminate distractions. Place the child near the teacher when appropriate. Introduce new materials and concepts gradually.

5. Motivate with success. Create a learning environment that ensures success. Build on the child's success and keep learning steps to attainable size—whatever is appropriate for each child.

6. Remediate weaknesses, teach to strengths. Identify what/where/how a child can do something and use that information to assist the child with what cannot yet be done.

7. Sequence tasks. Present instruction in small structured developmental units. Proceed from the known to the unknown by developmental steps, relating previously learned skills to new tasks. Krashen (1981) refers to this as $i + 1$ learning (i = what the student knows).

8. Use feedback. Feedback is a two-way street. Feedback from students can be used diagnostically to assess progress and modify the individ-

ual planning. Students need to receive feedback from teachers. The sooner the child receives feedback about a response, the more learning is facilitated. Feedback from the students to the teacher can facilitate the teacher's learning also.

9. Reinforce learning. Systematic reinforcement must be given as the desired behavior occurs. Reinforcement should be consistent and appropriate at all times. At the beginning stages reinforcement may be more frequent and gradually become more intermittent as skills are mastered. Students should continue to receive some form of reinforcement upon mastery to encourage the maintenance of the skill.

Step 5: Developing Individualized Lessons and Materials Appropriate to the Child's Exceptionality

The primary information source for this step is the existing special education curricula, which are quite extensive. Rather than duplicating this material, we will address the question of curriculum selection and development while urging the teacher to work closely with the special education specialist concerning exceptionality.

There are particular considerations in selecting culturally and educationally appropriate curriculum for Bilingual Special Education, as in any area. The key concerns in selecting appropriate curriculum for any area focus on the teacher, the student, the curriculum structure, and the materials. These four concerns must be addressed in terms of methodology, preparation, schedule, and level.

Teacher

Training. Has the teacher been trained to be competent in this content area? Has the teacher have a history of success or failure? How does the student respond to particular instructional assistance in working with these exceptionalities, cultures, or language groups? Does the teacher speak a language other than English? What languages, cultures, or exceptionalities will the teacher need training and assistance in? Has the teacher been trained to use certain materials and procedures?

Schedule. What are the specific time constraints for delivery of instruction? Will the child be placed in several programs/rooms daily or weekly while remaining primarily in the main room? Will the child be pulled out of the main room for specific or indefinite periods of time? Is the teacher expected to have the child at a certain skills level at a particular time?

Method. What methods or approaches does the teacher want to use or is the teacher presently using? What is the philosophical basis for teaching particular subjects? What is the teacher's philosophical basis for using particular techniques, such as behavior modification, individualization, or cooperative versus competitive rewards?

Student

Special Needs. What concepts and skills does the student need for achievement? Do any special characteristics—physical, psychological ethnic—imply special instructional techniques?

Current Level of Functioning. What is the student's level of performance within the sequence of needed skills and concepts? What is the prognosis for this student in terms of achievement in language acquisition, concept development, and physical development?

Method. What is the best instructional presentation for this study? Does a particular method

SAMPLE OBJECTIVE LESSON PLAN

Objective:

1. The students will be able to respond correctly to the question "Kia una pikau?" (Whose is this?)
2. The students will be able to tell the difference between "-aa" (his/her) and "aqa" (my).
3. The students will be able to use -aa and aqa correctly with "putukuq," "talliq," "tamluq," and "qamiquq" (toe, arm, chin, head).

Method:

1. Preskills: "Una cauga?" pattern and body parts.

T*: Points to toe and says "Una cauga?"
Pauses to see if students remember pattern, then says "Putukuq." Repeats, having children listen to pronunciation: "Una cauga? . . . Putukuq." Now has the children answer the question.

T: "Una cauga?"

S†: "Putukuq."

T: Points to arm, "Una cauga? . . . Talliq." Repeats and then has children answer. Repeats as necessary to determine that students know all the words: putukuq, tamluq, talliq, qamiquq.

b. New Pattern

T: "Now that we know what those parts are, let's learn how to tell whose they are. Listen! Kia una pikau?"
T asks twice while shrugging/acting question and pointing to toe. Then T points to self and says "Putukuqaqa!" (It's my toe). Repeats pattern while acting out questions.
"Kia una pikau? . . . Putukuqaqa." Chooses a student and tells her to point to her toe. T points to student's toe also and asks "Kia una pikau?"

S: "Putukaqa."

T: Has several students do this individually and as a group until pattern is established. Points to chin and says "Kia una pikau? . . . Tamluqaqa." Repeats, alternating with "Una cauga? . . . Tamluq" once or twice to establish contrast. Then points to one student's chin and asks "Kia una pikau?"

S: "Tamluqaqa."

T: Goes through this until all students know the pattern. "Now I can fool you. Kia una pikau?"—points to student's toe.

S: "Putukaqa."

T: "Una cauga?"

* T—teacher
† S—student
‡ Ss—all students

have a history of success or failure? How does the student respond to particular instructional techniques, for example, is the response positive or negative or does the child spend greater time on the task? How well does the student work in groups or individually? Does the student's particular learning style or cultural/linguistic background indicate that particular methods would be better than others?

Curriculum

Skills and Concepts. Can specific skills be identified as components of the concepts? Are

S: "Putukuq."
T: "Kia una pikau?"
S: "Putukaqa."
T: "I couldn't fool you. How about you? Una cauga?"—points to chin of another student.
S: "Tamluq."
T: "Kia una cauga?"
S: "Tamluqaqa."
T: Repeats this game with other students, then adds other body part words—talliqaqa, qamiquqaqa. "Now let's try something more. Una cauga?"—points to one student (S1) and tells him not to answer. "Una cauga?"
S2: "Qamiquq."
T: "Listen, Kia una pikau? Qamiquaqaa." Reminds students to listen while acting out asking others about S1. Points to the head of S1 and asks another student "Kia una pikau?"
S3: "Qamiquqaa."
T: Asks S2 while pointing to her head "Kia una pikau?"
S1: "Qamiquqaa."
T: Pointing to S1 head, asks others "Kia una pikau?"
Ss‡: "Qamiquqaa."
T: Repeats pattern with all words in the unit.

Evaluation: T has the students sit in a circle. Has them each take turns asking and answering the question "Kia una pikau?" both for their own body part and for their neighbors'. Procedure as follows (5 students):
S1 points to chin (or whichever part he wants)
S2 looks at S1 and asks "Kia una pikau?"
S1 answers "Tamluqaqa."
S2 turns to S3 and pointing to S1 chin asks "Kia una pikau?"
S3 answers "Tamluqaa."
S2 points to own head (or other part).
S3 asks "Kia una pikau?"
S2 answers "Qamiquqaqa."
S3 turns to S4 and pointing to S2 asks "Kia una pikau?"
S4 answers "Qamiquqaa."
S3 points to part, S4 asks and S3 answers "_____-aqa."
S4 turns to S5, pointing to S3 part, asks "Kia una pikau?"
S5 answers "_____-aa." S4 chooses part, S5 asks and S4 answers "_____-aqa."
S5 turns to S1, points to S4 part, asks, and S1 answers "_____-aa"
S5 chooses part, S1 asks, and S5 answers "_____-aqa."
Continued until all have had an opportunity to ask and answer both "my" and "her/his" body part.

curriculum concepts broken into individual skill steps? Will the teacher need to apply task analysis to the broad concept areas to elicit specific skill steps? Are the skills and concepts appropriate for the specific language, culture, and exceptional needs of the child?

Content. Does the content cut across several areas, such as language experience approach, or is it limited to one, for example, a phonetic reading program? Is the curriculum capable of being modified? Is it developmental (building on preskills and forming the foundation for further skills) and if so are preskills and developmental steps identified or assumed? If it is necessary to modify the developmental steps or global content, will the curriculum provide adequate content coverage and still meet the concept and skills needs of the student?

Method. Does the curriculum require a certain type of methodology or does it lend itself to a variety of methods? Is the prescribed methodology appropriate for the particular Bilingual Special Education child? Does the curriculum make allowances for individual student differences and provide suggestions for alternate presentations?

Materials

Level. Is the reading level indicated? Is it consistent throughout? Are there several levels? Are there several books for each level? Is the reading and interest level appropriate to the content?

Format. Is the form appropriate for student and teacher needs? If materials are in workbook or slide/tape format, will the student be able to use them appropriately? Are the expressive and receptive aspects appropriate for the content and the needs of the student? Is the material clear and easy to follow? Can the student work alone with these materials or must the teacher provide continuing direction? Are special ancillary materials or equipment required (for example, tape recorder or Language Master)? Does the material have multiple components? Can they be used independently? Can they be used for a variety of purposes? Will they need to be replaced? How frequently?

These curriculum concerns are useful in selecting and adapting materials not only to individual learning needs but also to different cultural and linguistic needs.

Step 6: Modifying Individualized Lessons and Materials Using a "Cultural Screen" and Sensitivity

By going through the curriculum selection considerations in Step 5, with particular attention to the cultural concerns discussed in Step 2, the teacher (in consultation with Bilingual Special Education resource people, if need be) should be able to select, adapt, and modify materials to meet the cultural and linguistic needs of the child.

The teacher should consider the following questions:

1. Are the pictures/objects familiar to the children, relevant to their learning needs and to their environment in and out of school? If introducing something new or "alien," the teacher should break up the lesson into smaller steps via task analysis. The teacher should provide plenty of demonstration and explanation and dissect one's own cultural assumptions in the lesson.

2. Does the child have the necessary preskills? The teacher should provide adequate review and develop preskills thoroughly before going on to the main lesson. For example, a lesson on clocks and time assumes the child comes to class with a common cultural understanding of time as composed of discrete sequential measurable units that move from the past (1:01 to now, 1:15; 1:15 to future, 1:22). The lesson may need to be dissected further than clock analysis and begin with time itself. The teacher should talk about day and night and seasons. The lesson can be moved to the sun and the progress of shadows; students may measure shadow movements. The teacher can invent or use own time measurement (the student's culture may have one different from "clock time"). Then clock measurement can be discussed as one other way to measure time and movement of the earth around the sun.

3. Are the words and phrases used to describe the lesson and materials familiar to the child? Are they culturally correct? Are the vocabulary words in the native language or an approved translation? If translated materials are used, are they literal translations or conceptual translations, or are annotations available? If literal, problems in comprehension may result. The teacher should consult the bilingual specialist about the meaning of materials that seem confused or peculiar. The teacher must feel confident of the meaning in both cultural contexts. For example, if using Coyote stories, the teacher must understand what these meant in traditional cultures and use the best translations available. The teacher should be aware of seasonal prohibitions or limitations on use (some tribes have a certain time of year they can be told). It may frighten, worry, or otherwise convince students of the teacher's disrespect of their culture if stories are used improperly or in fun when serious. Yet the teacher should use them in the class. In the right context they are an enriching experience for teacher and students alike.

4. Whenever materials possibly contradict the child's cultural beliefs, both sides should be discussed. The child may firmly believe that a hearing impairment or physical handicap or whatever is caused by being out of harmony with the natural order in some way. The child may even have had a native practitioner treat the condition using traditional methods. In teaching the child compensatory techniques such as of movement or hearing, the teacher should acknowledge the positive contributions of the cultural practitioner and explain that learning new ways adds to the child's power to deal with the exceptionality. Nothing is subtracted. The teacher must find ways to integrate cultural practices with teaching. Rarely if ever are native practices and beliefs actually harmful, and supporting children's belief in them while teaching new ways to deal with the exceptional condition may give the children more confidence in themselves and their cultural identities.

5. Are the methods used in teaching culturally appropriate?

a. In many cultures, children are taught that it is improper to volunteer or that it is unwise to speak or answer unless absolutely sure of the answer (no guessing or using make believe). The teacher can teach children to respond this way if it is a necessary part of teaching—but children cannot be expected to do so without developing the skill. The "pretend" or "what do you suppose" approach may create problems without adequate preparation. The teacher should always start with very real concrete actions and examples from the real life of students. Many Indochinese students newly arrived in the United States are not familiar with items using electricity and actions associated with the use of such items. The game/song "This is the way we _____ _____ _____" (wash our clothes, etc.) is very common in primary classrooms. Ironing, vacuuming, driving a car, or using washing machines would be confusing to children not exposed to the actions. The teacher should stick to common activities such as walking and running at first.

b. The teacher must be careful in using aggressive modern programming/teaching methods. These are frequently inappropriate for children from Asian and Native American cultures.

c. The use of masks and puppets without adequate preparation should be avoided. Putting on a mask and acting or speaking through the character has more serious meaning in many traditional cultures than in mainstream America. It can be a very effective teaching method, but the teacher must be sure of underlying structural meaning in both cultural contexts before using it.

6. The teacher's own cultural teaching screen should be analyzed. Are competitive or cooperative rewards used in lessons? Is the teacher rewarding or paying more attention to individual behaviors over the whole group's performance or cooperative behavior? Is the teacher rewarding attending to task or achievement at the expense of behavior and vice versa? Many cultures do not prize individual achievement or competition. Children are trained to be cooperative—to help one another in need, to blend into the group—and to believe that the group's success is more important than individual success. By singling out for praise or censure, by identifying individuals by name during lessons, or by using bulletin board displays of the best work or graphing progress publicly (Pat's horse is way ahead of the others; Marty's is way behind), the teacher may be motivating the children to not do their best, to feel ashamed of their best, and to believe that their best means little. Alternate means of rewarding or encouraging achievement can be tried. Participation can be rewarded. Lessons can be organized in such a way that "high/low" children are encouraged and rewarded for working together. "Cheating" is in the eyes of the teacher, not in the students helping one another. Everyone will produce something. Careful pairing of children with different skills—complementary learning styles, for example—may benefit all.

Step 7: Using Resource People for Assistance and Cooperation in Instruction and Coordinating Services

The extreme importance of coordinating the services of all those involved in the planning and implementation of the child's instruction must be kept in mind. All too often children are referred to special services without preplanned collaboration. This results in disjointed instructional efforts and the student never receives comprehensive attention to needs. Without reinforcement of the student's new skills in all instructional settings, the child never learns to generalize and apply the skills.

To truly coordinate services and familiarize oneself with culture and language needs, the teacher of the exceptional bilingual child must work with parents and cultural resource people. However, the teacher may feel concerned about being able to communicate effectively with resource people of these different cultures. Some valuable suggestions in cross-cultural communication are made by Scollon and Scollon (1980).

Scollon and Scollon suggest that the teacher should not dominate the conversation or talk too fast. They emphasize that being too intent, talking down to, and being overly boisterous are all impediments to cross-cultural communication. Scollon and Scollon recommend:

1. Listen until the other person is finished.
2. Allow extra time.
3. Avoid situations with many people interacting at one time.
4. Talk openly about communication and discrimination.
5. Seek help.
6. Learn to accept and appreciate difference.

Whether or not the children in the class are culturally different, whether they speak a different language or a variation of the "mainstream" language, and whether or not they have some exceptional characteristics, it is important to remember that they are all human children. They feel, eat, and think like any other people. Concerned, willing, culturally sensitive teachers are the key to successfully meeting their special needs while providing them with mainstream instruction.

Step 8: Evaluating the Child's Progress and Developing a New Individual Plan and Materials as Needed

Individual performance can be accessed in non-threatening group/culturally oriented ways. Games and other recreation or social activities can provide the observant teacher with quite comprehensive evaluative information. Such games and activities can be highly structured (as in the example at the end of the sample objective lesson plan on pp. 222–223) or very informal (as a free-time play period with children interacting naturally during which the teacher has encouraged a role-playing activity or introduced new toys or instructional play items). The teacher should find some traditional games or activities from resource people. For example, Eskimo dancing is a combination of stylized gesture and storytelling. It is often the humorous acting out of social or individual behavior situations, for example, a woman getting all dressed up with makeup and walking along so fancifully that she stumbles, a man jogging and getting more tired while a very old woman just keeps on going slowly but surely, or a particular hunter sneaking up on prey. Such dancing, with the accompanying singing and story and the preparation of the dance fans or clothes, can be used to teach cultural heritage, motor development, role playing, kinesthetic learning, and language development, and the final group performance is an opportunity for the teacher to observe how individuals are doing in those areas. Games, dances, songs, and theatrical performances from any culture are golden opportunities for such culturally appropriate teaching methods and evaluations. The teacher can combine art, language, social studies, math (rhythms, construction, measurements), various learning styles, and motor and physical needs into one integrated lesson and evaluation.

Summary

This chapter has discussed the eight steps involved in curriculum development for culturally and linguistically different exceptional children. Each step has been described and specific examples of implementation have been provided.

There are no simple steps to developing and adapting curriculum materials to meet the special needs of Bilingual Special Education children. It is a process of consciousness raising, a deliberate self-directed effort on the part of the concerned teacher to become culturally and linguistically sensitive as well as competent to deal with a range of exceptionalities. The development of cultural sensitivity and comprehensive teaching competencies are at the root of successful Bilingual Special Education curriculum development and adaptation. Without them, all our suggestions and examples are for naught.

Discussion Questions

1. Why is planning a critical part of the curriculum development process? Give examples of and contrast lessons without and with planning.

2. Explain how you would identify and familiarize yourself with the special learning needs of the children. Give specific examples for at least three exceptionalities.

3. How would you identify and familiarize yourself with the culture and language of a particular child? Children from numerous diverse backgrounds?

4. Give specific examples of resources to consult and use in becoming familiar with the culture of children from a Native American, Indochinese, and South American culture. Select and identify one specific tribe/country/group from each of these areas and list the available resources and how you could obtain or consult them.

5. What steps would you go through to develop an individualized instructional plan for a bilingual exceptional child?

6. Give a specific example of an individualized instructional plan for an exceptional child from a culture different from your own. Identify the age, grade, cultural background, level of development in both the native and the second language, and exceptionality. Describe what you might expect as long- and short-range objectives and how you might carry these out.

7. Develop a sample single-concept lesson plan for a bilingual child with a particular exceptionality. Identify age, grade, cultural/linguistic background, and exceptionality. Emphasize how you would individualize the lesson to accommodate the exceptionality.

8. Develop a sample single-concept lesson plan for an exceptional child from a culture/language background different from your own. Identify age, grade, exceptionality, cultural background, and level of development in both native and second language. Emphasize how you would individualize the lesson for the child's cultural/linguistic background.

9. How would you coordinate your classroom instruction for bilingual exceptional children with the instruction of specialists in bilingual and special education who are working with the child? Give a specific example of coordination of services, identifying child's age, grade, cultural/linguistic background, exceptionality, and the general instructional objectives.

10. How would you coordinate your instruction with the parents of a bilingual exceptional child from a culture different from your own? Describe how you would contact and communicate with them on an ongoing basis. Give a specific example. Identify cultural/linguistic background, resource persons you would involve, and the social/instructional objectives you would discuss.

11. Describe an informal evaluation. Give a specific example. Identify the instructional objective being evaluated and the procedure you would use. Identify age, grade, cultural/linguistic background, and exceptionality.

12. How would you evaluate bilingual exceptional children's progress on an ongoing basis? Describe in- and out-of-classroom procedures, resource persons you would consult, and how you would use the information in reviewing/revising your instructional plan.

References

Almanza, H. P., & Mosley, W. J. (1980). *A perspective on curriculum adaptations and modifications for culturally diverse handicapped children.* Unpublished paper.

Bland, E., et al. (1979). Availability, usability and desirability of instructional materials and media for minority handicapped students. *Journal of Special Education.* 13(2):157–167.

Bolander, M., Lamb, E., & Ramirez, J. L. (1981). *Coordinated services for handicapped LEP students.* Program developed for the Houston Independent School District.

Cazden, C. B., John, V. P., & Hymes, D. (1972). *Function of language in the classroom.* New York: Teachers College Press.

Center for Innovation in Teaching the Handicapped (1974). *Tips for Teachers.* Bloomington, IN: Indiana University.

Chall, J. (1967). *Learning to read: The great debate.* New York: McGraw-Hill.

Clark, C. M., & Yinger, R. S. (1980). *The hidden world of teaching: Implications of research on teacher planning.* Ann Arbor, MI: Michigan State University, Institute for Research on Teaching.

Collier, C. (1979). *Introduction to bilingual education.* Bethel, AK: University of Alaska (Kuskokwim Community College).

Collier, C. (1982). *Curriculum development for bilingual exceptional children.* Unpublished paper. University of Colorado.

Collier, C., & Hoover, J. J. (1987a). *Cognitive learning strategies for minority handicapped students.* Lindale, TX: Hamilton Publications.

Collier, C., & Hoover, J. J. (1987b). Sociocultural considerations when referring minority children for learning disabilities. *LD Focus.* 3(1):39–45.

Coolidge, L. (1982, February 25). Hellop yourselles to some millek: Breaking through the language barrier. *Tundra Drums,* 8.

Cornett, C. E. (1983). *What you should know about teaching and learning.* Bloomington, MN: Phi Delta Kappa Education Foundation.

Farnham-Diggory, S. (1972). *Cognitive processes in education.* New York: Harper & Row.

Feuerstein, R. (1979). *The dynamic assessment of retarded performers.* Baltimore: University Park Press.

Fromkin, V., & Rodman, R. (1978). *An introduction to language.* New York: Holt, Rinehart & Winston.

Gearheart, B. R., & Weishahn, M. W. (1984). *The handicapped child in the regular classroom.* 2nd ed. St. Louis: Mosby.

Hall, E. T. (1959). *The silent language.* Garden City, NY: Doubleday.

Hall, E. T. (1966). *The hidden dimension.* Garden City, NY: Doubleday.

Hall, E. T. (1976). *Beyond culture.* Garden City, NY: Anchor and Doubleday.

Hall, E. T. (1984). *The dance of life: The other dimension of time.* Garden City, NY: Anchor and Doubleday.

Hoover, J. J., & Collier, C. (1986). *Classroom management through curricular adaptations: Educating minority handicapped students.* Lindale, TX: Hamilton Publications.

Jones, R. L. (Ed.) (1976). *Mainstreaming and the minority child.* Reston, VA: Council for Exceptional Children.

Kagan, J. (1965). Reflection/impulsivity and reading ability in primary grade children. *Child Development.* 36:509.

Kluckhohn, C., & Leighton, D. (1962). *The Navajo.* rev. ed. New York: Natural History Library.

Krashen, S. D. (1981). Bilingual schooling and second language acquisition theory. In *School and language minority students: A theoretical framework.* Los Angeles: Evaluation Dissemination and Assessment Center, California State University.

McLean, G. D. (1981). *Bilingual special education programs: A needs study based on a survey of directors of bilingual education and special education in United States school districts receiving Tital VII ESEA funds.* Ph.D. dissertation. University of Colorado.

Mosley, W. M., & Spicker, H. H. (1975). Mainstreaming for the educationally deprived, *Theory into Practice.* 14:73–81.

Neithammer, C. (1977). *Daughters of the earth.* New York: Collier.

Pepper, F. C. (1976). Teaching the American Indian child in mainstream settings. In R. Jones (Ed.), *Mainstreaming and the minority child.* Reston, VA: Council for Exceptional Children.

Reed, I., et al. (1977). *Yupik Eskimo grammar.* Fairbanks, AK: University of Alaska, Alaska Native Language Center.

Scollon, R., & Scollon, S. B. (1980). *Interethnic communication.* Fairbanks, AK: University of Alaska, Alaska Native Language Center.

Shavelson, R., & Stern, P. (1981). Research on teachers' pedagogical thoughts, judgments, decisions and behavior. *Review of Educational Research* 51:455–498.

Spindler, G. D., and Spindler, L. (1978). *Education and cultural process: Toward an anthropology of education.* New York: Holt, Rinehart & Winston.

Woodward, M. M. (1981). *Indiana experiences with LEP students: Primarily with Indochinese refugee children.* Report to the Indiana Department of Instruction.

CHAPTER ELEVEN

Methods and Materials for Bilingual Special Education*

John J. Hoover
Catherine Collier

*Portions of this chapter are reprinted from *Classroom management through curricular adaptations: Educating minority handicapped students* by J. J. Hoover and C. Collier, 1986, Lindale, TX: Hamilton Publications. Reprinted by permission.

Objectives

- To describe the curricular environment for Bilingual Special Education
- To provide information about methods and materials appropriate for Bilingual Special Education
- To describe a variety of instructional interventions and strategies for use with bilingual exceptional children
- To provide guidelines for curricular adaptations in the culturally diverse special education classroom

In the preceding chapters on curriculum development and mainstreaming, various procedures and adaptation techniques have been discussed. The teacher working with culturally and linguistically different (CLD) children who are or may be exceptional (CLDE) needs to apply these suggestions in actual classroom settings in the most effective manner. This necessitates a variety of intervention and instruction techniques, strategies, and materials, and the knowledgeable use of these within the complete curricular environment. This topic is addressed within the framework of the more general definitions of curriculum that emphasize that curriculum is composed of several interrelated elements. We will discuss the curricular environment as a whole and the use of various instructional techniques, strategies, and materials particularly effective with CLDE children. The concept of the interrelationship among curricular elements is discussed relative to intervention from the prereferral level through placement in special education. The importance of effective curricular adaptations and adapting to meet special needs is addressed in this chapter, which also presents numerous teaching and behavior management techniques appropriate for adapting curriculum for CLDE learners. This chapter concludes with a discussion about criteria and guidelines for evaluating, selecting, adapting, and creating educational materials for CLDE learners.

Curricular Elements and Adaptation

The specific teaching and behavior management strategies to implement curriculum content, use instructional materials, manage behavior, and, in general, organize classroom instruction assist in determining the whole curriculum. Curriculum should be understood as all planned and guided learning experiences under the direction of the teacher (Wiles & Bondi, 1984) with intended educational consequences (Eisner, 1979). Although a general definition of curriculum is accepted and understood by most classroom teachers, the specific aspects that comprise curriculum are not as clear. In fact, many educators view the curriculum as merely the materials used in the classrooms. Materials are only one important element in the curriculum process. To effectively implement instruction for CLDE children, all aspects of the curricular environment must be addressed.

The total curriculum and curriculum implementation process involves consideration of four major elements: the *content* that is taught, the *instructional strategies* used, and *instructional settings* in the classroom, and the management of *student behaviors.* These four major areas within the whole curriculum must be understood relative to their relationship with one another as well as to individual student needs, linguistic and cultural heritages, and prior instructional experiences. As one acquires a more complete understanding of these four curricular elements, the appropriate selection and use of instructional methods and materials is maximized.

The element of content refers to the academic skills and knowledge associated with the various subject areas. This includes prerequisite skills needed to complete academic tasks as well as the expressive and receptive language skills in both languages necessary to comprehend and learn the content. The instructional strategies are the methods and techniques selected to assist students to acquire the content as well as manage behavior. The instructional settings refer to the settings in the classroom in which learning occurs. These include small and large group situations as well as independent work and one-to-one instructional situations. The student behaviors aspect of the curriculum refers to the CLDE students' abilities to manage and control their own behaviors under a variety of situations, learning activities, and groupings within the classroom. Each of these four elements is an individual factor that contributes to the success of education for CLDE students. These four elements are distinct aspects of the curriculum and often require adaptations in the total curricular implementation process.

Figure 11–1 illustrates a model that depicts the process of effective curriculum implementation for CLDE students through the curriculum adaptation process that will be described in a subsequent section. A circular figure is used to illustrate the continuous interaction among the four elements of curriculum comprising the curriculum implementation process. As shown in the figure, the four curriculum elements are first illustrated as individual elements. The four elements connect to the circular area depicting curriculum adaptation, which in turn connects with the innermost circle of effective curriculum implementation.

Although these four elements are distinct aspects of the total curriculum, the interrelationship among these elements provides the key to success when the total curriculum is implemented.

Problems, inconsistencies, and other events within a classroom that inhibit effective implementation of curriculum are frequently the result of problems associated with two or more of these curriculum elements. Although a problem

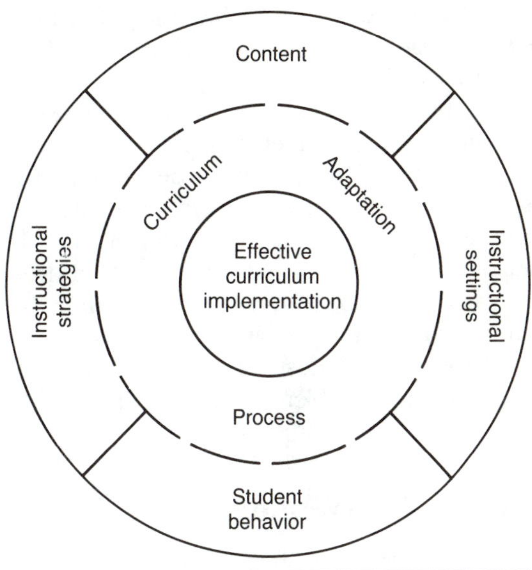

Figure 11–1
Integrative Model for Curriculum Implementation

Adapted from *Classroom Management Through Curricular Adaptations: Educating Minority Handicapped Students* by J. J. Hoover and C. Collier, 1986, p. 11, Lindale, TX: Hamilton Publications. Reprinted by permission.

limited to only one element of the curriculum is sometimes encountered, many CLDE students who experience problems within the classroom are having difficulty in more than one element within the total curriculum. However, all too often we concentrate our search for and solutions to academic and behavior problems within the individual elements without thinking through the possible interrelationships among the various elements.

By ignoring the interrelationships among the elements we frequently embark upon a path to improve learning or reduce behavior problems that is doomed to failure from the beginning. All too often teachers find themselves saying that they were sure that the problem was due to one of the curriculum elements (i.e., content, strategies), and after spending several weeks modifying or focusing upon the individual area or areas, they realize that something else was also contributing to the learning/behavior problems.

In many situations that "something else" pertains to the interrelationships among elements. As one element is addressed or adapted, each of the other three elements may also be affected. Thus, as one curriculum element is adapted or modified, each of the other three areas must also be addressed to determine the effects of the original adaptations on them, and if necessary, they must also be adapted to address potential problems that may arise.

Steps in Interventions

Before proceeding with the discussion of adaptations and methods and materials, a discussion about the topic of *when* these might be most useful in the student's program is necessary. As indicated previously the use of these techniques and strategies may occur from the prereferral through the placement steps.

Prereferral intervention for CLD students with learning and behavior problems is becoming the preferred method of meeting the needs of these children (Collier, 1987). Prereferral interventions are generally begun after a building level conference between the referring teacher and a teacher assistance team (sometimes the child study team with additional members), but before formal referral to staffing. This total process is illustrated in Table 11–1, which shows five steps. Each of these is discussed briefly. The major theme permeating the process outlined in Table 11–1 emphasizes the need to implement appropriate interventions at the prereferral level through placement into special education. The diagnostic interventions include curricular adaptions to one or more of the four curricular elements and classroom management techniques discussed in this chapter. Other diagnostic interventions have been discussed in other chapters throughout this book.

Step 1: Prereferral

After bringing the CLD child's learning and behavior problems to the attention of the teacher assistance child intervention team (TACIT), the referring teacher is assisted in implementing a number of instructional techniques and strategies that may resolve the child's problems. The members of the TACIT should include the classroom teacher, bilingual/English as a Second Language (ESL) specialist, special educator, Chapter I teacher, counselor, social worker, parent/advocate, and others. The TACIT discusses the child's needs with the teacher and proposes appropriate interventions. If the teacher needs assistance in implementing the interventions, the TACIT provides this help.

Step 2: Diagnostic Intervention

The suggested intervention techniques and strategies include those described in greater detail in the following section of this chapter. It is important to remember that these techniques and strategies may be used at any time and by any teacher working with a CLD or CLDE student. If implemented before staffing and placement, they are considered *interventions.* If implemented after staffing (Step 4) and placement (Step 5), they are considered part of the *individualized instructional plan.* Any of the service providers may be involved in implementing these intervention strategies, including the bilingual or ESL teacher or aide, the regular classroom teacher, the special educator, or other instructional personnel. The recommended interventions are:

1. Classroom management assistance
2. Curriculum adaptation
3. Psycho/social assistance
4. Physical assistance
5. Experiential assistance
6. "Slow learner" assistance
7. Language development

These interventions are described in this chapter and elsewhere in this book. During the intervention process, diagnostic information is collected about the child's response to the intervention strategies. A guide that may be followed in documenting information is shown in Table 11–2. If the child later must be referred for a formal staffing, this information will assist in making an appropriate placement and in identifying instructional goals and objectives. The diagnostic information is documented on the form relating to the CLD child's performance or behavior that is of concern to the TACIT. This includes questions relating to acculturation and language acquisition, examples of what the child can or cannot do in various settings, interventions attempted, how the child responded, patterns observed, and implications for further interventions or a referral to staffing.

Step 3: Referral

This refers to formal referral to staffing as discussed in Chapters 8 and 9. Referral is an important part of the placement decision making process (Ysseldyke & Algozzine, 1981). The TACIT members must all be involved in this decision to refer to staffing. Questions to be resolved during staffing may be drawn from the diagnostic intervention document (Table 11–2).

Step 4: Staffing

This is discussed in detail in Chapters 8 and 9. Table 11–1 summarizes the recommendations for appropriate staffing as developed in previous chapters.

Step 5: Placement

After the decision to place is made, the interventions listed under Step 2 are incorporated into the individualized instruction plan. Although Table 11–1 illustrates a more comprehensive process than this chapter addresses, it illustrates various opportunities where methods and materials for the CLDE student may be used throughout the entire process of referral, intervention, and staffing. If a decision to place a CLDE student is made, the cultural, acculturational, and sociolinguistic interventions outlined in Step 2 should be incorporated into the individualized educational plan (IEP).

Adapting the Four Curricular Elements

Curriculum adaptation is defined as adapting, modifying and/or supplementing the curriculum to meet the needs of individual students. The need to adapt curriculum in today's schools becomes readily apparent when one considers the similarities and differences among content, instructional strategies, instructional settings, and student behavior needs within a particular classroom.

Curriculum adaptations need to be an integral part of daily teaching if each CLDE student's needs are to be effectively addressed in the classroom. Because these special learners are educated in both special and regular education classrooms, special education teachers may be required to adapt curriculum in their classrooms as well as assist regular educators to adapt curriculum in the regular classroom. Therefore, the curriculum adaptation issues discussed in this chapter are applicable to both regular and special education classroom settings.

As previously discussed, many school districts or state legislatures have established mandated curriculum content that all students are expected to follow. Most, if not all, CLDE students are also expected to follow, to the extent possible, these sequentially oriented, mandated curricula. For the most part, through administrative or legislative mandates, the decisions concerning what to teach have already been made for teachers and students. Thus, for CLDE students

Table 11–1

Diagnostic Interventions in the Prereferral Through Placement Process of Culturally and Linguistically Different Children

Adapted from "Bilingual Special Education Curriculum Training" by C. Collier, 1987, p. 46. *Proceedings of the First Annual Symposium, Cross-Cultural Special Education Network,* Boulder, CO: University of Colorado. Reprinted by permission.

Building Level Step 1: Prereferral	Step 2: Diagnostic Intervention	Step 3: Referral	District Level Step 4: Staffing	Step 5: Placement
1. Teacher brings specific problem(s) to attention of TACIT (teacher assistance child intervention team). 2. Appropriate interventions are suggested by TACIT and implemented by teacher(s) with assistance from appropriate personnel. 3. TACIT may include classroom teacher, bilingual/ESL specialist, special educator, Chapter I teacher, counselor, social worker, parent/advocate, others	1. Classroom management assistance a. Academic interventions b. Behavior interventions c. Social/peer interventions d. Other teaching/behavior management strategies 2. Curriculum adaptation a. Special education adaptation b. Bilingual/ESL adaptations c. Cultural/linguistic adaptations d. Other curriculum adaptation 3. Psycho/social assistance a. Counseling b. Support groups c. Social services d. Social survival e. Cross-cultural counseling f. Acculturation assistance g. Other psycho/social aid 4. Physical assistance a. Medical b. Nutrition c. Sensory evaluation d. Environmental evaluation e. Other direct physical aid	If the problem is *not* resolved by interventions, and/or if as a result of these interventions, new patterns and indications arise, TACIT may try other indicated interventions or may recommend staffing.	Formal and informal assessment in regard to specific concern or suspected handicapping condition, taking into consideration: 1. Assess sociolinguistic competence and language proficiency in L_1 and L_2. 2. If primary language is *not* English, assess in the primary language. 3. If balanced bilinguals, assess in both L_1 and L_2. 4. If limited proficiency in either language, use sociolinguistic and nonlanguage-dependent measures in both languages. 5. Use a multidimensional approach by a multidisciplinary team. 6. Various optimization procedures should be tried.	1. No handicap determined. Go back to various alternative service options and intervention techniques. OR 2. Handicap determined: a. IEP development must include: 1) L_1/L_2 acculturation needs and who is responsible for services. 2) Integration of SE/BE services and resources. 3) How culture and language assistance is used in meeting special needs as well as needs of whole child. 4) Step 2: Interventions b. Support team may be aides, tutors, other resources. c. Coordinated service team may be special educator, bilingual/ESL specialists, acculturation specialist, and other resources.

5. Experiential assistance (due to mobility, trauma, etc.)
   a. High interest/low vocabulary
   b. School survival
   c. Metacognitive/learning strategies
   d. Sociolinguistic development
   e. "Remedial" basic skills
   f. Curriculum adaptation
   g. Other experiential adaptation

6. "Slow learner"
   a. Developmental curricula
   b. Modification of regular curricula
   c. Assistance to teacher: materials, schedule, etc.
   d. Training for teacher/parents/aides
   e. Bilingual tutor with special training
   f. Other learning/coping strategies

7. Language development
   a. First language (L_1) development
   b. Intensive L_1 to L_2 transfer/transition
   c. Intensive ESL
   d. First language CALP/ESL BICS
   e. CALP/BICS in English
   f. Interactive language strategies (INREAL)
   g. Socio/linguistic strategies
   h. Other linguistic assistance

8. Other

7. Review tests and procedures for culture specific bias.

8. Individualized education plan (IEP) should reflect the total needs, including acculturation, culture, and language needs.

9. Staffing team may include school psychologist, special educator, speech/language specialist, bilingual/ESL specialist, acculturation specialist, social worker, counselor, advocate, parent, others

d. Bilingual special educator, bilingual educator trained in special education or special educator trained in acculturation must be primary service provider.

Table 11–2
Diagnostic Intervention/Documentation

Adapted from "Bilingual Special Education Curriculum Training" by C. Collier, 1987, p. 47. *Proceedings of the First Annual Symposium, Cross-Cultural Special Education Network,* Boulder, CO: University of Colorado. Reprinted by permission.

$^*C_1$ = first culture; C_2 = second culture.

Questions About Child	Samples of Behavior	Interventions Attempted	Performances Outcomes	Patterns Observed	Conclusions and Recommendations	New Questions
What is present level of functioning in various academic and nonacademic activities?	L_1/L_2 C_1/C_2*	Interactive techniques; Cognitive learning strategies	How did child do in various settings?			
What can/can't child do?	Home and school	Cross-cultural communication strategies	How did child respond to various strategies?			
Appropriate versus inappropriate sociolinguistic behaviors?	Informal and formal; Records; Observations	Peer tutoring; Contracting	What could child do/not do with various behavior expectations?			
What is preferred mode of interaction (verbal and nonverbal)?	Interviews; Other interaction settings	Self-monitoring; Rewarding task completion; Individual instruction; Cooperative learning team				
Etc.	Etc.	Etc.	Etc.			

who have difficulty functioning within the prescribed curriculum, the issue at hand is not whether the mandated state/district curriculum is appropriate for these learners, but rather how best to help these special learners acquire what we are required to teach. Within this framework, curriculum adaptations for CLDE students refers specifically to modifying required content as well as adapting instructional strategies, instructional settings within the classroom, and behavior to improve student self-control. Methods for adapting the four curricular elements are the foundation upon which teaching techniques and strategies are built. Adaptations to any of the curricular elements will necessitate some modifications in the others. This continual adjustment is a crucial part of the effective instruction of CLDE students. In addition, when adapting one or more of the curricular elements, issues specific to CLDE students must be addressed and incorporated into the adaptations. Several of these issues within each of the four curricular elements are discussed.

Content

It is possible to use both first language (L_1) and second language (L_2) materials in a meaningful manner, either in direct instruction or as content reinforcement. If available, the teacher should obtain materials in both languages, preferably of similar content, and review for CALP (Cognitive/Academic Level Proficiency), relevance, and format. Also, it is important to consider the degree of field independence/field sensitivity necessary for the CLDE students to use the materials. When considering adaptations to content, the teacher should ensure that the selected material enhances subject area growth without penalizing students for gaps in their first and second language and limited English proficiency. The material should allow for integration of L_1 development, L_1 to L_2 transition, and L_2 acquisition, and be made available in the students' primary language. Material in either L_1 or L_2 should also be appropriate for the proficiency levels in various domains, including vocabulary, syntax, grammar, word attack, and oral paradigms. In addition, the students must possess Basic Interpersonal Communication Skills (BICS) in L_1 or L_2 necessary to ask questions about the content, and efforts should be made to ensure that the students do not experience culture shock as new materials and stimuli are introduced.

Instructional Strategies

Strategies that are selected and adapted should exhibit culturally appropriate cues and reinforcements as well as culturally appropriate motivation and relevance to the CLDE students. Some instructional strategies may produce distractions due to children's unfamiliarity with stimuli associated with the strategy. Teachers must also determine whether field-independent or field-sensitive strategies are more appropriate and select strategies accordingly. Additionally, the effects of acculturation experiences pertaining to various strategies must be considered as instruction is implemented for these special learners.

Instructional Settings

Using the setting that is most compatible with the CLDE students' home culture should be most effective in the early stages of instruction. The students should be taught how to participate in other less familiar and compatible settings as they become more comfortable with the culture of the public school. The quantity and quality of the verbal and nonverbal interactions that CLDE students are involved in are important elements in their cognitive and academic development and can be enhanced or discouraged by the teacher's selection of the instructional setting. The teacher must also consider the use of space and time in relation to the students' home culture. Depending on the degree of experience and familiarity with particular stimuli in the instructional setting, the teacher will need to adapt the manner in which students are introduced to new settings. Additionally, the selection of an instructional setting should consider the student's different cognitive/learning style as well as cross-cultural communication skills.

Student Behavior

In reference to student behaviors, it is necessary to consider the interaction of culture and language within the acculturation context and the possible effects of a handicap on this interaction. Teachers of CLDE students should possess cross-cultural communication skills and incorporate these into their instruction. Proficiency in cross-cultural communication facilitates appropriate student behaviors as these skills become effective learning and coping tools in the CLDE students' survival repertoire. Developing a sense of familiarity with the school culture and teaching the students appropriate sociolinguistic skills is an important element in CLDE students' development of self-control in the classroom. When modifications to student behaviors are being considered, these behaviors must be viewed relative to expected socioemotional development within the acculturation context.

Although determining the curriculum elements that require adaptations is difficult, the task of actually implementing the adaptations presents an even greater challenge to teachers of these special learners. The careful selection of various teaching and behavior techniques and cognitive learning strategies that will be used to implement the adaptations is the other main ingredient necessary to consider as one creates effective instruction for CLDE students.

Teaching and Behavior Management Techniques

Once curricular adaptations are determined to be necessary and the special needs of CLDE students have been considered, the challenge of actually adapting the curriculum while simultaneously meeting the special needs emerges. The appropriate selection and use of teaching and behavior techniques forms the base for effective curricular adaptations. This section describes a variety of techniques that may be used to achieve effective instruction through curricular adaptations while meeting the special needs of CLDE students.

Table 11–3 provides a variety of teaching and behavior techniques that may be employed to adapt curriculum elements and address the special needs of these students. Several key aspects about each technique are illustrated in the table. They are the desired outcomes when using each technique, an example for each strategy, and special considerations when using each technique with CLDE students. Although all the techniques described in this chapter may be used with any learner, they are discussed relative to adaptations particularly appropriate for CLDE students. Some of the techniques may already be an integral part of the whole curriculum process for some teachers. For these teachers, some of the techniques may not represent adaptations in the strict sense of the word. However, the various techniques and strategies described may be appropriately and effectively used to adapt curriculum to address the special needs of CLDE students.

Adapting to Meet Special Needs

Based on the issues discussed elsewhere in this book, several educational needs of CLDE students can be determined. These include needs associated with acculturation, interaction patterns, limited English proficiency, language development, nonverbal communication, language function, attention to task, concept development, locus of control, and perceptions of time and space. The use of teaching and behavior techniques with CLDE students is discussed relative to these special educational needs.

Acculturation. As previously discussed, students experiencing acculturation may find the learning environment in the public schools stressful and relatively unintelligible. The teacher in this circumstance should use teaching and behavior techniques that facilitate interpreting and explaining the learning environment and expectations to the students. The techniques should gradually introduce learners to the new element of activity in their environment through demonstration and explanation of the activity or item. As the students become more familiar with one new activity, they may be introduced to another activity. This is related to the observation that discovery learning techniques may not be effective with students experiencing acculturation without extensive demonstration and explanation of the roles, outcomes, and tasks expected of the student.

In many instances the teacher must lead the students through the process, showing them how to complete the task. This is followed by observing the students' completion of the task and checking for areas in need of further devel-

Table 11–3
Teaching and Behavior Techniques

Adapted from *Classroom Management through Curricular Adaptations: Educating Minority Handicapped Students* by J. J. Hoover and C. Collier, 1986, pp. 55–58. Lindale, TX: Hamilton Publications. Reprinted by permission.

Techniques	Desired Outcome	Examples	Special Considerations
Alternative methods for response	Students respond to questions or assignments in a manner compatible with their needs.	Allow a student who has difficulty with writing activities to tape-record answers in either the first language (L_1) or the second language (L_2).	Ensure that students know varied responses are acceptable.
Clear and concise	Reduce frustration in students due to unclear expectations; minimize ambiguity in classroom expectations.	Modify or break down general classroom rules into specific behavioral expectations to ensure that each student knows exactly what is meant by acceptable behaviors.	Limited English-speaking students may require pictures of the expected actions or role-played demonstrations of the expectations.
Contingency contracting	Improve motivation; clarify responsiblities, assignments, rewards.	Document in writing that the student will complete 20 math problems with 80% accuracy during the regular math period. Student will receive 10 minutes of extra free time if contract conditions are met.	The rewards for completing the contract must be culturally appropriate.
Individualized instruction	Learners are motivated and complete tasks appropriate to their needs, interests, and abilities.	IEP may state that student will be able to use particular sociolinguistic cues and responses in appropriate first culture (C_1) and second culture (C_2) settings.	IEPs must include language (L_1 and L_2) needs as well as those for identified handicap.
Learning centers	Students are able to reinforce specific skills while working at their own pace; individualization.	Create an area in the classroom where several different activities exist for reviewing sight works in both L_1 and L_2.	The learning center could have visual and auditory stimuli from the students' cultural backgrounds.
Modify presentation of abstract concepts	Students are gradually and systematically introduced to abstract concepts.	Supplement the presentations of abstract concepts with visual aids, manipulatives, examples from students' previous experiences, or other direct hands-on experiences.	This is an application of cognitive/academic development. The concepts as well as the language of cognitive and academic tasks must be taught and built upon students' prior cultural experiences.
Peer tutoring	Learning gains are experienced by both the tutor and the student being tutored.	A student who has mastered a list of sight words or math facts presents these items on flash cards to another student needing assistance in this area.	If the student needing assistance is limited English proficient, it would be most effective to have the peer tutor be bilingual in L_1 and L_2.

Continued

Techniques	Desired Outcome	Examples	Special Considerations
Planned ignoring	Reduction of possible confrontations over minor misbehaving; elimination of inappropriate behavior after a few moments.	Teacher elects to ignore some whispering between two students during independent work time.	This must be done consistently and with equal frequency with minority and nonminority students.
Planned physical movement	Prevent or minimize behavior problems in the classroom.	Allow students to move to a learning center or study booth for part of their independent work time instead of remaining seated at their desks for the entire time.	Effective technique if cultural variations in mobility and interaction patterns among students are considered.
Positive reinforcement	Increase the frequency of appropriate responses or behaviors.	Provide the student extra free time when a math or reading assignment has been completed.	Cultural as well as personal relevance must be considered.
Prompting	Increase the students' probability of generating a correct response.	Underline one letter of a pair of letters that a student is studying (e.g., *b* versus *d*). This helps focus the learner's attention on characteristics of both letters, thus reducing confusion.	Cues or prompts must be culturally appropriate and meaningful to the student.
Providing choices	Reduce fears associated with assignments; alleviate power struggles between teacher and student.	Select two different reading selections of interest to the student, both of which address the same desired objective. Allow the student to select one of them for the assignment. If student does not select either of these, introduce a third selection and ask student to choose.	Both L_1 and L_2 development should be incorporated into assignments where choices are provided.
Providing success	Improve confidence; student views self as a successful person.	Initially reduce the difficulty level of material and gradually increase the level as easier tasks are met with success.	Must consider L_1 and L_2 development to ensure success with academic tasks.
Proximity control	Increase students' time on task; reassure frustrated students.	Periodically circulate throughout the classroom during group or independent activities, spending time next to particular students.	Cultural implications of proximity must be considered as personal space varies considerably from culture to culture.
Role playing	Students learn to confront the reactions of others and ways to deal with the situations similar to the role-play event.	A specific problem, such as discrimination, is identified and described. Students role play how they would confront the problem and discuss their roles or behaviors upon completion.	This is an effective technique in assisting with the acculturation process.

Table 11–3
continuing

Techniques	Desired Outcome	Examples	Special Considerations
Self-monitoring	Reduce inappropriate behaviors; increase time on task; students assume responsibility for their own behaviors.	Instruct the students to record a check mark on a seprate sheet of paper each time they catch themselves tapping their pencils on their desks during spelling class.	This may assist minority handicapped students to learn behaviors appropriate to the culture of the school and classroom.
Shortened assignments	Complex or difficult tasks are more manageable to students.	Structure the presentation of weekly spelling words so two or three new words are introduced and studied each day throughout the week rather than presenting all words at the beginning of the week.	This technique may assist the teacher to check whether students have the preskills necessary for selected tasks.
Signal	Prevent minor inappropriate behaviors from escalating while not providing specific attention to the students' misbehaviors.	Flick the classroom lights on and off when the noise level in the class becomes too loud.	Students experiencing acculturation will have difficulty adjusting to unfamiliar signals.
Simplify reading	Students study content similar to other classmates but at a level commensurate with their reading abilities.	Provide student with lower level reading material that covers the same topic others are studying.	The materials can be in both L_1 and L_2 with different reading levels for either.
Student accountability	Students become aware of the connection between their actions and the consequences of these actions.	Establish rewards and consequences for completing work or exhibiting appropriate behavior, ensuring that these rewards and consequences are consistently implemented.	Limited English speaking students experiencing acculturation may require some role playing, mediation, or other teaching of expectations to best understand accountability.
Student input into curricular planning	Facilitate students' ownership in their education.	Allow students to select some specific topics to be covered in an upcoming unit of study.	Ensure that minority handicapped learners know how to contribute in the planning process.
Time-out	Regain control over self; student thinks about own behavior and behavioral expectations.	Remove a student to a quiet or time-out area for 3–5 minutes when student is unable to respond to a situation in a nonagressive manner.	Sociocultural implications of the time-out must be considered to ensure students understand the purpose of time-out.
Touch control	Increase time on task and awareness of one's behavior.	If a student is looking around the room during independent work time, gently tap student on shoulder as a signal to continue working.	As with proximity control, the cultural implication of the touching must be considered or the effect of this technique will be lost.

Table 11–3
continuing

opment. Teaching and behavior techniques appropriate for adapting curriculum to address this educational need include peer tutoring, prompting, providing success, positive reinforcement, establishing clear and concise expectations, learning centers, role playing, student input into curricular decisions, self-monitoring, or student accountability.

CLDE students often need to be taught how to behave appropriately in particular settings, as well as why certain behaviors are considered appropriate and others not appropriate. Specifically, the student may need to learn cultural values and behaviors pertaining to proximics (i.e., how close two people stand when interacting in various situations and roles), attitudes toward property and ownership, discrimination, attitudes towards handicaps and status, illustrations of how colors and clothing carry different meanings in different social contexts, and the interaction of sociolinguistic behaviors with other cues to convey meaning in the first culture (C_1) versus the second culture (C_2).

The most basic C_2 cultural values and behaviors must be taught first as survival skills for the CLDE student. These may include dressing appropriately, recognizing dangerous situations, recognizing to whom and where to go to receive assistance, how to ask for assistance, how to order and eat food appropriately, as well as contrasting similarities and differences between appropriate and inappropriate behaviors, in and out of school settings. Teaching and behavior techniques for implementing adaptations to curricular elements that address knowledge of cultural values and behaviors include peer tutoring, role playing, individualized instruction, providing choices, contingency contracting, positive reinforcement, clear and concise expectations, and proximity control.

Interaction Patterns. This educational need refers to assisting students to integrate C_1 and C_2 and to prevent the possible detrimental assimilation or rejection of C_2. This includes lessons in how to communicate without speaking the language, how to participate even when not completely understanding what is going on, the importance of interacting and participating while learning the new language and culture, as well as lessons on multicultural aspects of American society, the pluralistic nature of American heritage, and contributions of the student's culture to American culture and society.

Students should be encouraged to observe others and to respond to them even if they do not fully understand the occurrences. They may also be assigned a peer tutor who will explain the occurrences the student observes. It is also important to teach the students not to hesitate to participate and interact. Students learn to speak by speaking, learn appropriate actions by doing, learn to interact appropriately by interacting, and in turn are interacted with more frequently when they participate. Teaching and behavior techniques such as peer tutoring, student accountability, self-monitoring, role playing, or student input into curricular decisions may be appropriately used to address interaction needs of CLDE students.

Limited English Proficiency. As discussed by Cummins (1981), it takes one or two years for nonhandicapped CLDE students who do not speak English to learn basic interpersonal communication skills in English. As discussed previously, success in BICS should not be mistaken for proficiency in the type and depth of English used in the classroom. BICS should be fully developed to assist students to develop confidence and experience success in speaking English as a Second Language. This in turn forms the base upon which cognitive academic language skills are developed.

The teacher should use the students' current level of BICS for encouraging greater verbal communication in English through the use of such teaching and behavior techniques as role playing, prompting, and frequently requesting verbal responses in instructional activities. The content, instructional settings, and strategies of the curriculum must be adapted to allow and encourage this greater verbal discourse. To elicit more frequent and more proficient use of English as a Second Language, CLDE students must be given more frequent opportunities to use what English they have even though this may only be BICS-level English.

In reference to CALP in English, this may be developed within five to seven years in non-English speaking children in a regular English-speaking classroom setting (Cummins 1981). This proficiency is crucial to the academic achievement of the student and instruction in CALP should an integral part of the curriculum used with CLDE students. Strategies to use in adapting the curriculum for CALP development also include the use of peer tutoring, role playing, and frequent use of verbal interactions with the students. Students can role play particular school activities and personnel to become more familiar with the language used in these situations. Student accountability and self-monitoring are also useful teaching and behavior techniques as CLDE students become more proficient with CALP, but continue to need development.

Language Development. Language development needs of CLDE students include L_1 vocabulary development, L_1 discourse structure and topics, L_1 to L_2 code switching and L_2 and L_1 code switching in planned sequence, translation, contrastive analysis, or transformational grammar. This educational need may also involve revision or clarification, affirmation, acknowledging, commenting, or maintaining a topic in L_1 or L_2. A variety of teaching and behavior techniques and cognitive learning strategies may be used to adapt curriculum to meet these language-oriented needs. Some of the effective interventions include peer tutoring, prompting, alternate methods of response, role playing, modifying presentation of abstract concepts, providing success, positive reinforcement, contingency contracting, or individualized instruction. In addition, various interactive techniques may be used to develop language skills in L_1 and L_2. These include mirroring, parallel talk, self-talk, verbal reflection, and modeling. The reader is referred to INREAL (1984) and Collier and Hoover (1987) for a complete discussion of these strategies.

Nonverbal Communication. Much of expressive communication is nonverbal and CLDE students may be more at risk from misunderstandings of their nonverbal communications than of verbal communications (Hymes, 1970). Alternative methods of response, role-play situations, signal interference, and peer tutoring that focus on the nonverbal elements of the communication and situation are effective techniques to use in implementing adaptations to the curriculum when nonverbal communication skills require assistance. For example, students could act out (without words) the actions of another depicting a particular situation. The "audience" is instructed to generate a description of the situation and provide appropriate verbal discourse. Peers are instructed to cue CLDE students when their nonverbal communication is inappropriate or misunderstood.

Language Function. Teachers and students use language, but rarely learn how all the elements combine to achieve proficient communication. This does not mean just talking about grammar or syntax, but how grammar, syntax, or vocabulary function in the totality of communication. When the need arises to assist CLDE students to comprehend the function of language and its usage, appropriate curriculum adaptations include use of contrastive phoneme and morpheme (sound/symbol and meaning/symbol) analysis, use of communication with regular patterns, drawing students' attention to these patterns, and teaching how to use these patterns.

Learning centers, modifying presentation of abstract concepts, and self-monitoring are useful techniques to use when adapting curriculum to facilitate comprehension of language function. In addition, role-play situations may be developed in which students ask for directions from a person on the street versus requesting something from another family member. This will assist to illustrate the different functions of language as well as how language itself changes in different situations.

Attention to Task. CLDE students will vary in their willingness to work beyond the required time or to withstand frustration and possible failure. A highly persistent student may work until the task is completed and will seek any necessary assistance. A student with low persistence will demonstrate an inability to work on a task for any length of time or have a short attention span. It should be remembered that an abnormal persistence (i.e., perseveration) is also a learning and behavior problem. Teachers can use monitored observation to determine what, when, where, and with whom appropriate persistence is occurring. To address this educational need, adapt the instructional setting, instructional strategies, and content to continue to elicit the appropriate persistence as observed by the teacher.

Another facet of attention that should be considered is level of anxiety. An individual's level of apprehension and tension under stress conditions will affect attention to the task at hand. Students do better with challenging and difficult tasks if they are in a low-stress situation. Heightened anxiety (Collier & Hoover 1987) is one of the side effects of the acculturation process and must be addressed in the instruction of CLDE students. Teachers must adapt their instructional setting and content so that stress for the CLDE student is minimized and must use instructional strategies that do not produce more anxiety in the students.

This may be accomplished by using demonstration techniques and concrete cues to ensure knowledge of expectations, teaching students relaxation techniques before stressful tasks, and always prefacing new lessons with a review of previously successful learning experiences. Other techniques useful in conjunction with attention to task include planned physical movement, clear and concise expectations, time-out, touch control, providing success, prompting, simplifying reading level, alternative methods for response, contingency contracting, or planned ignoring.

Concept Development. This educational need pertains specifically to the ways in which students form and retain concepts. One aspect of this is conceptual tempo (i.e., the speed and adequacy of hypothesis formulation and information processing). Similar to other students, CLDE learners will fall somewhere along the conceptual tempo continuum of reflection versus impulsivity. Cultural factors as well as individual personality factors affect where students fall on this continuum. Some cultures encourage and expect more reflective behavior of learners. Other cultures encourage and expect more impulsive behavior of their children, regarding this as critical to the learning process.

The teacher should adapt the instructional setting, content, and strategies to the current conceptual tempo of the CLDE students and use various techniques and strategies to elicit desired school behavior gradually. The culturally sensitive use of contingency contracting, self-monitoring, and role play are effective in conceptual tempo development. It is also important for CLDE students to learn which conceptual tempo is appropriate and most effective in a particular setting.

Another consideration in conceptual style is breadth or style of categorization. The broad categorizer likes to include many items in a category and lessens the risk of leaving something out. The narrow categorizer prefers to exclude doubtful items and lessens the probability of including something that does not belong. Cognitive differences are also found when looking at whether students compartmentalize (relatively rigid categories) or differentiate (tendency to conceive of things as having many properties rather than a few). Differences in categorization are to be expected between cultural groups (Casson, 1981; Spindler, 1974). For example, students from different cultures may group food items in a variety of ways (e.g., color, time of day used, shape, type of utensil used).

To address these differences in concept development, the teacher must very clearly demonstrate the type of categorization that is expected and, if necessary, teach CLDE students how to make the desired categorizations. As previously discussed, some students may be unfamiliar with different "types" of items (e.g., fruit versus vegetable, insect versus animal). These complex categorization skills are common in primary classrooms and are based on assumptions of culturally similar cognitive understanding of concept formation. Teaching and behavior techniques to use in conjunction with development in this area include clear and concise expectations, alternate methods of response, and providing choices.

When considering cognitive development in curricular adaptations for CLDE students, it is important to remember that one of the side effects of acculturation is a resistance to change and new experiences. New activities should always be introduced in relation to previously and successfully learned tasks or skills. Techniques and strategies useful for this conceptual development include providing success, analogy, organization, shortening assignments, or simplifying the reading level of assignments.

Locus of Control. Locus of control refers to internal versus external perceptions of factors such as responsibility, success, or achievement. *Internal* persons think of themselves as responsible for their own behavior (i.e., their own efforts and abilities resulted in success or failure on a given task). *External* persons, on the other hand, view circumstances as events beyond their control (i.e., luck or other people are responsible for their successes or failures). CLDE students may display evidence of external locus of control due to the effects of acculturation. They may also display external locus of control due to continued failure to achieve in school no matter how hard they have tried. On the other hand, CLDE students may blame themselves (i.e., display internal locus of control) when failure is really affected by things beyond their control (e.g., their handicap).

Confusion in locus of control may be addressed by the teacher in various ways. For example, students may be taught to remind themselves that mistakes are only temporary, that mistakes help show them where they need to put more effort, and that they should congratulate themselves when they are successful. Other techniques that would be useful to address this area of need include student accountability, clear and concise expectations, student input into curricular planning, and self-monitoring.

Perceptions of Time and Space. Cultures deal with the environment in different ways. These differences must be considered by the classroom teacher when adapting the curriculum. For example, the teacher may adapt seating arrangements and the time of day for particular activities to make maximum use of the CLDE students' particular cultural orientations. The teacher should also be aware of differences in role expectations for males and females and appropriate "personal space." Various techniques and strategies enable the teacher to develop and teach school-appropriate role expectations within the instructional context, without penalizing the student for school or home differences. Role play, peer tutoring, alternate methods of response, and clear and concise expectations are useful techniques to use as perceptions of time and space require development.

Educational Materials

An integral component within the process of adapting one or more curricular elements is the appropriate selection and use of instructional materials. Materials are vehicles used in classrooms to study and learn knowledge, skills, and attributes associated with each of the curricular elements. This section provides an overview of criteria to follow when evaluating and selecting different materials, along with ideas for developing and adapting materials if commercial materials are inappropriate for specific situations.

Materials Evaluation and Selection

One primary objective in the materials evaluation and selection process is to select materials that are appropriate for the students who will use them and effective in the particular learning situation for which they are selected. Because an abundant amount of commercial materials exist and because use of some materials may not produce advertised results, careful evaluation of materials must accompany the selection of materials for CLDE students. When evaluating materials for selection and use, Weiderholt and McNutt (1977) discussed two types of evaluation that should be conducted: static evaluation and dynamic evaluation. Static evaluation relies upon various checklists or guidelines to analyze materials to determine their suitability for a particular group of students and situation. Dynamic evaluation is defined as evaluating material as it is being used by students once it has been selected through the static evaluation process. Dynamic evaluation of materials includes pre-post testing of the learners, observation of student interaction with the material, and reviews with students to gather their feedback about the material (Harris & Schutz, 1986). Dynamic evaluation is an ongoing process completed while students use selected materials. However, the process of evaluating and selecting materials begins with effective static evaluation.

Criteria for Materials Selection. Numerous authors have identified criteria important to consider in the materials evaluation and selection process (Morsink, 1984; Lewis & Doorlag, 1987; Harris & Schutz, 1986; Mandell & Gold, 1984). In discussing materials selection, Morsink (1984) wrote that these must match two general curricular areas. These include matching materials to content and to student needs. When matching to content, the teacher must consider the match between the structure of the specific content unit or subject area as well as to the objectives of the particular lesson or activity. A match between the material and the structure of the content area "implies that the material provides instruction that illustrates the major concepts in that subject" (Morsink, 1984, p. 108). Within the content of the subject area, the material must also match the specific objectives for which they are used.

Materials must also match student needs. Several criteria have been developed for selecting materials for special learners (Brown, 1975; Morsink, 1984). Factors that pertain to student needs and abilities that should be considered in materials selection include:

- Pacing of the material
- Format and readability
- Use and control of complex language
- Level of interest
- Potential for independent use

These and similar aspects of commercial material must be addressed as particular student needs are considered in the process of evaluating and selecting commercial material for CLDE students.

Materials Evaluation. In addition to general areas requiring consideration, various evaluation forms and checklists exist that address a variety of issues associated with evaluating materials for selection for use in the classroom. Most of these established evaluation forms include items that pertain to the criteria outlined earlier as well as other factors such as cost, durability, field testing, or bias of material. Figures 11–2 and 11–3 provide examples of two different forms available for evaluating and selecting materials.

Figure 11–2, developed from materials by Affleck, Lowenbraun, and Archer (1980), provides several general categories to address when analyzing materials. Each general category contains several questions that assist to determine if the material is appropriate to individual student needs as well as curriculum content and objective requirements. The evaluation form in Figure 11–3 encompasses the areas of:

- Instruction
- Practice
- Content
- Objectives
- Assessment
- Review
- Motivation
- Adaptability
- Physical characteristics
- Teacher directions and instructions

The materials evaluation form illustrated in Figure 11–3 provides a different type of form than illustrated in Figure 11–2. The evaluation form in Figure 11–3 was developed by Harris and Schutz (1986) and provides fewer items focusing in several general areas including:

- Prerequisite skills
- Thinking abilities
- Required functioning levels
- Individual or group instruction design
- Sequence of materials

Although not as comprehensive of an evaluation form as outlined in Figure 11–2, the brief materials evaluation form illustrated in Figure 11–3 may be useful for the selection of some individual materials that are not comprehensive in nature. The more comprehensive materials require more comprehensive evaluations before selection, and the materials evaluation form illustrated in Figure 11–2 is recommended for this task.

When considering materials for selection the teacher must also be cognizant of potential biases that may exist within both the printed and graphic material. Lemlech (1984) identified several issues that must be considered to determine potentially bias material. These issues include:

- Stereotyping cultures or ethnic groups
- Religious bias
- Sex bias
- Expression of diversity
- Specific material about minority groups
- Portrayal of the interrelationship among diverse groups

As materials evaluation and selection are completed, particular attention must also be directed at the potential biases that may exist within materials. Materials can be screened for biases before full evaluation in attempts to avoid efforts spent on the evaluation of material deemed biased in nature.

Instruction

Are instruction procedures for each lesson clearly specified?

Does the material provide a maximum amount of direct teacher instruction on the skills/concepts presented?

Does the direct teacher instruction provide for active student involvement and responses?

Are the direct instructional lessons adaptable to small-group/individual instruction?

Is a variety of cueing and prompting techniques used to elicit correct child responses?

When using verbal instruction, does the instruction proceed in a clear, logical fashion in both languages?

Does the teacher use modeling and demonstration when appropriate to the skills being taught?

Does the material specify correction and feedback procedures for use during instruction?

Practice

Does the material contain appropriate practice activities that contribute to mastery of the skill/concepts?

Are the practice activities directly related to the desired outcome behaviors?

Does the material provide enough practice for the slow learner?

Does the material provide for feedback on responses during practice?

Can the learner complete practice activities independently?

Does the material reduce the probability of error in independent practice activities?

Sequence of Instruction

Are the scope and sequence of the material clearly specified?

Are facts/concepts/skills ordered in a logical manner from simple to complex?

Does the sequence proceed in small steps, easily attainable by the handicapped learner?

Content

Does the selection of the concepts and skills adequately represent the content area?

Is the content consistent with the stated objectives?

Is the information presented in the material accurate?

Is the information presented in the material current?

Are various points of view concerning treatment of minorities and handicapped people, ideologies, social values, sex roles, culture, and socioeconomic class objectively represented?

Are the content and topic of the material relevant to the needs of the handicapped students as well as to the other students in the regular classroom?

Behavioral Objectives

Are objectives clearly stated for the material?

Are the objectives consistent with the goals for the whole classroom?

Are the objectives stated in behavioral terms including the desired child behavior, the criteria for measurement of the behavior, and the desired standard of performance?

Figure 11–2

Evaluation and Selection of Materials

Adapted from *Teaching the Mildly Handicapped in the Regular Class* by J.Q. Affleck, S. Lowenbraun, and A. Archer, 1980, pp. 125–127, Columbus, OH: Merrill Publishing Co.

Entry Behaviors
Does the material specify the prerequisite student skills needed to work with ease in the material?
Are the prerequisite student skills compatible with the objectives of the material?

Initial Assessment/Placement
Does the material provide a method to determine initial placement into the material?
Does the initial placement tool contain enough items to accurately place the learner into the material?

Ongoing Assessment/Evaluation
Does the material provide evaluation procedures for measuring progress and mastery of objectives?
Are there sufficient evaluative items to accurately measure learner progress?
Are procedures and/or materials for ongoing record keeping provided?

Review/Maintenance
Are practice and review of content material provided?
Are review and maintenance activities systematically and appropriately spaced?
Are adequate review and maintenance activities provided for the slow learner?

Motivation/Interest
Are reinforcement procedures built in or suggested for use in the program?
Are procedures specified for providing feedback to the student on the student's progress?
Has the program been designed to motivate and appeal to students?

Adaptability to Individual Differences
Can the pace be adapted to variations in learner rate of mastery?
Can the method of response be adapted to the individual needs of the learner?
Can the method of instruction be adapted to the individual needs of the learner?
Can the child advance to subsequent tasks when proficiency is demonstrated?
Can the learner be placed in the material at an individualized level?
Does the material offer alternative teaching strategies for students who are failing to master an objective?

Physical Characteristics of the Material
Is the format uncluttered?
Is the format grammatically correct and free of typographical errors?
Are photographs and illustrations clear, attractive, and consistent with the content and student experience?
Are the type size and style appropriate to the students?
Are auditory components of adequate clarity and amplification in both languages?
Are the materials durable?
Can the materials be easily stored and organized for classroom use?

Teacher Considerations
Is a teacher's manual or set of teacher guidelines provided?
Are teacher instructions clear, complete, and unambiguous?
Does the material specify the skills and abilities needed by the instructor to work effectively with the material?

Name of material: ______________________ Copyright date: __________
Publisher and address: ______________________
Price: ________ Grade level: ________ This analysis by: ______________ Date: ________
Subject or content area(s): ______________________

Structure and time estimates: ______________________
General goals of the material: ______________________
What is the cultural orientation of the material?

What is the language of instruction?

What prerequisite skills are needed?

What prerequisite language skills are needed?

What is the dominant modality of instruction?

What modalities are required for responses?

Is convergent or divergent thinking required?

Is the level of functioning concrete or abstract?

Is the material designed for individual or group instruction?

What parts of this material are consumable?

Are extra materials required?

Are skills logically sequenced?

Is there a suggested method for evaluating students' progress and/or performance?

Other comments:

Figure 11–3
Materials Evaluation

Adapted from *The Special Education Resource Program—Rationale and Implementation* by W.J. Harris and P.N.B. Schutz, 1986, p. 202, Columbus, OH: Merrill Publishing Co.

Creating and Adapting Materials

Although much commercial material exists, teachers of CLDE students may need to adapt material or create their own in an effort to meet prerequisite needs of CLDE students. If possible, commercial material should be used to avoid unnecessary work on the part of the teacher. Using commercial material allows the teacher to concentrate on actual teaching activities with learners and minimizes time required to deal with material once the selection process has been completed. However, the need to adapt or develop materials is not uncommon in today's classrooms for CLDE students.

Mandell and Gold (1984) suggested that because many educational materials reflect wide ranges of interest or abilities the need to adapt materials is frequently necessary. Several guidelines for adapting commercial material or developing teacher-made materials are discussed in the literature (Lewis & Doorlag, 1987; Mandell & Gold, 1984; Harris & Schutz, 1986). The following list contains suggestions from these and other sources for adapting or developing material. This list is not designed to be all-inclusive, and variations to these ideas may be required in order to meet individual needs.

- Adjust method of presentation of content of material.
- Develop supplemental material.
- Tape record directions or material.
- Provide alternatives for responding to questions in material.
- Rewrite brief sections of material to lower reading level.
- Outline material for student before reading and selection.
- Reduce the number of pages or items on a page to be completed by the student.
- Break tasks into smaller subtasks.
- Provide additional practice to ensure mastery.
- Substitute a similar, less complex task for a particular assignment.
- Develop simple study guides to complement required materials.

These and similar types of adaptations will allow CLDE students successfully to confront various materials used in the classroom. When combined with various curricular adaptation strategies previously discussed in this chapter, the adaptation of materials will allow students to have greater success in all areas within the total curriculum. The development of teacher-made materials such as study guides, game boards, or other supplemental material should be carefully completed to avoid unnecessary work for the teacher. However, similar to adapted material, carefully developed teacher-made materials can assist CLDE students successfully to address materials needed in school.

This chapter concludes with the presentation of several guidelines to facilitate the effective use of materials with CLDE students. These guidelines to facilitate the effective use of materials with CLDE students. These guidelines represent some of the many considerations teachers should bear in mind when evaluating, selecting, adapting, or developing materials for use by CLDE students:

1. Know specific language abilities of each student.
2. Include appropriate cultural experiences in material adapted or developed.
3. Ensure that material progresses at a rate commensurate with student needs and abilities.
4. Document the success of selected commercial material.
5. Adapt only specific materials requiring modifications and do not attempt to change too much at one time.
6. Attempt different materials and adaptations until appropriate education for all CLDE students exists.
7. Strategically implement materials adaptations to ensure smooth transitions into the new materials.
8. Follow some consistent format or guide when evaluating materials.
9. Be knowledgeable of particular cultures and heritages and their compatibility with selected materials.
10. Follow a well-developed process for evaluating the success of adapted or developed materials as individual language and culture needs of CLDE students are addressed.

Summary

This chapter has addressed the special needs of CLDE students with learning and behavior problems. A procedure for effective instruction through curricular adaptations that address these special needs has been presented. Materials selection and intervention techniques appropriate for meeting the special needs of CLDE students have been described and discussed. Appropriate use of methods and materials within the framework of adapting the four curricular elements will result in improved instruction for culturally and linguistically different handicapped students. Readers should consider a final thought and challenge—the challenge to look beyond simple solutions to complex curriculum problems through the study of the interrelationship among curricular elements, to achieve and maintain the most effective instruction necessary to promote a positive learning environment.

Discussion Questions

1. Describe the four curricular elements that must be addressed in the Bilingual Special Education classroom.
2. Explain the purpose of diagnostic intervention.
3. What steps would you go through to document instructional interventions?
4. Develop a sample diagnostic intervention plan for a bilingual child. Document the process you would use.
5. Select one teaching strategy and describe how you would use it with a bilingual exceptional child.

References

Affleck, J. Q., Lowenbraun, S., & Archer, A. (1980). *Teaching the mildly handicapped in the regular class.* Columbus, OH: Merrill Publishing Co.

Brown, V. (1975). A basic q-sheet for analyzing and comparing curriculum materials and proposals. *Journal of Learning Disabilities.* 8:409–416.

Casson, R. W. (1981). *Language, culture, and cognition.* New York: Macmillan.

Collier, C. (1987). Bilingual special education curriculum training. In *Proceedings of the First Annual Symposium, Cross-cultural special education network,* 46–47. Boulder, CO: University of Colorado.

Collier, C., & Hoover, J. J. (1987). *Cognitive learning strategies for minority handicapped students.* Lindale, TX: Hamilton Publications.

Cummins, J. (1981). Four misconceptions about the language proficiency in bilingual children. *Journal of the National Association of Bilingual Education.* 5(3):31–45.

Eisner, E. W. (1979). *The educational imagination.* New York: Macmillan.

Harris, W. J., & Schutz, P. N. B. (1986). *The special education resource program—rationale and implementation.* Columbus, OH: Merrill Publishing Co.

Hoover, J. J., & Collier, C. (1986). *Classroom management through curricular adaptations: Educating minority handicapped students.* Lindale, TX: Hamilton Publications.

Hymes, D. (1970). Bilingual education: Linguistic vs. sociolinguistic bases. In J. E. Alatis (Ed.), *Bilingualism and language contact* (pp. 69–76). Washington, DC: Georgetown University Press.

INREAL (1984). *INREAL specialist training packet.* Boulder, CO: University of Colorado.

Lemlech, J. K. (1984). *Curriculum and instructional methods for the elementary school.* New York: Macmillan.

Lewis, R. B., & Doorlag, D. H. (1987). *Teaching special students in the mainstream.* Columbus, OH: Merrill Publishing Co.

Mandell, C. J., & Gold, V. (1984). *Teaching handicapped students.* St. Paul, MN: West.

Morsink, C. V. (1984). *Teaching special needs students in regular classrooms.* Boston: Little, Brown.

Spindler, G. D. (Ed.). (1974). *Education and cultural process: Toward an anthropology of education.* New York: Holt, Rinehart, & Winston.

Weiderholt, J. L., & McNutt, G. (1977). Evaluating materials for handicapped adolescents. *Journal of Learning Disabilities.* 10:132–140.

Wiles, J., & Bondi, J. C. (1984). *Curriculum development: A guide to practice.* Columbus, OH: Merrill Publishing Co.

Ysseldyke, J. E., & Algozzine, B. (1987). Diagnostic classification in decisions as a function of referral information. *Journal of Special Education.* 15(4):429–435.

CHAPTER TWELVE

Mainstreaming and Bilingual Exceptional Children

Catherine Collier

- Definitions
- History of Mainstreaming Effort
- Mainstreaming
- Modes of Mainstreaming
- Teacher Competencies for Mainstreaming Bilingual Exceptional Children
- Suggestions for Mainstreaming Bilingual Exceptional Children
- Summary

Objectives

- To present a brief history and justification of mainstreaming as an educational strategy for both bilingual and special education programs
- To describe various models of mainstreaming in bilingual and special education programs as well as for exceptional bilingual children
- To describe the continuum mainstreaming model of educational services for exceptional bilingual children
- To describe various teacher competencies for mainstreaming exceptional bilingual children
- To provide practical suggestions for mainstreaming bilingual children with various exceptionalities

Mainstreaming has come to be the preferred means of providing exceptional children with equal access to appropriate education. In the form of transition programs, it is also the most common type of Bilingual Education for culturally and linguistically different children. This chapter discusses the history, need, and justification for mainstreaming modes, teacher competencies for these modes, and some suggestions for mainstreaming bilingual children with various exceptionalities.

Definitions

References to the mainstream are meant in the most general sense: the dominant population of a society and its culture and language. In this particular case the point of reference is Anglo-American and English. Mainstreaming means the integration of the "different" (e.g. exceptional and/or culturally/linguistically different) children into the regular classroom, and it implies a joint effort on the part of regular and specialized staff members. Mainstreaming is more than enrolling different children in regular classrooms. It involves an education placement procedure for children based on the belief that each such child should be educated in the least restrictive environment in which the child's needs can be satisfactorily met. The mainstreaming process recognizes the existence of a wide range of special needs varying in intensity and duration and the appropriateness of a continuum of educational settings for individual needs. Additionally, to the maximum extent possible, children should not be segregated by differences, whether due to exceptionality or to culture and language.

Mainstreaming and *least restrictive environment* are not synonymous. Although placement in a regular classroom is frequently seen as the least restrictive environment for a child with special needs, the child may benefit more by spending only part of the day in the mainstream and part of the day in special language and compensatory classes. Because these periods will vary proportionately depending on the child's special needs, mainstreaming should be viewed as a continuum of services. This is discussed in greater detail later in this chapter. Removal of the different child from the mainstream should occur only when the child's needs cannot be met satisfactorily in an environment including mainstream children. Reynolds and Birch (1986) state:

> Mainstreaming means that children who need special supports are receiving high quality special education while they enjoy the personal and social advantages of life in regular school classes with all the other neighborhood youngsters of their age. It also means that high quality regular education is going on at the same time. Further, it means that the regular teacher coordinates all pupil activities with the assistance of a staff of special educators, aides, the school principal, and

other specialists. Together with parents, these personnel make up a team whose central concern is topflight instruction for all children.

In bilingual and English as a Second Language (ESL) education, several mainstreaming models are used, some of which are immersion, maintenance, restoration, and transition. As with programs for exceptional children, these programs were developed to provide remedial, compensatory, or special education for culturally or linguistically different children under the impetus of equal educational opportunity as discussed in Chapter 1. These models will be discussed further in the section about modes of mainstreaming Bilingual Special Education children. To understand the mainstreaming concept, it is important to review the history and development of these programs for both exceptional and culturally or linguistically different children. Much of this history is addressed in greater detail in Chapter 4; the following section will briefly review this history.

History of Mainstreaming Effort

Before the 18th century anyone with discernible handicaps or socially defined differences was generally not accepted in the mainstream of society. People who were different from the mainstream in various ways were accused of being witches, possessed by spirits, heathen, or inferior human stock, and they were generally ostracized if not actually mistreated. They were generally not given any special training or education. The socially different, or handicapped, were "doomed to constricted lives . . . it was believed that they could not be taught, were not worth teaching, or could proceed on their own" (Reynolds & Birch, 1986).

Preindustrial education for the mainstream population was generally ethnically segregated religious and vocational preparation guided by local community needs (Parelius & Parelius, 1978). Few vocations accepted distinctly "different" people. Culturally different children were mostly left alone before 1800, except in those areas where mission schools operated (once the particular religious group had decided the natives were human enough to have souls).

In the 18th and early 19th centuries in North America, the mainstream population was fairly homogeneous by geographic location, being primarily Western European colonials living on lands wrested from the native population (U.S. Commission on Civil Rights, 1975). The native population either remained in or near the colonial settlement as slaves or indentured servants (for example, in the Southwest and West under the Spanish), receiving training commensurate with their expected duties, or were driven off to live their own "heathen" lives elsewhere. Those who wished to take up mainstream civilization did so through mission schools especially established to convert the heathens to Christianity. The emphasis of the nonreligious curriculum in these schools was to remediate or cure the native of "ignorance" and uncivilized ways. This is not dissimilar to the approach to education of exceptional children during this period. Whether handicapped or of diverse cultural backgrounds, these children were different and the difference needed to be cured.

Many changes during the 19th and early 20th centuries brought about the further development of special education programs to remediate or compensate for differences. Sociopolitical changes engendered by increased numbers of immigrants, technology, urbanization, the idea of free public education, and a general increase in the level of education were some of the factors in this development (Gearheart & Weishahn, 1984). A few segregated residential schools for the deaf, blind, and mentally deficient were established. In 1878 Alexander Graham Bell addressed the National Education Association, advocating that annexes be built onto public schools to provide special classes for the deaf, blind, and mentally deficient closer to home so that they would not have to attend far away institutions (Gearheart & Weishahn, 1984). This is similar to the gradual movement to educate Native Americans closer to home in this century.

During this time period, increasing numbers of immigrants arrived from Eastern Europe, Italy, and Asia. Special classes were set up to teach them the language and customs of the United States. Factories provided English language classes for workers and citizenship information in the native language of the workers was placed in pay envelopes. In the 1890s classes for educating immigrants were set up in New York City. Further, from 1907 to 1912 the YMCA held classes in 130 cities to teach the English language and American customs and history to immigrants. Additionally, in 1907 New Jersey passed a law providing for evening instruction in English and civics. Most of the programs were for adults only. The great majority of culturally different children in school—if they were in school at all—received no special consideration and were immersed in the mainstream of the public schools (U.S. Commission on Civil Rights, 1975).

Education of the different child in the first half of the 20th century was characterized by programs designed specifically for remediating or compensating for these differences. There was a gradual proliferation of programs in public schools. There were residential programs for severely handicapped, deaf, blind, and emotionally disturbed children and also for Native Americans. At first, many other different children were included in the regular classrooms, were taught with the regular curriculum, and were failed or retained until they could do the grade work. This did not work very well as a means of remediation or compensation for learning "handicaps," so special classrooms were evolved, separating the children with low achievement and behavioral problems from the regular classroom. After the 1920s separate special programs for many types of learning "handicaps" existed (Gearheart & Weishahn, 1984), but there were increasing questions about the efficacy of these programs (Dunn, 1968).

In the 1940s, at a conference, educators of culturally different children recommended an end to segregated schools and programs, improved teacher training, and better ESL programs (U.S. Commission on Civil Rights, 1975). In 1954 *Brown v. Board of Education* addressed the concern that when a state has undertaken to provide a benefit such as public education to the people, the benefits must be provided to all people (Jones, 1976). A five-year study of the education of culturally different children, conducted by the U.S. Commission on Civil Rights in the 1960s, concluded that the educational difference between these children and the mainstream was still severe and repeated the 1940 recommendations for an end to segregation, better teacher training, and improved language instruction (U.S. Commission on Civil Rights, 1975).

The second half of the 20th century has been a period of rapid and diverse development in the education of culturally and linguistically different and exceptional children (Gearheart & Weishahn, 1984). As discussed in Chapter 4, in 1963 P.L. 88–164 authorized federal funding for the handicapped, and in 1964 P.L. 89–10 established the Elementary and Secondary Education Act (ESEA) with provisions for federal funding for various special needs in education. The Civil Rights Act was passed in 1964, and P.L. 90–247, the Bilingual Education Act, was passed in 1968. In 1970 the Department of Health, Education and Welfare issued a memorandum requiring that school districts receiving federal funding provide assistance to language minority children. Failure to provide such assistance would constitute a violation of the Civil Rights Act of 1964 (U.S. Commission on Civil Rights, 1975).

The Education for All Handicapped Children Act of 1975, P.L. 94–142, established that all handicapped children between 3 and 21, regardless of type or severity of disability, shall receive a free appropriate public education, which includes special education and related services designed to meet their unique needs. The equal educational opportunity terms of P.L. 94–142 are similar in effect to the Supreme Court ruling in *Lau v. Nichols* (1974), P.L. 90–247 of 1968, and P.L. 93–380 of 1974, which established Bilingual Education programs under ESEA Title VII (Jones, 1976). All this legislation and litigation were to enable the different child to achieve equal educational opportunity via a program of transition into the mainstream program, or mainstreaming the different child.

Mainstreaming

As is clear from a detailed perusal of the terms of the bilingual and special education laws and litigation, the needs of exceptional and culturally/linguistically different children were not being met by either immersion in or segregation from the mainstream. As Dunn (1968) stated:

> The overwhelming evidence is that our present and past practices (of creating separate special classes) have their major justification in removing pressures on regular teachers and pupils at the expense of the . . . slow learning pupils themselves.

Beyond the various efficacy concerns of separate classrooms/programs versus mainstreaming (Dunn, 1968; Glass, 1980; Weininger, 1973), impetus for the integration of all children was gained as a result of studies that showed that as equal access to education via desegregation improved, the educational gap between minority and nonminority students narrowed considerably (Parelius & Parelius, 1978). In addition, tighter budgets for public schools have meant a consolidation of services and more comprehensive use of facilities. This process of comprehensive mainstreaming in public schools has also been encouraged by the deinstitutionalization of many children previously in residential facilities returning to the community and local schools, as well as by public school programs providing services to severely handicapped children remaining in residential facilities. In summary, the history of education for "different" children can be seen as one of progressive integration into mainstream programs. Heinz (1971) summarizes this as follows:

> From an historical perspective, special education may be viewed as developing through three successive stages: (1) treatment through the segregation and restriction of resources for survival appropriate for people called different; (2) caring for people regarded as different by providing resources required for their physical existence; and (3) instructing such people so that they may be incorporated into existing, dominant social systems.

The following sections will describe several modes of mainstreaming developed in response to this progressive mainstreaming effort.

Modes of Mainstreaming

The goals of mainstreaming are the complete social, physical, and instructional integration of all children. Jones (1976), Reynolds and Birch (1986), Gearheart and Weishahn (1984), Heward and Orlansky (1980), Hammill and Bartel (1986), and Lowenbraun and Affleck (1980) all address various models of mainstreaming exceptional children. There are also various models for mainstreaming bilingual children, similar in some respects to those for exceptional children. Models for both exceptional and bilingual mainstreaming are described subsequently.

The mainstreaming model increasingly common in public schools has "diversified staffing and offers many forms of individualized instruction to accommodate a variety of students with good results (Reynolds & Birch, 1986). Figure 12–1 illustrates this mode of mainstreaming (commonly referred to as the Cascade Model) with additions regarding Bilingual Education.

In practice, educational services for exceptional children may take several forms with varying degrees of mainstreaming, depending on the resources of the particular school district. Some of these may be illustrated as shown in Figure 12–2.

Usually, the mainstreamed exceptional child is referred by the regular classroom teacher, school counselor, or other personnel and, after assessment and a planning meeting, placed in the appropriate available program or programs. Most of these programs also include resource/itinerant consultants whose special services are available to the classroom teacher. Many public school programs are combinations of these models.

Models of bilingual/bicultural education programs are quite similar to the various models of services to exceptional children. These may be illustrated as shown in Figure 12–3. As can be seen, all of these models are designed to remediate or compensate for the difference of the learner from the mainstream. In the transition models, the goal is to return the child to the mainstream as soon as possible, that is, upon the acquisition of English or upon the remediation of the particular learning disability. Maintenance models seek to provide compensatory instruction and/or cultural identification while the child participates in mainstream instruction to the extent possible.

Frequently, programs in public schools are combinations of these models. In mainstreaming, it is preferable that all children have a place in the regular mainstream classroom, that all children begin school with the understanding that they have a "homeroom," that they have a place in the regular program, and that a specific regular teacher is "their" teacher. Although the bilingual exceptional child may spend periods of time in a special setting elsewhere, it is desirable that all students begin their education in regular classes. As much as possible, special services should be provided to them in the regular classroom setting. This can be accomplished through the use of Bilingual Special Education tutors, itinerant bilingual special teachers, and special consultants to the regular teachers. If the special services must take place outside the regular classroom, it should be in the least obtrusive method possible.

There is still considerable debate concerning how and where the bilingual exceptional child should be served. Some educators believe that all but the most severely handicapped or those with the least English proficiency should be mainstreamed. Others advocate continued special class placement for Bilingual Special Education children. In the case of limited English speakers, this is an especially sensitive issue. Most bilingual/bicultural education programs are designed to enhance the child's acquisition of English while providing uninterrupted achievement of general curriculum content. This is usually done through a combination of native language instruction in content areas and the ESL program. However, the bilingual or ESL instructor rarely has the training to adequately serve the special needs of exceptional children. Placing the handicapped child in the ESL or Bilingual Education classroom will not adequately serve that child's needs. However, placement part-time or full-time in the special education classroom will also be inadequate, because few if any special education teachers receive training in second

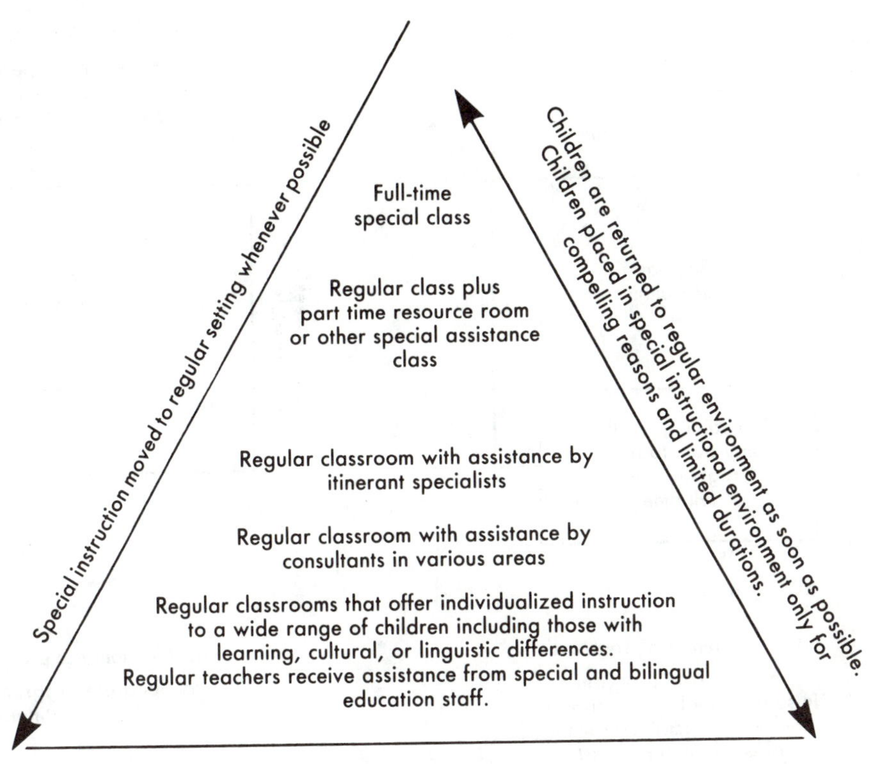

Figure 12–1
Cascade model

language and the special needs of the undergoing acculturation. To address these concerns for acculturation, language development, and acquisition, and to meet special learning needs of the bilingual exceptional child in a mainstream setting, a continuum approach to mainstreaming Bilingual Special Education children is proposed. The continuum provides a full spectrum of services available at particular periods during the instruction of the child. Table 12–1 illustrates this continuum model for mainstreaming bilingual exceptional children.

The key to the effective implementation of mainstreaming for bilingual exceptional children is an instructionally flexible, culturally sensitive teacher in every classroom. At best, the teacher should be fluent in the languages of all children in the class; at least, the teacher should be knowledgeable of and sensitive to children's various cultural and linguistic differences. Because more than two languages/cultures may well be represented in the classroom, the teacher must identify and contact appropriate resource personnel to assist in providing services to all the children in the class and to provide the teacher with information about the language and culture. Chapter 10 discusses this in more detail. Sensitivity and flexibility are two of the competencies the teacher of bilingual exceptional children must cultivate.

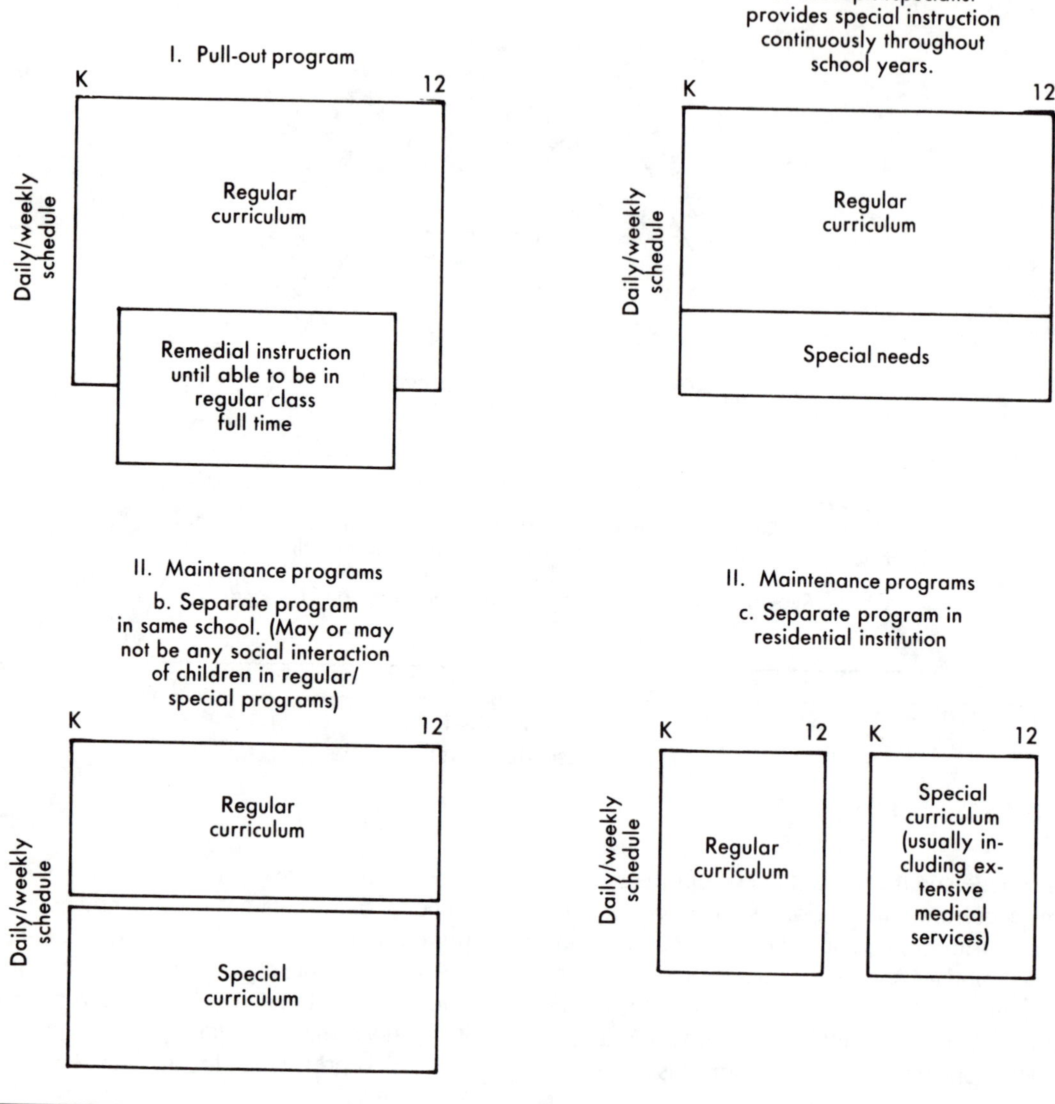

Figure 12–2
Special education mainstreaming models

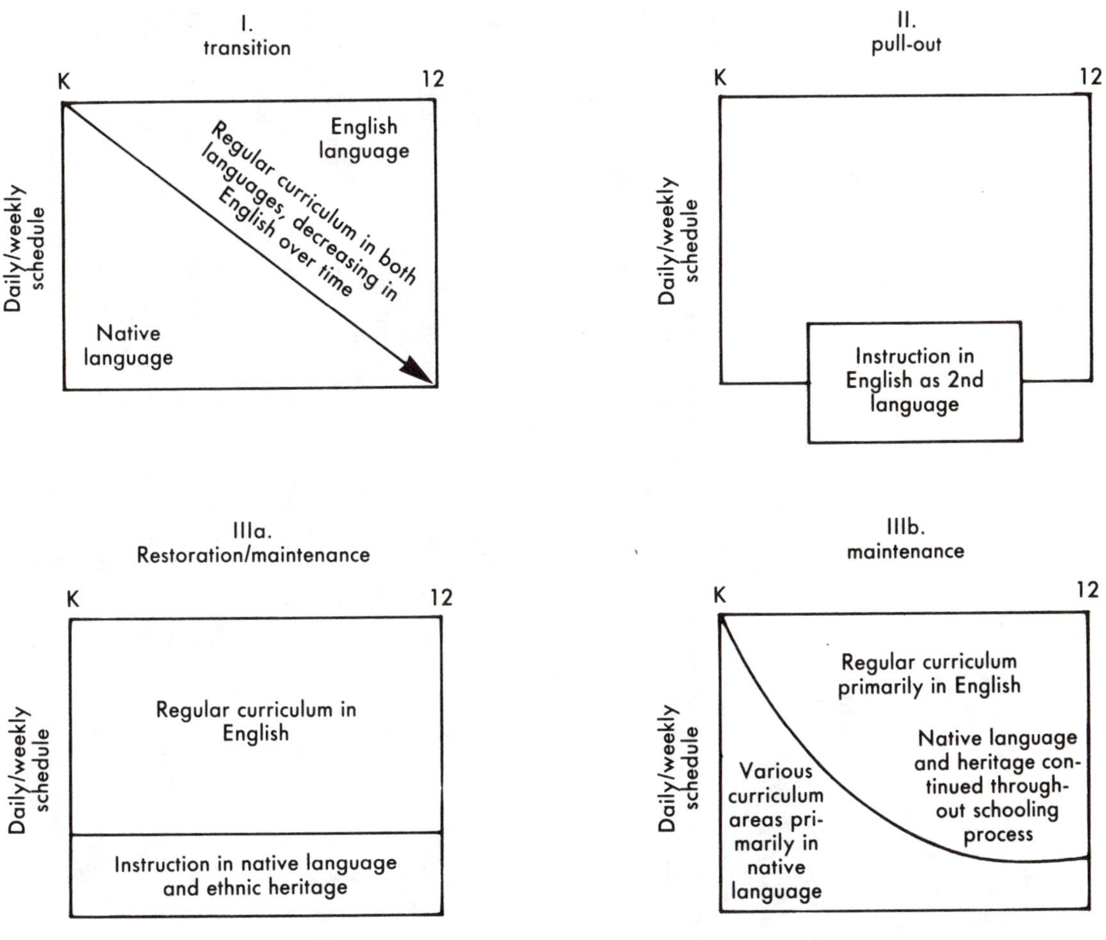

Figure 12–3
Bilingual/bicultural mainstreaming models

Teacher Competencies for Mainstreaming Bilingual Exceptional Children

The ability of a program to provide quality education for the bilingual exceptional child centers on the competence of its teachers in both the regular and the special classrooms. The majority of certified teachers have received a common core of professional preparation: history and philosophy of education and educational psychology. Upon these foundation courses are built skills courses that vary with extent and area of specialization. Reynolds (1980) recommends that a body of skills and knowledge be constructed that will prepare teachers "to function in the context of social mandates."

Table 12–1

Continuum Model for Bilingual Exceptional Children

Therapists, consultants, itinerants, bilingual/bicultural, special, and Bilingual Special Education resource personnel coordinate services with the child's primary teacher and each other at all levels.

Movement along this continuum of services is in either direction to meet the child's individual needs at various points in time

Hospital or home bound. Regular teacher may assist the home teacher and/or child via video and/or telephone. Home teacher speaks the child's native language, uses interpreter or bilingual tutor. Teaches English as a Second Language as part of oral language development.	Separate special schools. May be where particular exceptionalities are served, may be native language and culture schools (such as schools for the gifted, deaf, Japanese, or Native American). Teachers and staff at these schools should provide appropriate Bilingual Special Education as needed (also ESL) through the use of bilingual special educators or tutors.	Separate class in regular schools. May involve some interaction with other children. Student may spend most of day in the special education classroom with Bilingual Special Education and ESL pull-out classes or may spend most of the day in the bilingual class with ESL and special education pull-out classes. May have a Bilingual Special Education tutor while in special, regular, and ESL classes.	Regular class and special part-time classes. Student may spend most of the day in the regular class with pull-out classes for ESL, bilingual, special, and/or Bilingual Special Education classes as needed. Length of time attending each will vary. If teachers do not speak the native language of the child, Bilingual Special Education tutor would work with child in the native language to maintain and enhance content achievement.	Regular class with itinerant services. Student remains in regular classes. Therapists, ESL, bilingual, special, and Bilingual Special Education itinerant tutors and/or teachers work with the student within the regular instructional context. Curriculum used comes from regular sequence, though teacher and itinerants may cooperate on appropriate modifications.	Regular class. Linguistically and culturally appropriate instruction with the use of both English and native language. Teacher may consult with Bilingual Special Education staff for assistance with materials. May require assistance of Bilingual Special Education tutor on special occasions. May require consultation with school counselor knowledgeable of the psychological side effects of acculturation.

If there is a Bilingual Special Education class in the school, the child would spend most of the day in it with the assistance of a native language tutor as necessary.	Counselors or tutors fluent in the native language and knowledgeable of effective acculturation process (culture shock) would work with the child to enhance cross-cultural development. Requires close teamwork by all educators to ensure coordination and continuity.	Use of native language tutors may be necessary on occasion for maintenance of content achievement. Use of cross-cultural counselors, peer counseling support sessions may be necessary on occasion for assistance with the acculturation process.

> The contents of the knowledge, skill, and practice would be derived, in significant parts, from the intent of the mandates to assure equality of educational opportunity for all handicapped, disadvantaged, and other minority group children as provided in Public Law 94–142 and other recent laws and adjudications.

As discussed earlier in this book, individualization of education for exceptional children is one such mandate of the current philosophy of education. P.L. 94–142 provides for an individual instructional plan to be written for each student. In the past these have been IEPs (individual educational plans). Recent changes in legislation may modify the present rather rigid structure of IEPs. Therefore the following discussion is a general guide for teachers developing individual instruction plans, where using IEPs, another format, or more informal individualizing. An individual instructional plan should specifically outline what is to be taught by whom, how it is to be taught, and how it will be evaluated. All the teachers/tutors working with the bilingual exceptional child must be aware of and involved in the IEP. It is especially important that the IEP include objectives and service information in language, vocational and acculturation needs, and exceptional needs.

The ability to develop and implement individual instruction plans is a critical competency for all teachers working with bilingual exceptional children in the mainstreaming process. The development and implementation of these plans for bilingual exceptional children demand instructional flexibility, broad knowledge, and cultural sensitivity. Implementing an individual instruction plan means adapting the regular curriculum to the needs and abilities of individual culturally and linguistically different exceptional (CLDE) children. This process is discussed further elsewhere in text. To achieve ongoing individualization, the school must provide teachers with various resources, some of which are outlined on the continuum model shown in Table 12–1 and some of which are discussed elsewhere in text. In addition to the consultants and special support staff, resources should also include a wide range of differentiated instructional materials and appropriate facilities and space. Given adequate resources, the teacher's ability to develop and implement individual instruction plans remains the core of an effective individualized program, the heart of mainstreaming. Specific suggestions for components of individualized instruction are detailed in Chapter 11.

Reynolds (1980) gives 10 "clusters of capabilities" in which teachers need to be trained to become competent in achieving effective individualization. The 12 competencies that follow are adapted from these clusters:

1. All teachers should have a general knowledge of curriculum principles, guides, and structures from preschool through secondary school levels. The means and procedures by which curriculum is developed and adapted in a cross-cultural setting should be understood.

2. All teachers should be competent in teaching the basic skills (defined to include literacy, life maintenance, and personal development skills) and in collaborative practice with specialists in basic skills instruction. Basic skills in both the native and second cultural contexts must be considered.

3. All teachers should be proficient in class management procedures, including applied behavior analysis, cross-cultural communication strategies, crisis intervention techniques, and cognitive affective climate.

4. All teachers should be proficient in consultation and other forms of professional communications, as both initiators and receivers, to establish and maintain responsible cross-cultural interactions with parents, bilingual tutors, colleagues, and administrators.

5. All teachers should have skills and sensitivity for dealing with parents and siblings of bilingual exceptional students.

6. All teachers should be able to convey to students the attitude that they bear some of the responsibility for their social environment and must be willing to help one another within a multicultural environment.

7. All teachers should be able to manage the social structure of multicultural classes by generating cooperative, mutually helpful behavior among the students. (Teachers need specific insights into and skills for developing heterogeneously cooperative grouping procedures and peer and cross-age tutoring.)

8. All teachers must have an understanding of bilingual exceptional children, or school procedures for accommodating children's special needs, and of the functions of specialists who serve bilingual exceptional children.

9. All teachers need to learn the procedures for referrals, the responsibilities involved, and the ways to capitalize on referral resources in behalf of better education for individual pupils.

10. All teachers must be skilled in making systematic, cross-cultural observations to provide data and undergird judgments for the referral and individualization process.

11. All teachers should be competent in the assessment of the individual student's educational needs and in adapting instruction to the individual.

12. All teachers, in their personal commitments and professional behavior with pupils, parents, and colleagues, should exemplify the same consideration for all individuals and their educational rights as are called for in Public Laws 94–142 and 90–247, the Civil Rights Act of 1964, *Lau v. Nichols* (1974), and in the Rehabilitation Act of 1973. These include the right of individual students to due process in all school placement decisions, to education in the least restrictive environment, to education in English as a second language, to the use of the native language to facilitate this transition, and to carefully individualized education.

Further teacher competencies are given in Table 12–2. These are from Bergin (1979) and illustrate actual responsibilities and the corresponding competencies of a Bilingual Special Education teacher. Baca (1981) delineated additional teacher competencies for working with bilingual exceptional children. These may be achieved through use of resource personnel and materials, in addition to the individual teacher's abilities, where the existing situation is such that the teacher has not yet mastered all of these competencies. The following five competencies are summarized as ideal recommendations for teachers working with bilingual exceptional children:

1. In the area of language it is preferable that the teacher should be able to (a) understand and speak the native language of the student, (b) read and write the native language at an acceptable level of competency, (c) teach any part of the curriculum in English and in the native language of the student, and (d) communicate with parents in their native language regarding the academic progress of their child.

2. In linguistic competence, it is preferable that the teacher (a) understand the theory and process of first and second language acquisition, (b) deal with specific areas of interlanguage interference and positive transfer, (c) understand phonological, grammatical, and lexical characteristics of both languages and their implications for classroom instruction, and (d) distinguish between local dialects and the standard language.

3. For competence in the assessment area, the teacher should be able to (a) administer a vari-

Table 12–2
Teacher Competencies and Responsibilities

Recommended competencies for Bilingual Special Education teachers	
Needs	**Competencies**
Development of nondiscriminatory testing tools	Skills to develop procedures and instruments to identify learning problems of limited English proficient handicapped children
	Understanding the relationship and differences between screening and assessment (placement instruments)
	Knowledge and interpretation of intelligence tests, free of cultural stereotypes
	Knowledge of diagnostic and achievement instruments by academic subjects
	Knowledge of language assessment and evaluation tools
	Knowledge of language proficiency measures
	Knowledge of sociocultural differences from a positive standpoint
Cross-cultural sensitization of special educators	Awareness of cultural and linguistic differences from a positive standpoint
	Knowledge of different teaching and learning styles
	Ability to communicate cross-culturally
Diagnosis of language disorders	Ability to distinguish between non-English dialect variations and transference into English
	Knowledge of bilingualism/biculturalism
	Knowledge of child language development theories
	Knowledge of speech or language disorders in the child's vernacular language
	Knowledge of language assessment tools
Development of bilingual/bicultural educators into special educators	Standard state certification requirements in special education areas
	Language skills and cross-cultural communication
Parent counseling and training	Language skills and cross-cultural communication
	Thorough knowledge of special education in the particular disability of the child

ety of language dominance/proficiency tests, (b) conduct a nondiscriminatory comprehensive diagnostic assessment, (c) evaluate the child from a social/emotional perspective, (d) evaluate the child from a perceptual/motor perspective, and (e) construct and use criterion-referenced measures.

4. In the instructional area, teachers should be able to (a) prepare individualized instructional plans based on student needs, (b) individualize instruction of several students and coordinate large and small group instruction concurrently, (c) adapt curricula to meet the needs of bilingual handicapped children, (d) revise materials and activities to make them more linguistically and culturally appropriate for bilingual handicapped children, (e) construct instructional materials to enhance the curriculum for bilingual exceptional students, (f) recognize the learning characteristics of various handicapping conditions, (g) select the proper bilingual instruc-

Recommended competencies for Bilingual Special Education teachers

Needs	Competencies
School and community counseling services	Understanding parental child-rearing practices and attitudes toward their handicapped children
	Ability to deal with parental fears and frustrations
	Knowledge of interpersonal skills for communication
	Ability to work with ethnic/linguistic communities
Assess students	Knowledge of diagnostic process and ability to use the results
	Ability to provide special educational assessments based on observations of students, criterion-referenced tests, and conferences with referring teachers
Participate in core evaluations and review conferences	Ability to articulate a theoretical and practical base for decision making
	Ability to formulate general and specific objectives in behavioral terms
Provide direct services to special needs LEP students	Ability to use individualized instruction techniques to intervene effectively
	Ability to use different types of materials for different levels of achievement
	Knowledge of methodology for teaching students of different second language proficiency levels
	Ability to adequately use ready-made materials; ability to adapt and design other materials according to the needs of LEP students
	Ability to communicate effectively with the students in their native language
	Familiarity with the regular bilingual curriculum
Confer with other assessors, parents, and regular bilingual teachers	Ability to form consultation relationships with parents and colleagues
Provide quarterly progress reports	Ability to chart student progress and write concise progress reports that reflect program success/failure
Provide support and training for parents and colleagues	Ability to create a climate for exchange; ability to arrange or conduct inservice training for parents and regular teachers

tional approach for each situation, and (h) assess readability levels of materials both in English and in the native language.

5. In the area of culture, the teacher should be able to (a) establish rapport with children from a variety of cultural backgrounds, (b) listen to children and understand the cultural perspective they have, (c) understand the cultural significance of various exceptionalities, (d) utilize community resources for bilingual exceptional children, (e) advise parents of their due process rights relative to their child's education, and (f) counsel parents regarding various aspects of their child's exceptionality.

All of the competencies adapted from Reynolds (1980), Bergin (1979), and Baca (1981) should become the goals of teachers working with bilingual exceptional children. Working with children with special needs is an ongoing learning experience for all professionals. Part of this ongoing learning is sharing suggestions and resources. The following section provides practical suggestions for working with bilingual children with various exceptionalities.

Suggestions for Mainstreaming Bilingual Exceptional Children

Among several things the teacher of bilingual exceptional children must keep in mind in mainstreaming are (1) level of language competence in both native and second languages, (2) degree of cultural identity and acculturation, (3) degree and type of exceptionality, (4) age at onset of exceptionality (birth or acquired) and chronological age, (5) level of achievement, (6) measured intellectual ability in both languages, (7) social maturity in both native and second culture, (8) presence of multiple handicaps, (9) mobility, (10) wishes of student and parents, and (11) availability of services.

All these variables will affect where the child is placed in the continuum of services. Most of this information will come to the teacher through consultation with parents and special support staff members. As mentioned in Chapter 10 there are also various informal ways to assess some of these. Once the teacher has identified each student's needs and abilities, the teacher should develop an individual instructional plan for each student in conjunction with parents and other teachers responsible for instructing the child. The child should be encouraged to take part in the meeting whenever possible. Other resource people who work with the child are also frequently included in the planning meeting. This team planning process of parents and educators was discussed briefly in Chapter 10.

Reynolds and Birch (1986) provide teachers with guidelines for conducting such a planning conference. These may be summarized as:

1. Keep the proceedings simple. Avoid jargon and emphasize curricular decisions.
2. Clarify the purposes of the conference; set an agenda and hold strictly to it.
3. Make the arrangements for all participants as comfortable as possible.
4. Encourage the parents and the persons closest to the child to be the most active participants.
5. Try very hard to agree on plans for special education and related services that the parents can accept, at least for a trial period.
6. Give first attention to accommodations in the child's regular class. Consider pull-out programs only for compelling reasons.
7. Specify the ways in which parents can be helpful immediately and in the long run.
8. Clarify rights to appeal decisions about the plan, to secure additional studies of the child, and to see school records.

The basic elements of an individual plan for a bilingual exceptional child are:

1. The child's current educational status including all service programs the child is receiving (ESL, Bilingual Education, etc.).
2. Goals including adaptation to acculturation and growth in both the first and second language that must be realistic in regard to the time necessary—possibly months or years may be involved.
3. Sequence of short-term instructional objectives leading up to each goal.
4. List of instructional and service requirements to allow the program to operate including balance between the first and second language, as well as who will assist with acculturation needs.
5. An indication of how much and what aspects of the program will be in the mainstream.
6. The program's duration.

7. The realistic criteria and schedule for evaluation of its effectiveness.

8. A statement of the role of parents in relation to the plan.

9. The specification of changes to be made in the physical, social, and instructional situation including the first and second languages and the cross-cultural adaptation.

In developing and implementing an individualized plan for the bilingual exceptional child, the teacher must develop curriculum using the considerations discussed in Chapters 10 and 11. Some of these are cultural relevance, underlying cultural and linguistic concepts, acculturation assistance, and individual learning styles. In addition to the cultural and linguistic considerations discussed in detail in previous chapters, the teacher should be aware of special situations and needs that will be effective in dealing with particular exceptionalities. Following are some suggestions for working with particular exceptionalities in the regular or mainstream classroom. These are organized in sections addressing:

1. Perceptual/emotional concerns
   a. Emotionally disabled
   b. Learning disabled
2. Communication concerns
   a. Speech impaired
   b. Hearing impaired
3. Intellectual concerns
   a. Mentally retarded
   b. Gifted and talented
4. Physical environment concerns
   a. Physically/neurologically handicapped
   b. Vision impaired

The general characteristics of each exceptionality are given. (Labels and generalizations should be avoided, however. All children exhibit some of these characteristics sometimes. The teacher should look for persistent patterns of behavior.) Also included are suggestions for instruction, remediation, and compensation where appropriate. These are given in greater detail in Chapter 11. These activities should be coordinated with the services provided by the special and bilingual staff members.

Perceptual/Emotional Concerns

Learning and emotional disabilities are grouped under one rubric for several reasons. First, behavior problems are frequently associated with learning disabilities and in some cases it is difficult to separate the two as "cause and effect." There is a closely integrated relationship between the child's perceptual difficulties (receiving, processing, and expressing information in specific learning tasks) and the child's behavior in the classroom. In addition, cultural factors are especially important in the assessment of an instructional program for these two exceptionalities. Emotional and learning disabilities are probably the areas most affected by cultural interpretation.

What is acceptable behavior in given situations and what and how children are instructed vary considerably from culture to culture. The common identification of a learning disability is a significant discrepancy between ability and achievement, and because these are usually assessed with reference to English language instruments and Anglo-American cultural expectations, there may be some legitimate questions raised about what this term means in regard to the culturally and linguistically different child (Collier & Hoover, 1987). The same questions may be raised with regard to the identification of emotional disability in the culturally and linguistically different child (Hoover & Collier, 1985). What is unacceptable and aberrant behavior in Anglo-American culture may be appropriate in another culture in a particular situation.

Also, consideration must be given to the social and psychological difficulties encountered by the culturally different child in the acculturative process.

Emotionally Disabled. All teachers have to handle a variety of behavior problems in class. For example, the aggressive child, the withdrawn child, and the daydreamer all are found in most classrooms. All these behaviors, from passive to aggressive and from manic to depressive, require the teacher to attend to the individual child's emotional needs while at the same time dealing with the less serious, mainstream, up-and-down behavior of average students. Behaviors characteristic of emotionally disabled children are seen in all children during stressful moments. It is the frequency and intensity of these behaviors that indicate a serious disturbance. A child may exhibit some of these characteristics temporarily in response to the acculturation process or consistently as a culturally appropriate response within the child's culture (Hoover & Collier, 1985). Assessment and treatment should always be carried out with this in mind.

Hammill and Bartel (1986) provide various strategies for assessing behavior problems, among them direct observation (analysis of child's work, anecdotal records, and activity checks), behavioral checklists and inventories, procedures for examining interaction in the classroom, and standardized tests. The teacher should also consult with the parents and siblings when appropriate. The regular classroom teacher can generally get assistance in these assessment areas from the support staff, Bilingual Special Education teacher, and therapists. The teacher should talk to resource people from the same cultural background as the child. Some behaviors that may appear strange in the mainstream classroom may reflect acceptable behavior in the child's out-of-school environment and not emotional disturbance (Hoover & Collier, 1985). Following are some characteristic behaviors used as indications of emotional disability.

- Depression, hypochondria, regression (such as thumb sucking)
- Overly dependent behavior
- Compulsive behaviors (overly meticulous about arrangement of objects, cleanliness, etc.)
- Being accident-prone (seems to enjoy attention drawn to injuries)
- Feelings and moods that are out of proportion to the provocation or situation in which they occur
- Conversations with self or imaginary figures
- Extreme anxiety
- Refusal to verbalize but ability to do so in native language or English
- Strong uncontrollable fears or frequent crying
- Seeming distracted, dreamy, or extremely withdrawn
- Aggressive behavior

The child's ability to learn may be submerged by emotional disturbance. Remediation involves developing insight, self-esteem, and acceptable social behavior. This must be done within the context of the child's home and community cultural values. Once the emotional disturbance is diminished, the child should be able to benefit from various learning strategies. If the behavior persists, in both the school and the home environment, professional counseling may be necessary. The counselor should understand the child's culture, be able to speak the child's native language, and understand the acculturation experience.

Children experiencing acculturation may exhibit troubling behaviors that are normal side effects of the adaptive process, such as withdrawal or defensiveness in certain situations.

These behaviors will diminish as the child receives assistance with and adapts to the cross-cultural situation.

Many teachers ask themselves "why me?" when they have an especially troubled or troublesome student in their class. Teachers should keep in mind that there are many positive educational benefits to mainstreaming the emotionally disabled child. Some of these are (1) the opportunity for the child to observe appropriate behavior within a given cultural context; (2) the opportunity for the child to observe and participate in cross-culturally appropriate emotional expression; (3) the opportunity for the child to see similarities to and differences from other children; and (4) the opportunity for the child to interact with and receive support from peers in a multicultural setting. The main key to working with emotionally disabled children is showing care and concern about the child. The teacher's approach, positive or negative, is what counts the most. Positive reinforcement of the child's successes and appropriate behaviors should be coupled with a friendly and encouraging attitude.

Some techniques useful in managing behavior problems in class are the following:

1. The teacher should not let the situation get out of hand. The teacher should stop the problem behavior before the entire class is disrupted.

2. Appropriate behavior should be positively reinforced, in a culturally appropriate manner.

3. Tasks should be organized to provide a variety of activity and orderly transition from one activity to another. Materials should be culturally/linguistically relevant and interesting.

4. Learning or activity centers, time-out areas, or quiet areas should be used. These are useful when the child has completed tasks early or when the child needs to be alone. (Children might even use a punching bag to let out their frustrations—then be moved to one of the quiet areas before continuing lessons.)

5. The teacher should be consistent.

6. What is appropriate/inappropriate in what situations and the consequences of inappropriate behavior should be demonstrated. Role play is useful as a way to demonstrate these situations.

Learning Disabled. *Learning disability* is not a term used to define temporary or minor learning problems. It refers to severe discrepancies between ability and achievement. P.L. 94–142, the Education for All Handicapped Children Act of 1975, defines learning disability as follows:

> . . . a disorder in one of the basic psychological processes involved in understanding or in using language, spoken or written, which may manifest itself in an imperfect ability to listen, think, speak, read, write, spell, or do mathematical calculations. The term includes such conditions as perceptual handicaps, brain injury, minimal brain dysfunction, dyslexia, and developmental aphasia. The term does not include children who have learning problems which are primarily the result of visual, hearing or motor handicaps, or mental retardation, or of environment, cultural, or economic disadvantages.

The common and most cited characteristic of learning disabled children is a significant discrepancy between achievement and overall ability (intelligence and other measures of ability). As discussed previously, measures of intelligence/ability may be quite inaccurate for the culturally different child. The characteristics of the learning disabled are sometimes hard to identify. The following characteristics are intended as general guides. Children with learning disabilities may exhibit several but not all of these:

- Hyperactive or hypoactive
- Appears to hear but is not able to follow oral instructions or complete tasks assigned orally in both the second and native languages

- Lacks ability to organize: written tasks, speech, self-care
- Short attention span, distractible
- Auditory or visual memory problems
- Poor perceptual/motor coordination
- Poor language skills in both native and second languages
- Sporadic behavior—calm one day, very hyperactive the next
- Reverses words, numbers, letters, and phrases in both languages
- Difficulty in performing mathematical calculations
- Extreme difficulty in writing in both languages
- Appears to see and read but is not able to follow written instructions or complete visual tasks.

None of these characteristics should be taken as single predictors of learning disability. An illustrative account of the problems of identifying and teaching learning disabled children is provided in the box on pp. 278–279. This is a firsthand account by a person who was learning disabled as a child. It is important to assess the child in the native language and to consider cultural factors in the testing situation itself. Instruction usually involves presenting materials in a modified step-by-step manner and teaching to the child's strengths.

Gearheart and Weishahn (1984) provide 10 principles as general guidelines for working with the learning disabled child. These may be summarized for the bilingual exceptional child as follows:

1. There is no single correct method to use. The teacher should try a variety of approaches, methods, and cross-cultural strategies.

2. All other factors being equal, the method to use is something new to the child. The teacher may use a method that looks and feels different to the child, but must be sure to explain and demonstrate the procedure.

3. Some type of positive reinforcement and reconditioning should be implemented. Success must be planned. Consultation with a cultural specialist may enhance appropriate teaching.

4. High motivation is a prerequisite to success; deliberate consideration of the affective domain is essential. Cultural differences in this must be accommodated.

5. The existence of nonspecific or difficult-to-define disabilities, particularly with older children, must be recognized. What may exist is significant educational retardation and negative attitudes toward school as a result of earlier problems.

6. Complete accurate information about the child's learning strengths and weaknesses is essential. When one problem is discovered it should not be automatically assumed that it is the major cause of the learning and behavior problems. A balance of what the child can and cannot do is important information.

7. Symptoms often associated with learning disabilities do not necessarily indicate the presence of learning disabilities or predict future learning disabilities. Many of these symptoms are normal by-products of acculturation.

8. Educational time and effort must be carefully maximized for the child. Specific learning abilities should be developed within a framework of the deficient academic area(s): First language development, second language acquisition, and assistance with acculturation must be a part of this effort.

9. Learning disability planning should be based on a learning theory or theories to be most effective.

10. Both process- and task-oriented assistance and remediation are critically important.

Multisensory technique is a useful approach for the teacher in mainstreaming learning disabled bilingual children. The teacher presents words or numbers (the approach is primarily used in reading and math remediation) in such a way that the child can hear, see, feel, and then say it alone. The language in which the child has the best oral/aural proficiency is used. The teacher writes the word or number in crayon (a rougher texture than pencil), clay, glue or other tactile substance. Cursive script is usually used because it provides a connected "whole" feeling of the word as a single entity rather than a group of separate letters. The teacher says the word aloud while writing it, and the child repeats it. If the teacher does not speak the child's language, a bilingual tutor or peer may assist. The child traces the word or number with a finger in contact with the crayon or substance in which it is written, saying the word or number aloud while tracing it. This activity can be done in the native language and in English as part of teaching the child English as a Second Language. This is done until the child can write the word without referring to the paper.

Teachers may use manipulative objects and methods while talking about what they are doing and then have the children tell what they are doing as they work out the calculation or problem. Again, the use of first native and then second language is recommended. In a simpler form, teachers may use many objects illustrative of a particular lesson or topic that the children can feel and talk about with the teacher or tutor. A word of caution about multisensory technique: Some types of neurological dysfunction may lead to a tendency for the brain to "overload" if there are too many stimuli arriving simultaneously. This is not an indisputably established fact but the possibility of this type of reaction to multiple stimuli should be kept in mind. Feuerstein (1979) suggests that children with learning disabilities must be taught how to respond appropriately to various stimuli in their environment and that this mediated learning can be of great benefit in improving children's academic achievement.

Other approaches to working with learning disabled children is the consideration of learning styles as discussed in Chapter 10 and the instructing techniques in Chapter 11. Some children learn more from what they see and touch than from what they hear. Some children learn to read their native language more quickly through phonetics or sound analysis and some learn through the whole-word or sight-word approach. Some have difficulty seeing the forest for the trees, attend to the individual items, and do not see the underlying similarities and relationships. Some have difficulty seeing the trees for the forest: figure/ground confusions or difficulty discriminating individual objects from a group. Tactile and kinesthetic approaches are useful in singling out objects from a group or background. Activities in taxonomy and categorizing are useful in identifying groups and generalizations, although care must be taken to consider cultural differences in what is similar and different. The oral rhythms and intonations of both languages and the use of native songs are also very useful in teaching learning disabled bilingual children. Sometimes song and drama can enhance the multisensory approach and may also greatly assist the development of memory skills.

The comments in Chapter 10 and 11 in regard to the difficulties in identifying and working with learning and emotional disability in culturally and linguistically different children must be carefully considered by all teachers attempting to mainstream these children.

Communication Concerns

Speech Impaired. Speech impairment does not refer to linguistic or language difference or to

. . . THEN THEY TOLD ME YOU HAD TO CUT ON THE LINES* . . .

First of all, I grew up in a time when we didn't have all the labels that we have now for disabilities; for example, a learning disabilities label did not exist. When I look retrospectively at my life, I realize that I had a bona fide learning disability. When I entered the third grade, I was a nonreader. My auditory memory skills had helped me so much that it was impossible to catch me before. Everybody thought I was reading from the page; but I was actually reciting, playing back what I had heard, utilizing other cues such as pictures and getting my buddies to give me the key words that started the sentences. If I got the key word that started the sentence, I could rattle off the rest. But in the third grade they took the pictures away from the readers. I hadn't started to associate text and topics and sentences with page numbers up in the corner. So by that time I was just lost. But reading was not the only problem I had.

I couldn't do math either. My problem is one that is visual-spatial orientation; and when you put a math problem down on paper, the numbers have to be lined up properly. I knew what it meant to subtract, and to multiply and divide; and I could handle it as long as it was verbal—"7 times 7" or "6 times 3"—no problem. Basically I learned the problems by heart. That was easy. But once you get past the two-digit numbers and up into the hundreds, all of a sudden you had to put it down on paper. I couldn't place a number that had to be subtracted beneath the column that it had to be subtracted from. I couldn't put the carried-over digit in the right place; they hung all over the place. It was impossible for me to do even a simple sum because the numbers sat all over the piece of paper. Whey they finally found out it was not the basic operations I had problems with, but the alignment on paper, they modified their approach. I was introduced to little grids that helped me set the problems up and that countered my visual problems just fine.

I went through all kinds of things. I was in a classroom for the mentally retarded for a while. Yet when I look back on the early years, I did not realize how different I was. When I went to nursery school, at age five, my mother was still dressing me. I couldn't tie my shoes; I couldn't zip a zipper; I couldn't button buttons. My buttons would be misaligned because it was impossible for me to do this visual act. I have learned now that if you want the two upper ones unbuttoned, you unbutton them after you have buttoned up the whole dress. I didn't know that other kids could dress themselves. They knew how to put a coat on. They had to teach me to put my coat on by laying it on the floor, and then I would go lie down on it and put it over my head to arrange the sleeves correctly. Otherwise, it simply couldn't be done.

And when I got into school, they handed me scissors. First of all, I couldn't do the movement of the scissors to open and close them—that rhythmic sequential movement you've got to have. Once I got that

the problems non-English-speaking children have in acquiring English as a Second Language. However, there may be some problems in articulation in learning a new language and the suggestions given below may be helpful.

Speech differences become a handicap when (1) they interfere with communication, (2) they cause the speaker to be maladjusted, and (3) they call undue attention to the speech (as opposed to what the person is saying) (Gearheart & Weishahn, 1984). People may have speech impairments in any language. To be considered a speech impairment in a bilingual child, the problem must be apparent in both languages. The impairment of speech may be caused by several conditions, some of which are cleft palate or lip, cerebral palsy, central nervous system damage, or deformities of the mouth or nose.

Some characteristic behaviors the teacher should use as possible additional indications of a speech problem are:

- Omits initial or final sounds of words in both native and second language down (and it took a long, long time) I felt that I had conquered the world. That's when they told me you had to cut on lines! Once I could cut, I thought I could cut all over the place because I was so proud of the fact that I had mastered it. The other kids were cutting dolls, and I would look at them and think there was something magic in their bodies that made it possible, and that that magic just wasn't given to me.

I cut a friend's hair off one day. I was constantly in trouble. There was no way to restrain me. The teacher would come over to me and I would start singing, because it would make her so mad that I would get thrown out of the room. I would have to go sit out on the stairs, and then I could just fantasize. I had a lot of stories in my head; at that time I could tell oodles of stories. If I could just get the teacher to expel me from the room, I could fantasize my whole day away. I had learned that there were certain things that I could do—for example, if I spilled my milk—that would get me out for the rest of the day. If I started singing when I wasn't supposed to, by 9:15 I could be out of the room. So basically I had all of the nonadaptive strategies, things kids learn how to do to get out of the mess they're in. And as long as you can get out of the mess, you can have a modicum of self-esteem.

But there comes a time when you are on the other side of your learning disability. You can select to do things that take advantage of your strengths. When I had the opportunity to do this, I found out I really could learn languages. I got A's in language, and they counterbalanced the F's I got in gymnastics, art, and geometry.

When you get into high school you can select more. Do you want to go the math/science route, or do you want to concentrate on the language complement? Then when you get to college, you select again; and when you get to graduate school you are working completely in an area suited to your strengths. By that time you are out of it, because you know not to select something you cannot handle. For example, the only sport I do today is swimming. That is the only sport I can handle because it is not visually-spatially oriented. I can make all the choices now that I understand I don't have to be just like you. I am a person, and I have strengths and weaknesses just as you do. If you are willing to accept me as I am, then maybe I can give you something in return.

*From "... Then they told me you had to cut on the lines ..." by E. H. Wiig, 1980. In W. L. Heward & M. D. Orlansky. *Exceptional children: An introductory survey to special education* (pp. 80–81). Columbus, OH: Merrill Publishing Co. Elizabeth H. Wiig is now professor of speech pathology at Boston University. Dr. Wiig is the author of two textbooks and over 50 research articles dealing with language disorders in children and adolescents. She speaks six languages fluently. This accounting of her childhood memories will help to clarify the definition of "learning disability."

- Substitutes sounds (teacher needs to identify cultural substitutions and eliminate them from consideration as an impairment)
- Is hesitant to participate orally in class in native language (may not participate in English until more proficiency is gained—not a problem of impairment)
- Has malformation of the oral cavity with speech impediment apparent in both languages
- Distorts sounds—has some voice disorders apparent in both languages:

  Hoarse

  Too loud, too soft (cultural factors may be involved—it may be appropriate in a given situation in the child's culture)

  Raspy or gravelly

  Nasal
- Stutters or is nonfluent in communicating in both languages. Some of this behavior may occur temporarily when the child is first learning English, especially if the child is placed under a lot of stress to speak the unfamiliar language perfectly.

Where a true speech impairment exists, the teacher should consult with a speech therapist to obtain suggestions regarding classroom activities and procedures that will support and reinforce the objectives of the child's individual educational program in speech. The speech therapist will have the primary responsibility for remediation of the (noncultural) speech element. Both the speech therapist and the teacher may work with the ESL specialist on specific second language learning needs (for example, phonemic discrimination, new articulation patterns, and new rhythmic patterns) and bilingual specialist on first language development and transfer skills.

Because speech is closely related to hearing ability, the first step the teacher must take with a child showing speech problems is to see if the child has received a recent audiological examination and the results of the examination. If a hearing problem is indicated, the teacher should follow the suggestions given in the section on hearing-impaired children, and work with the audiologist to remediate the hearing to the extent possible. The teachers working with speech-impaired bilingual children should coordinate services with the speech clinician and Bilingual Education teacher. In general, the speech clinician will provide the remedial instruction for the speech impairment and the bilingual teacher will assist with language problems, which are part of the second language learning process. Following are some suggestions for working with speech-impaired children in the regular and/or bilingual education.

Stuttering or Nonfluency. This is a rather noticeable speech problem and thus receives more attention than its actual frequency would call for. There are many theories about the causes and treatments for stuttering but no general agreement. Some specialists believe the problem is organic or neurological and others that it is behavioral. Reynolds and Birch (1986) make several suggestions for working with children with stuttering or other nonfluency problems. The two following points are adapted from their suggestions:

1. Conflict or excitement tends to increase stuttering. The teacher should expect and not be surprised by what happens to speech under such conditions. The teacher should help children learn consciously to control their activity and emotional states while talking in either language.

2. Children who stutter should be treated like other children. They should have opportunities to ask questions and the teacher should take the time to listen. The teacher should not fill in words for them anymore than for any other child. Such behavior will be a model for the stuttering pupil's classmates.

Articulation Problems. The following suggestions address articulation problems and apply to instruction in both the native and second languages.

1. Child must become able to discriminate between accurate and inaccurate pronunciations—must become able to "hear" errors.

2. Teachers could use a tape recorder or Language Master. Correct sound in initial, middle, and final positions in words should be given.

3. Teachers should provide good speech models, in both the native and the second languages, if possible. Speech is imitative. Teachers must evaluate their own speech and should work with tutors, parents, and peers to provide good models in both languages.

4. Child must learn to produce correct sounds in both languages. Teachers could motivate learning through culturally appropriate games, songs, and behavior shaping (progressive approximations of correct sound).

The teacher should use culturally appropriate reinforcement to motivate the child to use newly learned sounds in both languages. Puppets, rhymes, and songs, for example, are all helpful in integrating and encouraging correct speech patterns.

Speech and language are a basic human faculty necessary for participation in society and culture. It is extremely important that children learn to communicate to the best of their ability and be given the opportunities to use what modes of communication they have. The best thing the classroom teacher can do for children is to give them time to get their thoughts out and plenty of opportunities to initiate and respond to verbal interactions. The teacher in the mainstream classroom must be careful to provide these opportunities for all children and encourage all children in the classroom to communicate, whether in English or in another language, with gestures, or with whatever means appropriate.

Hearing Impaired. As with speech, hearing becomes a teaching concern when it becomes a social adjustment or communication problem. Many people have various degrees of hearing impairment. The teacher should watch for:

- Tilting or turning head to hear
- Cupping hand around ear
- Hesitance in participating in oral/aural activities in native language, also talking very little or in brief sentences in native language (may exhibit this behavior in second language situations until greater proficiency is achieved. This behavior may also be culturally appropriate in speaking to an adult)
- Complaints of frequent earaches, colds, and similar ailments
- Watching lips of speakers
- Failing to respond to loud noises
- Small group achievement but failure to do well in large group or space (may be cultural factor)
- Showing confusion in following group activities and discussions in native language
- Appearing withdrawn, not interacting very much with peers (may exhibit this behavior if new to the culturally different classroom—also if few of the children are from the same culture)

If hearing impairment is diagnosed, the teacher may be working with the assistance of specialists in teaching the child to use a hearing aid, cued speech, or other compensatory techniques, depending on the severity of the impairment. The teacher should modify and adapt curriculum and instruction to include broader academic areas, usually within the mainstream classroom as much as possible. Attention is also being given to the development of special learning strategies in enhancing memory and generalization from experience. The teacher will need to make certain classroom modifications to accommodate the hearing-impaired child in the mainstream classroom. To make the appropriate modifications, the teacher should become knowledgeable of the nature of the loss, the amount of residual hearing, and the ways in which the child communicates. The teacher should gain familiarity with the child's unique speech patterns to facilitate communication and decrease the child's embarrassment of being continually asked "What?" or asked to repeat.

A useful suggestion in working with the hearing-impaired child in the regular classroom is to use another child as a listening partner. This can be a rotating assignment in the room, although the partner should be a child who speaks the same languages as the hearing-impaired child if possible. It is important that the partner provide assistance only when needed; otherwise the hearing-impaired child may become overly dependent on the classmate. The partner sits next to the hearing-impaired child and ensures that the child is turning to the correct page and taking accurate notes, or provides other appropriate assistance.

Another classroom modification is to allow the child to sit as close as possible to the source of sound in oral/aural instruction with an unobstructed view of the speaker's face. This should be within 5 or 10 feet; the child should not have to look up constantly. Also, the location of the source of sound should be varied, but the child should be able to observe activities.

The teacher should be knowledgeable about the care and use of hearing aids. Hearing aids help compensate for hearing loss by amplifying sounds. They cannot replace the natural ability to hear, so the teacher must not expect "normal" hearing ability when the child wears a hearing aid. However, hearing aids are very helpful in allowing the child to use whatever hearing is available, and children should be encouraged to use them when possible and appropriate. The teacher should be sensitive to possible cultural attitudes toward the hearing impaired within the child's culture. It is also a good idea for the teacher to keep extra batteries at school so the child does not have to go without hearing when the battery goes dead during the school day.

The child should be encouraged to learn to observe face and body gestures, lip formation and movement, and other environmental clues to facilitate understanding of what is going on. This is why it is important that the child sit with an unobstructed view of the speaker. The child should not sit where it is necessary to look into a light source, for example, the windows, or a dark or shadowed area. Generally, it is best to have the light source behind the child and on the speaker. In assisting the child to observe and "read" gestures and lip movements, the teacher should not use exaggerated gestures or speech patterns and should be sensitive to cultural differences in body language. The child needs to learn to "read" naturally and appropriately in both native and second cultural contexts. Gestures should be used but objects should be kept away from the face whenever possible. Facial hair can obscure facial and lip movement. The teacher should face the group when speaking and should encourage other children to face the hearing-impaired child when speaking.

The teacher should consult with the special education staff and hearing specialists about the use of cued speech with the child. This is a combined total communication technique easily integrated into the regular classroom routine.

Intellectual Concerns

Mental Retardation. Mental retardation has been defined as "significant subaverage general intellectual functioning existing concurrently with deficits in adaptive behavior and manifested during the developmental period" (Kirk & Gallagher, 1984).

It should be understood that this discussion relates to the 80% to 90% of the retarded population who may be considered mildly, moderately trainable, or educable retarded. The care of the severely or profoundly retarded usually is not the responsibility of regular school personnel, although many districts have special self-contained classrooms or separate schools for children needing a highly specialized learning environment. Of the mildly to moderately retarded children found in regular schools, the following characteristics may be observed:

- Difficulty in generalizing and understanding abstractions (given in native language)
- Overall academic retardation—significantly below grade level in all subjects
- Immaturity evidenced in play and other interests both in and out of school
- Sensory and coordination problems
- Easily frustrated
- Vocabulary of a much younger child in the native language (in English this may indicate only the relative proficiency level attained so far)

- Slower growth and development patterns
- Poor self-help skills (as understood by the particular culture)

Many of these behaviors may be the temporary result of experiential differences and should be carefully assessed in the native language and cultural context of the child. A visit with the parents (with an interpreter if needed) would provide information about the child's adaptive behaviors and developmental history within the cultural context.

The retarded child in the mainstream classroom should be identified by multiple criteria and not by IQ alone. Some of these criteria are level of language development in both native and second languages, level of socialization in both cultures, emotional maturity, and academic achievement, as well as IQ. Most commonly the instruction of the retarded has been primarily through reduced academic expectations and emphasized functional skills needed for work and community living. Recently, however, the education of the retarded has included broader academic areas, usually within the mainstream classroom as much as possible. Attention is also being given to the development of special learning strategies in enhancing memory and generalization from experience.

The regular teacher with mentally retarded children in the classroom should not attempt to require any child to perform tasks for which the child lacks the prerequisite skills. The teacher should provide opportunities for the development of such skills and provide simplified programs and activities. Games and physical activity, such as throwing beanbags or jumping rope, will assist in general motor development and improvement in coordination. Blindfold "guess what it is" games will aid sensory development and language development. Carefully individualized sequenced instruction will assist in all academic areas. Teaching bilingual retarded children cross-cultural associations and generalizations will increase their ability to understand abstractions in both settings. Other cognitive learning strategies are given in Chapter 11. Some frustrations are unavoidable and indeed to some extent are part of growth and development. Learning to deal with difficulties is to be encouraged. However, the teacher needs to reduce the number of possibly frustrating situations that may be of little benefit at that particular time.

Retarded children are capable of learning quite a bit and the teacher should neither underestimate their abilities nor overpower them with unrealistic expectations. Cultural attitudes toward the retarded vary and these differences must be considered in regard to their effect on the retarded bilingual child.

Gifted and Talented. Gifted and talented children were generally perceived for many years as able to proceed on their own. Many teachers joyfully hold them up as examples to the rest of their class, to the unhappiness of both the gifted and the not gifted. These children need special opportunities in the mainstream classroom if they are to develop their great potential and retain their creative and gifted abilities.

Culturally and linguistically different children who are intellectually gifted frequently have their special educational needs overlooked because of their temporary inability to speak the language of the classroom. The characteristics of these children may be summarized here, as adapted from Kirk and Gallagher (1984):

- Has unusually advanced vocabulary and communicative ability in native language
- Is keen and alert observer, displays a great deal of curiosity
- Strives toward perfection, is not easily satisfied with own work
- Often passes judgment on events
- Displays keen sense of humor

- Is self-confident with other children as well as with adults
- Tends to dominate others

These characteristics must be considered within the child's cultural context and assessed through observation of the child outside of as well as in the classroom and in the native language and cultural setting. Table 12–3 further illustrates characteristics of the gifted or talented child.

The identification of giftedness by the use of IQ alone is currently discouraged and seen as inappropriate especially for culturally different children. Far more than IQ is involved in identifying and defining giftedness. In addition, serious questions have been raised about the efficacy of IQ and intelligence testing in general (Gould, 1982). As discussed in Jones (1976) the usual intelligence measures have been found to be culturally biased and inappropriate for any child not representative of the mainstream population, especially the bilingual exceptional child.

Intelligence tests are still used as part of the identification of giftedness, but they must be administered whenever possible in the native language of the child and be used along with a variety of other measures and procedures. These include tests of creativity and achievement and recognition as exceptional by teachers, parents, or other students.

Basic skills need to be taught to the gifted as to all students; however, these should be enriched by such activities as inquiry and research techniques. The lessons should not be repeated over and over in various sequences as may be necessary for other children. The ability to investigate and pursue meaningful inquiries is a fundamental skill that may enhance the development and education of the gifted and talented. Various cognitive learning strategies are also useful for culturally gifted different children (Collier & Hoover, 1987). Two common approaches in the mainstreaming of gifted and talented bilingual children are enrichment and acceleration, either of which may be done in a direct, indirect, or self-directed manner. As in all individualization and mainstreaming, the teacher must remain flexible and tolerant of a variety of differences in learning styles. Enrichment occurs when the teacher provides experiences and opportunities for gifted bilingual children to investigate topics of interest in greater detail and depth than in the standard curriculum. These topics of investigation may be built upon the ongoing activities in the mainstream classroom but allow the gifted bilingual child to go beyond the limits of the regular instructional curriculum. There must be structure and guidance in this investigation; the limits and outcomes expected from the child must be defined. Enrichment in cross-cultural curricular elements is especially useful for bilingual gifted children.

Some of the approaches to acceleration given in Heward & Orlansky (1980) may be summarized as follows:

Early admission to school

Grade skipping

Concurrent enrollment in both high school and college

Advanced placement tests

Early admission to college

Content acceleration (giving youngsters the opportunity to move through a particular curricular sequence at their own rate)

Early acceleration may be possible for the LEP gifted. After the child has a good grasp of English, acceleration may be considered. Heward and Orlansky note that acceleration does not cause the problems of social and emotional adjustment often attributed to it. Acceleration combined with enrichment seems to be very beneficial in the mainstreaming of bilingual gifted children.

Table 12–3
Characteristics of the Gifted*

From *Exceptional children: An introductory survey to special education* by W. L. Heward and M. D. Orlansky, 1980. Columbus, OH: Merrill Publishing Co.

*These lists were developed with the assistance of graduate students at The Ohio State University.

Two Sides to the Behavior of the Gifted	
List A	**List B**
Expresses ideas and feelings well	May be glib, making fluent statements based on little knowledge or understanding
Can move at a rapid pace	May dominate discussions
Works conscientiously	May be impatient to proceed to next level of task
Wants to learn, explore, and seek more information	May be considered nosey
Develops broad knowledge and an extensive store of vicarious experiences	May choose reading at the expense of active participation in social, creative, or physical activities
Is sensitive to the feelings and rights of others	May struggle against rules, regulations, and standardized procedures
Makes steady progress	May lead discussions "off the track"
Makes original and stimulated contributions to discussions	May be frustrated by the apparent absence of logic in activities and daily events
Sees relationships easily	May become bored by repetitions
Learns material quickly	May use humor to manipulate
Is able to use reading skills to obtain new information	May resist a schedule based on time rather than task
Contributes to enjoyment of life for self and others	May lose interest quickly
Completes assigned tasks	
Requires little drill for learning	

Physical Environment Concerns

For both physical and visual handicaps the child's mobility and ability to physically interact with the environment are very important concerns in the classroom. Another consideration is the cultural attitude toward persons with such impairments, which can vary considerably from culture to culture. Handicaps that affect mobility were and are of special concern in traditionally nomadic or agricultural cultures. Many culturally different children come from such rural cultures and may have special social/psychological needs if visually or physically handicapped.

Physically/Neurologically Handicapped. This is an extremely diverse group of children and it is difficult to characterize them under a single set of criteria. Characteristics vary according to the handicap and may include:

- Muscular weakness or paralysis
- Lack of muscle control (may additionally affect speech and communicative ability)
- Poor coordination
- Curved spine
- Inability to walk
- Lack of bowel/bladder control
- Use of orthopedic aids, such as braces or wheelchairs
- Use of prostheses
- Breathing difficulties

- Easily fatigued
- Seizures
- Depression associated with health problems of long duration

Physically or neurologically handicapped children may require modifications in the physical, social, or instructional aspects of the public school environment. Physical modifications may be ramps and wider doorways for wheelchairs. Social and instructional modifications may primarily involve training the mainstream children to accept and communicate with the handicapped and using special equipment in the classroom. As Gearheart and Weishahn (1984) state:

> Children grouped under this category range from the cerebral palsied . . . to the child with asthma and the child born without a limb. One child may have limited use of his arms but have good use of his legs, another may have use of all extremities but have considerable trouble breathing, and another may be generally weak because of a progressive condition. One may be completely mobile in the classroom, another mobile with the use of crutches, or still another confined to a wheelchair.

Most commonly included under physically or neurologically handicapping conditions are:

Cerebral palsy. Disturbances of voluntary motor function (paralysis, extreme weakness, lack of coordination, involuntary convulsions, and little control over arms, legs, or speech).

Epilepsy. Convulsive disorder characterized by sudden, uncontrollable attacks or seizures during which the child loses consciousness and muscular control. May be grand mal seizures (convulsions), petit mal (brief loss of consciousness), or psychomotor (period of aimless or inappropriate behavior).

Muscular dystrophy. Fatal disease characterized by progressive gradual weakening of muscle tissue. This slow deterioration of the voluntary muscles ends in a state of complete helplessness and death.

Spina bifida. Congenital malformation of the spine. The bones of the spine fail to close during fetal development and result in various degrees of paralysis and incontinence, impaired autonomic nervous system, and absence of sensation below the level of the spinal defect.

Paralysis, leukemia, rheumatic fever, allergies, asthma, arthritis, amputation, diabetes, and hemophilia are examples of other physical handicaps that the teacher needs to be prepared for in the mainstreaming program. The teacher should consult with the school nurse and parents about accommodating these conditions. Cultural attitudes toward the handicap should also be considered. Some handicaps are perceived as more or less severe than others. There may be culturally prescribed treatments that the child must follow, as well as medical treatments.

All of these conditions may have to be accommodated within the regular classroom. Sometimes this means physical provisions for wheelchairs, standing tables, walkers, crutches, and other special equipment. It may mean careful preparation of the other children in the class for special aspects of the conditions such as seizures, incontinence, and disordered speech patterns. Heward and Orlansky (1986) make this observation:

> Some teachers find that simulation or role-playing activities can be useful in building understanding and acceptance of the child with a physical disability. Nondisabled children may, for example, have the opportunity to use wheelchairs, braces, crutches, or other adaptive devices. This may increase their awareness of some of the obstacles faced by the disabled child. They should learn appropriate terminology and know how to offer the correct kind of assistance when needed.

Reynolds and Birch (1986) provide some guidelines for working with physically or neurologically handicapped children. These may be adapted for culturally and linguistically different children as follows:

1. All children should begin school in regular and bilingual/ESL classes unless there are insurmountable transportation problems.

2. Keep schooling in both the bilingual education/ESL and regular classroom a continuous and full-time process adjusted in intensity to the child's vitality level and reaction speed.

3. Pupils should attain self-regulation with regard to exertion and scheduling of activities.

4. Organize educational programs in terms of pupils' educational needs; match both short- and long-range instructional designs to the pupils L1—L2 transfer needs, acculturation, cognitive learning styles, and their present and projected cross-cultural educational achievements.

5. Make technology the servant of pupils and teachers.

6. Provide expert cross-cultural educational assessment, instruction, and counseling all along the way.

Many children with physical or neurological handicaps will need to be mainstreamed in a "maintenance" program (see Figures 12–2 and 12–3). That is, they will require a special period of time throughout their school years to work with therapists. This necessitates careful coordination between regular and special staff members and ongoing consultation with parents and specialists.

Vision Impaired

The teacher should refer the child immediately for testing and evaluation of sight when the child shows consistent signs of visual impairment.

Some characteristic behaviors the teacher should watch for as indications of possible visual problems are:

- Squinting, covering, or shutting one eye
- Frequent rubbing of the eyes
- Difficulty in writing on lines (check native orthography)
- Complaining of eyes itching or burning, dizziness, blurriness
- Eyes that are crossed, swollen, inflamed, "wiggly"
- Poor motor coordination, tripping or stumbling a lot
- Holding book too close or too far from eyes
- Seeming overly sensitive to light
- Being unable to distinguish colors (teachers should consider possible different cultural identification of colors)

Upon evaluation and determination of specific need areas, the regular and special education teachers should work together closely to provide a continuum of services as outlined earlier in this chapter. In the early grades or stages of instructing the vision-impaired bilingual child, the child may need extensive assistance from a resource or special education teacher. This teacher can provide intensive instruction and orientation to various ways of writing (such as Braille or typing) and reading (Braille or magnifiers) and means of mobility (the use of cane, arms, or sounds). If the teacher does not speak the language of the child, a Bilingual Special Education tutor may be necessary. As the child becomes skilled in these areas, the child may need an occasional session with the itinerant teacher to develop and maintain compensatory skills while participating in the regular classroom.

Some special educational materials that may be beneficial with bilingual vision-impaired children are:

- Molded relief maps and globes
- Abacuses
- Geometric forms in three dimensions
- Clocks with raised faces
- Braille rulers or large/raised numbered rulers
- Magnifiers of various types
- Writing guides
- Raised line writing paper
- Braille or large-print books and papers
- Scale models

The teacher should use open seating and allow the child to sit where necessary to see most clearly for different lessons. Lighting and physical obstacles in travel paths should also be considered in the physical environment. The arrangement of the room may be changed as often as necessary, if the teacher makes sure that the vision-impaired child is oriented to the changes. Other children in the class can assist in this orientation. As the child must depend on sound to a great extent, the noise level in the classroom should be kept reasonably low. A space where the child can store necessary equipment should be provided. Lessons with many visual aids should be supplemented with specific verbal explanation through a native interpreter if necessary. This should be accompanied by taking the child through the motions where appropriate, not just by relying on verbal descriptions of what the child has to do. Examples of this are in physical activities and games or in the use and manipulation of concrete objects in math and science lessons.

Lessons should be varied from close to far work, visual to auditory and motor activities. The child should also be allowed to take short rests between visual activities or may even be given a break within an activity requiring long periods of close visual work. The teacher should also be careful always to address the child by name when speaking to aid the child. Also, because the child may not see facial expression or gestures, the teacher should use physical contact (where and how culturally appropriate) such as pats or hugs for positive reinforcement along with verbal praise for a job well done. The regular classroom teacher should be sure not to overprotect or underestimate the bilingual child with impaired vision.

Summary

Working with bilingual exceptional children in the regular classroom can be a rewarding experience for both the children and their teacher. This mainstreaming approach to the education of bilingual and exceptional children has developed over several years, and recently attention is being focused on providing services to children who are both bilingual and exceptional. The continuum mainstreaming model is presented here as an appropriate way to provide these services.

The continuum of services proposed provides for bilingual exceptional children to be mainstreamed into regular classrooms while receiving special assistance via bilingual and special education resource personnel. This special assistance is to be provided proportionate to the child's specific needs and continued for as long as necessary. The regular classroom teacher should coordinate instructional efforts (using the suggestions in the text) with resource personnel and parents.

All children benefit from individual, sensitive, appropriate instruction. As more schools develop mainstreaming programs, regular teachers will find more exceptional children from diverse cultural and linguistic backgrounds in their classrooms. A teacher competent in flexible instructional methodology and culturally sensitive interpersonal communication will find working with bilingual exceptional children an enriching and positive teaching experience.

Discussion Questions

1. Give your own definitions of mainstreaming.

2. Give your own definition of least restrictive environment.

3. What do you consider the two most important points in the history of the mainstreaming effort? Identify and describe them, give dates or eras when they occurred, and tell why you think they are important.

4. Contrast and compare the development of mainstreaming in bilingual and special education. What are some similarities and differences in their development?

5. Contrast and compare the mainstreaming models of bilingual and special education programs. What are some similarities and differences in these programs?

6. Using the continuum mainstreaming model, how would you provide services to a specific bilingual exceptional child? Give two examples of specific children from cultural/linguistic backgrounds different from your own. Identify age/grade, exceptionality, cultural/linguistic background, and level of development in both native and second languages.

7. The continuum model provides for movement in either direction. Give an example of a bilingual exceptional child placed in the regular classroom who may require more specialized assistance. Give an example of a bilingual exceptional child placed in a separate special program who may be moved into a less restricted environment. Identify age, exceptionality, cultural/linguistic background, and level of development in both native and second languages.

8. Select five teacher competencies that you consider most important for effective mainstreaming of bilingual exceptional children. Identify, describe, and explain why they are essential in the mainstreaming process.

9. Develop example (single-concept) lesson plans for working with bilingual children with the particular exceptionalities listed. Identify the age, cultural/linguistic background, and level of language development in both languages. Emphasize how you would accommodate for each exceptionality. Be sure instructional objective, methodology, and evaluation procedure are clearly described.

a. Emotionally disturbed
b. Gifted and talented
c. Hearing impaired
d. Learning impaired
e. Mentally retarded
f. Physically/neurologically handicapped
g. Speech impaired
h. Vision impaired

References

Baca, L. (1981). *Bilingual special education teacher competencies.* Paper prepared for Association of Colleges of Teacher Education, Bilingual Special Education Project.

Bergin, V. (1979). *Special education needs in bilingual programs.* Rosslyn, VA: National clearinghouse for Bilingual Education.

Brown V. Board of Education of Topeka (1954). 347 U.S. 483, 74 S.Ct. 686, 91 L.Ed. 873.

Collier, C., & Hoover, J. J. (1987). *Cognitive learning strategies for minority handicapped students.* Lindale, TX: Hamilton Publications.

Dunn, L. M. (1968). Special education for the mildly retarded: Is much of it justifiable? *Exceptional Children.* 35:5–22.

Feuerstein, R. (1979). *The dynamic assesment of retarded performers.* Baltimore: University Park Press.

Gearheart, B. R., & Weishahn, M. W. (1984). *The handicapped student in the regular classroom.* 2nd ed. St. Louis: Mosby.

Glass, G. V. (1980). *Effectiveness of special education.* Paper presented at the Working Conference of Social Policy and Educational Leaders to Develop Strategies for Special Education in the 1980's, Racine, WI.

Gould, S. J. (1982). *The mismeasure of man.* New York: Norton.

Hammill, E. E., & Bartel, N. R. (1986). *Teaching children with learning and behavior problems.* Boston: Allyn & Bacon.

Heinz, R. W. (1971). Special education: History. *The encyclopedia of education, vol. 8.* New York: Free Press.

Heward, W. L., & Orlansky, M. D. (1980). *Exceptional children: An introductory survey to special education.* Columbus, OH: Merrill Publishing Co.

Hoover, J. J., & Collier, C. (1985). Referring culturally different children: Sociocultural considerations. *Academic Therapy.* 20(4):503–509.

Jones, R. L. (Ed.). (1976). *Mainstreaming and the minority child.* Reston, VA: Council for Exceptional Children.

Lau v. Nichols (1974). 414 U.S. 563.

Lowenbraun, S., & Affleck, J. Q. (1980). *Teaching mildly handicapped children in regular classes.* Columbus, OH: Merrill Publishing Co.

Parelius, A. P., & Parelius, R. J. (1978). *The sociology of education.* Englewood Cliffs, NJ: Prentice-Hall.

Reynolds, M. C. (Ed.) (1980). *A common body of practices for teachers: The challenge of Public Law 94–142 to teacher education.* Minneapolis: University of Minnesota.

Reynolds, M. C., & Birch, J. W. (1986). *Teaching exceptional children in all of America's schools.* Reston, VA: Council for Exceptional Children.

U.S. Commission on Civil Rights (1975). *A better chance to learn: Bilingual bicultural education.* Washington, DC: U.S. Government Printing Office.

Weininger, O. (1973). Integrate or isolate: perspective on the whole child. *Education.* 94:139–147.

Wiig, E. H. (1980). ... Then they told me you had to cut on the lines ... In W. L. Heward and M. D. Orlansky, *Exceptional children: An introductory survey to special education.* Columbus, OH: Merrill Publishing Co.

CHAPTER THIRTEEN

Educational Consultation as a Service Delivery Option for Bilingual Special Education Students

Kathleen C. Harris
Timothy E. Heron

*With the permission of authors and publishers, portions of this chapter were adapted from *The educational consultant: Helping professionals, parents, and mainstreamed students* (2nd ed.), by T. E. Heron and K. C. Harris, 1987. Austin, TX: Pro-Ed, and from "Meeting the needs of special education high school students in regular education classrooms," by K. C. Harris, P. Harvey, L. Garcia, D. Innes, P. Lynn, D. Munoz, K. Sexton, and R. Stoica, 1987, *Teacher Education and Special Education,* 10(4):143–152.

The first author thanks Laura Garcia for her help in constructing the example of a consultation program for LEP exceptional students.

Objectives

- To define the term *consultation*
- To discuss the roles of the educational consultant
- To discuss how direct and indirect services can be provided to students, teachers, and administrators through the overlapping roles of the educational consultant
- To clarify the skills needed by the educational consultant to serve LEP exceptional students
- To present a model for educational consultation applicable to LEP exceptional students

The Need for Educational Consultation

Since the enactment of P.L. 94–142, the Education for All Handicapped Children Act of 1975, an increasing number of exceptional students have been integrated into the regular classroom. This is due in large part to the strong commitment in this law for the provision of educational services within the least restrictive environment.

By definition, limited English proficient (LEP) students are exceptional students. Hence, they are entitled to the same appropriate educational programming as all other students receiving assistance under P.L. 94–142. Also, as LEP students they are eligible to receive services under the Bilingual Education Act. Consequently it is necessary to coordinate programs for LEP exceptional students among bilingual/English as a Second Language (ESL) educators, special educators, and regular educators.

For approximately the last 15 years, educators have identified educational consultation as a way to facilitate the coordination of programs for exceptional students in the least restrictive environment (e.g., Adelman, 1972; Bauer, 1975; Evans, 1980; Friend, 1984; Haight & Molitor, 1983; Heron & Harris, 1987; Lilly, 1971; Lilly & Givens-Ogle, 1981; McKenzie et al., 1970; Miller & Sabatino, 1978; Powell, 1982; Spodek, 1982). Therefore, educational consultation is worthy of scrutiny as a vehicle for providing educational services to LEP exceptional students.

In this chapter, we will discuss the role of the educational consultant, including the methodology for providing direct and indirect services; clarify the skills needed by the educational consultant to serve LEP students; and provide a model and an example of a collaborative educational approach for LEP exceptional students.

The Role of the Educational Consultant

As discussed in Heron and Harris (1987), consultation has acquired a variety of definitions that vary depending on the target of the consultation or the nature of the consultation activities (cf. Bergan & Tombari, 1976; Friend, 1985; Robinson, Cameron, & Raethel, 1985). Effective consultation is a collaborative, voluntary, mutual problem-solving process that leads to the prevention or resolution of identified problems.

Given this definition, the educational consultant assumes three primary and overlapping roles: providing technical assistance, coordinating services, and communicating (Goldstein & Sorcher, 1974) (See Figure 13–1). Each of these roles will be addressed in the next sections and we will discuss how the consultant can provide technical assistance directly and indirectly.

Providing Direct Technical Assistance

Technical assistance can be provided in two ways, directly and indirectly, and it can be delivered to students, teachers, parents, and admin-

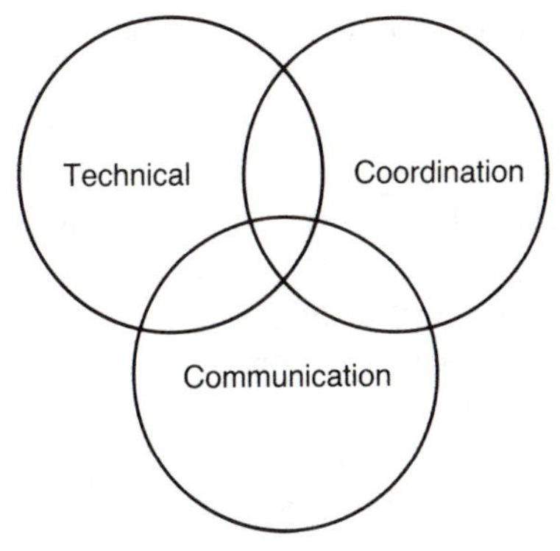

Figure 13–1
The three overlapping roles of a consultant: providing technical assistance, coordinating programs, and communicating to other professionals, parents, and students.

Adapted from *Changing Supervisor Behavior* by A. Goldstein and M. Sorcher, 1974, New York, Pergamon. Copyright © 1974 by Pergamon. Reprinted by permission.

istrators. Direct service includes any task where the consultant actually works with an individual without a mediator. For example, the consultant can work individually with a student, teacher, or administrator to change behavior. Direct service to students can be performed through many activities, including team teaching, conducting individual assessments, and providing counseling. According to Bergan (1977), direct service to students is usually conducted subsequent to a referral. Additional information is required, and the consultant is called upon to obtain that information and to communicate it to those individuals (professionals and parents) with whom the student interacts.

Let us assume that Maria, a limited English proficient (LEP), learning disabled, seventh-grade student, is referred for special services because of adjustment problems in the classroom. After a discussion with the classroom teacher, the consultant determines that Maria's adjustment problems involve her interactions with other students during small group activities. She does not finish her portion of an assignment, and consequently her group is not able to complete the whole task. As a result, she is ignored by her peers.

In this example, the consultant provides direct service on two levels. First, the consultant conducts an observation of the small group activity to determine the type of assignment Maria was to complete and the nature of the interactions she has with her peers. Next, the consultant discusses the situation with Maria directly. During the interview, Maria indicates that she feels uncomfortable performing several of the tasks. She has to read, take notes, and compile her portion of the project for the other group members. She wants to do the assignment but feels frustrated at being so slow. Though she communicates well in English with her peers, it takes Maria longer than her peers to read and comprehend the English reading assignments and then write her portion of the assignment.

After collecting this information, the consultant works with the teacher and Maria to develop a procedure whereby she can complete her group assignments in a timely fashion. The plan is that Maria will tape-record her portion of the assignment rather than write it. Although Maria still has trouble reading her portion of the group assignment, she uses a tape recorder to make notes on major points as she reads. These notes are later transcribed and edited for her report. The consultant and the teacher will then conduct observations of Maria and her peers during small group activities to determine whether the plan facilitates positive interactions between Maria and her peers.

Direct service to teachers can be conducted with an individual teacher, small groups of teachers, or a whole school staff. The intent of direct, technical consultation could be to help a teacher prevent or solve a particular student problem, increase the teacher's level of awareness regarding curriculum issues, or conduct observations of teacher behavior. The goal of direct service to teachers is to improve a teacher's skill so that, in turn, the teacher will be more proficient in dealing with student problems. Newcomer (1977) states that the consultant's "ultimate goal is not to remediate a particular child's learning problems, but to prevent certain problems from developing and provide the regular educator with the additional skills and competencies required to undertake remedial activities independently" (p. 161).

Direct consulting service to teachers is maximally effective when teachers want to change their own behavior. This perception by the regular teacher is a precondition to effective consultation. The consultee (the teacher) perceives the situation to be outside direct control and requests assistance. In some cases, the consultee may have the skills required to do the job, but because of extraneous factors, these skills are not evident. For example, a bilingual teacher may be able to individualize instruction for students if the class size is not too large. If additional students are added to the roster—especially if those students have handicaps—the bilingual teacher's ability to provide individualized instruction may decrease, and the services of a consultant may be requested to help individualize instruction for all students effectively and efficiently.

Direct consulting services for teachers can be rendered in several ways: conducting observations in classrooms, modeling, providing inservice training, conducting evaluations, and providing referrals for support services within and outside the school system.

Conducting Observations. Consultants can be of great assistance to teachers when they conduct observations for the purpose of qualifying and quantifying student and teacher behavior. A consultant can serve as another pair of eyes and ears and help a teacher determine who receives the teacher's attention and under what circumstances.

Skinner (1979) conducted a study that illustrates this point. A regular education teacher expressed interest in having an observer in the classroom because of concern about the uneven amount of attention students in the classroom were receiving. Baseline data were collected on six students in the classroom (two high achieving, two low achieving, and two learning disabled students). After five sessions, the consultant met with the teacher to discuss the observational findings. The teacher believed that student 3, one of the learning disabled students, did not receive enough teacher-initiated statements, while student 2, a nonhandicapped student, received a disproportionate share of initiations. The teacher indicated that the remaining four students received an appropriate number of initiations.

Beginning with week 6 of observation for student 3 and week 11 for student 2, the consultant met with the teacher to show the data on teacher initiations. The observation plus feedback phase was successful in modifying the teacher's interactions with each of the two students. The student who had received too many initiations was now receiving fewer and vice versa.

Skinner's (1979) approach to resolving this teacher's problem was successful for several reasons. First, his observational data were accurate and reliable. Second, he was able to relate to and interact with the classroom teacher. Third, he had consulting experience. As Brown (1977) stated, few professionals who express a desire to become consulting teachers have preservice training in consultation, or have the skill to provide realistic alternatives for a range of management problems. Skinner was able to combine his experiences and skill to help resolve the teacher's problem.

Modeling. Modeling, defined as physically showing an instructional procedure to another person, is an effective procedure to use when the teacher has some prerequisite skills already in the repertoire, holds the model in esteem, and perceives the model as competent (Bandura, 1971; Cooper, Heron, & Heward, 1987). Modeling can be performed at any stage in the consultation process.

A form of modeling, referred to as surreptitious or covert modeling, can affect teacher performance (Brown, Reschly, & Wasserman, 1974). During covert modeling the consultant performs a desired classroom behavior in the presence of the teacher but without necessarily saying, "Watch what I do, and you do the same." According to Brown, Reschly, and Wasserman (1974), this procedure can be effective, even though no specific directional prompts are issued. The main advantage of surreptitious modeling is that the chances for a potentially negative "expert-subordinate" relationship between the consultant and the teacher are reduced or eliminated. Because verbal prompts are not given, the teacher does not experience the feelings of inferiority or incompetence that Oldridge (1977) indicates teachers could experience during the consultation process if the consultant is viewed as an expert and the teacher is viewed as a subordinate.

Providing Inservice Training. The need for continued teacher inservice training, defined as the process whereby additional skills are acquired to maintain or improve instructional effectiveness, is well recognized (Joyce & Showers, 1980; Speece & Mandell, 1980). However, few educators agree on the best method to provide this training. Shaw and Shaw (1972) state that regardless of the method for delivering inservice, the training will be effective only when the participants want to learn a new skill or method. If participants are forced to attend inservice programs in which they have no interest, it is unlikely that learning will be efficient.

Consultants can provide teachers with informal inservice training by giving them reliable and credible feedback as soon after the teaching act as possible (Van Houten, 1980). Brophy and Good's research (1974) seems to indicate that an effective inservice consultation strategy is to make teachers aware of their established, but inappropriate, behavior or interaction patterns with students. Brophy and Good offer a nine-point intervention program for the consultant (see Table 13–1).

Two important functions for the consultant to consider when providing technically competent inservice training are found in points 2 and 3 in Table 13–1. Essentially, these points state that the consultant should try to focus on a few teacher behaviors at a time and find comparison groups that demonstrate good teaching technique, communicating that the teacher already has some of the skills the consultant is trying to reinforce. Teachers are more likely to have confidence in the consultant who reinforces them for the positive instructional behaviors they have instead of criticizing them for what they lack.

If positive instructional behaviors do not occur or occur only occasionally, the consultant might try to reinforce approximations of the desired behavior (e.g., "I noticed the way Lamar smiled when you publicly praised his accomplishment in science. I bet that same strategy would work for Margie, who seems to like your attention."). The consultant is attempting to extend a demonstrated positive approach to another situation where the likelihood of success is high. The essential message the teacher gets when receiving inservice consultation using Brophy and Good's approach (1974) is that the teacher has teaching competencies and skills that can be employed in other situations to prevent or solve problems. The teacher does not perceive an expert-subordinate relationship because the

Table 13–1
Brophy and Good's Model for Intervention in the Classroom

From *Teacher-Student Relationships: Causes and Consequences* (pp. 292–295) by J. E. Brophy & T. L. Good, 1974, New York: Holt, Rinehart & Winston.

1. Collect behavioral data on a representative sample of students or the entire class but maintain separate records for each individual student.
2. Identify explicit problems or possible developmental points that appear in the data.
3. If possible, find contrast groups to show good teaching behavior, making it possible to ask teachers to extend to new situations behavior that is already in their repertoire rather than to ask them to perform new behaviors.
4. Express interest in the problem, but allow teachers to give explanations before suggesting changes.
5. Pinpoint differences in teaching behavior with contrasting students and suggest change in teaching behavior with target students as a possible corrective step.
6. If the teacher is agreeable, engage in mutual problem solving until explicit treatment procedures are agreed upon.
7. Specify exactly what the teacher will do to attempt to change student behavior.
8. Arrange to get posttreatment data to evaluate success in changing teacher and student behavior and to examine the data for radiation effects.
9. Hold a debriefing session with the teacher to review the results of the study and to gain valuable clinical data from the teacher.

consultant's role has been deemphasized in the process (Idol, Paolucci-Whitcomb, & Nevin, 1986) and the consultant has reinforced the teacher for appropriate instructional behavior.

Conducting Evaluations. Consultants who provide technical assistance to teachers with respect to evaluation procedures perform a direct service of immeasurable importance. Not only can an evaluation plan determine whether a given treatment or intervention was effective, but the data collected during the course of the program evaluation might prove helpful in future situations (Alpert, 1977). For example, suppose a bilingual teacher successfully implemented a peer tutoring activity with a hearing-impaired student in the class. The knowledge gained during the tutoring session could be invaluable if the teacher decided to use a peer tutoring program with other students.

Program evaluation can be categorized as formative or summative. Formative evaluation is conducted during the actual implementation of the program (the intervention mutually agreed on by the teacher and the consultant). In formative evaluation the consultant determines whether the plan is being implemented as intended and the effectiveness of the plan for changing behavior. Formative evaluation allows for midcourse correction. If the plan is implemented as intended, yet no functional effect on the targeted behavior is noted, another strategy can be initiated immediately.

Summative evaluation is conducted at the end of the intervention. The question the consultant seeks to answer then is, "Did the plan have a functional effect?" If the teacher's (or student's) behavior changed a significant amount in the desired direction and adequate controls were used to eliminate competing explanations for the change, then the consultant can be reasonably confident that the plan accounted for the change.

Gersten and Hauser (1984) contend that evaluations of special education programs should produce information useful for program improvement. Measurements should be used that are sensitive to the process as well as program outcomes. These authors discuss the use of behavioral observations and teacher ratings as viable outcome measures. They argue that two critical areas need to be assessed to improve evaluation results: program implementation and measurement of outcome. Assessing program implementation is important for two reasons: (1) It provides information on the extent to which the program was implemented as intended; and (2) the data can be used to establish the relationship between the program and its intended outcome, that is, how much or what quality of the intervention is associated with what level of outcome.

This combination of formative and summative evaluation can be used for groups and individuals. For example, the individualized educational plan (IEP) process demands a yearly or summative evaluation. However, short-term objectives for each annual goal and methods for evaluating those objectives are also written into an IEP. If during implementation these short-term objectives are not being met, steps can be taken to modify the educational program. The appropriateness of the instructional methodology or the assessment instrument itself may be examined. Rather than waiting a year to determine whether the IEP has been successful for the student, a formative evaluation of short-term objectives can indicate program success or failure and suggest alterations in the IEP that could increase the probability of overall success.

The following suggestions for planning and conducting program evaluation activities are offered to the educational consultant:

1. Clearly identify program goals (Knowlton, 1983; Maher, 1983).

2. Clearly identify desired outcomes of the program (Knowlton, 1983) as well as the process of program implementation.

3. Specify measurable objectives that will reflect desired program outcomes as well as the process of program implementation.

4. Evaluate the usefulness of program evaluation activities, that is, the extent to which the efforts serve the program development and improvement needs of users (Maher & Bennett, 1984).

5. Assure the propriety of evaluation activities, that is, the legal and ethical considerations (Maher & Bennett, 1984).

6. Assure the accuracy of program evaluation data collection activities, that is, assure that activities are technically defensible (Maher & Bennett, 1984).

7. Identify the resources available within or outside the institution to conduct program evaluation (Knowlton, 1983).

8. Include, as a source of evaluative information, consumers of the program.

Providing Referrals. The consultant may not be able to solve all classroom-related problems, even with the assistance of a sensitive and competent teacher. Therefore, it is important for the consultant to be able to work with the teacher and other professionals who may be in a position to help. An example is the case where a student's language problem might be based on hearing problems. The consultant might involve an audiologist and a speech therapist in determining the most appropriate intervention for the student. Also, in the case where a student's problem in school extends into the home and disrupts the family life, counseling services might be recommended. Consultants who work within specific geographic regions should be familiar with the referral resources of the community, including child protective services, mental health agencies, parent assistance programs, and counseling or clinical services.

Administrators often seek the advice of consultants to help solve problems related to policy design, short- and long-term planning, inservice training for staff, services to handicapped and minority children, and a host of other topics. Before service can be provided, the consultant must have a clear idea of the objective the administrator has in mind. The consultant must be certain that the objective is measurable and know the time frame in which the administrator wants the problem addressed. For example, the administrator might state in broad terms that all the teachers in the district's Bilingual Special Education program should be competent in certain classroom management techniques. The consultant must help to determine the terminal objectives by ascertaining which techniques are most important to master at this time (e.g., individual or group approaches, positive reinforcement or positive reductive techniques). Once this is established, the consultant must determine a procedure to measure the terminal objective and the time constraints for achieving the objective. In addition to obtaining information from the administrator, it is also important for the consultant to share information with the administrator. In our example, the administrator is interested in improving the classroom management skills of the teachers. If this is accomplished through inservice training, the consultant should share with the administrator that the teachers' reactions to the inservice plan are important. The consultant should also clearly establish a role in this program as a facilitator and not as an administrator. As Hughes (1980) indicates, consultants must avoid alienating any organizational or philosophical factions within the school. Obtaining consensus and avoiding confrontations are important objectives for the consultant.

Consultants can perform other functions at the administration level as well. For example, they may assist with establishing and maintaining open communication between teachers and administrators. They may serve as a resource for innovative program planning, applying for and receiving grants-in-aid for experimental education research projects. They may participate in advisory meetings to design districtwide policy on a range of topics, including the provision of appropriate services for bilingual exceptional students.

Although the reasons for the interaction between the administrator and the consultant may vary, the nature of the interaction should follow a consistent path: determine the goals, identify the resources, establish the consultant role, implement the program, and evaluate the results.

Providing Indirect Technical Assistance

Indirect service includes any task where the consultant works with a mediator who in turn works to change the target individual's behavior. Indirect services can be provided to students, teachers, and administrators.

Indirect services to students are accomplished by providing direct services to teachers or parents or both. Providing teachers and parents with recommendations for intervention, helping to design instructional materials, or referring a teacher to another agency for additional student assistance are examples of indirect services, because the student benefits indirectly from the consultant's intervention. As mediator, the teacher or parent actually conducts the intervention.

The main advantage of providing indirect services to students is that the consultant can serve more pupils. Time constraints and the physical limitations of travel preclude the consultant from attending personally to every student who might need assistance. With indirect service, the consultant provides technical assistance to the teacher or the parent, who in turn provides the direct service. Also, when providing the teacher or parent with technical assistance indirectly, the consultant sets the occasion for the teacher or parent to use the newly acquired skills in a preventive, problem-solving mode. The teacher will learn to use the skills to prevent problems rather than waiting for a problem to surface and then seeking the assistance of the consultant. Finally, indirect service sets the occasion for the teacher to generalize the skills to other students or situations in the future.

The primary disadvantage of providing indirect service to students through a mediator is that it is difficult to ascertain conclusively the effects of the intervention. Is improved student performance directly related to the new instructional material or teaching procedure employed by the teacher?

Indirect services can also be provided to teachers. Indirect service to teachers occurs when the consultant provides direct service to an administrator (or other agent) who in turn serves the teacher. In this case, the administrator would be the mediator and the teacher would be the target. When a consultant assists an administrator with classroom placement decisions, ecological or physical design arrangements, scheduling, or staff development, teachers receive indirect service. Indirect services to teachers share many of the advantages and disadvantages of indirect service to students. Consultants should work indirectly with teachers through an administrator but recognize the pluses and minuses of the service.

When a consultant provides an indirect service to an administrator, the administrator is the target and another agent serves as the mediator. For example, an indirect service to an administrator would be provided when a consultant improved the curriculum decision making of teachers, and they in turn influenced the administrator to adopt a particular textbook series that would better meet the needs of LEP handicapped students.

Coordinating Services

As previously discussed, LEP handicapped students are entitled to special education, Bilingual Education, and regular education services. Therefore, determining the most appropriate program for a LEP handicapped student requires coordination of services. According to Martinez (1982), it is necessary to establish communication between departments of Bilingual Education/ESL and special education. These departments must agree that there is a need to develop specialized programs. They must commit resources and energy to work cooperatively to identify, design, implement, and evaluate programs. The role of the consultant involves coordinating services with resource personnel.

Coordinating services can be accomplished in two major ways: by facilitating the individualized education plan and by managing resources.

Facilitating the IEP. Facilitating the IEP means that the consultant assumes responsibility for ensuring that all aspects of the IEP (identification through evaluation) are completed in a timely fashion and that all persons associated with completing the IEP participate fully. Turnbull, Strickland, and Brantley (1982) are emphatic that the consultant ensure full participation by all members of the IEP committee, especially teachers:

> An initial step to foster coordination is the involvement of persons responsible for implementation in the initial decision-making process of IEP development. A major consideration is to involve the teachers of the handicapped student in the development of the IEP. . . An important system of checks and balances occurs when persons responsible for implementation participate in the planning process. (p.231)

The IEP process is also facilitated by careful monitoring during implementation. Monitoring can occur at several levels. For instance, by using formative evaluation techniques, student progress can be monitored by determining whether the student's present level of achievement improved since the IEP was developed. Is the student able to complete tasks or assignments that could not be completed before? Likewise, how does the student perceive the implementation of the IEP? Is the student (or parent) satisfied with the rate of progress? Finally, are the methods used to reach established goals consistent with good practice? When measures are taken to determine if the goals, procedures, and outcomes of an intervention program are acceptable, the social validity of the program is being monitored.

Monitoring can also be applied to the procedural aspects of the IEP. Are students evaluated or reevaluated according to the established time lines? Are IEP meetings held annually? Are all due process measures followed? Monitoring of IEP goals, procedures, and outcomes should not be undertaken merely to identify problem areas. According to Turnbull, Strickland, and Brantley (1982), data analysis during the monitoring phase of the IEP should identify those factors of the program that work successfully. Turnbull, Strickland, and Brantley (1982) state the importance of collecting these data:

> There is a tendency to point out problems, yet rarely to highlight the successes. Educators and parents need reinforcement; they need to be recognized for a job well done. The systematic improvement of mechanics associated with the IEP process can be fostered by building on strengths and ensuring that the participants are commended for their success. (p. 240)

Managing Resources. Two major resources that consultants can coordinate are personnel and information. When coordinating information, the consultant should be familiar with curriculum materials and instructional strategies appropriate for LEP handicapped students and share this information with teachers in an appropriate way, for example, through demonstration of the technique or material or by actually team teaching with the student's teacher. For instance, based on the identified needs of a student, a peer tutoring program might be needed. For another student, team teaching might be the method of first choice, allowing the student to receive more individualized assistance from a bilingual teacher. For a third student, a home-based education program might have to be devised so that skills learned in school can be practiced at home. The management of personnel in each of these illustrations—the students, another teacher, or the parents—is the consultant's role. Another aspect of this role is to evaluate the resources available to the team.

Using procedures for formative and summative evaluation, the consultant may want to apply the guidelines provided by Benavides (1985) for analyzing the educational resources available for LEP handicapped students. Benavides (1985) suggests a five-stage process.

First, the objectives of the service delivery must be specified. In the case of services for LEP handicapped students, a goal of the service delivery system may be that all LEP handicapped students be provided appropriate education by certified teachers who are bilingual and biliterate in the student's native language.

Second, the consultant will determine the resources available to accomplish the objectives. In this case, the consultant would want to take a frequency count of the number of LEP handicapped students in special day classes, mainstreamed regular education settings, and mainstreamed Bilingual Education settings. The consultant would also want to determine the number of certified teachers in each of these settings and their level of proficiency in different languages.

Third, if the resources are not sufficient to provide the necessary services, the consultant must determine alternatives. For example, the consultant may decide that pairing bilingual and biliterate paraprofessionals with certified monolingual English teachers may provide a satisfactory alternative.

Fourth, the consultant evaluates the resources available to implement the alternative goal, using procedures similar to those used to evaluate resources. The consultant would also want to determine what additional staff training may be required to implement the alternatives and estimate the cost and effectiveness of implementing the alternative plan.

Fifth, the alternative plan is implemented. The consultant would evaluate the effectiveness of the alternative plan, considering formative and summative evaluation procedures.

The consultant may also want to consider developing short- and long-term plans. For example, a suitable alternative may not be possible with existing resources. The consultant may develop interim alternatives (e.g., sharing of paraprofessionals between the bilingual and special education departments) until the educational staff is adequately trained to implement a more effective service delivery program for LEP exceptional students.

It is important for the consultant to consider the adequacy of resources to meet the needs of LEP handicapped students and initiate programs that may be necessary to improve the quality of service. One way the quality of service can be improved is by the consultant fulfilling the final primary role, communicating effectively.

Effective Communication

According to Parsons and Meyers (1984), communication is defined as a "condition in which the message perceived and responded to by the receiver corresponds to the one intended by the sender" (p. 57). Davis (1983) considers communication as the transfer of any thought, feeling, or need between people through a verbal or nonverbal channel. Figure 13–2 shows a model of communication in which meaning is conceived, encoded, and sent by the sender, and received, decoded, and comprehended by the receiver.

According to Parsons and Meyers (1984), consultants should be aware that "miscommunication" can occur at any stage in this model because of conditions existing at the time of communication (interfering stimuli), a faulty mechanism during the communication act itself (inappropriate translation, culturally confusing gestures) or a lack of background knowledge or experience of the receiver (parent's lack of familiarity of the culture of U.S. public schools).

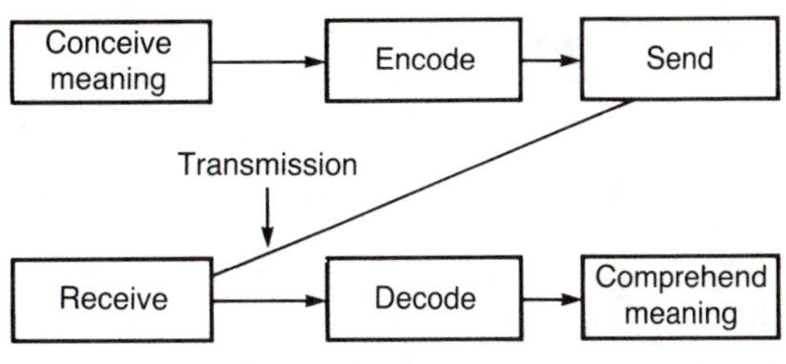

Figure 13–2
A communication model illustrating the sequence by which a message is conceived, encoded, sent, received, decoded, and comprehended.

Adapted from *Interpersonal Communication in Organizations* by O. Baskin and C. Aronoff, 1980, Santa Monica, CA: Goodyear.

To establish and maintain effective communication, the consultant must accomplish several interrelated objectives, including gaining acceptance, establishing credibility, providing feedback, and disseminating information (Evans, 1980; Goldstein & Sorcher, 1974; Idol, Paolucci-Whitcomb, and Nevin 1986; Speece & Mandell, 1980).

Gaining acceptance. Gaining acceptance and establishing rapport are important components of effective consultation (Brown, Wyne, Blackburn, & Powell, 1979; Idol, Paolucci-Whitcomb, & Nevin, 1986). Without the acceptance of the group, even the most skilled consultant will be ineffective. Gaining acceptance and establishing rapport can be accomplished in several ways. First, Idol, Paolucci-Whitcomb, and Nevin (1986) recommend, in part, treating others with respect, shifting credit for ideas and accomplishments to others, and willingly sharing information and learning with others. Second, acceptance can be achieved when consultants participate fully in school or agency functions (serving on committees, assisting with sport or club activities). Serving in this capacity provides visibility and demonstrates to peers a commitment to the overall educational process. Finally, the consultant can gain acceptance by clearly defining, or having a superior define, the role the consultant will play in the school. Letting colleagues know what the consultant can and cannot do decreases the likelihood that misconstrued expectations, which could jeopardize acceptance into the social community of the school or agency, will arise.

The consultant should realize that gaining acceptance takes time, even when the process described is implemented. It is almost never achieved immediately by the newcomer. It has to be earned, and time is an important factor. As Laurie, Buchwach, Silverman, and Zigmond (1978) discovered after working with teachers in a secondary level mainstreaming program over several years:

> Our experience . . . has shown us that mainstream teachers can be helped to provide more individualized educational programs for learning disabled students . . . But [it] took four years to accomplish, with one special educator in each high school assigned full time to the task of working with mainstream teachers. While these results suggested that our long-term goal of effectively mainstreaming learning disabled adolescents might be achieved, they also demonstrate that the task we have undertaken is a formidable one . . . To help mainstream educators develop the attitudes, skills, and knowledge necessary to meet the challenges of PL 94–142 . . . [we] must extend our influence through direct involvement with mainstream teachers. (p. 71)

Establishing Credibility. Establishing credibility means that the consultant is perceived as a believable person by colleagues. The consultant is thought of as a knowledgeable person who is able to apply effective interventions. According to Hawisher and Calhoun (1978), the consultant must have a thorough knowledge of the dynamics of the regular classroom to establish credibility:

> The [consultant] skilled in teacher-to-teacher consultation has the ability to relate to the classroom teacher in that he is able to recognize those problems of tedium, those problems of an exceptional nature, and those problems imposed by varying aptitudes and abilities of 30 or so active students. Without these understandings of the classroom, the [consultant] will not be able to establish credibility and will not be able to influence the classroom teacher to attempt new techniques or approaches. (p. 143)

Providing Feedback. Providing feedback to teachers or parents serves as a mechanism to verify whether the message was received as intended. Davis (1983) indicates that feedback can be obtained by asking the other party to restate the communication using different words and analyzing the verbal and nonverbal behavior of others during the communication. For example, suppose a teacher said to a consultant, "Noma has not been behaving very well in the classroom lately," to which the consultant replied, "If I understand what you are saying, Noma's behavior has been disruptive." The consultant's reply attempts to provide feedback to the teacher that the intent of the message is understood. At this point, the teacher can either verify that the meaning was understood ("Yes, that is what I mean") or further refine the original statement ("Well, it's not that she has been disruptive, only that she is not paying attention as she used to do"). In either case, the consultant's feedback statement has served a useful purpose.

Nonverbally, the consultant must be cognizant of body position, posture, gestures, or other signals that might provide feedback that the intended message is not likely to be received correctly. A good example of how this happens occurs when a teacher and a consultant attempt to squeeze a mini-consultation into a cramped time frame. If the teacher is organizing papers, setting up equipment, or quickly reviewing lesson plans, it is likely that shuffling papers, poor eye contact, or physical distance will preclude the message from being received well. In this situation, the consultant is receiving nonverbal feedback that this is not the best time to try to discuss the matter.

Speece and Mandell (1980) state that teachers or parents might not have the prerequisite skills to communicate effectively. Yet all parties involved in the communication interaction should have the necessary prerequisite skills to communicate effectively and efficiently. Therefore, it is important that all parties receive the help they need to learn effective communication skills. This may be accomplished through training sessions involving role playing, videotaping, or modeling. For instance, in the example above with the harried teacher and consultant, a role-playing situation might be designed whereby the consultant would say, "I recognize that this is not the best time to discuss the problem. Can I call you later today to discuss it?"

Further, Speece and Mandell (1980) believe that administrators must recognize the importance of consultant-teacher feedback exchanges and provide time during the school day for thse interactions to take place. If consultant-teacher interactions occur only on the run the full value of consultation will not be achieved.

Disseminating Information. According to Cooper, Heron, and Heward (1987), "Practitioners have legal and ethical responsibilities to share data with learners, and these responsibilities extend to parents and guardians when the learners are minors and/or dependents" (p. 588). But dissemination can be defined in a broader context to include all information relative to the education program for which the consultant is responsible. Using this broader perspective, the consultant can disseminate information in several useful ways. Informally, the consultant can talk about the program with teachers, parents, or administrators. Informal conversations that occur in the hallways, lounge areas, and parking lots of school buildings provide a valuable medium through which information flows. Formal means of communication can occur through established districtwide newsletters, school newspapers, or specially audiotaped announcements accessible through a home-school communication system (cf. Weiss et al., 1982). Likewise, a broader professional or parental audience can be reached through conferences, journal articles, television, or print media.

When providing oral or written communication to an audience, the consultant should be mindful of the audience's background knowledge, experiences, language, and vocabulary. The words and context of a description of a new Bilingual Special Education program before a school board would be stated entirely differently for teachers, parents, or students. The content of the message would be the same, but the manner in which the content is expressed would change.

With any audience it is helpful to program for redundancy; that is, provide several ways to communicate the same message and define terms or clarify meaning with examples at every opportunity. For example, suppose that special and bilingual teachers of LEP learning disabled elementary students wanted the consultant to advertise a new reading program for the students. The consultant might present the program to the school board and the Parent Teacher Association, submit an article to the school or community newspaper, and enlist faculty cooperation by presenting a slide/tape show at the teachers' meeting. For each communication medium the consultant would define the scope and sequence of the reading program and state how it would fit within the existing structure of the school and the community.

Because of the need to coordinate services and communicate among monolingual and bilingual experts in various areas (special and regular education teachers, Bilingual Education teachers, and related service personnel) the LEP handicapped student may also need the services of an interpreter.

Working with an interpreter. According to Medina (1982), "The main function of an interpreter . . . is to make it possible for all participants to communicate with one another despite language and culture differences. The interpreter . . . facilitates communication" (p. 34). Interpreters generally facilitate communication for school personnel by interpreting during parent conferences, parent interviews, and testing situations. However, bilingual paraprofessionals, secretaries, and other staff members may also be asked to serve as interpreters for monolingual English teachers and students who do not speak English. Because individuals who are not trained as interpreters may be asked to serve as interpreters, it is important for the consultant to be familiar with the skills needed by interpreters and the skills needed by educators to work successfully with interpreters.

Medina (1982) lists several minimal qualifications for interpreters. The interpreter should be bilingual and biliterate with proficiency in both English and the target language. The interpreter should also be able to adjust to different levels of language use (i.e., the interpreter should be able to function if the situation involves colloquial language or literary language). This also necessitates that the interpreter be familiar with the appropriate educational terminology, the culture of the school, and the culture of the student. Finally, and most important, the interpreter should be familiar with the ethics of interpretation. This includes maintenance of the confidentiality of information and interpreting responses and questions without elaboration.

The following represents a modification of Langdon's discussion (1983) of skills one should have when working with interpreters. First, the educator should be familiar with the dynamics of interpretation. This includes familiarity with procedures for establishing rapport with multicultural participants, knowledge of the kinds of information that can easily be interpreted and not lost in the interpretation process, understanding of the authority position of the educator, use of appropriate and culturally sensitive nonverbal communication methods, and understanding of the need to obtain translations that do not include the personal input of the interpreter. Second, the educator should be able to plan and conduct pre- and post-sessions with the interpreter. During these sessions, the educator orients the interpreter to the purpose and procedures of a given educational situation. Third, the educator should be able to help the interpreter follow ethical procedures of interpretation.

If the person responsible for interpreting and the educator involved in the interpretation process do not have the necessary skills to work together successfully, the consultant should seek resources and training for the educational staff. This is most important if the services provided the educational staff will directly affect the adequacy of the educational program for LEP handicapped students.

Additional Skills Needed by the Educational Consultant

Aside from being able to fulfill the roles mentioned previously, educational consultants who want to assist in the implementation of appropriate services for LEP exceptional students must have an additional set of skills. They must be well grounded in the knowledge of curriculum and instructional strategies.

To help design an appropriate curriculum for a LEP exceptional student, the consultant must consider several factors: the language proficiency of the student, the culture of the student, the regular education curriculum, and the Bilingual Education curriculum. Whether the student is in a special education setting or a mainstream setting, it is necessary to determine the appropriate language of instruction and the extent of the student's cultural identity to develop a curriculum that is culturally meaningful to the student. Also, if the student is in a special education setting, it will be necessary to incorporate relevant components of the regular education and Bilingual Education curricula to ensure that the student receives an appropriate program. Finally, central to the consultant's knowledge of curriculum and instructional strategies are the concepts of instructional design, pacing, task analysis, feedback, self-management, and generality of behavior change. Curriculum and instructional strategies for LEP handicapped students are addressed elsewhere in this text; the reader is also referred to the work of Cooper, Heron, and Heward (1987) and Heron and Harris (1987) for a thorough description of curriculum and instructional strategies.

A Model of Educational Consultation

The triadic model of educational consultation represents a way in which school consultation can be conceptualized. This model is not intended to be representative of all models that might be used with teachers, parents, or students. Rather, it and the accompanying example illustrate how educational consultation services can be used in a collaborative program for LEP handicapped individuals and groups.

Triadic Model

The triadic model (Figure 13–3), in its most basic form, is a linear sequence that portrays the relationships among the consultant, the mediator or consultee, and the client or target. The bracket that connects the consultant and the mediator represents the collaborative consultation process.

The triadic model describes a functional rather than an absolute sequence for consultation. That is, any teacher, parent, or administrator could serve as the consultant. The only requirement for serving as a consultant is that the individual possess the knowledge, skills, or abilities needed to work collaboratively with the mediator or the target. A bilingual teacher, paraprofessional, or parent could serve as the mediator. The mediator has access to the target student and has some influence over the student, while the consultant serves as a catalyst to activate the mediator. The target is the individual (or group) for whom the consultative service is intended, or any other person involved with the consultation (Tharp & Wetzel, 1969).

Principles of Collaborative Consultation

According to Idol-Maestas, Nevin, and Paolucci-Whitcomb (1984), four principles of collaborative consultation form the basis of the triadic model: team ownership, recognition of individual differences, application of reinforcement, and data-based evaluation.

Team Ownership. Team ownership is indicated in the two-way arrow shown in Figure 13–3. Both equality and parity must exist between the consultant and the mediator for the triadic model to work effectively. According to Idol-Maestas, Nevin, and Paolucci-Whitcomb (1984), equality is demonstrated when both parties listen, respect, and learn from each other. Parity exists when the knowledge and skills of both parties are blended.

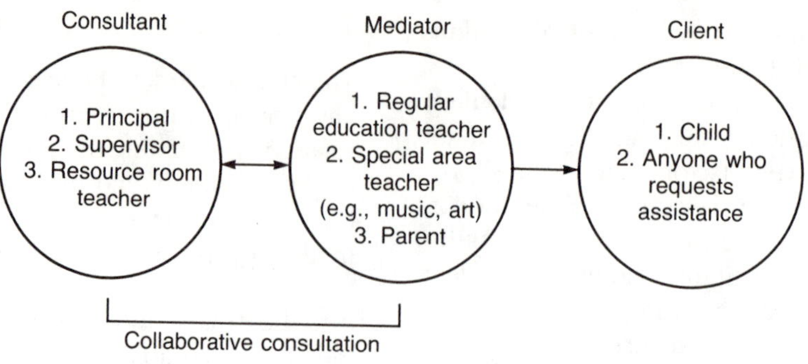

Figure 13–3
The triadic model of consultation showing individuals within each role
From *Behavior Modification in the Natural Environment* (p. 47) by R. G. Tharp and R. J. Wetzel, 1969, New York: Academic Press. Copyright © 1969 by Academic Press. Reprinted by permission.

Recognition of Individual Differences. Individual differences must be recognized because the principle of collaborative consultation focuses on the effect of change on the mediator and target. That is, implicit in the implementation of the triadic model is that a change in procedure occurs. For some individuals, making a change in a routine is uncomfortable. The consultant's role in the collaboration process is to be sensitive to effects of change on the mediator and the target and to make transitions as nonthreatening as possible.

Application of Reinforcement. Application of positive reinforcement is a distinguishing feature of collaborative consultation within the triadic model. A basic tenet of this approach is that new behaviors are learned when their occurrence is followed by reinforcement. So, not only does the consultant use liberal amounts of reinforcement when teaching the mediator new behaviors, but also the mediator learns to use ample reinforcement with the target individual.

The emphasis on reinforcement does not mean that other behavior change principles or procedures are not used. Many educators have written extensively on how behaviors can be changed using a variety of acceleration and deceleration approaches (cf. Cooper, Heron, & Heward, 1987). The point is, positive reinforcement is a key principle in behavior development.

Data-Based Evaluation. Data-based evaluation is the fourth principle of collaborative consultation in the triadic model. The model is evaluated by determining the extent to which improved performance in the mediator and target is achieved. So success can be analyzed using a variety of qualitative and quantitative measures (cf. Kerr & Nelson, 1983; Tawney & Gast, 1984). Specifically, the consultant has two evaluative measures to index when using the triadic model. The first measure is the extent to which the mediator acquires the knowledge or skill presented by the consultant. The second measure is whether the application of this knowledge or skill affects student performance. Gains may be obtained by the mediator when little or no improvement in student performance is realized. As Heath and Nielson (1974) indicate, the relationship between the specific performance of the teacher and the achievement of the student is uncertain. But, as Idol-Maestas, Nevin, and Paolucci-Whitcomb (1984) indicate, failure to achieve results should be interpreted as a procedural or system failure, not as a failure due to the inherent deficits of the learner.

Example of a Consultation Program

The following description of a program for LEP learning disabled students is an adaptation of a program implemented at a high school in southern California (Harris et al., 1987).

This program is based on a consultation model in that services for LEP learning disabled students are provided according to the principles of collaborative consultation and use a combination of direct and indirect services. The program is implemented in five stages: development of program philosophy, identification of teachers, articulation of program, program scheduling, and program evaluation.

The consultants in the program are the special educators in the high school (the three resource specialists, the special day class teacher, the speech and language specialist, and the school psychologist). The program is designed to serve all LEP learning disabled students in the school (approximately 80). The resources available to implement the program are the special educators, the bilingual/ESL educators, the regular educators, the special education paraprofessionals, and the bilingual paraprofessionals. Among the staff available to implement the program are a combination of monolingual and bilingual (Spanish) speakers.

Development of Program Philosophy. Before implementing the program, the consultants meet to develop their program philosophy. A firm program philosophy is important for the successful implementation of the program. Essentially, the philosophy of the program includes the following: a need to serve special education and low-ability students (those students who are not achieving at a satisfactory level in school but who are not eligible for special education services), a desire to address the development of language proficiency as part of the program, a desire to serve students in mainstream classrooms as this is the least restrictive environment, and a desire to serve as a resource to the mainstream classroom teacher. Based on this philosophy, the goal of the program is to provide services to LEP learning disabled students in mainstream classrooms. These students will only be removed from the mainstream classroom when it is not possible to provide the services they need in the mainstream classroom. This program will be implemented with all the LEP learning disabled students in the school.

Identification of Mainstream Teachers. The consultants choose only a portion of all the teachers in the school (approximately 30) to work with during the first year of the program. The consultants choose teachers with the following characteristics: they teach classes in which the LEP learning disabled students had been or could be mainstreamed, they are familiar with the consultants, they are willing to work with the consultants, and they and the consultants feel mutual professional respect and credibility. The mainstream teachers who participate in the program teach bilingual/ESL classes in basic reading, English, math, social sciences, and biological sciences.

Articulation of Program. Before program implementation, the consultants meet with the mainstream teachers to discuss and refine the program. The meeting is held at the beginning of the school year. The consultants present themselves as a team. They discuss the philosophy of the program and explain that they wish to serve the LEP learning disabled students and the mainstream teachers in the mainstream classroom. The consultants describe the services they would be able to implement in this program: (1) student support in the mainstream classroom, (2) student support outside the mainstream classroom, (3) teacher support in the mainstream classroom, and (4) teacher support through collaborative planning. Examples of specific activities in each of these areas can be found in Table 13–2.

During the discussion, the following issues are addressed: difficulty of content, difficulty of material, grading, behavior problems, and collaborating with the consultants. The consultants and the mainstream teachers discuss ways in which these issues could be addressed in this program. By the end of the initial presentation of the program, both consultants and mainstream teachers adopt the philosophy of the program, identify activities that could be conducted to implement the program, and identify procedures that could be used to help meet concerns raised regarding program implementation.

Table 13–2
Consultant Activities

Adapted from "Meeting the needs of special high school students in regular education classrooms," by K. C. Harris, P. Harvey, L. Garcia, D. Innes, P. Lynn, D. Munoz, K. Sexton, and R. Stoica, 1987, *Teacher Education and Special Education,* 10(4): 143–152. Reprinted by permission.

Consultant Activities
Student Support in Mainstream Classrooms
Clarifying directions and instructions of teachers
Helping students take class notes
Counseling students
Student Support Outside Mainstream Classrooms
Counseling students
Note-taking/Study-skills sessions
Helping students study for tests
Reading tests to students
Coordinating home and school activities
Teacher Support in Mainstream Classrooms
Team teaching
Developing and implementing behavior management strategies
Teaching small groups of students
Teaching individual students
Establishing cooperative learning groups
Teacher Support Through Collaborative Planning
Collecting and summarizing student background information
Analyzing student behavior
Discussing consultant and teacher roles
Analyzing teaching
Evaluating lessons
Modifying curriculum
Developing and supplying materials

Program Scheduling. This program is a schoolwide effort. Therefore, scheduling for program implementation must reflect how each student in the program will be served by all staff members. The criteria used to develop a preliminary schedule include the following: in-class support for those mainstream teachers who have the largest concentration of LEP learning disabled students, the allocation of most of the consultants' time in the mainstream classrooms, and the allocation of some time for collaborative planning with mainstream teachers as well as among the consultants. Because this is a schoolwide program and consultants share responsibility for students, it is important that consultants have time to discuss among themselves the performance of individual students as well as their ongoing evaluation of program implementation.

During the initial implementation of the program, the consultants spend time observing and helping the mainstream teachers. This is done so that the role each consultant takes in each mainstream classroom could be identified. After implementing the preliminary schedule for a few weeks, the schedule can be modified based on the identified needs of the mainstream teachers and the students. For example, some mainstream teachers may want more in-class assistance from the consultants than they are receiving. Therefore, time spent in some mainstream classrooms may be increased even though there is not a high percentage of LEP learning disabled students in those classrooms. Examples of schedules can be found in Tables 13–3, 13–4, and 13–5.

Table 13–3
Sample Student's Schedule

C = Consultant
P = Paraprofessional
BL = Bilingual

Adapted from "Meeting the needs of special high school students in regular education classrooms," by K. C. Harris, P. Harvey, L. Garcia, D. Innes, P. Lynn, D. Munoz, K. Sexton, and R. Stoica, 1987, *Teacher Education and Special Education,* 10(4): 143–152. Reprinted by permission.

Course	Monday	Tuesday	Wednesday	Thursday	Friday
Applied Math—BL	C1		C1		
Int. Bio. Sci.—BL	P1	P1	P1		C3
ESL	C2		C2		
Reading		C1		C1	
World Civ.—BL			C4		C4
Phys. Ed.					

Table 13–4
Sample Paraprofessional's Schedule

BL = Bilingual

Adapted from "Meeting the needs of special high school students in regular education classrooms," by K. C. Harris, P. Harvey, L. Garcia, D. Innes, P. Lynn, D. Munoz, K. Sexton, and R. Stoica, 1987, *Teacher Education and Special Education,* 10(4): 143–152. Reprinted by permission.

Period	Monday	Tuesday	Wednesday	Thursday	Friday
2	Int. to Bio. Sci.	Int. to Bio. Sci.	Int. to Bio. Sci.	ESL	ESL
3	Resource room	Resource room	Resource room	Resource room	Resource room
4	ESL	Clerical	ESL	Clerical	Clerical
5	Clerical	Clerical	Clerical	Applied Math—BL	Clerical
6	Clerical	Applied Math—BL	Clerical	Applied Math—BL	Clerical

Table 13–3 provides a sample student's schedule for a week. This LEP learning disabled student is in mainstream classes for all six periods of the school day. The student receives support from either consultants or paraprofessionals in the mainstream class every day of the week and in five out of six classes. As can be seen in this table, the student receives direct service from four of the six consultants during the course of a week. The student receives the most direct service in those classes that are most difficult (e.g., introduction to biological sciences).

Table 13–4 provides a sample paraprofessional's schedule for a week. This paraprofessional arrives in time for the second period of the school day. Most of the paraprofessional's time is spent in the mainstream classroom (40% of the week) or performing clerical activities (40% of the week). For only 20% of the time

Table 13–5
Sample Consultant's Schedule

CP = Collaborative planning
BL = Bilingual

Adapted from "Meeting the needs of special high school students in regular education classrooms," by K. C. Harris, P. Harvey, L. Garcia, D. Innes, P. Lynn, D. Munoz, K. Sexton, and R. Stoica, 1987, *Teacher Education and Special Education,* 10(4): 143–152. Reprinted by permission.

Period	Monday	Tuesday	Wednesday	Thursday	Friday
1	IEP	CP with teachers	World Civ.—BL	CP with consultants	World Civ.—BL
2	IEP	CP with teachers	Reading	CP with consultants	Reading
3	Resource room	Reading	Resource room	Reading	Resource room
4	Applied Math—BL	Applied Math—BL	CP with teachers	Applied Math—BL	CP with teachers
5	Applied Math—BL	Resource room	CP with teachers	Resource room	CP with teachers
6	Applied Math—BL	Reading	Applied Math—BL	Reading	Applied Math—BL

does the paraprofessional provide support to LEP learning disabled students outside the mainstream classroom (i.e., resource room).

Table 13–5 provides a sample consultant's schedule for a week. As can be seen by this schedule, half of the consultant's time is spent in the mainstream classroom working with all students needing assistance (including LEP learning disabled students). The consultant spends about 27% of the time in collaborative planning and 17% providing services to LEP learning disabled students outside the mainstream classroom. Only 6% of the consultant's time is necessary for the referral/classification process (i.e., reserved for IEP meetings).

Program Evaluation. The consultants design the program evaluation to measure the impact upon the mediators (the mainstream teachers) as well as the targets (LEP learning disabled students). This can be done in a number of different ways. In the study conducted by Harris et al. (1987), the consultants administered questionnaires to mainstream teachers and students and also evaluated grades collected from student files. The student questionnaires included the following topics: students' preference for mainstream classrooms, students' comfort with consultants in the mainstream classroom, students' satisfaction with program, and students' perception of academic and behavioral performance. The teacher questionnaires included the following topics: teachers' comfort with consultants in the mainstream classroom, teachers' satisfaction with the program, and teachers' perceptions of students' academic and behavioral performance. The results of the Harris et al. study (1987), which was an evaluation of a similar program to that described here, was overwhelmingly positive. The students reported that they liked school, they felt as if they were achieving in school, they liked being in mainstream classrooms, and they liked working with consultants in the mainstream classrooms. The mainstream teachers felt comfortable with the consultants in their classrooms. They reported that the consultants were encouraged to work with all students in the class and to use their own discretion when working collaboratively in the mainstream classroom. In addition, all mainstream teachers felt that collaborative planning with consultants was helpful.

The consultation program described here incorporates several elements discussed in this chapter. Consultants provide teachers and students with direct as well as indirect services. In addition, this program incorporates components of collaborative consultation as described by Idol-Maestas, Nevin, and Paolucci-Whitcomb (1984). That is, the consultants work with the mainstream teachers in clarifying activities that are conducted to implement the program, thereby achieving team ownership. The individual differences of teachers and students are accommodated in the program scheduling and variety of services offered within and outside the mainstream classroom. Finally, the consultants evaluate the program through the following activities: formative evaluation through ongoing weekly discussion of student progress as well as teacher and consultant behavior during consultant collaborative planning sessions, and summative evaluation through inspection of student grades and administration of teacher and student questionnaires.

Summary

This chapter presented educational consultation as a service delivery approach for LEP exceptional students. With the need to provide effective programs for LEP exceptional students within the least restrictive environment, educational consultation becomes viable as a service delivery option for these students.

Educational consultation is essentially a collaborative, voluntary, mutual problem-solving process that leads to the prevention or resolution of educational problems. The skilled educational consultant capitalizes on the knowledge and experiences of those with whom the consultant works, ensuring that the educational program that is implemented is jointly designed and has the widest possible support.

The educational consultant assumes three overlapping roles: providing technical assistance, coordinating services, and communicating effectively. Through these roles, the consultant may provide direct and indirect services to students, teachers, and administrators. Additionally, the educational consultant must possess the knowledge of appropriate curriculum and instructional strategies that extends their role considerably with all providers of educational services for LEP exceptional students.

In this chapter, a model of educational consultation and an application of this model for LEP exceptional students was presented. The components of this model included principles of collaborative consultation (team ownership, recognition of individual differences, and data-based evaluation), as well as a description of ways in which educational consultants can be involved in providing direct and indirect services. This model was offered as an example. It was not meant to be inclusive of all possible models of educational consultation. Rather, it was provided to assist the reader in conceptualizing a consultation approach for LEP exceptional students. The reader is encouraged to think about different ways in which educational consultation can best meet the needs of LEP exceptional students and develop approaches to meet specific needs. Indeed, one of the key components of collaborative consultation is the ability to recognize and accommodate individual differences.

Discussion Questions

1. How is the consultation process defined?
2. What are the pros and cons of providing indirect services to LEP exceptional students?

3. What skills must the educational consultant possess to work effectively with personnel who provide services to LEP exceptional students?

4. Why is it important for the consultant to establish a role in the consultation process before service is delivered?

5. Discuss how the educational consultant might enhance the cooperation between bilingual educators, special educators, and regular educators to provide educational services to LEP exceptional students in mainstream classrooms.

6. Describe a process for evaluating a program for LEP exceptional students. What components of effective program evaluation have been incorporated into the evaluation plan?

7. Describe a model for educational consultation that would be effective for LEP exceptional students. What are the characteristics of this model that make it particularly appropriate for LEP exceptional students?

References

Adelman, H. S. (1972). The resource concept—Bigger than a room. *Journal of Special Education*. 6:361–367.

Alpert, J. L. (1977). Some guidelines for school consultants. *Journal of School Psychology*. 15(4):308–319.

Bandura, A. (1971). *Social learning theory*. New York: General Learning Press.

Bauer, H. (1975). The resource teacher—A teacher consultant. *Academic Therapy*. 10:299–304.

Benavides, A. (1985). Planning effective special education for exceptional language minorities. *Teaching Exceptional Children*. 17(2):127–132.

Bergan, J. R. (1977). *Behavioral consultation*. Columbus, OH: Merrill Publishing Co.

Bergan, J. R., & Tombari, M. L. (1976). Consultant skill and efficiency and the implementation and outcomes of consultation. *Journal of School Psychology*. 14(1):3–14.

Brophy, J. E., & Good, T. L. (1974). *Teacher-student relationships: Causes and consequences*. New York: Holt, Rinehart & Winston.

Brown, D., Reschly, D., & Wasserman, H. (1974). Effects of surreptitious modeling upon classroom behaviors. *Psychology in the Schools*. 11(3):366–369.

Brown, D., Wyne, M. D., Blackburn, J. E., & Powell, W. C. (1979). *Consultation: Strategy for improving education*. Boston: Allyn & Bacon.

Brown, V. L. (1977). "Yes, but . . ." A reply to Phyllis Newcomer. *Journal of Special Education*. 11(2):171–177.

Cooper, J. O., Heron, T. E., & Heward, W. L. (1987). *Applied behavior analysis*. Columbus, OH: Merrill Publishing Co.

Davis, W. E. (1983). *The special educator: Strategies for succeeding in today's schools*. Austin, TX: Pro-Ed.

Evans, S. B. (1980). The consulting role of the resource teacher. *Exceptional Children*. 46:402–404.

Friend, M. (1984). Consulting skills for resource teachers. *Learning Disability Quarterly*. 7:246–250.

Friend, M. (1985). Training special educators to be consultants. *Teacher Education and Special Education*. 8(3):115–120.

Gersten, R., & Hauser, C. (1984). The case for impact evaluations in special education. *Remedial and Special Education*. 5(2):16–24.

Goldstein, A. P., & Sorcher, M. (1974). *Changing supervisor behavior*. New York: Pergamon.

Haight, S. L., & Molitor, D. I. (1983). A survey of special education teacher consultants. *Exceptional Children*. 49:550–553.

Harris, K. C., Harvey, P., Garcia, L., Innes, D., Lynn, P., Munoz, D., Sexton, K., & Stoica, R. (1987). Meeting the needs of special education high school students in regular education classrooms. *Teacher Education and Special Education*. 10(4):143–152.

Hawisher, M. F., & Calhoun, M. L. (1978). *The resource room: An educational asset for children with special needs*. Columbus, OH: Merrill Publishing Co.

Heath, R. W., & Nielson, M. A. (1974). The research basis for performance-based teacher education. *Review of Educational Research*. 44:463–484.

Heron, T. E., & Harris, K. C. (1987). *The educational consultant: Helping professionals, parents, and mainstreamed students.* 2nd ed. Austin, TX: Pro-Ed.

Hughes, J. A. (1980). A case study in behavioral consultation: Organizational factors. *School Psychology Review.* 9(1):103–107.

Idol, L., Paolucci-Whitcomb, P., & Nevin, A. (1986). *Collaborative consultation.* Rockville, MD: Aspen.

Idol-Maestas, L., Nevin, A., & Paolucci-Whitcomb, P. (1984). *Facilitator's manual for collaborative consultation: Principles and techniques.* Reston, VA: National RETOOL Center, Teacher Education Division, Council for Exceptional Children.

Joyce, B., & Showers, B. (1980). Improving inservice training: The message of research. *Educational Leadership.* 3(5):379–385.

Kerr, M. M., & Nelson, C. M. (1983). *Strategies for managing behavior problems in the classroom.* Columbus, OH: Merrill Publlishing Co.

Knowlton, H. E. (1983). A strategy for rational and responsive program evaluation. *Teacher Education and Special Education.* 6(2):106–111.

Langdon, H. W. (1983). Assessment and intervention strategies for the bilingual language-disordered student. *Exceptional Children.* 50(1):37–46.

Laurie, T. E., Buchwach, L., Silverman, R., & Zigmond, N. (1978). Teaching secondary learning disabled students in the mainstream. *Learning Disability Quarterly.* 1:62–72.

Lilly, M. S., & Givens-Ogle, L. B. (1981). Teacher consultation: Present, past, and future. *Behavioral Disorders.* 6:73–77.

Lilly, S. M. (1971). A training based model for special education. *Exceptional Children.* 37:745–749.

Maher, C. A. (1983). Goal attainment scaling: A method for evaluating special education services. *Exceptional Children.* 4:529–536.

Maher, C. A., & Bennett, R. E. (1984). *Planning and evaluating special education services.* Englewood Cliffs, NJ: Prentice-Hall.

Martinez, O. (1982). Developing a plan for coordinating bilingual and special education services: San Jose Unified School District Plan. *Proceedings of the Conference on Special Education and the Bilingual Child.* (pp. 106–111). San Diego: National Origin Desegregation Lau Center, San Diego State University.

McKenzie, H. S., Egner, A. N., Knight, M. F., Perelman, P. F., Schneider, B. M., & Garvin, J. S. (1970). Training consulting teachers to assist elementary teachers in the management and education of handicapped children. *Exceptional Children.* 37:137–143.

Medina, V. (1982). Issues regarding the use of interpreters and translators in a school setting. *Proceedings of the Conference on Special Education and the Bilingual Child* (pp. 31–37). San Deigo: National Origin Desegregation Lau Center, San Diego State University.

Miller, T. L., & Sabatino, D. A. (1978). An evaluation of the teacher consultant model as an approach to mainstreaming. *Exceptional Children.* 45:86–91.

Newcomer, P. L. (1977). Special education services for the "mildly handicapped": Beyond a diagnostic and remedial model. *Journal of Special Education.* 11(2):153–165.

Oldridge, O. A. (1977). Future directions for special education: Beyond a diagnostic and remedial model. *Journal of Special Education.* 11(2):167–169.

Parsons, R. D., & Meyers, J. (1984). *Developing consultation skills.* San Francisco: Jossey-Bass.

Powell, T. H. (1982). Mainstreaming: A case for the consulting teacher. *Journal for Special Educators.* 17:183–188.

Robinson, V. M., Cameron, M. M., & Raethel, A. M. (1985). Negotiation of a consultative role for school psychologists: A case study. *Journal of School Psychology.* 23:43–49.

Shaw, S. F., & Shaw, W. K. (1972). The in-service experience plan, or changing the bath without losing the baby. *Journal of Special Education.* 6(2): 121–126.

Skinner, M. E. (1979). *Effects of an in-service program on the attitudes, knowledge, and student-teacher interaction patterns of regular classroom teachers.* Unpublished master's thesis. Ohio State University, Columbus, OH.

Speece, D. L., & Mandell, C. J. (1980). Interpersonal communication between resource and regular teachers. *Teacher Education and Special Education.* 3(4):55–60.

Spodek, B. (1982). What special educators need to know about regular classrooms. *Educational Forum.* 46:295–307.

Tawney, J. W., & Gast, D. L. (1984). *Single subject research in special education.* Columbus, OH: Merrill Publishing Co.

Tharp, R. G., & Wetzel, R. J. (1969). *Behavior modification in the natural environment.* New York: Academic Press.

Turnbull, A. P., Strickland, B. B., & Brantley, J. C. (1982). *Developing and implementing individualized education programs.* 2d ed. Columbus, OH: Merrill Publishing Co.

Van Houten, R. (1980). *Learning through feedback.* New York: Human Sciences Press.

Weiss, A. B., Cooke, N. L., Grossman, M. A., Ryno-Vrabel, M., Hassett, M. E., Heward, W. L., & Heron, T. E. (1982). *Home-school communication.* Columbus, OH: Special Press.

CHAPTER FOURTEEN

Parent and Community Involvement in Bilingual Special Education

Objectives

- To understand the need for parent and community involvement in Bilingual Special Education
- To describe the parent-school relationship
- To explain how present-day parent education programs were affected by historical factors
- To examine the relationship between attitudes of parents and the handicap of their children
- To describe the ATSEM model for bilingual parent involvement
- To describe suggestions for enhancing bilingual parent involvement in a school setting

The Need for Parent Involvement

The importance of parents and communities cannot be overemphasized. Indeed, society could not survive if some people decided not to care for their children. Infants cannot survive without being cared for by someone who provides for their basic needs.

The manner in which infants are cared for and reared varies across all ethnic and cultural groups. The child, the parent, and the community work together in the child-rearing process such that each child's experience is unique. The crucial bond between child and parent significantly emphasizes the role of the parent.

Though parents must play many roles within their own cultural group, in child rearing there are some responsibilities that are consistent across all cultural groups. For example, every child must be fed, clothed, kept warm and comfortable, touched, and involved in some type of communication to develop physically, emotionally, cognitively, and socially.

The rearing of children requires considerable nurturance. Many assume that parenthood is a natural condition, that a new parent automatically becomes a nurturing mother or father. As a result, society has not demanded that parents have the necessary skills and competencies that would ensure adequate child rearing. Parenting skills should be based on some basic understanding of child development, within its cultural context.

Many factors are involved in becoming a nurturing parent, such as the bonding between parents and the child, previous learning experiences, and community conditions that foster a positive parent-child relationship. Some parents have not experienced a positive role model, so that the rearing of children is difficult, especially if the child is exceptional. Parents such as these need assistance as well as their own support system. When a child is born, the need for parenting skills has just begun.

Throughout childhood, a child is involved with many significant adults, from parents, teachers, paraprofessionals, doctors, nurses, and social workers to administrators, psychologists, and counselors. They are involved with the child and family and can assist in the child's development.

For the linguistically and culturally diverse population, it is almost impossible to develop a school curriculum that is continuous for all children. It is, however, possible to work toward enhancing support systems that affect the child's continuous development. The family and the home are the first and the primary support system for the child. Secondary support systems include the schools, community centers, local businesses, recreation centers, clubs, and churches. They could join forces in an effort to provide for a nurturing environment.

This is, unfortunately, more difficult to accomplish. When children come to school they exhibit a unique set of behaviors, mannerisms, and characteristics. For example, they may be sad, happy, depressed, dependent, independent, outgoing, or timid. When they get to school they find a wide variety of teachers, from creative, open, and stimulating ones to structured, closed, and authoritarian ones.

Families, on the other hand, are just as varied, from disorganized, unstable, restrictive families to organized, stable, extended, enriching, or bilingual ones. All of these variables need to fit into the sequence of development. The schools aim not for perfection but for flexibility within a cultural context. This is a tremendous challenge to schools, families, and communities and one toward which all must work.

Rights and Services Available to Parents of Bilingual Exceptional Children

Many parents are unaware of the rights and services available to them as parents of bilingual exceptional children. It is the responsibility of teachers and other school personnel to share these rights and services with them. One of the primary needs of parents of bilingual exceptional children has been the need for information (Marion, 1979; Dillard, Kinnison, & Peel, 1980). Some educators have assumed that this need of bilingual parents has been met through involvement with the schools. Parents and bilingual exceptional children will need to have the basic tenets of P.L. 94–142 explained to them. Others may have little knowledge of their rights and responsibilities under the law. Another group of parents may not have even heard of P.L. 94–142.

According to Haring and McCormick, (1986), educators working with these parents should be aware that the law requires each state to:

1. Make available a free, appropriate public education to all handicapped children between the ages of 3 and 21.
2. Locate and identify all children who have handicaps, evaluate their educational needs, and determine whether those needs are being met.
3. Develop an individualized education plan (IEP) for every handicapped child in the state.
4. Submit to the federal government a state plan for the education of handicapped children and revise the state plan yearly.
5. Describe the means by which handicapped children will be identified and referred for diagnosis.
6. Avoid using racially or culturally discriminatory testing and evaluation procedures in placing handicapped children; administer tests in the child's native language.
7. Protect the rights of handicapped children and their parents by ensuring due process, confidentiality of records, and parental involvement in educational planning and placement decisions.
8. Provide a comprehensive system for personnel development, including inservice training programs for regular education teachers, special education teachers, school administrators, and other support personnel.
9. Educate handicapped and nonhandicapped children together to the maximum extent appropriate. Handicapped children will be placed in special classes or separate schools only when education cannot be achieved satisfactorily in regular classes, even with special aids and services.

Other requirements provide for a private school program at no cost for handicapped children when an appropriate education cannot be provided in the public schools. In the law first priority is given to handicapped children who are not receiving any education and second priority is given to the most severely disabled children who are receiving only minimal education.

One important requirement is stated frequently to parents but is not always explained. The requirement of right to due process has become so widely used by educators that they assume all parents are familiar with its meaning. Parents have the right to be notified of any decision affecting their child's educational placement.

Federal Law and Parent Involvement

According to P.L. 94–142 parents have many rights that protect them and their children with respect to special education. This is evident in Figure 8–1, which shows that parents of bilingual exceptional children are included at every step of the assessment process.

From the very beginning, parents have a right to be informed of concerns about their child before any evaluation or special education placement. When the parents agree to allow the school to evaluate their child, they have a right to be informed of what tests will be given and must give written consent for the evaluation.

When the evaluation has been completed, parents must give written consent for their child to be placed in a special education program. The individualized education plan is written with the participation of the parents, and an interpreter must be included at all stages if the parents speak a language other than English.

However, it appears that parent involvement in the special education program placement meeting is minimal and is not encouraged (Ysseldyke, Algozzine, & Mitchell, 1982). In addition, parents for the most part were unable to understand much of what was being discussed.

Parent involvement can be increased at special education meetings and IEP conferences. One strategy that has proven successful is the presence of a parent advocate at all meetings. This appears to be particularly successful with bilingual parents.

Another strategy that appears helpful is the use of encouragement and positive feedback whenever parents do participate.

Feelings and Attitudes of Parents of Bilingual Exceptional Children

Parents react differently and sometimes unpredictably to the birth or the diagnosis of a child with an exceptionality. Reactions are a result of feelings. Parents may experience anger, resentment, fear, guilt, or despair because their child is exceptional. In addition, for the parent of a bilingual exceptional child, these feelings occur within a socioeconomic, linguistic, and cultural context. For example, one young Vietnamese mother explained her child's mental retardation as a punishment to her because she had dishonored her family by marrying against her father's wishes.

To work effectively with parents of bilingual exceptional children, the educator must be able to recognize these feelings and be willing to accept them, given their socioeconomic and cultural context. It is usually easier for the educator to view the exceptional child objectively than it is for the parents. The educator deals with the child on a day-to-day basis, whereas the parents deal with the child at least 75% of the school day.

Parents of severely disabled children may be faced with a lifetime of care. It is not recognized that there is a need to offer parents relief from the constant care that is often required. Foster parents, substitute grandparents, and knowledgeable volunteers are becoming more available to assist parents (Chinn, Winn, & Walters, 1978).

Considerable evidence shows that the attitudes of parents do have a significant impact on their children. Although the development of a child's self-concept can be described as a series of stages possibly related to cognitive maturity, it is likely that one's self-perception is the result of modeling. If so, a positive self-concept will be developed through behaviors that have been reinforced by parents and significant others during the child's development (Dillard, Kinnison, & Peel, 1980).

Characteristics that were punished or not reinforced will lead to the development of a negative self-concept. Ausubel (1974) found that children's self-concepts develop according to the pattern of parental rewards and punishments. When objective success is stressed rather than the child's physical, social, and emotional needs, the child's self-concept is affected.

The literature on attitudes of parents of exceptional children also indicates that these attitudes have significant effects. Eyman, Dingman, and Sabagh (1966) showed that parents' attitudes, along with education and socioeconomic status, were positively related to how quickly their child was institutionalized. These factors were more significant than the nature of the child's handicap.

Children of deaf parents appear to do quite well in a residential placement, whereas deaf children of hearing parents do not (Schlesinger & Meadow, 1972). The reason is not clear. Perhaps hearing parents place a deaf child in an institution out of frustration, while deaf parents do so in support of a deaf subculture. If this is true, it might be because deaf children have had better social interaction with deaf parents than hearing parents with their deaf children.

Dingman, Eyman, and Windle (1963) found that mothers of mildly handicapped children had more protective child-rearing attitudes than parents of severely handicapped children. Another study (Klausner, 1961) revealed differences between parents of noninstitutionalized and institutionalized handicapped children. Parents of noninstitutionalized children were described as domineering and used more restrictive child-rearing practices.

Worchel and Worchel (1961) demonstrated that some parents were rejecting of their handicapped children. This study compared the attitudes of parents toward both handicapped and nonhandicapped children. The findings suggested that parents project more negative attitudes toward their handicapped children than toward their nonhandicapped children.

Although examining parental attitudes is valuable, it may also be to valuable to examine the conditions under which parental attitudes vary. Barber (1963) found that attitudes of parents of handicapped children were not significantly affected by the sex of the handicapped child. There were, however, effects related to the intellectual capacity of the child and the socioeconomic status of the family.

Parents from lower socioeconomic classes were described as having child-rearing attitudes associated with defensiveness, aggressiveness, dominance, authoritarianism, and rejection of their children. These parents had similar attitudes toward normal children. The difference appeared to be one of degree. These attitudes appeared more pronounced with a handicapped child. It appears that the basic attitudes these parents have intensify following the birth of a handicapped child.

Takeguchi (1967) also reported on a study examining socioeconomic status and parental attitudes. He found that parents of educable and trainable retarded children had similar conceptions of "mental retardation," "educable mentally retarded," and "my own child," regardless of social class. However, the term "trainable mentally retarded" was found to be related to socioeconomic status. Low socioeconomic status parents perceived this term significantly lower than parents of higher socioeconomic status.

Religion is another variable related to parental attitude. Zuk et al. (1961) reported on the relationship between religious belief and maternal acceptance of handicapped children. The results indicated a low but positive correlation between the two variables. Mothers who rated themselves higher with respect to religious practice frequently expressed attitudes that were more accepting of handicapped children.

It appeared to the investigators that Catholics were the most intensely religious parents when compared to other religious groups. This finding appeared related to their failure to associate blame with the birth of a handicapped child. Thus the parents can more easily accept a handicapped child.

Hoffman (1965) made similar findings. He also reported that Catholic families tended to be more accepting of the handicapped child. However, his explanation was not related to guilt but to suffering. He suggested that the Catholics' belief in suffering as a part of life made the acceptance of a handicapped child more bearable.

Christian Scientists, on the other hand, tended to deny the diagnosis while fundamental Protestants were characterized by guilt.

While socioeconomic status and religious belief appear to be important factors in the attitudes of parents of exceptional children, the nature of this relationship is not clear. One major hindrance is just how socioeconomic status and religious belief are defined. Another question is whether attitude differences are a result of guilt or of religious belief. A final question is whether the socioeconomic differences found were the result of the stress of low socioeconomic environments or of socioeconomic status itself.

Suggestions for Bilingual Parents

A parent of a bilingual exceptional child is the primary helper, observer, record keeper, and decision maker for the child and should be treated as such. It is the parent's right to understand the child's diagnosis and the specific reasons for the treatment recommended with respect to the child's educational placement. Changes in the treatment of the child or educational placement cannot take place without the approval of the parent (Haring & McCormick, 1986).

Becoming as well informed as possible so that the child's progress can be checked depends on the parent's ability to work with the school staff involved with the child. Some resistance to being included in the diagnostic or decisionmaking processes may be encountered. The way a bilingual parent handles that resistance is important. It is always helpful to remember that parents know their child better than anyone else and should be crucial members of the diagnostic team.

The following are other suggestions that might be helpful for parents when involved with school staff. For example, it might be helpful for the parent to find a friend who can assist with the various diagnostic visits and results—someone who speaks the language of the parent, has rapport with the parent, and understands the parent's role as the principal monitor of the child's progress throughout life.

A bilingual parent should be encouraged to keep anecdotal records. When the parent becomes aware that the child has a problem, a notebook should be started, which includes names, addresses, phone numbers, dates of visits, the persons present during the visits, and notes on what was said.

Records of questions asked and answers should be kept, as well as any recommendations. Records of phone calls, including the dates, the purpose, and the result, may prove helpful. Though not essential, it is useful to make important requests by letter and to retain copies. Such documentation by the parents may be critical in obtaining the services their child needs. It might also assist the program director in making a decision with respect to educational programming for the child.

Without accurate records of the person spoken to, when the contact was made, what was discussed, and how much time elapsed between the request and the response, the parent will be at a disadvantage. No one can be held accountable for conversations or meetings with persons whose names and titles a bilingual parent does not remember, for dates forgotten, for topics not clearly remembered.

Understanding the terms used by bilingual special education services staff is crucial. Staff members routinely should translate terms into more understandable language. The staff members could also be asked to give examples of what they mean. Bilingual parents should not leave the office of the staff member until they are sure they understand what was said and can explain it to someone else. (Dillard, Kinnison, & Peel, 1980).

Bilingual parents should ask for all copies of their bilingual exceptional child's records. They should learn as much as they can through books and articles about the exceptionality and examine school files, in their native language, whenever possible.

Bilingual parents would also benefit from talking frequently and frankly with as many professionals as they can find. Talking with other parents would be helpful, as would joining a parent organization. By talking with other parents with similar experiences, bilingual parents might gain a perspective on their child's exceptionality. An added benefit might be the moral support they receive by knowing other parents have similar experiences.

Bilingual parents might also get information from parent organizations about available services for their child. They should keep in mind that a particular program might not help their child even though it helped someone else's child. A visit to the program would also be valuable for the bilingual parent.

Bilingual parents should stay in contact with the classroom teacher. They should be aware of what is being done in the classroom so that they can reinforce these activities at home. They might share what they have read with the teacher. They might also ask for directions, ideas, advice, and suggestions. Together the parent and the teacher are a team, working for the benefit of the child. The goal should always include the child.

Bilingual parents would benefit from listening to their children. Only children can give their own point of view. Children should know that being different is okay, and they will learn most from the example of their parents. Bilingual parents might help their children to think of problems as situations that can be solved if people work on them together and with some direction.

Involving Bilingual Parents of Exceptional Children

Parental involvement in special education programs for exceptional children has long been an important aspect of a quality program for these children. Unfortunately, not all efforts have been successful. Attitudes of professional personnel and lack of skills in working with parents are related to this lack of success. These two factors are so closely connected that it is almost impossible to determine what causes what. For example, a parent might view a teacher as an "expert," thereby creating distance and possibly apprehension on the parent's part.

A programmatic effort involving family members of exceptional children has enabled some investigators to prescribe a set of assumptions leading to the development of a model for family involvement in an education program

(Karnes, Hodgins, & Teska, 1969; Karnes, Zehrback, & Teska, 1971). According to these assumptions, family members:

1. Are concerned about the development of their child
2. Can develop human relations skills
3. Are willing to devote time for interaction with their child
4. Will participate if their objectives are consistent with those of the school
5. Will participate if they are involved in the decision-making process
6. Will participate when instruction is individualized and conducted by competent personnel
7. Are willing to apply new ideas and techniques to other family members
8. Will develop more positive attitudes when the involvement is successful
9. Will need less assistance from supportive staff as they become more knowledgeable and skillful

The ATSEM Model

From these assumptions, the ATSEM model (see Figure 14–1) was developed (Karnes, Hodgins, & Teska, 1969; Karnes, Zehrbach, & Teska, 1971). A new model based on the ATSEM model was developed that might be more applicable for bilingual families of exceptional children.

This model is designed to be flexible because the needs of bilingual family members vary on a multitude of unique problems. The ATSEM model derives its label from the initials that stand for the five main areas: *acquaint, teach, support, expand,* and *maintain.*

The acquaint phase is a process of involving the bilingual family member in activities that enhance the development of the child, both at home and at school. For example, involving bilingual parents as parent/community aides might have an impact both on the children and on the school.

The teach phase is also a process. During this phase, bilingual family members learn a set of procedures and techniques that help them teach the child new skills and behaviors. These skills would be developed by providing the bilingual family members with individualized instruction designed to teach the parents how to teach their child.

The third phase of the model, the support phase, is a time during which the bilingual family member needs emotional, social, or economic support. This support may help the bilingual parent learn how to obtain services from the Division of Services for Crippled Children, to complete high school via a general education development test (GED), to seek additional help from Aid to Dependent Children (ADC), or to seek help from a mental health facility. This phase ends when the bilingual family members indicate that they no longer need additional supportive help.

The bilingual parents enter the expand stage when they feel emotionally, physically, and socially comfortable and are able to expand their relationship with the child. For example, a bilingual parent coming to the child's classroom for the first time to tell a story from Choctaw folklore, without fearing that the child will be upset or otherwise embarrassed by the family member's presence, may indicate such growth.

The maintain phase of the model has many components. Some bilingual parents in this phase might require continued reassurance to maintain this level of functioning. The maintain phase can be used to help bilingual parents acquaint other bilingual parents with the program. Vietnamese parents, for example, bring other Vietnamese parents to the school to introduce them to the bilingual program, to view school projects and activities, and to see what effect the school has had on their children.

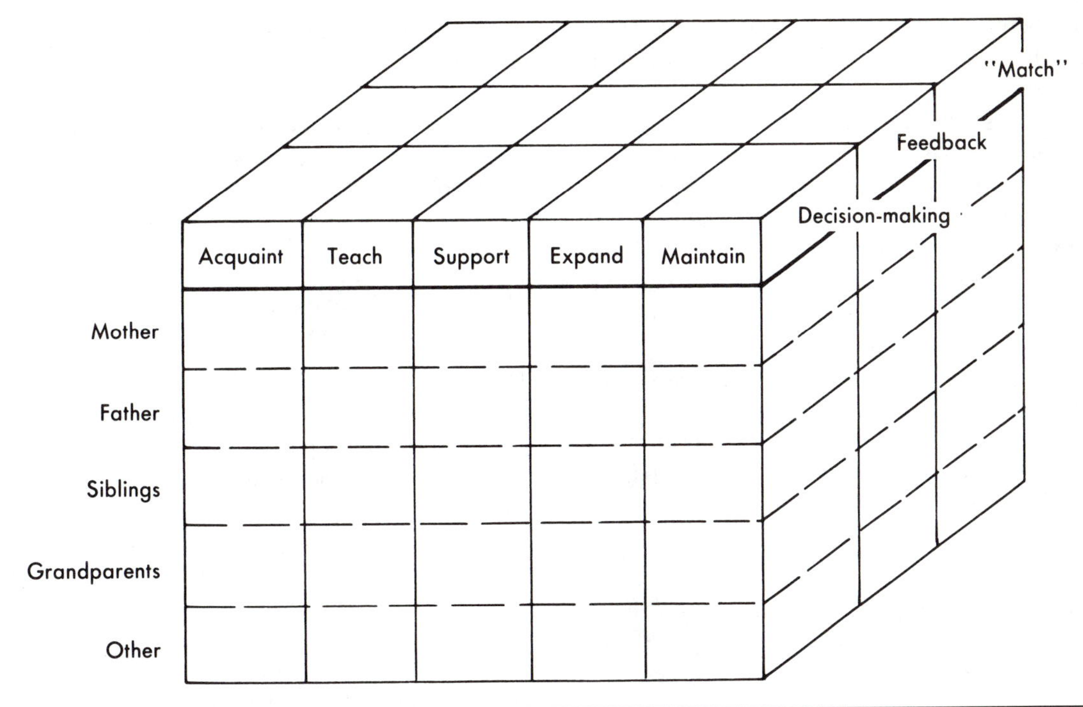

Figure 14–1
The ATSEM model for parent involvement

Adapted from "Investigations of Classroom and At Home Interventions." vol. 1, *Research and Development Program on Preschool Disadvantaged Children, Final Report,* by M.G. Karnes, A.S. Hodgins, and J.A. Teska, 1969, Bethesda, MD: ERIC Document Reproduction Service [ED0366630].

Overall, the ATSEM model is a process-oriented model that focuses on bringing bilingual family members into contact with a program and then involving them actively in the program. The program appears to function best when all family members are involved. In addition, there is evidence that older siblings can assist in the development of younger exceptional children (Karnes, Zehrbach, & Teska, 1971).

Suggested Activities for Developing Bilingual Parent Involvement

Anderson and Safar (1967) suggest that parent involvement in school activities is determined by the following factors:

1. The extent of participation allowed by the school decision-making unit
2. The leadership of the school-community
3. The skills and knowledge of the parents about the school curriculum
4. The degree and quality of parent participation
5. The influence of the parent group on the administration of the school

To initiate and maintain parental support, it is important that bilingual exceptional parents feel a bond with the school and a significant feeling of comfortableness within the school setting. More frequently, these parents have a feeling of uncomfortableness within the school setting. School staff members enhance these feelings of not belonging by excluding parents from various school activities because they have minimal education.

Parents, are, however, a wealth of resources and with some assistance could be actively used within the classroom. Their experiences in such areas as school, vocations, peers, language and linguistic differences, and cultural and socioeconomic differences could richly enhance the children's awareness of the community and the uniqueness of each individual.

There are, however, some things school staffs can do to foster parent involvement. Nelson and Bloom (1973) suggest some parent involvement activities that might enhance parent participation:

1. Study groups that focus on the child, including topics such as child development, child-rearing practices, and other childhood concerns
2. Task groups formed to develop school-community activities
3. Advisory groups organized to assist the school in providing educational services to limited English-proficient students
4. Informal home gatherings designed out of mutual concern such as grades, academic achievement, or other school-community issues
5. Classroom resources for topics, experiences, or training that might be relevant to the curriculum
6. School-community paraprofessionals assisting classroom teachers, nurses, administrators, or community agency staffs
7. Tutors for students in academic subject areas
8. Curriculum developers for materials that reflect and promote the diversity of school-community cultures

For bilingual parents to be successfully involved in these suggested activities, school staffs must sincerely believe that such efforts are necessary, valuable, and in the best interest of the school. A school's efforts at parent involvement cannot be successful if a majority of its staff is not convinced it has merit and does not actively participate.

Other services such as child care, transportation, interpreters, newsletters, and coffee times might be considered to promote bilingual parent involvement.

Generating Bilingual Parent Support

If bilingual parents are provided with positive information about their child's learning, they are more likely to participate in school-related activities. Thus it becomes important for educators to develop ideas, strategies, and procedures for establishing communication and trust with bilingual parents of exceptional children (Dillard, Kinnison, & Peel, 1980).

One of the most important ways to establish this communication and trust is through the involvement of the bilingual parent in every aspect of the exceptional child's education. The dialogue established between the parent and teacher may be the single most important thing accomplished. How well the classroom teacher and other support staff within the school can accomplish this will determine how much support will be obtained in the future.

A reasonable management plan should be part of the assessment outcome. The bilingual parents should receive suggestions, directions, and techniques in how to live with their handicapped child on a day-to-day basis, considering the needs of the child, the capacities of the family, and the resources of the community. Here again, how well this plan is developed and presented to bilingual parents will affect their continued participation at the school.

Information about bilingual community resources is extremely important. The first step would be providing them direction on how to go about getting what they need within their community. Directing them to a local parent organization, community center, or club might be helpful. In addition, sharing with a bilingual parent where cultural events and native foods relative to their background might be found would establish a bond between the teacher and the parent. Similar assistance would allow the bilingual parent to feel accepted and a part of the community.

Through such activities, bilingual parents might begin to feel more comfortable within the school setting and participate in more school-related activities.

Additionally, in generating active bilingual parental support, it is necessary for school staffs to involve bilingual parents in resolving school-community issues and concerns. The following procedures might prove helpful:

1. Identify the issue as clearly and objectively as possible.
2. Identify alternatives that are realistic and plausible. Examine these alternatives, select one, and put it in the form of an objective to be accomplished.
3. Identify and develop a support group, as well as others who would be willing to work to accomplish the objective.
4. Identify parents, resources, or other individuals who might be helpful in accomplishing this objective.
5. Identify the activities necessary to achieve the objective, including duties and responsibilities for each group member.
6. Review and modify the steps in the plan as necessary until the objective is reached or reasonably resolved.

This procedure could be used to address such issues and concerns as parent involvement, Bilingual Special Education, school attendance, drug abuse, vandalism, racial conflict, community resources, school achievement and attitude, as well as other concerns affecting the school community.

Through a collaborative effort with active participation by parents and educators, issues of concern to the school could be resolved for the benefit of the children as well as the school and community.

Summary

Parents play a crucial role in the lives of their children. Children cannot survive without care. Together the child, parent, school, and community work in the development of the child. As the child grows, the school plays an increasingly important role in the development of the child.

To enhance the child's development, the child's support system must work together. The primary support system is the home, followed by schools, community centers, and churches. The challenge is for the child's support systems to work together in behalf of the child.

In discussing parent involvement, the importance of parents' attitudes toward handicaps was pointed out. Research indicates that socioeconomic status and religious belief are related to the attitude of the parent about the handicap.

The ATSEM model was presented for involving parents of handicapped children. The process begins with an acquaint phase to maximize the child's growth both at school and at home. It then proceeds through teach, support, expand, and maintain phases.

Finally, eight activities were presented that a school might initiate for developing parent involvement.

Discussion Questions

1. Explain what role parental involvement plays in the educational process of children.
2. Identify the child's support systems and explain their roles.
3. Explain the value of parental involvement for the child within the school setting.

4. In general, discuss how parents' attitudes might affect their bilingual exceptional children.

5. Discuss the five phases of the ATSEM parent involvement model.

6. Discuss five ways in which bilingual parents of exceptional children might be involved in a school setting.

References

Anderson, J. G., & Safar, D. (1967). The influence of differential community perceptions on the provision of equal educational opportunities. *Sociology of Education.* 40:219–230.

Ausubel, D. P. (1974) Perceived parent attitudes as determinants of children's ego structure. *Child Development.* 15:173–183.

Barber, B. M. (1963). A study of the attitudes of mothers of mentally retarded children as influenced by socioeconomic status. *Dissertation Abstracts.* 24:415.

Chinn, P. C., Winn, J., & Walters, R. H. (1978). *Two-way talking with parents of special children: A process of positive communication.* St. Louis: Mosby.

Clasky, M. (1973). *Together: Schools and communities.* Boston: Advisory Council of Education.

Dillard, J. M., Kinnison, K., & Peel, B. (1980, July). Multicultural approach to mainstreaming: A challenge to counselors, teachers, psychologists, and administrators. *Peabody Journal of Education.*

Dingman, H. F., Eyman, R. K., & Windle, C. D. (1963). An investigation of some child-rearing attitudes of mothers with retarded children. *American Journal of Mental Deficiency.* 67:899–908.

Eyman, R. K., Dingman, H. F., & Windle, C. D. (1966). Association of characteristics of retarded patients and their families with speed of institutionalization. *American Journal of Mental Deficiency.* 71:93–99.

Haring, N. G., & McCormick, L. (1986). *Exceptional children and youth: An introduction to special education.* Columbus, OH: Merrill Publishing Co.

Hoffman, J. L. (1965). Mental retardation, religious values, and psychiatric universals. *American Journal of Psychiatry.* 121:885–889.

Karnes, M. G., Hodgins, A. S., & Taska, J. A. (1969). Investigations of classroom and at home interventions, vol. 1. *Research and development program on preschool disadvantaged children, final report.* Bethesda, MD: ERIC Document Reproduction Service (ED036663).

Karnes, M. B., Zehrbach, R. R., & Teska, J. A. (1971). A new professional role in early childhood education. *Interchange.* 2:89:105.

Klausner, M. (1961). The attitudes of mothers toward institutionalized and non-institutionalized retarded children. *Dissertation Abstracts.* 22:915–916.

Marion, R. L. (1979, January). Minority parent involvement in the IEP process: A systematic model approach. *Focus on Exceptional Children.* 10:1–14.

Nelson, R. C., & Bloom, J. W. (1973). Issues and dialogue: Guiding parent involvement. *Elementary School Guidance and Counseling.* 8:48–49.

Schlesinger, H. S., & Meadow, K. P.: *Sound and sign: Childhood deafness and mental health.* Berkeley, CA: University of California Press.

Takeguchi, S. L. (1967). A comparison of the conceptions and attitudes of parents of mentally retarded children concerning the subgroups of mental retardation as influenced by socioeconomic status. *Dissertation Abstracts.* 27:4342–4343.

Worchel, T. L., & Worchel, P. (1961). The parental concept of the mentally retarded child. *American Journal of Mental Deficiency.* 65:782–788.

Ysseldyke, J. E., Algozzine, B., & Mitchell, J. Special education team decision making: An analysis of current practice. *Personnel and Guidance Journal:* 60:308–313.

Zuk, G. H., et al. (1961). Maternal acceptance of retarded children: A questionnaire study of attitudes and religious background. *Child Development* 32:525–540.

CHAPTER FIFTEEN

Bilingual Special Education: Issues in Policy Development and Implementation

James Bransford
Leonard M. Baca

- General Policy Development
- Models for Policy Development
- Critical Issues Affecting Policy Development
- Current Federal Requirements for Serving LEP Handicapped Children
- Strategies for Influencing Policies
- Suggested Policy Options
- Planning and Implementation
- Future of Bilingual Special Education
- Summary

Objectives

- To understand the need for and importance of policy development
- To become familiar with the process as well as various models for policy development
- To be aware of the various federal requirements as they relate to serving LEP handicapped students
- To review and critique various policy options for Bilingual Special Education
- To compare and contrast program planning and implementation strategies
- To discuss the future of Bilingual Special Education

Policy has been defined as a "purposeful cause of action followed by an actor or set of actors in dealing with a problem or matter of concern" (Anderson, 1975). Public policy is described as a definitive course of action adopted or pursued by a government (or other like body) in response to an articulated or perceived public concern (Lewis & Wallace, 1984). Public policies are formally developed by public officials such as legislators, judges, administrators, and board members. Using this definition as a point of departure, one can see that there exists today an extensive public policy at both the federal and the state level that addresses the education of all handicapped children (Ramirez & Pages, 1979). This is based on laws such as the Education for All Handicapped Children Act of 1975 (P.L. 94–142) and Section 504 of the Rehabilitation Act of 1973 (P.L. 93–112) and various state statutes. There is also an officially articulated public policy dealing with the education of limited English proficient (LEP) students. This policy comes primarily from the Bilingual Education Act of 1968 as amended in 1974 and 1978 (P.L. 95–561) and related state statutes. Also important in this context is the 1974 U.S. Supreme Court decision of *Lau v. Nichols* (1974). The interpretation of these federal and state directives leads to the conclusion that handicapped LEP students must be afforded the opportunity of receiving bilingual and special education services.

Although many of our nation's school districts have been providing effective special education and Bilingual Education services for several years, only in the past few years have educators begun to address the complexities involved in merging special education services with bilingual methodology for an increasing number of LEP handicapped students nationwide. A broad set of policies exist at the federal and, to a limited extent, at the state level. However, there is an absence of well-developed written policies for Bilingual Special Education at the local school district level.

Any new program within a tax-supported institution, such as a public school system, can benefit from the establishment of policies related to that program. Bilingual Special Education programs and services are no exception. Carefully formulated policies can help provide the support, direction, parameters, and guidelines that are needed to implement a successful Bilingual Special Education program. The formal establishment of educational policy is of utmost importance. If policy is not planned, developed, and adopted in a formal and systematic manner it will be established through default rather than through intent. For example, if a school district did not adopt a policy regarding girls' athletics there would in fact be a policy of benign neglect, and consequently little if any formal participation of girls in athletics. Likewise, if a school district has no policy for the provision of bilingual services to LEP handicapped children there will probably be no bilingual services for these children. The purpose of this chapter is to underscore the importance of policy formulation for Bilingual Special Education by discussing various issues related to policy development and implementation. Specifically, this chapter will discuss the general background for policy development, along with the description of policy development models. This will be followed by the presentation of the critical issues affecting policy development. The current federal requirements will be discussed along with suggested strategies for influencing policy. A number of policy options and some guidelines for program planning and implementation will be presented. Finally, there will be a discussion of the possible future directions of Bilingual Special Education.

General Policy Development

Policy has been defined as the outcome of decision-making processes set in motion to respond to existing stimuli or challenges (Dunn, 1986). Thompson (1976) referred to policymaking as the sum of the processes in which all the parties involved in and related to a social system shape the goals of the system. The process includes all the factors that tie the various parties together and facilitate their adjustments to one another and to the environmental factors affecting them.

These factors include structural factors relating to the more permanent, unchanging elements of the community, such as population characteristics, economic base, and established organizations; cultural factors, or the value commitments of the community at large; and situational factors, or short-term special issues that may arise from time to time in a community. In educational policymaking, these environmental factors are impacted by a number of distinct features that may be unique to the American educational system:

- Decentralization of the educational system, with shared responsibility for developing and implementing educational policy among local, state, and federal governmental and related entities
- Regionalism, or differences in politics and public policies among various states and geographic areas
- Diversity, or the many cultural and economic variances among different American communities

Traditional View

The literature refers to two major views relative to policymaking. The traditional view is a strictly legal perspective. Policymaking is viewed as a responsibility, as stated by law, of elected representatives. In the realm of education the most prominent elected body is the school board. The people elect school board members to serve as their representatives and give them the power to make school policy. The board, in turn, hires a superintendent or other administrator and delegates to that official the authority to administer board policy. The superintendent or other official, with this delegated authority, organizes the work and hires and directs teaching and other staff to carry out specific duties. Policymaking is seen as completely separate from administration (Thompson, 1976).

The traditional view does not take into consideration the many variables that are working constantly and simultaneously to shape policymaking. Many groups both within and outside the schools influence policy development. These groups include students, parents, economic groups (taxpayers), business groups, religious groups, parent organizations, teachers, labor organizations, professional associations, community and college groups, regional education associations, and local, regional, and federal governmental bodies.

Systems Approach

The other major view is the systems approach to educational policymaking. This view considers the many variables that influence policymaking.

Besides those groups already mentioned, this view looks at economic factors, demographics, resources, state of technology, and costs. It considers social and cultural factors such as social beliefs, religious beliefs, state systems, individual motivation for education, cultural issues, political administration structures, influence and power structures, degree of governmental stability, and political and administrative organization of the schools. The systems approach also considers social-psychological factors, including attitudes, beliefs, and values of teachers, administrators, and other staff; their educational backgrounds and roles, and the different group affiliations and group strengths that may prevail, in addition to individual motivation and intellectual abilities of the total school population, including the students (Thompson, 1976).

Views of Policymaking

Within these two general views rest two competing images of policymaking: the academic image and the image of policymaking as a pragmatic art. The academic image holds that policymaking is a systematic, rational process of finding the best solution to a social or educational problem. Tremendous importance is placed on the power of information and analysis to influence decisions. The pragmatic art view sees decision making occurring in a context of uncertainty, conflicting values and interests, and incomplete information. Negotiation, compromise, and incremental solutions are considered part of the decision-making or policymaking process (Takanishi, 1981).

This latter image, coupled with the systems approach described earlier, seems to reflect the reality of educational politics better than the other system reviewed. They certainly relate more to the adaptive process described by Bebout and Bredemeier (1963). Policymaking, they contend, goes through a process that involves identification, or feeling of oneness with other individuals or groups; bargaining, or a system of exchanges in which one attempts to get something from someone by convincing that person that it is beneficial to accede to the request; and using legal bureaucratic mechanisms that, as a last resort, in most cases means getting what one desires by narrowing the alternatives so that the competing individual or group has no choice but to comply.

In effect, in educational policymaking as in politics generally, some individual or group of individuals wants something from government or other agencies and builds a coalition of influences to get it. Other people with different preferences join one another to block or modify the designs of the primary group. They strategize and develop certain tactics that are intended to provoke decision makers and those in power to determine the winners and losers by passing laws and issuing executive and judicial orders. This process is said to be continuous. As soon as a decision is made on a specific issue, new discussion begins on other issues (Thompson, 1976).

The decision-making process leading to policymaking is seen as working in a series of social relationships including both formal and informal decision makers. Individuals who may be pursing their particular interests interact with one another in a series of social situations. From these contacts they come to know and understand one another's attitudes, views, and position on the various issues. Consensus is established as positions are discussed and negotiated and friendships develop. Because much of the activity leading to formal decisions only takes place in the social milieu, little input is received or considered from individuals or groups not included in these events. As a result, policymaking may reflect the interests of groups or individuals whose influence then extends to major segments of political, economic, educational, and social life (Hughes, 1967).

This process of formulating policy or making decisions in informal and social settings is practiced by government representatives at all levels, state education agency officials, other agencies, various associations and groups, institutions of higher education, and the courts. In education each group must influence the other to influence policy. The process—through identification, bargaining, negotiation, accommodation, rules and laws, pressure and coercion, appeals to common loyalties, partnerships, shared ideals, history, and friendships, as well as the use of rational argument—leads directly to specific policy development (Dunn, 1986).

Models for Policy Development

Models are fundamental to policymaking and policy analysis. The creation of precise and manageable processes designed to produce information about the consequences of proposed actions are at the very heart of decision making. Although most models cannot predict the consequences of specific actions with the assurance of some of the best scientific models, they do produce information that assists in understanding situations more clearly (Quade, 1982).

A number of models, theories, views, and approaches have been developed to analyze policymaking and decision making. These models and theories are critical to the total process of policy formulation and to the meaningful explanation of policy actions (Anderson, 1984).

As defined in earlier sections of this chapter, policymaking involves a pattern of actions extending over time and requiring a number of decisions. Policy serves to clarify and organize thought and provides an understanding of policy decisions. Policy is rarely synonymous with a simple decision, which involves, in its simplest form, a choice among competing alternatives. Models are used to identify these alternatives.

Anderson (1984) identifies a number of what he terms "theoretical approaches" that, although not developed specifically for the analysis of policy formulation, have been modified to address policymaking in general and decision making as the logical extension of policy development. Of those models or theories referred to in Anderson's analysis, which included both group and elite theory as well as functional process theory, the political systems theory provides the most comprehensive perception of general policy development.

Political Systems Theory

Policy from the perspective of the political systems theory may be viewed as the response of a political or quasipolitical system to demands emanating from the system's environment. Input from that environment, which includes all conditions and events external to the system, consists of demands and supports. Demands are defined as all claims made to somehow satisfy the needs and interests of individuals and groups within that specific environment. Support is provided when these same individuals or groups accept the decisions and outcomes made by officials authorized by the political system in response to the demands. Policy output, through feedback, leads to new demands, which in turn produce additional policy actions on a continuous loop basis (Anderson, 1975).

Easton Model

Anderson's Public Policy Model mirrors to a great extent the Easton Model developed and refined by David Easton. The Easton Model also identified the interaction of environmental inputs with outputs and feedback. This model, however, placed supreme importance on the understanding of the complexity of the environment. Those interventions through which values are authoritatively allocated for a society, according to Easton, are differentiated from other systems because of the uniqueness of system environments. Easton divided the environment itself into two parts, which he described as the intrasocietal and the extrasocietal (Easton, 1965).

The first part consists of those systems in the same society as the political system under analysis but extracted from the system itself. Intrasocietal environmental factors include sets of behaviors, attitudes, and ideas such as the economy, the culture, social structures, and personalities of role players; all of which are functional segments of the society and components of the political system. The extrasocietal environmental factors include all those systems that lie outside the society itself and that are functional components of what Easton terms an international society. The United Nations is an example of an extrasocietal environmental factor (Easton, 1965).

From these environmental sources arise significant influences that contribute to possible stress on the political system. These influences are termed disturbances emanating from the environment that act upon the environment and attempt to change it. These disturbances or input are raw material, according to Easton, that flow into the conversion process. The process reflects those decisions made by authorities who have special responsibilities for converting demands into outputs in response to demands. Feedback depicts the effects of any decision or change in the environment (Easton, 1965).

Easton's model is presented in Figure 15–1. Because Easton goes into such depth and specificity in describing his model, it is difficult in a few pages to discuss adequately the process he has to a great extent developed and refined. Thompson (1976) has successfully captured Easton's thinking when he describes the political systems theory:

> The political system as part of a broader social system receives input from the environment in the form of demands and support which are converted through a series of conversion processes into outputs or authoritative rules and actions. In turn, the outputs of the system affect the environment and, as feedback, may result in another demand or input on the system.

Although Easton's model attracts wide attention from individuals supportive of a systems approach to policymaking and decision making, the work of Rakoff and Schaefer (1970) in expanding the Easton Model focuses more directly on the process of policymaking. The fundamental concern behind Rakoff and Schaefer's adoption of Easton's work is the assumption that the process itself matters. They are clearly concerned with what happens to inputs as they work their way toward becoming outputs.

The creation of public policy involves the environment, procedures, resources, time, and outcomes. To present it simply as inputs/outputs and feedback, they argue, does not seem to enhance a true understanding of how policymaking occurs.

Figure 15–2 graphically describes Rakoff and Schaefer's model of the policymaking process.

The environment is recognized as a dominant force. Specific requests for political or government actions go through a two-step process. The first step simply entails some acknowledgment of a condition. The second step identifies a perceived condition of need. The perceived needs can then be transformed into political demands requiring a response from the system. These demands undergo political transformation in three distinct phases: aggregation, adoption, and application.

Aggregation involves the collection, weighing, and ordering of the demands. This is in effect a prioritizing, since no system can deal with all demands imposed on it. Adoption is the formal process by which a decision of "go" or "no go" is reached on the demand. Application is the actual carrying out of the decision.

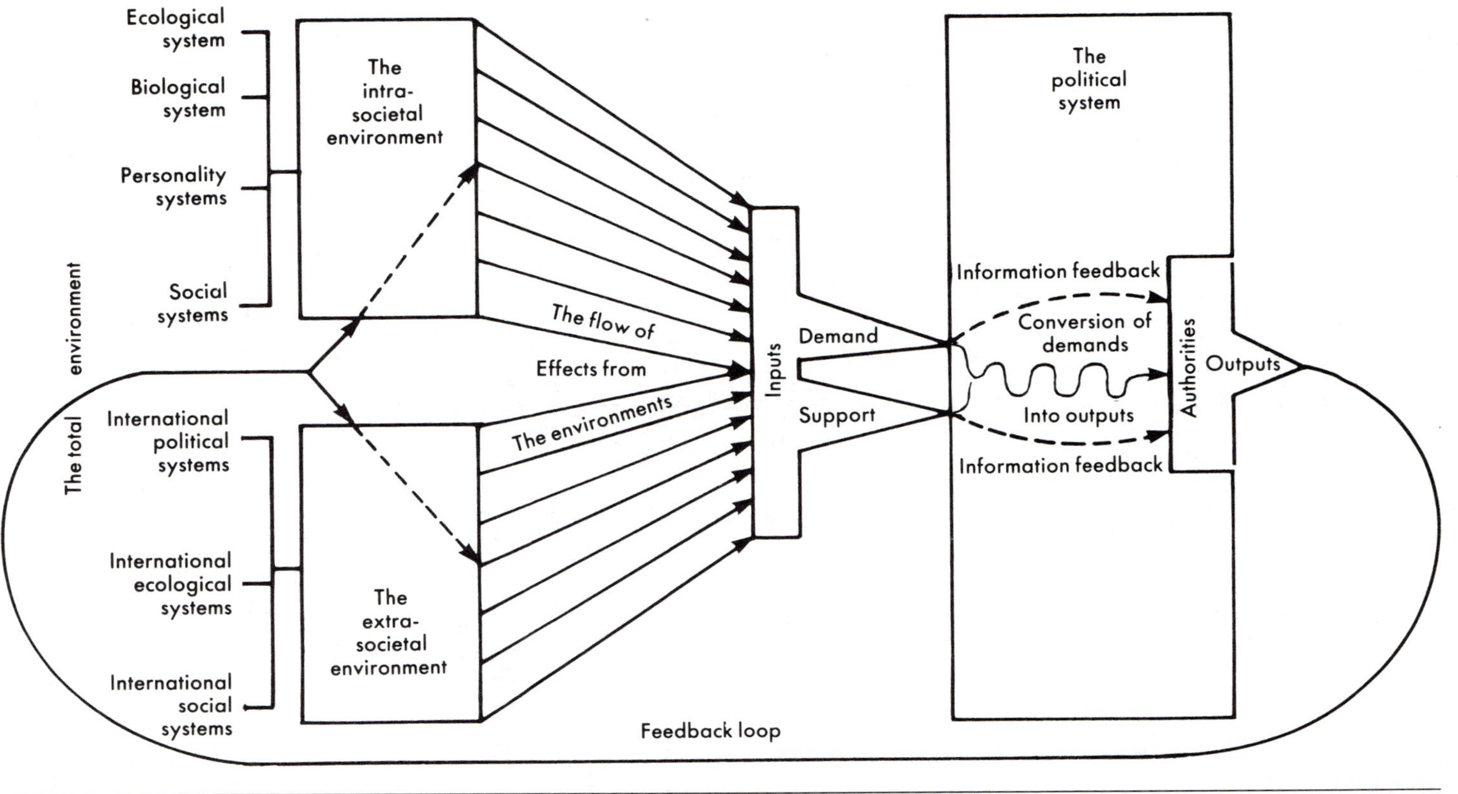

Figure 15–1

Easton's model. A dynamic response model of a political system

From *A framework for political analysis* by D. Easton, 1979, Chicago: University of Chicago Press. Copyright 1965, 1979 by David Easton. Reprinted by permission.

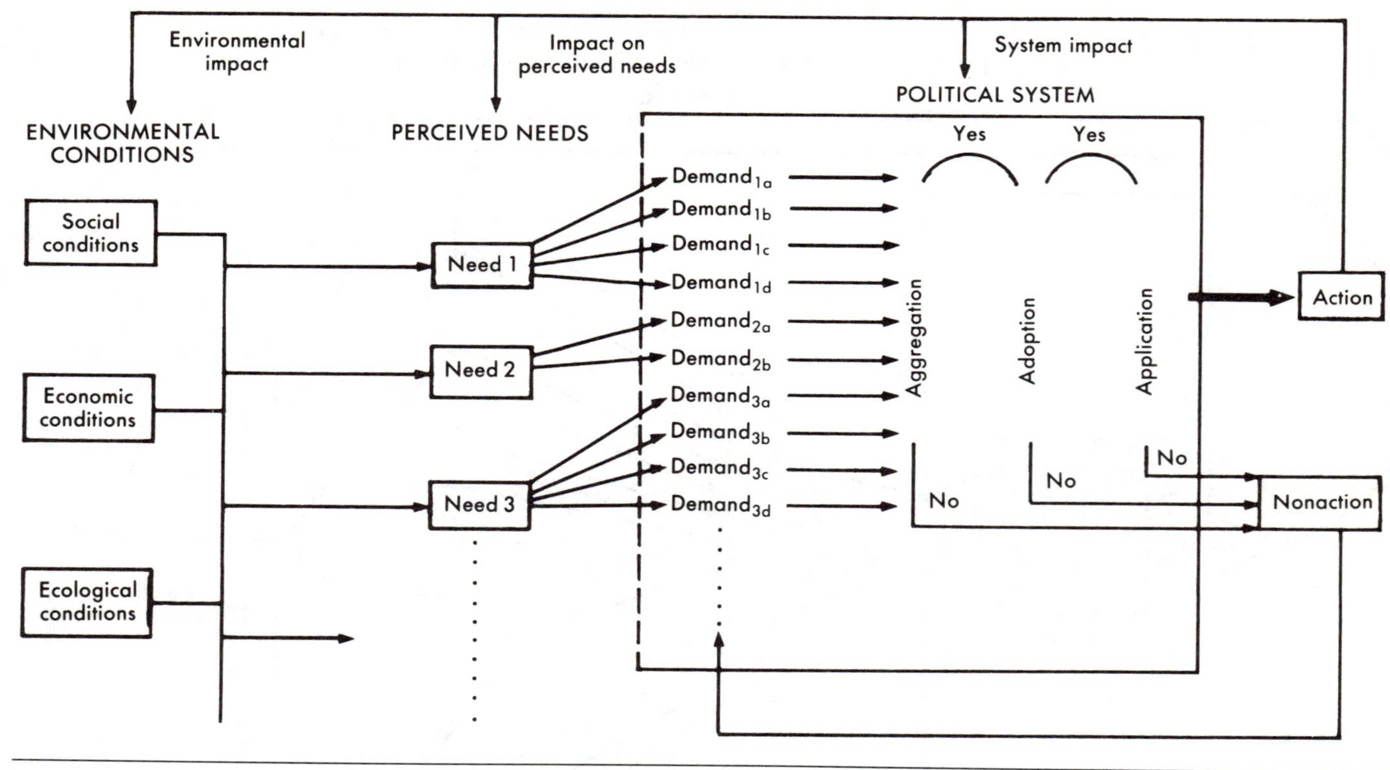

Figure 15–2

A model of the policymaking process

From "Politics, policy, and political science: Theoretical alternatives" by S. H. Rakoff and G. F. Schaefer. Copyright 1970 by Geron-X, Inc. Reprinted by permission.

In the educational arena a variety of groups interact in an attempt to establish or influence educational policies that they support. These groups are considered components of that environment which Easton, Rakoff, and Schaefer find so important. The composition, size, number, and relative influence of these groups differ depending on the issues, but in education generally, including Bilingual Special Education, one can expect that school-based personnel, state and local government entities, and special interest groups are all playing a particular role as inputs in this policymaking process.

Decisions relating to all program functions or activities in the area of Bilingual Special Education can best be explained by understanding the particular model of policy development and revamping the complex relationship and interaction that occurs in the total environment.

Critical Issues Affecting Policy Development

The critical issues most directly impacting policy development in the area of Bilingual Special Education are those that most critically affect education generally. In effect, these issues or problem areas can be categorized under several major issues:

- Economic needs or financing
- States' rights issues or local control
- Planning and implementation
- Training needs
- Effectiveness of Bilingual Special Education

The most visible and critical problem facing special population educational/training programs today relates to the cost of the programs, especially in light of massive cutbacks in federal funding and the inability or unwillingness of state and local governments to assume the costs associated with these programs. The nation is faced with the problem of decreasing gross national product and real net income and spiraling budget deficits. High unemployment and underemployment figures, concern for interest rates, increasing costs of government services, reduced federal expenditures for education generally, the shift from categorical funding to block grants and budget balancing plans like those required by Gramm-Rudman are just some of the issues associated with the problem of financing educational programs for the disadvantaged or handicapped.

Related to these economic issues and contributing to the problems of addressing the needs of special student populations are radical changes in political party policies and philosophies toward education, reduced federal pressures for equity in education and training programs, the unwillingness of special interest groups to return to spending levels of the past, expanding role of state government in educational support, the support for private school efforts to offer equivalent services at public expense, disparities in local funding that result in unequal educational opportunities, increased competition from special interest groups for fewer available dollars, the population shift resulting in a change in the numbers of people supporting public education, decrease in the numbers of children entering the schools especially in the large urban areas, the geographic conflict and competition for available funds from other than government sources, and the reduced interest and advocacy for public education from the general population (Jones & Ferguson, 1981).

The issue of who is to pay for the education of the Bilingual Special Education students has not undergone extensive study. More information on the costs associated with educating the bilingual child is available. The Department of Education estimated that Bilingual Education costs an additional 12% over funds appropriated for education generally. The American Institute of Research stated in a highly controversial study that it costs an additional $376 during the school year to educate a child eligible for Title VII funds. A survey of state departments of education by the National Conference of State Legislatures indicated the cost of providing Bilingual Education programs to be between an additional $10 million and $20 million annually. The costs associated with the identification and assessment of eligible students was estimated to reach between $6 million and $9 million for that activity alone. Educational programs for limited English proficient handicapped students would add significantly to these costs (Takanishi, 1981).

One additional problem associated with financing Bilingual Special Education relates to the distribution of students. The Education Commission of the States (1979) found that special education students are distributed unevenly throughout the states and the distribution was not related to the property wealth, population density, or minority populations of the reporting school districts. In essence the less affluent districts, those situated in the larger urban areas, serve greater numbers of eligible students than do the districts that were better able to support special programs.

States' Rights Issues

The shifting responsibility for the education of special populations from the federal government to states and local agencies does not bode well for the Bilingual Special Education students. Although the states have assumed the largest share of the funding responsibility (64%) as compared to the local school district share (30.1%) or the federal share (5.9%), the states are seemingly unable to pick up any additional costs primarily assumed by the federal government (ECS, 1979).

This inability to assume the additional cost of educating the Bilingual Special Education student produces very special problems for the state and local school districts that have made a major issue of states' rights in the area of education. One of the basic arguments used by states' rights advocates is that educating the young has long been the recognized constitutional responsibility of the states and local school districts (Thompson, 1976).

In this argument the states' rightists say that the Tenth Amendment to the Constitution gives the power and responsibility for the education of the populace to the states. The Department of Education, they argue, goes beyond the intent of any laws by issuing specific or prescriptive guidelines to the local school districts and has therefore usurped the power of the states and local school boards to determine educational methodologies and curriculum policy (Takanishi, 1981).

The intervention of federal governmental entities and the courts in what are perceived to be local educational issues is seen by these defenders of local control as greatly complicating an already serious problem. As one spokesperson for the Center for Applied Legislation stated (Takanishi, 1981):

> The proposed rules greatly underestimate and oversimplify the complexity of the task of educating language minority youngsters by attempting to prescribe one educational solution for all.

Planning and Implementation

These problems are exacerbated by the lack of coordination between federal and state agencies in initial planning, implementation, and evaluation of programs. Very little information sharing takes place. Guidelines for program monitoring are usually ambiguous and weak. Federal requirements and court mandates often conflict with existing state laws and, in most cases, funds appropriated for carrying out programs of instruction are inadequate to accomplish the task (Alexander & Nava, 1976).

Questions such as the following are rarely addressed:

- What is the rationale for proper services or activities?
- What types of programs are already available?
- What type of teacher is needed?
- What kind of teacher training is necessary?
- How do federal and state requirements interface?
- What changes will current policy need to undergo?
- What are the long-term expectations of the program?
- What costs are associated with the program?
- What kind of community commitment exists?
- What are the long-range financial obligations?
- What alternative funding resources exist?

As a result of this lack of coordination and planning, resources—both human and material—may not even be identified, much less mobilized. Federal and state requirements and expectations run counter to one another, and the schools, caught in the middle of the imbroglio, fail to meet the goals of addressing individual student needs. Students are therefore denied a meaningful opportunity to participate in an appropriate educational experience, resulting in a loss of human potential.

Program Effectiveness

The final issue treated relates to the effectiveness of both Bilingual Education and Bilingual Special Education. Little research has been carried out on any long-term basis in Bilingual Special Education. Much research exists, however, on Bilingual Education generally. Although much of this research provides positive evidence of the effectiveness of such programs (Barrera-Vasquez, 1953; Blank, 1973; Modiano, 1968; Richardson, 1968; Troike, 1978; Tucker, 1972), highly publicized studies, like the 1977 American Institute of Research evaluation of Title VII Programs, provide deadly political ammunition to opponents of Bilingual Education. Many of these antagonists oppose the concept for a variety of political reasons but base their offense on the question of effectiveness. Thus, as is the case with other highly controversial topics, Bilingual Education is under constant scrutiny and continuous attack with only a limited chance of ever receiving unbiased, politically free evaluation.

Current Federal Requirements for Serving LEP Handicapped Children

Chapter 4 of this text reviews the legal background related to Bilingual Special Education. The interest here is simply to list and summarize the specific programmatic requirements that are based on the various laws and judicial decisions. Once these basic requirements are established, policy strategies and policy options will then be considered. To validate the accuracy of the following requirements the Office of Civil Rights was contacted (Gutierrez, 1982). With their help the following list of requirements was formulated. Although the list is accurate, it is not an official and formalized statement of the federal government. The following information was taken in part from an ERIC Exceptional Child Education Report (Baca & Bransford, 1982).

1. Every state and its localities shall provide or make available a free appropriate public education for all handicapped children aged 3 to 18. (P.L. 94–142, Section 504 of the Rehabilitation Act of 1973. Section 504 does not refer to specific ages.)

2. Every school district shall conduct a language screening at the beginning of each school year for all new students to determine if there is the influence of a language other than English on the child (*Lau,* 1974).

3. If the initial screening did find the influence of a language other than English, then a language assessment shall be made to determine language dominance and proficiency (*Lau*, 1974).

4. If it is determined that a child is both handicapped and of limited English proficiency, an individualized education plan (IEP) shall be developed that reflects the child's language-related needs (Title VI, P.L. 94–142, Section 504).

5. When a child is evaluated, the instruments used shall be appropriate and the testing shall be nondiscriminatory (P.L. 94–142, Section 504).

6. Tests and other evaluation materials must be validated for the specific purpose for which they are used and should be administered by trained personnel in conformance with the instructions provided by their producers (P.L. 94–142, Section 504).

7. Tests and other evaluation materials must be tailored to access specific areas of educational need. There should not be a total reliance on tests designed to provide a single general intelligence quotient (P.L. 94–142, Section 504).

8. Tests must be selected and administered to ensure that, when administered to a student with impaired sensory, manual, or speaking skills, the test results accurately reflect the student's aptitude, achievement level, or whatever other factor the test purports to measure rather than reflecting the student's impaired sensory, manual, or speaking skills (P.L. 94–142, Section 504).

9. In interpreting evaluation data and in making placement decisions, information shall be drawn from a variety of sources, including aptitude and achievement tests, teacher recommendations, physical condition, social or cultural background, and adaptive behavior (P.L. 94–142, Section 504).

10. The parents of a child shall be informed of all due process rights in their native language. An interpreter shall be provided at all meetings if the parents cannot communicate in English (Title VI, P.L. 94–142).

11. The handicapped child of limited English proficiency shall be provided with a program of instruction that addresses the child's unique needs, including language-related needs (P.L. 94–142).

Strategies for Influencing Policies

As has been seen, public policy development and implementation are part of a complex political process. Although the primary developers of policy are elected and appointed officials such as legislators, governors, judges, board members, and administrators of agencies or programs, it is important that they be in communication with their constituents. In other words, policymakers should know the needs and concerns of the people most affected by the policies they are formulating. With this in mind, advocates of LEP handicapped children can use several strategies in their efforts to shape these policies. In discussing these specific strategies it is helpful to relate them to the various components of policy development. Anderson (1984) describes five such components, including policy demands, policy decisions, policy statements, policy outputs, and policy outcomes.

Policy demands in this context are the policy priorities as perceived by the public. Strategies for teachers and parents include conveying their major concerns or demands to the policymakers. This can be done on an individual basis through letters and through presentations at school board meetings. Another effective strategy in this regard is at the group or organizational level. Professional teacher organizations or parent groups could make their collective concerns known to policymakers.

Policy decisions in this context are the decisions made by public officials and administrators that in effect result in policy formulation. Included here is the decision to introduce a bill to the legislature or to seek school board approval for the establishment of program guidelines for Bilingual Special Education services. Possible strategies here include various forms of persuading key officials and administrators of the political and moral value of being an advocate of equal educational opportunity for all children, including LEP handicapped students.

Policy Statements

The third component of policy development is policy statements. These statements include legislative acts or statutes, executive orders, court decisions, rules and regulations, or even public speeches by key officials (Edwards, 1980). More often than not, these official policy statements are generic and difficult to interpret and apply at the local school district level. For example, how does *Lau v. Nichols* (1974) apply to LEP handicapped students in Laguna, NM? An important strategy here is to request a clarification of a higher-level policy principle as applied to a local school's practices. For example, a teacher or parent could request that the local director of special education clarify how the district implements the nondiscriminatory testing requirements of P.L. 94–142 with LEP children. Likewise, a parent group could request this clarification. Oftentimes a policy clarification request such as this will highlight the absence of local policy guidelines and thus call attention to the need for developing a local policy.

Policy Outputs

Another phase of policy development is the policy outputs. This refers to what is actually done as compared to what the policy says should be done. For example, a school district policy might state that a LEP handicapped student's language and cultural needs should be reflected in the student's IEP. However, if a number of LEP students' IEPs are examined, it may be found that there is very little information on how these students' language and culture needs are to be met. A strategy in this regard is to request a review of existing policy outputs from time to time. This request might be more effective if it came from a state or local advisory committee.

Policy Outcomes

The final aspect of policy development is referred to as the policy outcomes, the actual benefits provided to the LEP child, the child's family, and society at large. In other words, has the policy worked as it was intended to work? This is in effect the accountability component of policy development. An important strategy in this regard is to encourage program directors to include this concern in the annual program evaluation. This could also be viewed as a cost benefit analysis. Are the benefits to the LEP handicapped child, the child's family, and society at large worth the special education intervention and investment? Although this is difficult to measure it is advisable to provide such information to policymakers whenever possible.

Training and Coordination

The strategies for influencing policy are addressed to individual teachers, parents, and school administrators, as well as to professional educational organizations. To have maximum impact these individuals and organizations need training and orientation. This training can be provided by any number of political action groups. We recommend that this training be requested from professional organizations with good track records in governmental relations, such as the Council for Exceptional Children, the American Speech and Hearing Association, and the National Education Association. It is equally important to seek out training from legal advisory groups such as ASPIRA, the Mexican American Legal Defense and Education Fund (MALDEF), and the Native American Rights Fund (NARF).

In addition to seeking training on policy shaping, it is important for local groups to support the efforts of organizations such as those listed. In this arena they are the experts. They have highly trained and specialized staff who are well versed in the process of policy formulation. These individuals are also excellent sources of information regarding policy matters.

Suggested Policy Options

Every school district is unique in terms of location, size, makeup of student population, teaching staff, financial resources, and many other variables. Because of the unique character of each school district it is not advisable or possible to design a comprehensive set of model policy statements that would have broad applicability across many districts. The following policy options are presented to highlight issues that may need policy clarification and direction. These policy options may also serve to stimulate a dialogue relative to the need for policy on a number of different topics related to Bilingual Special Education services. These policy options are not meant to be adopted by school districts as they stand. They must be revised and rewritten to fit the unique needs of a particular school district. Finally, because every policy contains within it both positive and negative implications, an attempt is made to point out the possible positive and negative effects of each option. These policy options are taken in large part from a policy options report prepared for the Council for Exceptional Children (Baca, 1980).

Screening

Every school district shall assure that each of its schools conducts a uniform language screening for all new students at the beginning of each school year to determine if there is the influence of a language other than English on any of the children.

Potential Positive Effects. This option will increase the number of students identified as being in need of special language-related services. It will assure that all schools within the district use the same criteria and procedures for identifying students who may be of limited English proficiency and should assist all school districts in complying with the *Lau* (1974) decision.

Potential Negative Effects. It will add an additional requirement to school districts already burdened with excessive bureaucratic red tape and another level of identification and assessment to an already overly identified and assessed population. It may also take time away from much needed instruction.

Language Dominance/Proficiency Testing

Every school district will provide language dominance/proficiency testing for those students who have been identified through the screening process as needing further language assessment.

Potential Positive Effects. This option will provide teachers with a better indication of each student's first and second language abilities for instructional purposes, contributing important language proficiency information to the IEP staffing team. It will provide baseline information to help teachers arrive at decisions regarding when to initiate first and second language reading instruction.

Potential Negative Effects. This option will create a requirement for which there are no language dominance/proficiency tests in certain languages, thus creating additional testing requirements for an already overburdened staff. It will add another financial burden to already stringent budgets.

Acceptable Tests

Every school district shall adopt a list of acceptable language dominance and proficiency tests in the various languages necessary. In the event that instruments are not available in certain languages, alternate methods of language assessment should be suggested.

Potential Positive Effects. The use of poorer quality instruments or procedures will be minimized. Low-incidence languages will be included.

Potential Negative Effects. Technical data on validity and reliability are not available for some language assessment instruments. Having proper instruments and procedures identified does not ensure that they will be properly administered.

Parent Notification

Every school district will assure that parents or guardians of LEP students are notified in their native language regarding permission to test, IEP participation, and due process rights.

Potential Positive Effects. This will facilitate meaningful parent participation and informed consent. It will help school districts comply with P.L. 94–142 and will show parents that the school district acknowledges and respects their native language.

Potential Negative Effects. It may be difficult for school districts to find translators who could help formulate parent notices in low-incidence and rare languages. Even though notices are sent in the parents' native language, the parents may not be able to read these notices; in effect, providing information in this manner to parents does not mean that meaningful communication has taken place.

Individualized Education Program Development

Every school district shall assure that each LEP handicapped student and the student's parents or guardians are provided with an IEP in both English and the family's primary language and that an interpreter will be used if necessary to communicate effectively the meaning and content of the IEP to the parents or guardians.

Potential Positive Effects. This option will promote meaningful parental involvement in the educational process and demonstrate the district's willingness to acknowledge the family's primary language. It will help the district document its compliance with P.L. 94–142.

Potential Negative Effects. Language interpreters in some of the low-incidence languages may be difficult to find. This option may tax an already overstrained budget and the procedure may slow up the staffing process and delay the implementation of the needed instruction.

Testing Guidelines

Every school district shall establish guidelines that will assure that appropriate testing instruments are used and that all testing will be nondiscriminatory in terms of language, culture, and handicap.

Potential Positive Effects. The assessment of handicapped children of limited English proficiency will be improved. Assessment practices within each school district will be more consistent for this group of students, resulting in more districts being in compliance with P.L. 94–142.

Potential Negative Effects. There is no assurance that guidelines will be updated from time to time, since the state of the art is not sufficiently advanced to assure that the guideline will be effective. In addition, the personnel needed to do the job may not be available.

Bilingual Advocate

Every school district shall designate a bilingual specialist or specialists who will participate in all staffings for LEP handicapped children.

Potential Positive Effects. All LEP handicapped children will have an advocate on the staffing team. Every IEP will include provisions related to language needs, and services for LEP handicapped children will be improved.

Potential Negative Effects. The specialist may have limited knowledge of the particular handicap or of the various languages in the district. This may add another additional expense to an already strained budget.

Establishing Primary Need

Each staffing team will have the responsibility for determining if the student's principal obstacle to learning in the regular classroom is the handicap or the language difference.

Potential Positive Effects. This will help ensure that the proper remedial emphasis is placed in the area of greatest need, facilitating the proper placement of the student and the developing of the IEP.

Potential Negative Effects. It is sometimes difficult to separate the impact of the handicap from the impact of the language difference, thus the lesser of the two needs may be considered unimportant and the child may not receive appropriate services.

Use of Parents' Language

Every school district shall print parent due process rights in the appropriate target languages and shall compile a list of available interpreters for the various languages.

Potential Positive Effects. Printed material in the various languages will be readily available at the time of the staffings. A pool of interpreters will be available when needed for staffings, and the meaningful involvement of linguistically different parents will be improved.

Potential Negative Effects. School districts may not hire bilingual staff if they can use community people. In addition, some languages do not have an orthography and thus material cannot be printed.

Comprehensive Services

Every school district shall design and implement a plan with various alternatives for serving the handicapped child of limited English proficiency.

Potential Positive Effects. This option should help ensure that appropriate programs are provided for LEP handicapped students by providing a variety of alternative programs that will allow the staffing team the opportunity of selecting the most appropriate program. It will assist school districts in complying with *Lau* (1974), as well.

Potential Negative Effects. School districts may not have the expertise and recources to carry out this policy option. The staff needed may not be available in many parts of the country, and providing a range of alternative programs may be too idealistic.

Establishing Primary Responsibility

When the student's primary need has been established, the student will become the primary responsibility of the appropriate program, that is, Bilingual Education or special education.

Potential Positive Effects. The lines of responsibility will be clearly established and proper follow-up and restaffing will be assured. This will promote the use of the least restrictive environment.

Potential Negative Effects. Additional red tape may not be justified. Special education may view Bilingual Education as encroaching into its area of responsibility.

Use of Existing Services

The school principal will ensure that, whenever possible, handicapped students in need of Bilingual Education will use the existing services of the bilingual program in the school building.

Potential Positive Effects. This should help reduce duplication of effort and personnel. It would also keep the student in the local school rather than require busing to a special program and would help bilingual programs become more accessible to handicapped students.

Potential Negative Effects. Existing bilingual programs may not be able to meet the students' needs, resulting in a fragmentation of the students' education. It may also encourage matching the student to the program, rather than matching the program to the student.

Bilingual Special Education

When the number of LEP handicapped students is large enough, a school district shall design and implement a Bilingual Special Education program.

Potential Positive Effects. Students will be assured of an appropriate educational experience. They will not be relegated to fragmented "pull-out" programs (programs that pull or remove children from the regular classroom for supplementary instruction). Teachers in these programs will be trained in both special education and Bilingual Education methodology.

Potential Negative Effects. Properly trained personnel may not be available to staff such a program. In addition, the term *large enough* is open to a wide range of interpretations.

Parent and Community Involvement

Any school district planning to develop a Bilingual Special Education program shall involve parents and community members in the planning of the program.

Potential Positive Effects. When parents are involved in the planning of the program, they are more supportive of the program and more likely to assist as volunteers for the program, contributing particularly in the areas of language and culture.

Potential Negative Effects. If the role of parents and community members is not clearly defined, conflicts may result. Some parents may act more like observers than participants.

Accessibility

Every school district with an existing bilingual program will, as a matter of policy, make it available to handicapped children of limited English proficiency.

Potential Positive Effects. This will encourage placement in the least restrictive environment, promote the maximum use of existing resources, and be more cost effective.

Potential Negative Effects. It may deter some districts from implementing a Bilingual Special Education program because regular bilingual teachers may not be prepared to accept handicapped children into their classrooms.

Removal of Barriers

Every school district with an existing bilingual program will make every effort to remove any barriers that may prevent handicapped students of limited English proficiency from meaningful participation in the program.

Potential Positive Effects. This option will promote placement in the least restrictive environment while helping to sensitize teachers and administrators to the needs of the handicapped. It will make existing bilingual programs accessible to the handicapped.

Potential Negative Effects. Barriers may be interpreted very narrowly to mean only physical barriers, and some districts may feel their responsibility ends there.

Supplementary Services

Every school district with an existing bilingual program will make every effort to provide supplementary services and materials to make it more responsive to handicapped children of limited English proficiency.

Potential Positive Effects. This will serve to improve the quality of services for the handicapped student of limited English proficiency with the mainstream of education, be more cost effective, and encourage more placements in a least restrictive environment.

Potential Negative Effects. It may deter some districts from going a step further to establish a Bilingual Special Education program.

Minimum Services

When no bilingual programs or services are available or accessible, the school district shall, at the very minimum, provide a native language tutor for every handicapped LEP child.

Potential Positive Effects. Handicapped LEP children will be assured of a minimum level of services because every school district will be accountable for at least a minimum effort in meeting the needs of the handicapped child of limited English proficiency.

Potential Negative Effects. This may deter some districts from providing more comprehensive services. This minimum standard may be too low in certain instances.

Exit Criteria

A school district's exit criteria for a Bilingual Special Education program shall be the same as the exit criteria for the regular bilingual program in terms of language dimension.

Potential Positive Effects. This will assure fair and equitable treatment of the handicapped LEP child and will assist the district in adopting fair and consistent policies.

Potential Negative Effects. Because children in a Bilingual Special Education program are following a program based on an IEP rather than program criteria, it could potentially pose a problem. In addition, the goals of a Bilingual Special Education program may not be compatible with a maintenance philosophy that might exist in some regular bilingual programs.

Inservice Training

Every school district shall provide inservice training for the teachers, aides, and administrators who work with handicapped LEP students.

Potential Positive Effects. The skills of existing staff will be improved, helping to bridge the gap between bilingual and special education and improving the quality of services provided to children.

Potential Negative Effects. Identifying trainers with the proper background may be difficult, and this may deter some districts from hiring new teachers with the appropriate training.

Teacher Certification/Endorsement

State departments of education certification units will set up the criteria for certifying or endorsing Bilingual Special Education teachers in consultation with representatives from local school districts and college or schools of education.

Potential Positive Effects. The establishment of standards will encourage schools of education to begin offering the appropriate training, thereby improving the quality of teacher training and ultimately improving the quality of services provided to handicapped children of limited English proficiency.

Potential Negative Effects. The use of existing standards may allow for more flexibility. If such is the case, the additional bureaucratic red tape may not be justified.

Teacher Training

Schools and colleges of education in high impact areas will revise their training programs to include training experiences for teachers who will work in Bilingual Special Education programs.

Potential Positive Effects. Teachers now in short supply will become more available. Colleges will become more responsive to needs in the field, more easily placing their graduates and leading to improved quality of services to the handicapped child of limited English proficiency.

Potential Negative Effects. Colleges may not have the appropriate faculty to accomplish the task. Also, such an approach may add an additional year to the training program.

Planning and Implementation

Earlier in this chapter the current federal requirements for serving LEP handicapped children were delineated. This section will discuss practical measures for planning and administering services for this population of students. Issues such as student identification, needs assessment, personnel competencies, program implementation, and instructional resources will be treated from a nontheoretical standpoint. This will allow ideas discussed earlier to be viewed from a more practical perspective. Some of this material could be adapted and refined to meet the needs of a local school or school district.

The first step in the planning process is the recognition of the need for this type of program or services. The existence of special learning problems among this population needs to be identified, and steps to solve these learning difficulties should be taken through appropriate program development and correct student placement. The placement and assessment of students into the proper learning environment are of critical importance. The persons responsible for placement should review the referral process and all testing procedures for any bias. Cultural and linguistic factors should also be carefully considered in viewing the student's regular program before a referral is made.

After determining that students have been properly identified as needing Bilingual Special Education services, a thorough needs assessment should be completed. This part of the planning process requires a review of existing programs, funding, staff, and materials to see how they can be better used in meeting the needs of these students. Linkages with existing programs such as special education, Bilingual Education, and remedial reading must be formed to increase effectiveness. Funding sources should also be reviewed to determine length and amount of support in addition to flexibility of allocation.

Along with knowing the programs and funding available, it is necessary to find out the existing human resources. To do this, personnel competencies need to be documented. Each staff position involved with the program needs to be evaluated. Questions such as the following need to be answered:

- What are the bilingual abilities of individuals staffing special education and other positions in the district?
- How can personnel with a bilingual and/or special education background be best used?

A thorough evaluation of personnel information is an indispensable part of the planning process. Once the evaluation has occurred, effective use of personnel is an equally vital part of the implementation aspect of the program. It should also be noted that all personnel involved in this program should be aware of their roles. For the program to proceed in a smooth manner, all staff responsible for its success should be informed of their functions.

After the skills of the staff are determined, a plan must account for variables such as student separation time from peers in the standard curriculum, service delivery models, monitoring procedures, instructional techniques, evaluation policies, and exit assurance criteria. The evaluation of the program's effectiveness should be ongoing to make adjustments to improve the program.

Another integral aspect of the planning process is the allocation of material and instructional resources. However, before the acquisition of new materials, an evaluation of available materials should be conducted. This inventory clarifies which items the district has to assist the program and those items it needs to order. Items in these categories can range from inservice materials to consultants for training. This determination of resources should complete the assessment process. Once the needs are understood, the progess of planning and implementing the program becomes easier.

Following are some planning forms (Figures 15–3 to 15–6) that can be modified and adapted as needed to fit the needs of local schools and districts. These instruments are designed for planning and monitoring a Bilingual Special Education program. With careful evaluation they can provide effective feedback in the areas of pupil population, personnel skills, program planning, and materials management.

Future of Bilingual Special Education

Because bilingual special education is a relatively new and still emerging concern within education it can easily be viewed in a futuristic context. A futurist has been defined as "a person who makes other people's futures more real for them" (Kierstead & Dede, 1979). In this sense bilingual special educators, as well as those involved in Bilingual Special Education policy formulation, are futurists. Dede (1979) has indicated that the field of educational futures resembles a tree. The trunk is the present and the branches are the different alternative futures. As futurists, when we move up the trunk to the branches, or from the present to the future, we have eliminated some alternative futures. The branch we are on becomes the present and many new branches or futures remain ahead of us.

Bilingual Special Education can be viewed as an emerging branch on the tree of general education. The future direction of Bilingual Special Education depends to a great extent on what happens to general education and to special education as well. On the other hand, the future of Bilingual Special Education will also be affected by the way it is planned for and directed in and of itself. With this in mind, some of the issues that may affect the future of general education as well as Bilingual Special Education will be discussed.

A very common way of relating to the future of education is to analyze some of the past as well as current practices within the field of education. One obvious historical practice in education has been and continues to be the crisis response to social problems. For example, not too many years ago the widespread problem of drug abuse prompted schools to develop drug education programs and classes. The racial and ethnic tensions of the 1960s prompted the implementation of ethnic studies and multicultural education. The pollution of our natural resources resulted in environmental education. The same could be said of many other educational innovations such as energy education, sex education, and even the back-to-the-basics movement. Although some of the educational changes that have occurred through this crisis model have been beneficial, a better approach is needed.

Future Trends

Educational futurists stress the importance of planning education in the context of the impact of the major future trends. Shane (1977) stresses that the following factors will influence future educational practices:

1. A continued acceleration in the rate of change.
2. Greater complexity of life because of new technological breakthroughs.
3. A need to reassess our present concepts of growth.
4. Continued pressure for human equity in all areas.
5. Increased governmental debt and capital deficits.

These factors will definitely affect the future of education in our society. Our purpose here is not to discuss them at great length but rather to illustrate the complexity involved in discussing the future of education. The future financial support of education, for example, is very directly related to the factor of increased governmental debt and capital deficits. Reynolds and

Form I—Student Identification

CATEGORY	K		1		2		3		4		5		6		7		8		9		10		11		12	
	LEP	NON-LEP	LEP	NON-LEP	LEP	NON-LEP	LEP	NON-LEP	LEP	NON-LEP	LEP	NON-LEP	LEP	NON-LEP	LEP	NON-LEP	LEP	NON-LEP	LEP	NON-LEP	LEP	NON-LEP	LEP	NON-LEP	LEP	NON-LEP
Emotionally disturbed																										
Specific learning disabled																										
Hard of hearing																										
Deaf																										
Deaf-Blind																										
Educable mentally retarded																										
Trainable mentally retarded																										
Severely mentally retarded																										
Speech impaired																										
Orthopedically handicapped																										
Other health impaired																										
Multiply handicapped																										
Gifted and talented																										
Other (specify)																										
Total																										

Figure 15–3
Form I—Student Identification

Form II – Bilingual and Special Education Personnel

PERSONNEL TYPE	FULL-TIME EQUIVALENT	
	BILINGUAL	NOT BILINGUAL
Bilingual teachers		
Bilingual teacher aides		
Teacher of the educationally handicapped		
Teacher of the emotionally handicapped		
Teacher of the hearing impaired		
Teacher of the learning disabled		
Teacher of the mentally retarded		
Teacher of the multiply handicapped		
Teacher of the physically handicapped		
Teacher of the vision impaired		
Vocational teacher		
Special education teacher aides		
Diagnostician		
Psychologist		
Child find coordinator		
Social worker		
Guidance counselor		
Speech and language clinician		
Audiologist		
Bilingual special education teacher		
Other (specify)		
Total		

Figure 15–4
Form II—Bilingual and Special Education Personnel

Form III – Program Planning

	CURRENT POLICY		POLICY NEEDED	
	YES	NO	YES	NO
1. The methods your school district uses to contact parents for their participation in the Individual Education Plan meeting are: a. Letter				
b. Home visitations				
c. Telephone				
d. Note home via child				
e. Other (specify)				
2. All written notification is in: a. English				
b. English and oral interpretation/translation				
c. Native language of the parents				
d. Other modes of communication (e.g., sign, braille) if applicable				
e. Other (specify)				
3. The following persons participate in the IEP meeting for a child in your school district: a. Child's teacher				
b. A person from agency other than the child's teacher who is qualified to provide or supervise the provision of special education				
c. One or both of the child's parents				
d. The child where appropriate				
e. Other individuals at the discretion of the parent or agency				
f. A member of the evaluation team or someone knowledgeable about evaluation procedures				

Adapted from Ramirez, B., and Pages, M.: Special education program for American Indian exceptional children and youth, Reston, Va., 1979, Council for Exceptional Children.

Figure 15–5
Form III—Program Planning

Form III – Program Planning – cont'd

	CURRENT POLICY		POLICY NEEDED	
	YES	NO	YES	NO
g. Bilingual advocate				
h. An interpreter where appropriate				
i. Other (specify)				
4. The following are components of the IEP for a child in in your school district: a. A statement of the child's present level of educational performance				
b. A statement of annual goals, including short-term instructional objectives				
c. A statement of the specific special education and related services to be provided to the child				
d. The extent to which the child will be able to participate in regular educational programs				
e. The projected dates for initiation of services and the anticipated duration of the services				
f. Appropriate objective criteria and evaluation procedures and schedules for determining, on at least an annual basis, whether the short-term instructional objectives are being achieved				
g. A description of the child's learning style				
h. Intervals for which objectives are written				
i. Explanation of why placement is the least restrictive one feasible				
j. Name and title of IEP meeting participants				
k. Criteria under which the child returns to the regular program or least restrictive alternative				
l. Name and title of personnel required to provide the special services				
m. Designation of responsible person to act as liaison to ensure this plan is followed				

continued

Figure 15–5
continuing

Form III – Program Planning – cont'd

	CURRENT POLICY		POLICY NEEDED	
	YES	NO	YES	NO
n. Other (specify)				
5. If the primary language spoken by the child is other than English, there is a provision made in the IEP as to which language to use for classroom instruction until the child can profit from English instruction				
6. The decision in regard to which language should be used for the child's initial instruction is made by: a. Parents				
b. IEP meeting participants				
c. Other (specify)				
7. If the parents have not participated in the development of the IEP, the following are contained in the parental notice of recommended program: a. A detailed description of the proposed IEP				
b. An explanation of how the IEP was developed				
c. The reasons why the proposed program is deemed appropriate for the child				
d. The reasons why the proposed program is the least restrictive program setting appropriate for the child				
e. A list of the tests, reports, or evaluation procedures on which the proposed program is based				
f. A statement that the school reports, files, and records pertaining to the child are available to them for inspection and copying				
g. A description of the procedures that parent(s) should follow to appeal the placement decisions				
h. A guarantee that the child will be temporarily continued in present placement (unless the child is a danger to himself or others) if proposed action is rejected by parent				
i. An explanation of procedures to be followed if the child cannot remain in his current placement even temporarily				

Figure 15–5
continuing

Form III – Program Planning – cont'd

	CURRENT POLICY		POLICY NEEDED	
	YES	NO	YES	NO
j. Other (specify)				
8. It is the policy of your school district to require written approval of the proposed IEP for their child				
9. If the parents agree to the proposed placement, the child is placed within 14 days				
10. IEPs are reviewed: a. End of each grading period (quarterly)				
b. Twice a year				
c. Once a year				
d. Other (specify)				
11. The following are considered as part of the review: a. Whether the child has achieved the goals set				
b. Whether the child has met the criteria that indicated readiness to enter a less restrictive program				
c. Whether the program the child is in should be modified to render it more suitable to the child's needs				
d. Other (specify)				
12. Your school district's follow-up procedures for bilingual children who go from the special education program to the regular program are: a. Monitoring of student progress by the special education teacher				
b. Monitoring of student progress by the bilingual administrator, coordinator, or specialist				
c. Written progress reports by regular teacher				
d. Written progress reports by special education teacher				
e. Other (specify)				

Figure 15–5
continuing

Form IV—Management of Resources for Bilingual and Special Education

	YES QUANTITY	NO	TO BE ACQUIRED
Your school district or instructional materials center has: A. Bilingual curriculum materials			
B. Bilingual special education curriculum materials			
C. Bilingual films			
D. Bilingual literature			
E. Information or referral services			
F. Filmstrips			
G. Audio tapes			
H. Instructional games			
I. Audiovisual materials			
J. Overhead projections			
K. Competency examinations			
L. Pupil evaluations			
M. Basic textbooks			
N. Records			
O. Inservice materials			
P. Supplemental services			
Q. Teacher development materials			
R. Other (specify)			

Figure 15–6
Form IV—Management of Resources for Bilingual and Special Education

Birch (1982) point out that schools in the United States as well as throughout the Western world are facing a serious problem of meeting expanding educational needs with fewer dollars.

Coupled with the declining resources is the changing role of the federal government in supporting education. This can be viewed from the policy perspective of increased emphasis on local control as well as from the administrative perspective of block granting. In terms of categorical programs like the education of the handicapped and Bilingual Education, this means that local school administrators will have more flexibility and control in how they choose to design their educational programs. The trend toward block grants means that the hard-fought battles for financial support and quality programs at the federal level will have to be repeated again at the state and local levels. Another implication of this policy for the future is that services for the handicapped and the limited English proficient will be viewed less as separate categorical programs and more as the responsibility of the local school district. This will be a welcome change, assuming that these services are given adequate support.

Another factor that will influence the future of education is the continued pressure for human equity in all areas. Regardless of what educational changes occur in the future, the principles related to equal educational opportunity as well as the basic educational rights of all children will continue to receive priority consideration.

Projections for Bilingual Special Education

Looking specifically at the future of Bilingual Special Education, some projections can be made.

1. The number of LEP handicapped children will more than likely increase at a greater rate than the rest of the student population. This will be due to the increased number of foreign students coming into the United States. The probable lower socioeconomic background of these students will also be a contributing factor.

2. Psychological and diagnostic testing procedures for the LEP handicapped will continue to improve as research and training efforts improve and as more bilingual professionals become available.

3. There will be an increasing trend to classify LEP handicapped children by their educational needs rather than by the current medical model. This will come about because of the trend away from categorical funding and the increasing concern over the negative stigma attached to the present classification system.

4. Individualized educational plans (IEPs) for LEP handicapped students will increasingly reflect the language and culture needs of these students. This will occur because of improved preservice and inservice training and because of continued litigation.

5. Bilingual Special Education instruction in self-contained classes will be kept to a minimum. Bilingual Special Education resource rooms will continue to be used to a limited extent. The majority of LEP handicapped children will be served in regular classrooms with a variety of support services uniquely designed and based on the resources of each individual school.

6. There will be increased emphasis on early intervention with the LEP handicapped child. This will be based on demonstrated educational and cost benefits of early childhood education.

7. The use of educational technology with the LEP handicapped student will become important as the appropriate hardware and software become more readily available.

As was mentioned earlier, the future of Bilingual Special Education rests primarily on the future of regular education. The American educational system is in need of reform. The public schools must develop the capacity to respond to an ever-increasing range of individual differences. All students in our schools should be treated as unique individuals. Individualized educational programs should be developed for every child in our schools. When this is done, the future of Bilingual Special Education will be the present.

Summary

The chapter provided a general background on policy development and described various policymaking models that could be used in the development of federal language policy. Critical issues affecting policy development were discussed, as were suggested strategies for influencing policy at the national level. Policy options directly related to Bilingual Special Education were proposed along with some specific guidelines for Bilingual Special Education program planning and implementation. Several projections on the future direction of Bilingual Special Education were included for reader consideration.

Discussion Questions

1. Discuss the viability of two Bilingual Special Education service alternatives in your local school district.

2. Select two groups influencing policy development in your local school district and survey their opinions of Bilingual Special Education.

3. Answer, in detail, two of the questions found on p. 333.

4. Are there any additions or subtractions needed to the federal requirements mentioned in this chapter? If so, name and explain them.

5. Discuss in detail the positive and negative aspects of any three of the policy options as applied to your local school district.

6. Using the criteria mentioned by Shane (found on page 347) or your own philosophy, state the outlook for Bilingual Special Education in your local school district.

References

Alexander, D. J., & Nava, A. (1976). *A public policy analysis of bilingual education in California.* San Francisco: R & E Research Associates.

Anderson, J. E. (1975). *Public policy-making.* New York: Praeger.

Anderson, J. E. (1984). *Public policy and politics in America.* Monterrey, CA: Brooks-Cole.

Baca, L. (1980). *Policy options for insuring the delivery of an appropriate education to handicapped children who are of limited English proficiency.* Reston, VA: Council for Exceptional Children.

Baca, L., & Bransford, J. (1982). *An appropriate education for handicapped children of limited English proficiency.* An ERIC Exceptional Child Education Report, ERIC Clearinghouse for Exceptional Children. Reston, VA: Council for Exceptional Children.

Barrera-Vasquez, A. (1953). The Tarascan Project in Mexico. In *Use of vernacular language in education.* Paris: UNESCO.

Bebout, J. E., & Bredemeier, H. C. (1963). American cities as special systems. *American Institute of Planners Journal.* 29(2):64–75.

Blank, M. (1973). A tutorial language program to develop abstract thinking in socially disadvantaged preschool children. *Child Development.* 39:379–389.

Dede, C. (1979). The state of the union in educational theory. In F. Kierstead, and C. Dede, (Eds.), *Educational futures: Sourcebook, I.* Washington, DC: World Future Society.

Dunn, W. N. (Ed.) (1986). *Policy analysis: Perceptions, concepts, and methods.* Greenwich, CT: Jai Press.

Easton, D. (1965). *A framework for political analysis.* Englewood Cliffs, NJ: Prentice-Hall.

Education Commission for the States (ECS). (1979). *Special education finances: The interaction be-*

tween state and federal support systems, Denver: Education Finance Center.

Edwards, A. (1980). Policy research and special education: Research issues affecting policy formation and implementation. *Exceptional Education Quarterly.* 2(2):96–102.

Gutierrez, L. (1982, January). Personal interview.

Hughes, L. W. (1967, May). Know your power structure. *School Board Journal.* 26:84–92.

Jones, P., & Ferguson, J. (1981, March). *Trends in school finance at the national, state, and local levels.* Paper presented at the American Education Finance Association, New Orleans, LA.

Kierstead, F., & Dede, C. (Eds.) (1979). *Educational futures: Sourcebook I,* Washington, DC: World Future Society.

Lau v. Nichols (1974). 414 U.S. 563.

Lewis, D., & Wallace, H. (Eds.) (1984). *Policies into practice.* Exeter, NH: Heineman.

Modiano, N. (1968). Bilingual education for children of linguistic minorities. *American Indigena.* 28:405–414.

Quade, E. S. (1982). *Analysis for public decisions.* New York: Rand.

Rakoff, S. H., & Schaefer, G. F. (1970). Politics, policy, and political science: Theoretical alternatives. *Politics and Society.* 1(1):51–77.

Ramirez, B., & Pages, M. (1979). *Special education programs for American Indian exceptional children and youth: A policy analysis guide.* Reston, VA: Council for Exceptional Children.

Reynolds, M. C., & Birch, J. W. (1982). *Teaching exceptional children in all America's schools.* Reston, VA: Council for Exceptional Children.

Richardson, M. W. (1986). Two patterns of bilingual education in Dade County, Florida. In I. E. Bird (Ed.), *Foreign language learning: Research and development.* Menesha, WI: George Banta Co.

Shane, H. G. (1977). *Curriculum change toward the 21st century.* (pp. 16–20). Washington, DC: National Education Association.

Takanishi, R. (1981). *Preparing a policy-relevant report: Guidelines for authors.* Los Alamitos, CA: National Center for Bilingual Research.

Thompson, J. T. (1976) . *Policymaking in American public education: A framework for analysis.* Englewood Cliffs, NJ: Prentice-Hall.

Troike, R. C. (1978). *Research evidence for the effectiveness of bilingual education.* Rosslyn, VA: National Clearinghouse for Bilingual Education.

Tucker, G. R., et al. An alternate days approach to bilingual education. In J. E. Alatis (Ed.), *Report of the 21st Annual Round Table Meeting of Linguistics and Language Studies.* Washington, DC: Georgetown University Press.

APPENDIX

A Case Study Using Diagnostic-Intervention Process

For the reader to get a better idea of just how the diagnostic-intervention process might operate, a case study is presented. The case study will follow the phases as diagrammed in Figure 8–1. This is an actual case of a student currently enrolled in a large urban school in Colorado. Her name and the names of other significant individuals have been changed.

Irene Torres is a 13-year-old student in fourth grade at Del Pueblo Elementary School. Her teachers indicated that she was having numerous academic, social, and particularly communication problems. She was referred for special education intervention because her teachers thought that she had significant learning and possibly emotional problems.

The box on pp. 360–361 is the student referral form for Irene. The form reveals that Irene is a bilingual Spanish-speaking student, with Spanish being the primary language spoken in the home, according to the classroom teacher, Ms. Hooper.

An important comment by the teacher indicates that the student had some health problems that appeared to be quite significant. Though the reason for her visits to the hospital was not reported, it can be assumed that Irene was receiving some type of care, most probably for her kidney condition.

Irene's academic history showed she recently arrived in the school district from Puerto Rico where she was having some academic problems in third grade because of attendance problems. It seems likely that this "poor health" condition was again related to her kidney problems.

Irene's grade level in English was beginning second grade, and the teacher emphasized poor oral language skills. No specific academic scores were available for her in Spanish, though one would suspect some problems in Spanish also because her grades were marginal in Puerto Rico. A question to raise here is just where Irene stood academically, because her classroom teacher said she had trouble understanding her.

A strength for Irene was her ability to work independently for considerably long periods on classroom assignments. On the other hand, her ability to get along with groups of children was strained and might have been related to her health, language, culture, emotional state, adjustment to a new country, or a combination of all of these.

Referring person: Judy Hooper Title Teacher Date Oct. 12, 1981

Parent contacted by: Judy Hooper Title Teacher Date Oct. 13, 1981

Pupil's name Irene Torres Birth date 5-14-68 Age 13

Address 6705 S. Grant Phone # 555-2716 day none evening

Parent/guardian Martha Torres

School Del Pueblo Elementary Grade 4th Room # 112 Teacher Judy Hooper

Primary language spoken in the home mostly Spanish

Is student bilingual: yes X no ______

Basis for determination of bilingualism: Teacher aide spoke with mother

Health problems known Irene has missed a lot of school since she enrolled because of kidney problems. She goes to Colorado General Hospital at least twice a week according to the nurse.

Academic history (include schools attended, grade levels, and most recent grades earned).
Escuela Primaria de Santa Maria (in Puerto Rico) grades K–3
3rd grade–mostly C & D grades. Teachers report she missed a lot of school in 3rd grade because of poor health. She was recommended to be retrained but mother refused. She was not in any special programs in Puerto Rico.

Student Referral Form

Though the teacher's description of the presenting problem lacked some specificity (and was typical of many referrals), the primary problem seemed to be academic, with an emphasis in reading and math skills. Just how much Irene understood in English appeared limited with her primary language facility in Spanish, according to the bilingual teacher aide.

Ms. Hooper took some steps to help Irene, all of them useful. The teacher pointed out that Irene was referred to the Bilingual Education program and apparently was having some positive experiences there because she reported that Irene liked the classroom and the teacher.

Overall, thus far the information suggested that Irene's current problem in Ms. Hooper's

Academic functioning level

Reading: 2.2 grade level
Spelling: 2.0 grade level
Math: 2.3 grade level

Irene has poor word attach skills, has trouble blending sounds and reads very slowly. She also mispronounces words and seems not to understand much of what I say to her.

Student strengths (be specific and examine academic, social, emotional, and other areas).

Irene is very persistent. She tries very hard to complete the work that I give her. She can work independently for an hour if I let her. She follows directions fairly well, though I usually have to repeat them a couple of times for her.

Behavior functioning level (be specific)

Irene can work by herself very well. However, she has noticeable problems in small or large groups. She hits children for no reason and yesterday nearly struck another student in the eye with a pencil after she called her stupid. She seems immature and has trouble making friends. It looks like she doesn't know how to go about making friends.

Describe the presenting problem (be specific)

Irene first entered my class on September 3, 1981. She was very quiet and shy for a couple of weeks and would not speak at all. I did not know she was bilingual for a couple of days. Her records say she had some English skills. Her reading skills are lower than the skills of my lowest reading group (beginning 3rd grade). Her math is the same way. Her first day in a reading group (after informally testing her) she had trouble sorting out basic words like "cat," "see," "dog," "rat," "jump." Though she seems to understand more in Spanish (according to my bilingual teacher aide) I think her problem is more severe than just language.

Describe the measures you have taken to resolve the problem

The first thing I did once I knew she was bilingual was to sit her next to Kathy, a bilingual student who is very sharp. That did not work out too well as they could not get along very well. I moved her to another table where she is sitting next to a girl she seems to like and who is in her reading group. My aide works with her in reading and math every day for an hour.

I referred Irene to the Bilingual Education program, and she goes to Mrs. Armijo everyday for an hour. Irene tells me she likes Mrs. Armijo and likes going to her room.

class could be related to one or a combination of several factors that include (1) recent arrival from Puerto Rico, (2) primarily a Spanish-speaking home, (3) second language learning, (4) learning disability in Spanish, (5) situational problem related to adjustment to new environment, (6) emotional difficulties, (7) cultural differences, and (8) health problems. Which one of these was specifically related to her present state could not be readily determined without additional information.

In a meeting of the assessment committee, it was recommended that observational data, interview data, and other pertinent school records be obtained about Irene.

Pages 362–364 contain the observational and interview data about Irene. The classroom observation (pp. 362–363) reveals that Irene

Student's name: Irene Torres School: Del Pueblo Elem. Grade 4th Room # 112

Teacher's name: Judy Hooper

Student's needs: Irene needs assistance in academic areas particularly reading and math. Also needs to develop better social skills.

Time of day: morning Length: 60 min.

Classroom setting (be specific, including approximate number of students, seating, organization of classroom, daily schedule, etc.)

At the time of the observation reading was in progress and there were 28 students in the class. Two groups were in progress, one with the teacher, Ms. Hooper, and one with her aide, Mrs. Valdez. Fifteen students were at their seats completing assignments from the previous day and were waiting their group's turn for reading. Ms. Hooper has a stimulating room and there are many pictures, class papers, posters, and wall hangings. It has a warm and relaxed atmosphere.

Specific activity (reading, math, etc.; size of group, etc.)

Two groups of reading were in progress. Ms. Hooper's group had eight students and Mrs. Valdez, a teacher aide, had five students. Irene was with Mrs. Valdez.

Management instructional techniques of teacher (be specific, including use of positive or negative reinforcement, verbal and nonverbal cues, etc.; teacher-child interactions, how teacher presents materials, use of questions, student responses, etc.)

Both Ms. Hooper and Mrs. Valdez provide a lot of positive reinforcement in their groups. They smile frequently and encourage the students. Mrs. Valdez has the lowest reading group and each child is reading a sentence or two from the reading book. The atmosphere is relaxed but the students seem restless and all are quite fidgety including Irene.

Observation of student's behavior with independent seat work assignments (be specific, including how well student completes work, attending to task, etc.)

Classroom Observation

was observed in the morning for an hour. Reading groups were in progress and Irene was in a group of five students with the teacher's aide, Mrs. Valdez. The classroom seemed to have a warm and relaxed atmosphere with many stimulating materials on the walls and bulletin boards.

During the time in the reading group, Irene was seen to have some difficulty, and at one point she hit a student when she was laughed at for mispronouncing a word. Other students in the group were seen as restless and fidgety, including Irene.

At her seat she worked quietly and only occasionally spoke to a neighbor by her desk. Other students in the same reading group finished their seatwork 15 to 20 minutes sooner than Irene. Her assignments were mostly correct.

In a conversation with the observer, Irene said that reading was difficult for her, which was an embarrassing comment for her to make.

Following her reading group, Irene went to her seat to complete an assignment given to her by Mrs. Valdez. While at her seat she sat quietly without disturbing anyone for 25 minutes. A glance of her work showed that most of it was correct. However, the other group members finished 15–20 minutes before her.

Observation of student's behavior in group situation (be specific, including group size, types of interactions between student and other group members etc.)
In her reading group of five students, Mrs. Valdez has each student read a few sentences and then asks some questions for students to answer. Irene received help with her reading and had trouble pronouncing words. She seemed embarrassed and hit one student when he laughed when she mispronounced a word.

Observation of student's interactions with peers as they relate to the classroom or other education setting (be specific, including how conversations are initiated, who initiates conversation, how the student responds, etc.)
Irene was seen talking to another student while at her desk. She asked her a question about the reading assignment and they both laughed. She seems much more relaxed at her seat and is friendly with Maria, who sits next to her.

Additional comments
Being in the reading group seems to be embarrassing and painful for Irene. While she was at her seat, I asked her if reading was difficult for her, she became embarrassed and said "yes."

Does the classroom teacher believe that the student's behavior during the observation period was typical of the student's everyday school performance?

Yes __X__ No ______

Observer: Albert Howard Title: Social Worker

Date: October 19, 1981

Information on p. 364 suggests that Irene's academic problems were significantly related to her perceptions of her own competencies in reading. She appeared to know that she did not read as well as others in the classroom and found this difficult to admit or accept. She would not accept any students making fun of her reading and would hit them. The teacher's concern was particularly noticeable for the time Irene had to spend to complete her reading assignments at her seat. Taking so much longer than others in her group must have been frustrating and upsetting for her.

Remarkably, her behavior at her seat was well controlled and disciplined and she certainly exerted considerable effort in completing those assignments.

The referral interview summary (p. 364) was obtained by two different individuals. A bilingual Spanish-speaking social worker was asked to interview Irene and her mother on separate occasions. This was decided because the primary language spoken in the home was Spanish.

Ms. Hooper believed that Irene's extreme slowness in reading and math was more related to a severe learning disorder than to her bilingual background; she thought Irene should have been considered for special education intervention. The teacher seemed adamant and thought

Student's name: Irene Torres School: Del Pueblo Elem. Grade 4th Room # 112

Teacher's name: Judy Hooper

Interviewer for: Albert Howard Teacher Bob Pera (Bil. Social Worker) Student Bob Pera (Bil. Social Worker) Parent

Date of Interview for: 10-21-81 Teacher 10-22-81 Student 10-23-81 Parent

Teacher interview (ask general open-ended questions such as: What is your main concern about the student? What could be done to help the student? etc.)

Teacher thinks that Irene has severe academic problems that are not just related to her Spanish background. Her progress in reading and math is extremely slow and below that of any other student in class. She thinks that Irene has a severe learning disorder that will be evident even in Spanish. At this time, she feels that Irene should seriously be considered for the special education learning disabilities program plus continued help from the Bilingual Education program.

Student interview (ask general open-ended questions such as: What do you enjoy doing at school, at the playground, and at home? What subjects are most enjoyable? What makes them enjoyable? What subjects are most difficult? What makes them difficult? etc.)

Irene reports that reading is very difficult and embarrassing for her. She says that she can read in Spanish but prefers to play or do something else rather than read. She enjoys music, art, and recess the best during the day at school. They are the most enjoyable since she can just enjoy them and not have to worry about doing math.

Parent interview (ask general open-ended questions such as: How do you see your child's progress at school? What subjects do you think your child enjoys most and least? How does your child get along at home, at school, and in the neighborhood? etc.)

Mom states that Irene began having trouble at school about the middle of third grade at Escuela Primaria de Santa Maria in Puerto Rico. She thinks Irene dislikes most academic subjects mainly because she missed a lot of school in third grade because of severe kidney infections. Also, the medicine that Irene was taking seemed to make her tired and drowsy in school. At home and around the neighborhood she gets along well and has several friends near their home that also speak Spanish.

Referral Interview Summary

a severe problem would be noticeable in Spanish as well. The teacher also recommended a learning disabilities program for Irene.

Irene admitted that reading was difficult and frustrating for her to the point that she did not read, in English or Spanish, as a hobby or for recreation or relaxation. At school she enjoyed subjects that did not require reading to any great extent.

Mrs. Torres revealed that a significant health history could be contributing a great deal to Irene's problems. As a student in her native Puerto Rico, Irene missed many school days because of poor health. Her kidney condition apparently was quite severe and the medication she was taking had obvious side effects.

Members of the assessment staff obtained the school records for Irene Torres. Looking at the cumulative folder revealed that in third grade Irene missed 87 school days. Though the total number of school days on the folder was not reported, if one assumes roughly 180 days, then Irene missed nearly half of the school year. Comments by the classroom teacher showed that Irene had major surgery twice during the school year and was hospitalized for three weeks on each occasion.

Irene's medical records were extensive and indicated that Irene's kidney problems were related to a birth defect that required corrective surgery. Following a second operation in May 1981, Irene did not return to school. Her last reported medical visit, according to the records, was July 7, 1981, and she was normal in all vital areas. Medication was discontinued and normal activity was recommended by the doctor.

This medical information and the mother's report of Irene's physical state were not totally in agreement, because Mrs. Torres suggested that Irene was still suffering from her kidney disorder and the records indicated just the opposite.

After careful examination of the records, the teachers thought that additional information was necessary in order to best meet Irene's physical, social, and academic needs. Mrs. Torres was invited to attend a meeting at school to discuss the information thus far obtained and to discuss the recommendation for additional assessment.

During the home-school conference, Mrs. Torres was asked about Irene's present physical state and whether it was consistent with the medical records for July 7, 1981. Mrs. Torres stated that Irene still was quite ill and would wake up sick and nauseous and be unable to get out of bed. She was, however, taking no medication but had scheduled appointments to go to Colorado General Hospital for checkups.

To obtain a more comprehensive and accurate picture of Irene's functions, a three-pronged assessment process was recommended that included a medical and developmental history, a language proficiency scale, and an educational assessment.

For the medical and developmental history, an appointment was scheduled by the school nurse at Colorado General Hospital for a complete physical. Second, the medical model portion of the System of Multicultural Pluralistic Assessment (Mercer, 1979) was administered by the school nurse. Results of the physical examination showed that Irene's physical state was normal and no dysfunction was noted with her kidneys; normal school activity was recommended by the physician. The System of Multicultural Pluralistic Assessment, Medical Model portion (Mercer, 1979) identified Irene as being "at risk" in one of the six areas assessed, the health history inventory.

Irene was then administered the Language Assessment Scale (De Avila & Duncan, 1975) in English and in Spanish to determine her language proficiency. In English Irene scored basically as a non-English speaker (Level I, apparent linguistic deficiencies) and had significant deficits in the four systems (phonemic, referential, syntactical, and pragmatic), with the most severe deficiencies in the last two systems. In Spanish she scored as a near-fluent Spanish speaker (Level IV), with particular strengths in the last three areas.

Irene was then administered the Inter-American Series, Tests of General Ability, and Tests of Reading (Manuel, 1950). Results indicated that Irene's math and reading skills were at a mid-third grade level in Spanish.

These data were presented at a home-school conference and a question was raised as to whether continued assessment was necessary. The general consensus at the conference was that additional assessment was not necessary. It was recommended instead that the following be provided:

1. A minimum of two hours each day of bilingual instruction from the bilingual resource teacher.

2. A referral to the school nurse to assist Irene and her mother to better understand Irene's health needs.

3. A consultation between the bilingual resource teacher and Irene's classroom teacher to aid the teacher to better meet the educational needs of her students.

4. A follow-up of Irene's progress in one month to determine how well she was doing.

References

De Avila, E. A. & Duncan S. E.: (1975). *The language assessment scale.* Corte Madera, CA: Linguametrics Group.

Manuel, H.: (1950). *Inter-American series.* Austin, TX: Guidance Testing Associates.

Mercer, J. R.: (1970). *System of multicultural pluralistic assessment.* New York: Psychological Corp.

SUBJECT INDEX

NAME INDEX